Teaching and learning in the secondary school

Edited by
Bob Moon and Ann Shelton Mayes
at The Open University

London and New York
in association with
The Open University

First published 1995
by Routledge
11 New Fetter Lane, London EC4P 4EE

Simultaneously published in the USA and Canada
by Routledge
29 West 35th Street, New York, NY 10001

Reprinted 1994, 1995, 1996
Selection and editorial matter: © 1994 The Open University

Typeset in Garamond by Florencetype Ltd, Stoodleigh, Devon
Printed and bound in Great Britain by
Biddles Ltd, Guildford and King's Lynn

British Library Cataloguing in Publication Data
A catalogue record for this book is available from the British Library

Library of Congress Cataloguing in Publication Data
A catalogue record for this book is available from the Library of Congress

ISBN 0–415–10250–2

Contents

Foreword

The form of teacher education is one of the most debated educational issues of the day. How is the curriculum of teacher education, particularly initial, pre-service education to be defined? What is the appropriate balance between practical school experience and the academic study to support such practice? What skills and competence can be expected of a newly qualified teacher? How are these skills formulated and assessed and in what ways are they integrated into an ongoing programme of professional development?

These issues have been at the heart of the development and planning of the Open University's programme of initial teacher training and education – the Postgraduate Certificate of Education (PGCE). Each course within the programme uses a combination of technologies, some of which are well tried and tested while others, on information technology for example, may represent new and innovatory approaches to teaching. All, however, contribute in an integrated way towards fulfilling the aims and purposes of the course and programme.

All of the PGCE courses have readers which bring together a range of articles, extracts from books, and reports that discuss key ideas and issues, including specially commissioned chapters. The readers also provide a resource that can be used to support a range of teaching and learning in other types and structures of course.

This series from Routledge, in supporting the Open University PGCE programme, provides a contemporary view of developments in primary and secondary education and across a range of specialist subject areas. Its primary aim is to provide insights and analysis for those participating in initial education and training. Much of its content, however, will also be relevant to ongoing programmes of personal and institutional professional development. Each book is designed to provide an integral part of that basis of knowledge that we would expect of both new and experienced teachers.

Bob Moon
Professor of Education, The Open University

Part I

Introduction

Chapter 1

Developments in secondary education
An introduction

Bob Moon and Ann Shelton Mayes

Three major Acts of Parliament have shaped the development of secondary education in the twentieth century. The first, in 1902, laid the foundations of a national system of secondary education, the second, in 1944, required local education authorities to provide universal and free secondary education for all pupils of secondary age, and the third, in 1988 (developed further by legislation in 1993), introduced a national curriculum and gave schools the possibility of obtaining greater autonomy than was possible under local education authority control. These dates and Acts are English, apply almost equally to Wales, are usually replicated in Northern Ireland, and have had a broad, although less direct influence, in Scotland.

Each of these major pieces of legislation in 1902, 1944 and 1988 precipitated national debate and controversy. The curriculum regulations that accompanied the 1902 Act, for example, were pushed through in a form that for many ignored the need for a new scientific technical orientation to counter the overtly academic emphasis of the public schools. In 1944 the system of selection at 11-plus into grammar, secondary modern and, in a few areas, technical schools, that came to characterise the implementation of the Act, fuelled political and academic disputation. In 1988 the Education Reform and associated subsequent Acts have aroused fierce oppositional forces who denigrate the erosion of local accountability and democracy and the introduction of, as they are characterised, overly formal and prescriptive forms of testing and assessment.

The formal record of major legislation, however, and even the informal record of surrounding debate only capture in part the evolution of ideas and practice within the secondary school system. Equally they bypass the fortunes of the private, independent sector of secondary education which, although responsible for less than 10 per cent of the secondary population, has exerted considerable influence on the development of the education system in general.

Looking back over the last few decades, it is possible to identify a number of important themes that are barely represented in the passage of parliamentary legislation. The introduction of the comprehensive school system, for example, and the erosion of the seemingly incontrovertible ideas about intelligence that were developed through the 1950s and 1960s.

The gradual introduction of comprehensivisation was also associated with a period of questioning about the social and academic organisation of schools. Influential studies such as David Hargreaves' (1967) *Social Relations in a Secondary School*, Lacey's (1970) *Hightown Grammar*, and the more recent study by Stephen Ball (1981) *Beachside Comprehensive*, explored the explicit and implicit social structures that frame a child's experience of schooling. Most significantly they pointed to the influence, sometimes unfair influence, that school systems of organisation, ability grouping and so forth had on the attitudes and achievement of certain groups of pupils. And, in particular, there was a concern about the relationship between achievement, under-achievement and socio-economic class. Stubbornly, despite all the optimism of those who advocated the introduction of comprehensive schooling, the overall record of attainment for children from the less wealthy socio-economic groups remained a concern.

More recent work, for example that done by Peter Burnhill and colleagues in the University of Edinburgh, has pointed to the need to look over a much longer time span than was allowed in the early evaluations of the comprehensive school system (Burnhill, 1990). The differences that occur, for example, when a generation of parents, who themselves went to comprehensive school, have children going through the secondary school system produce some significant changes in outcomes.

Critical scrutiny, however, of the internal and social organisation of secondary schools has led to innovation and change that have retained a significant influence today. The move towards *mixed-ability classes*, for example, arose from a concern about the academic and social impact of streaming and setting. Ability grouping, it was argued, merely replicated the selective system inside the comprehensive with all the same consequences for pupil self-esteem and academic achievement. Many schools, particularly in the early secondary years, abolished grouping or setting by ability and developed more individualised and resource-based forms of classroom organisation. This has been, and remains, politically and educationally controversial, although the grounds of debate are beginning to change as new ideas about the concept of ability come to redefine teaching and learning strategies (see Chapter 3).

Alongside the interest in academic organisation, schools became increasingly concerned with the social and personal support given to pupils. Pastoral systems and tutoring have been a characteristic of secondary education since its inception, borrowed in part from the traditions of the nineteenth century private/'public' boarding schools. The need, however, to develop a more *active tutorial role* for the teacher, liaising with other agencies outside the school, reflected a growing recognition through the

1970s and 1980s, of the need to link social as well as academic responsibilities in the organisation of the school.

Many secondary schools also set out to establish forms of *community schooling*. The aim was not only to provide public access to facilities and resources, but also to create a change in the character and atmosphere of the school. The school for many people, especially parents, was seen as alien territory, and any way of 'breaking down the barriers' had the potential to produce a more positive stance towards schooling and education in general. Community education goes back further than the recent history of comprehensive schools. Henry Morris, for example, in Cambridgeshire in the 1930s opened a series of community colleges that have thrived across all the vicissitudes in national policy (Rée, 1984). Mason in Leicestershire restructured the whole of secondary education around the concept of community-based schooling (Fairbairn, 1980). Community schooling, however, was taken up in the 1970s in places like Manchester and Coventry to provide the basis for a regenerated urban education (Moon, 1983). This paralleled developments in primary schools where a number of educational-priority urban areas were designated and experimental community-based approaches adopted (Midwinter, 1970).

The same period that saw debates about mixed-ability teaching, more active tutoring and community schooling was also the era of the curriculum development project. All subjects of the secondary curriculum became the focus of project development by national teams. A national agency, The Schools Council, was an important provider of funds although the early impetus for such work came from private sources such as the Nuffield Foundation. A number of the projects were very successful and have continued in revised form through to the 1990s. 'Nuffield Science', 'Schools Council History', 'Geography 16–19' are phrases heard in secondary school staff rooms today and all with their origins in this period. The rate of take-up of materials and ideas, however, as economic pressures increased, came to be critically evaluated. The Schools Council, made up of representatives from the Teachers Associations, local education authorities and other interest groups, was abolished in the early years of the first Thatcher government. By then the interest in modernising the curriculum had shifted from looking at subjects to looking at the whole curriculum. In 1976, James Callaghan made a much reported speech at Ruskin College, Oxford, where he questioned the variety and type of curriculum to be found in schools and he gave a first Prime Ministerial indication of a wish to legislate some form of curriculum framework for schools.

The first significant government intervention, however, in the curriculum of secondary schools, came through two developments in the 1980s. The first was the introduction of the GCSE to take the place of the old GCE and CSE examinations. National criteria for the GCSE subjects were laid down and the possibilities opened up for new types of syllabus design using continuous assessment, modular structures, and a range of other new approaches to examining. This involved a significant input to staff retraining and in-service development, and national training days and funds were set aside specifically for this purpose.

The second intervention came via what was then called the Manpower Services Commission, an agency responsible to the Department of Employment rather than Education. The Technical and Vocational Education Initiative (TVEI) was a series of development programmes which LEAs and schools bid for against specific criteria. The aim was to provide a more technical and vocational curriculum in the final, compulsory, years of secondary schooling for pupils of all levels of attainment. Pilot projects were eventually extended to most secondary schools, although it was the first schools in the first projects that had a really significant injection of resources. Many local and national evaluation reports appeared. In ways that paralleled the experience of the Schools Council there is some indication of a relatively low level of impact on the system. A study at the University of Newcastle (Hopkins, 1990), for example, suggested that involvement in TVEI did not have much impact on subsequent pupil interests and careers. But again the proviso must be added that the evaluations may have come too soon, that in schooling, new ideas and new ways of working have a rather longer period of gestation than can be expected in a two- or three-year project cycle of evaluation.

The introduction of the national curriculum in 1988 overshadowed the extension phase of TVEI with schools turning their attention to the implications of implementing a detailed statutory framework across the full range of prescribed secondary subjects. The legacy of TVEI lives on in most secondary schools particularly through more fully developed links with industry and commerce, in a number of the vocationally related GCSE programmes and in a rethinking of the courses available for 16- to 19-year-olds. The introduction of the GCSE and of the TVEI programme were major concerns for secondary schools in the 1980s. In the current decade a further range of issues has come to the fore, driven in part by responses to the legislation programme in the late 1980s and early 1990s and the ongoing debate about national competitiveness in European and world markets (see Chapter 32). The introduction of the *national curriculum*, for example, has provided the major focus for professional development. Many aspects of the plans have been controversial. The ten-subject model of curriculum, the level of detail in which the subjects have been prescribed, the approach to assessment and testing and the timetable and style of implementation have all been vigorously questioned. The requirements of the national curriculum have, however, created a more explicit concern for planning across the curriculum, monitoring pupil progress and evaluating how successfully and effectively the school as a whole is in sustaining and improving pupil attainment. Achieving an appropriate balance between national and school-based curriculum responsibilities presents one of the major challenges for secondary schools in the 1990s.

A second issue could be titled *community relations*. Secondary schools have become increasingly responsive to their local communities. The reasons for this are many. A new generation of teachers has come to recognise more fully the wider role schools should play in the community. This embraces a range of activities. The hundreds of 15- or 16-year-olds who go into local businesses and shops, banks and so forth, as part of work experience schemes are one example. The increased number of school community newspapers or newsletters is another. Other pressures have pointed for different reasons in the same direction. The policy of the Conservative government in the 1980s and 1990s was to give parents and pupils more choice, literally to 'shop around' for schools and the community image of schools has had to take account of that dimension. Sensitivity to community in most schools, however, is more than public relations. The shift of style and tone, the acceptance of new commitments and responsibilities by both the school and local communities, have provided new networks of alliance and social integration.

The devolution of responsibilities through schemes for locally managing resources or for schools to acquire direct grants from government rather than the LEA have increased lay and governor participation in school-based decisions. There are, as with the national curriculum, important areas of disagreement about the purpose of such policies. Is competition or co-operation the model within which local schools should work together? Are there ways of judiciously balancing the strengths of both? If parents are to retain a degree of choice in the schools their children attend, on what criteria and information should such choices be based? Importantly, as many would argue, what does choice mean given the geographical and institutional variations in secondary schooling that exist? Like curriculum, a range of issues that secondary schools will be addressing in the 1990s.

A third issue is the style and form of *relationships or ethos inside secondary schools*, pupil to pupil, pupil to teacher, teacher and pupil to other adults working in the school. Many older adults remember their secondary schools in terms of a 'spare the rod and spoil the child' type of philosophy. If not literally, then metaphorically through a plethora of rather arbitrary rules and regulations. The importance of establishing caring relationships, firm but fair maybe, but with a genuine commitment towards pupils and their personal growth, has become more explicit. The importance of the teacher's tutorial role has grown. Many schools now provide organised opportunities and moments (a summer term Activities week or day, charity walks) where a more relaxed and informal moment helps build up new dimensions to any relationship. This, of course, is not a recent phenomenon but it is increasingly accepted as a significant element in defining the quality of the school in local community terms, and through the criteria now being used for school inspection.

Research on school effectiveness (see Chapters 18 and 38) has shown how important school ethos or climate is to pupils' attitudes to school and to their attainments. How this evidence can be further built on is one of the most important issues for sustained secondary school improvement.

The identification of these three themes, *curriculum, community relations* and *school ethos*, represents one analysis of trends in secondary education. Other observers may detect alternative or complementary trends. Some would argue that the way secondary and primary schooling have become politicised through the 1980s and 1990s, and in particular the high-profile reform agenda given to education by successive Conservative governments, require a more pessimistic analysis. The focus, they might argue, would be more on issues such as teacher morale, the resource level allocated to education and the problem of a policy process based on an illusionary 'harking back' to some golden age where standards were high and respect for the authority of the teacher went unquestioned.

It is difficult, looking back over the last century, to find a time when schooling was anything other than political and each age and era has a plethora of press-cuttings and Hansard entries to point to the particular issues around which debate has revolved. The task of teaching in secondary schools continues, influenced, sometimes significantly, by changes in policy and resourcing, but evolving in a context of ideas in measure independent of particular national concerns.

This book focuses on these wider issues of teaching in secondary schools. Most of the contributions came from contemporary writing. A number do address the political context of the day, although it is not the aim here to provide support or critique to particular political interventions. All, however, explicitly or implicitly reflect certain value positions, and the contribution from Brian Simon included in this introductory section, is one example. Simon asks the question *why no pedagogy in England*?, and he points to a range of historical and social factors that have nourished, in his terms, a rather amateur approach to the task of teaching. The Parts that follow, and the contributions in each provide some responses to Simon's question, which focuses, like this book, on teaching and the teachers' professional role.

Part II looks at *learning* and the redefining of learning, attainment and potential that is reflected in much contemporary analysis. Part III examines *teaching* and the parallel rethinking of the teaching role, tasks and professionalism that is taking place. *Classrooms* provide the focus for Part IV, issues of organisation and management, the crucial role of language in classroom interaction and the impact of information technology on the classrooms of the future. Part V explores how learning and teaching are focused through the *curriculum*, and how assessment within the curriculum has come to have increased importance in recent years. Finally, in Part VI, the analysis moves to *schools* and a selection of readings that address the central issue of school reform and school improvement.

REFERENCES

Ball, S. (1981) *Beachside Comprehensive: A Case Study of Secondary Schooling*, Cambridge: Cambridge University Press.

Burnhill, P., Garner, C. and McPherson, A. (1990) 'Parental education, social class and entry to higher education, 1976–1986', *Journal of the Royal Statistical Society*, Series A, 152(2): 233–48.

Fairbairn, A. N. (1980) *Leicestershire Plan*, London: Heinemann Educational Books.

Hargreaves, D. H. (1967) *Social Relations in a Secondary School*, London: Routledge & Kegan Paul.

Hopkins, D. (ed.) (1990) 'TVEI at the change of life', in *Multilingual Matters: Learning from Unwelcome Data*, Newcastle: Newcastle University.

Lacey, C. (1970) *Hightown Grammar: The School as Social System*, Manchester: Manchester University Press.

Midwinter, E. (1970) *Education: A Priority Area*, London: NUT.

Moon, B. (1983) *Comprehensive Schools: Challenge and Change*, Windsor: NFER.

Rée, H. (1984) *The Henry Morris Collection*, Cambridge: Cambridge University Press.

Chapter 2

Why no pedagogy in England?

Brian Simon

The term 'pedagogy' is used here in the sense of the 'science of teaching' (OED). The title of the chapter is meant to imply that no such science exists in England; the fact that the term is generally shunned implies that such a science is either undesirable or impossible to achieve. And such, it is argued, is the situation in England.

The contrast here with other European countries, both west and east, is striking. In the educational tradition of the Continent, the term 'pedagogy' has an honoured place, stemming perhaps particularly from the work and thinking of Comenius in the seventeenth century, but developed and elaborated in the nineteenth century through the work of Pestalozzi, Herbart and others. The concept of teaching as a science has strong roots in this tradition.

Not so in England. It is now one hundred years since Alexander Bain published *Education as a Science* (1879). Since then, less and less has been heard of this claim. The most striking aspect of current thinking and discussion about education is its eclectic character, reflecting deep confusion of thought, and of aims and purposes, relating to learning and teaching – to pedagogy.

It may be useful to advance an interpretation as to why the concept of 'pedagogy' has been shunned in England, and why instead our approach to educational theory and practice has tended to be amateurish, and highly pragmatic in character.[1] Relevant here is the practice and approach of our most prestigious educational institutions (historically speaking), the ancient universities and leading public schools. Until recently, and even perhaps today, these have been dominant, both socially and in terms of the formation of the climate of opinion. It is symptomatic that the public schools, in general, have until recently contemptuously rejected the idea that a professional training is in any sense relevant to the job of a public schoolmaster. Although toying with the idea in the late nineteenth century, the Headmasters Conference has never adopted a positive attitude to such training, which traditionally has been seen as perhaps relevant and important for an elementary school teacher, but certainly not to someone taking up the gentlemanly profession of teaching in a public school. This was seen, perhaps, not so much as a job anyone from the middle or upper middle class could do, but as something those who wished to teach, having the appropriate social origins including a degree at Oxford or Cambridge, could learn, through experience, on the job. Certainly no special training was necessary.[2]

The reasons for this are clear. The public schools developed as a cohesive system from the mid- to late 1860s serving the new Victorian upper middle class; indeed they played a major role in the symbiosis of aristocracy and bourgeoisie which characterised the late nineteenth century. As Honey makes clear, these schools were centrally concerned with the socialisation of these classes which could not be effectively undertaken in the home. This, he argues, is why, in spite of the epidemics, outrageous bullying, sexual dangers and insanitary conditions to which their pupils were exposed (and all of which took their toll), the popularity of these schools mounted irresistibly at this time (Honey, 1977).

The result has been that education, as a subject of enquiry and study, still less as a 'science', has, historically, had little prestige in this country, having been to all intents and purposes ignored in the most prestigious educational institutions. As Matthew Arnold tirelessly pointed out over one hundred years ago, in France, Prussia and elsewhere the problems of education for the middle class were taken really seriously. In Britain, on the other hand, everything was neglected; a laissez-faire pragmatism predominated.[3] This situation has, to some extent, been perpetuated. The dominant educational institutions of this country have had no concern with theory, its relation to practice, with pedagogy. This is the first point to establish.

But this, of course, is only part of the picture, if an important one. For while the public schools expressed, at least in their practice, a total disregard for pedagogy, in fact a systematic, rational approach was being developed elsewhere – as an indigenous growth within the system of elementary education, and specifically in the last decade of the nineteenth century, just as this system 'became of age', as it were, after its establishment in 1870. This is an interesting and relevant phenomenon, and worth serious attention for its lessons today.

The context of what was, in fact, a serious attempt to integrate theoretical knowledge with the practice of education is to be found in the work of the advanced School Boards in the main industrial cities at this time. Described as 'citadels of radicalism' by Elie Halévy, the French historian, these, with their higher grade schools, pupil-teacher centres, and technical institutions of various kinds (some of which supported, or merged with local universities) were now, in cooperation with the Technical Education Boards established after 1888, deliberately developing cohesive systems of education with an organic relation between the various stages, having the perspective of covering the whole field from infant school to university. This potential development was sharply cut off and circumscribed by a series of administrative and legislative measures brought in by a deeply Conservative government in the period 1899–1904.[4] But through the 1890s, such a perspective appeared realisable. Now at last the mass of the children had been brought into the schools; buildings erected (some of them massive), teaching developing as a profession. The so-called 'extravagance' of the School Boards, as seen by such as Sir John Gorst (and the Tories generally), had some basis in fact. The outlook was optimistic. This was the context of the quite sudden, and apparently rapid, development of educational theory and practice – of positive, all-embracing, pedagogical means.

The social context of this development has been outlined; its theoretical context is equally important. This is personified – or crystallised – in Alexander Bain's *Education as a Science*, published in 1879, reprinted six times in the 1880s, and a further ten times before 1900. Examination of a number of student-teacher manuals, which proliferated in the 1890s, indicates their indebtedness to Bain's approach – or the extent to which they shared common interpretations both of theoretical issues relating to education, and of the practice of teaching.

Of course the theories, and the practices, advocated by Bain and the authors of these manuals, had their limitations as well as theoretical weaknesses. That goes without saying. But, in the 1890s, the approach was serious, systematic, all-embracing. The pedagogy of this specific decade pointed the way to universal education, and was seen as such by its progenitors. What happened? Why was this embryo pedagogy not systematically developed? What went wrong?

First, the social and political context underwent an abrupt change, as indicated earlier. The development referred to took place within the *elementary* system, but one having for a short period a realistic perspective of organic growth. This was the backcloth, the crucial feature, of this movement as a whole. The administrative and legislative events of 1899 to 1904, almost traumatic in their effects, put a stopper on this, and apart from abolishing the School Boards, confined elementary education within precise limits, setting up a system of 'secondary' schooling parallel to, but quite separate from, the elementary system.

This created a new situation. A positive pedagogy based on scientific procedures and understanding and relevant for *all* was no longer seen as appropriate, or required. Intellectual development in the elementary schools was now at a discount (in parallel with the public schools, but for different reasons). The social-disciplinary ('containment') function of elementary education was now especially emphasised. The soil required to nurture a science of education no longer existed.

However, with the demise of the elementary school as the ground of pedagogy, there now emerged the new local authority-controlled systems of secondary education; it seems to have been into these new systems that the most advanced local authorities put their main efforts. These new systems, although strictly contained in their development by the central authority (the Board of Education), and designed specifically for what can best be described as the lower middle class (all such schools had to charge fees), were the only growth points permitted in the new dispensation. The more advanced local authorities, determined to extend educational provision, approached this new field with energy and developed a considerable pride in the school systems so created.[5]

It was the establishment, and rapid development of this new system of secondary schools which underlay new developments in the theory and practice of education. This system insistently required a pedagogy – the development of effective pedagogical means. Thus we find, in the period 1900–1914, a renewed concern to develop a relevant pedagogy and it is this that lies behind the great interest in, almost the discovery of, the work of Herbart, and of the Prussian educators who had developed Herbartianism into a system – itself a phenomenon of some interest.

Until now, the rational foundation for pedagogical theories – for the concept of education as a science – had lain in associationist psychological theories concerning learning. These were espoused by Bain, as we have seen, and underlay his whole approach; as also by Herbart and his protagonists (or elaborators). So it was theory and practice based on these ideas which gave rise both to the positive, or optimistic, pedagogics of the 1890s relating to elementary education, and to those of the period 1900–1920 relating to the new system of secondary education. But it was just at this period that new approaches came to predominate in the field of psychology which either relegated associationism to the background, or denied its significance altogether.

The two major influences leading to the demise of associationism as a major determinant of pedagogy were, on the one hand, the rise of philosophic idealism which denied the material basis of mind and decisively rejected the model of human formation of the strict materialists of the late eighteenth century (with its emphasis on man as the passive product of external stimuli); and, on the other hand, the triumph of Darwinism with its emphasis on heredity (Murphy, 1938, pp. 109–113). With the latter is linked Galton's work (*Hereditary Genius* was published as early as 1869), the rise of the eugenics movement with its associated theories (the Eugenics Education Society was founded in 1908), and the work of the Galton Laboratory at University College, London, associated with the names of Pearson, Spearman, and later Cyril Burt. 'No request is more frequently made to the psychologist', wrote Burt in 1921, when he was educational psychologist to the London County Council, 'than the demand for a simple mental footrule' (Burt, 1921, p. 1). It was precisely this that the psychologists were now ready to supply.

The demands of the system and the movement of ideas now coincided. In the field of educational theory psychometry (or mental testing) now established its hegemony which lasted over forty years from the 1920s. The triumph of psychometry tied in with a new stress on individualism after World War I and a kind of reductionist biologism, both of which are central to the thinking of Sir Percy Nunn whose *Education, its Data and First Principles* was the central student manual of the interwar years.[6] For reasons which will be discussed later, this spelt the end of pedagogy – its actual death. If education cannot promote cognitive growth, as the psychometrists seemed to aver, its whole purpose or direction was lost. 'Othello's occupation gone', as Hayward, an LCC Inspector, once put it.

This, I suggest, is the background to our present discontents. For a combination of social, political and ideological reasons pedagogy – a scientific basis to the theory and practice of education – has never taken root and flourished in Britain. For a single decade in the late nineteenth century in the field of elementary education; for a similar short period early this century in secondary education, pedagogic approaches and analyses flowered – though never in the most socially prestigious system of the public schools and ancient universities. Each 'system', largely self-contained, developed its own specific educational approach, each within its narrowly defined field, and each 'appropriate' to its specific social function. In these circumstances the conditions did not, and could not, exist for the development of an all-embracing, universalised, scientific theory of education relating to the practice of teaching. Nor is it an accident that, in these circumstances, fatalistic ideas preaching the limitation of human powers were in the ascendant.

EDUCATION AND THE TECHNOLOGICAL REVOLUTION

The main objective of this paper is to argue first, that we can no longer afford to go on in the old way, muddling through on a largely pragmatic, or historically institutionalised basis, tinkering with this and that, but that a really serious effort can and should now be made to clear up current confusions and dichotomies. Second, in spite of what must surely be temporary setbacks in the provision of educational facilities, the conditions now exist for a major breakthrough in terms of pedagogy. This statement is made on the basis of two contemporary developments, the one structural, the other theoretical. Of major importance here is the insistent tendency towards unification of the historically determined separate systems of schooling through the transition to comprehensive secondary education. This has been accompanied, in the realm of ideas or theory, by a shift in the concern of educators and psychologists from static concepts of the child (derived from intelligence testing) towards dynamic and complex theories of child development. Both open new perspectives relating to the grounding of educational theory and practice on science (or on scientific procedures).

A REVITALISED PEDAGOGY?

What, then, are the requirements for a renewal of scientific approaches to the practice of teaching – for a revitalised pedagogy?

First, we can identify two essential conditions without which there can be no pedagogy having a generalised significance or application. The first is recognition of the human capacity for learning. It may seem unnecessary, even ridiculous, to single this out in this connection, but in practice this is not the case. Fundamentally, psychometric theory, as elaborated in the 1930s to 1950s, denied the lability of learning capacity, seeing each individual as endowed, as it were, with an engine of a given horse-power which is fixed, unchangeable and measurable in each particular case, irrevocably setting precise and definable limits to achievement (or learning).[7] It was not until this view had been discredited in the eyes of psychologists that serious attention could be given to the analysis and interpretation of the *process* of human learning.

The second condition has been effectively defined by Professor Stones in his helpful and relevant book *Psychopedagogy*, sub-titled 'Psychological Theory and the Practice of Teaching' (1979). It is the recognition that, in general terms, the process of learning among human beings is similar across the human species as a whole. The view on which Stones's book is based is that 'except in pathological cases, learning capability among individuals is similar', so that 'it is possible to envisage a body of general principles of teaching' that are relevant for 'most individual pupils'. The determination, or identification, of such general principles must comprise the objectives of pedagogical study and research (Stones, 1979, p. 453).

One further point may be made at the start. The term 'pedagogy' itself implies structure. It implies the elaboration or definition of specific means adapted to produce the desired effect – such-and-such learning on the part of the child. From the start of the use of the term, pedagogy has been concerned to relate the process of teaching to that of learning on the part of the child. It was this approach that characterised the work of Comenius, Pestalozzi and Herbart.

Both the conditions defined above are today very widely accepted among leading psychologists directly concerned with education and with research into human cognitive development. When Bruner claimed, in a striking and well-known statement, that 'any subject can be taught to anybody at any age in some form that is both interesting and honest', he was basing himself on a positive assessment of human capacity for learning, and deliberately pointing to the need to link psychology with pedagogy. In an essay aimed at persuading American psychologists of the need to concern themselves with education – to provide assistance in elucidating the learning process for practising educators – he stressed his central point, 'that developmental psychology without a theory of pedagogy was as empty an enterprise as a theory of pedagogy that ignored the nature of growth'. 'Man is not a naked ape', writes Bruner, 'but a culture clothed human being, hopelessly ineffective without the prosthesis provided by culture'. Education itself can be a powerful cultural influence, and educational experiences ordered and structured to enable people more fully to realise their humanity and powers, to bring about social change – and so create a world according to their felt and recognised objectives. The major problem humanity faces is not the general development of skill and intelligence, but 'devising a society that can use it wisely' (Bruner, 1972, pp. 18, 131, 158).

When writing this, Bruner was clearly concerned with social change, and with the contribution that pedagogical means might make to this, as we must be in Britain in face of the dramatic social challenge that technological change now presents. And in considering the power of education, rightly ordered, to play a central part in this, it may be as well to recall that, while the simplified and certainly over-mechanist interpretations of the associationist psychologists of the nineteenth century are no longer acceptable in the form, for instance, expressed by Alexander Bain (and his predecessors), yet the concept of learning as a process involving the formation of new connections in the brain and higher nervous systems has in fact not only retained its force, but been highly developed by neuro-physiologists and psychologists specifically concerned to investigate learning. Among these, perhaps the greatest contribution has been made by A. R. Luria in a series of works relevant to teaching, education and human development generally; but perhaps particularly in his work on the role of language in mental development, and in his theory of the formation of what he calls 'complex functional systems' underlying learning (Luria, 1962).

> It is now generally accepted that in the process of mental development there takes place a profound qualitative reorganisation of human mental activity, and that the basic characteristic of this reorganisation is that elementary, direct activity is replaced by complex functional systems, formed on the basis of the child's communication with adults in the process of learning. These functional systems are of complex construction, and are developed with the close participation of language, which as the basic means of communication with people is simultaneously one of the basic tools in the formation of human mental activity and in the regulation of behaviour. It is through these complex forms of mental activity . . . that new features are acquired and begin to develop according to new laws which displace many of the laws which govern the formation of elementary conditioned reflexes in animals.

The work and thinking of both Luria and Bruner (as representative of their respective traditions) point in a similar direction – towards a renewed understanding both of the power of education to effect human change and especially cognitive development, and of the need for the systematisation and structuring of the child's experiences in the process of learning. And it is precisely from this standpoint that a critique is necessary of certain contemporary standpoints, dichotomies and ideologies, and, in particular, of the whole trend towards so-called 'child-centred' theories, which have dominated this area in Britain basically since the early 1920s, to reach its apotheosis in what is best called the 'pedagogic romanticism' of the Plowden Report, its most recent, and semi-official expression.

It may be unfashionable, among educationists, to direct attention specifically to this point, more particularly because a critique of 'progressivism' was central to the outlook expressed in the Black Papers in the late sixties and early seventies; but to make such a critique does not imply identification with the essentially philistine and a-theoretical standpoint of the Black Paperites, as I hope to establish. Indeed the dichotomies which these and other critics sought to establish, for instance between progressive and traditional approaches, between the 'formal' and 'informal', do not reflect the options now available, nor even contemporary practice as it really is.

The basic tenets of child-centred education derive in particular from the work of Froebel who held that children are endowed with certain characteristics or qualities which will mature or flower given the appropriate environment. The child develops best in a 'rich' environment. The teacher should not interfere with this process of maturation, but act as a 'guide'. The function of early education, according to Froebel, is 'to make the inner outer' (Froebel, 1912, p. 94). Hence the emphasis on spontaneity, as also on stages of development, and the concomitant concept of 'readiness' – the child will learn specific skills and mental operations only when he is 'ready'.

That there is a fundamental convergence between this view and the theories (or assumptions) embodied in Intelligence Testing has been overlooked; nevertheless it is the close similarity between both sets of views as to the nature of the child which made it possible for both to flourish together in the period following World War I and after. Intelligence Testing also embodied the view that the child is endowed with certain innate characteristics; in this case a brain and higher nervous system of a given power or force – Spearman's 'Mental Energy or Noegenetics' (Spearman, 1927), and that the process of education is concerned to actualise the given potential, that is, to activate and realise the 'inner' (in Froebel's sense). Both views in fact deny the creative function of education, the formative power of differential educational (or life) experiences. The two trends come together strikingly, for instance, in the work of Susan Isaacs who, on the one hand, firmly believed in the scientific truth of the doctrines of Intelligence Testing, and, on the other, forcefully propagated Froebelian approaches, which she considered particularly appropriate for advanced (middle-class) children with high 'intelligence' (Isaacs, 1932 pp. 25, 28–29; 1963, pp. 41–42).

The theoretical, or pedagogical stance of the Plowden Report represents an extension of these ideas. In their re-interpretation of the conclusions derived from psychometry they reject the concept of total hereditary, or genetic, determination. Development is seen as an interactional process, in which the child's encounters with the environment are crucial. Yet Plowden takes the child-centred approach to its logical limits, insisting on the principle of the complete individualisation of the teaching/learning process as the ideal (even though, from a pedagogic standpoint, this is not a practical possibility in any realistic sense). In their analysis the hereditary/ environmental interactional process is interpreted as exacerbating initial differences so greatly that each child must be seen to be unique, and be treated as such. The matter is rendered even more complex by their insistence that each individual child develops at different rates across three parameters, intellectual, emotional and physical; and that in determining her approach to each individual child each of these must be taken into account by the teacher. The result is that the task set the teacher, with an average of 35 children per class when Plowden reported, is, in the words of the report itself, 'frighteningly high' (Plowden, 1967, I paras 75, 875).

I want to suggest that, by focusing on the individual child ('at the heart of the educational process lies the child'), and in developing the analysis from this point, the Plowden Committee created a situation from which it was impossible to derive an effective pedagogy (or effective pedagogical means). If each child is unique, and each requires a specific pedagogical approach appropriate to him or her and to no other, the construction of an all-embracing pedagogy, or general principles of teaching becomes an impossibility. And indeed research has shown that primary school teachers who have taken the priority of individualisation to heart, find it difficult to do more than ensure that each child is in fact engaged on the series of tasks which the teacher sets up for the child; the complex management problem which then arises takes the teacher's full energies. Hence the approach of teachers who endeavour to implement these prescripts is necessarily primarily didactic ('telling') since it becomes literally impossible to stimulate enquiry, or to 'lead from behind', as Plowden held the teacher should operate in the classroom. Even with a lower average of 30 children per class, this is far too complex and time-consuming a role for the teacher to perform.[8]

The main thrust of the argument of this chapter is this: that to start from the standpoint of individual differences is to start from the wrong position. To develop effective pedagogy means starting from the opposite standpoint, from what children have in common as members of the human species; to establish the general principles of teaching and, in the light of these, to determine what modifications of practice are necessary to meet specific individual needs. If all children are to be assisted to learn, to master increasingly complex cognitive tasks, to develop increasingly complex skills and abilities or mental operations, then this is an objective that schools must have in common; their task becomes the deliberate development of such skills and abilities in all their children. And this involves importing a definite structure into the teaching, and so into the learning experiences provided for the pupils. Individual differences only become important, in this context, if the pedagogical means elaborated are found not to be appropriate to particular children (or groups of children) because of one or other aspect of their individual development or character. In this situation the requirement becomes that of modifying the pedagogical means so that they become appropriate for all; that is, of applying general principles in specific instances.

What is suggested here is that the starting point for constructing the curriculum, or children's activities in school, insofar as we are concerned with cognitive development (the schools may reasonably have other aims as well) lies in definition of the objectives of teaching, which forms the ground base from which pedagogical means are defined and established, means or principles which underlie specific methodological (or experiential) approaches. It may well be that these include the use of co-operative group work as well as individualised activities – but these are carefully designed and structured in relation to the achievement of overall objectives. This approach, I am arguing, is the opposite of basing the educational process on the child, on his immediate interests and spontaneous activity, and providing, in theory, for a total differentiation of the learning process in the case of each individual child. This latter approach is not only undesirable in principle, it is impossible of achievement in practice.[9]

In a striking phrase Lev Vygotsky summed up his outlook on teaching and learning. Pedagogy, he wrote, 'must be oriented not towards the yesterday of development but towards its tomorrow'. Teaching, education, pedagogic means, must always take the child forward, be concerned with the formation of new concepts and hierarchies of concepts, with the next stage in the development of a particular ability, with ever more complex forms of mental operations. 'What the child can do today with adult help', he said, 'he will be able to do independently tomorrow'. This concept, that of the 'zone of next (or "potential") development' implies in the educator a clear concept of the progression of learning, of a consistent challenge, of the mastery by the child of increasingly complex forms – of never standing still or going backwards. 'The only good teaching is that which outpaces development', insisted Vygotsky.[10] Whether the area is that of language development, of concepts of number and mathematics – symbolic systems that underlie all further learning – or whether it covers scientific and technological concepts and skills as well as those related to the social sciences and humanities, appropriate pedagogical means can and should be defined, perhaps particularly in areas having their own inner logical structures. In this sense, psychological knowledge combined with logical analysis forms the ground base from which pedagogical principles can be established, given, of course, effective research and experiment.

This chapter has been strictly concerned with cognitive development, since it is here that technological/scientific and social changes will make their greatest impact and demands. But for successful implementation of rational procedures and planning, in the face of the micro-processor revolution, more than this needs consideration. There is also the question, for instance, of the individual's enhanced responsibility for his own activities; the development of autonomy, of initiative, creativity, critical awareness; the need on the part of the mass of the population for access to knowledge and culture, the arts and literature, to mention only some aspects of human development. The means of promoting such human qualities and characteristics cannot simply be left to individual teachers, on the grounds that each individual child is unique so that the development of a pedagogy is both impracticable and superfluous. The existing teaching force of half a million have, no doubt, many talents, but they need assistance in the pursuit of their common objective – the education of new generations of pupils. The new pedagogy requires carefully defined goals, structure, and adult guidance. Without this a high proportion of children, whose concepts are formed as a result of their everyday experiences, and, as a result, are often distorted and incorrectly reflect reality, will never even reach the stage where the development of higher cognitive forms of activity becomes a possibility. And this implies a massive cognitive failure in terms of involvement and control (responsible participation) in the new social forms and activities which the future may bring.

NOTES

1 The English failure to take pedagogy seriously is stressed in an article on the subject in an educational encyclopaedia of a century ago. Interest in pedagogy 'is not held in much honour among us English'. The lack of a professional approach to teaching means that 'pedagogy is with us at a discount'. This, it is held, 'is unquestionably a most grievous national loss. . . . Without something like scientific discussion on educational subjects, without pedagogy, we shall never obtain a body of organised opinion on education.' (Fletcher, 1889, pp. 257–258).

2 An exception here was R. H. Quick, author of *Essays on Educational Reformers* (1869), a public schoolmaster himself who fought hard for professional training and who appears to have been largely instrumental in setting up the Cambridge Syndicate which organised (prematurely) the first systematic set of lectures on education in an English university; those delivered at Cambridge in 1879–1880 (see Storr, 1889, pp. 349–388). For a young teacher's experience of 'learning on the job' in the 1930s see Worsley, 1967, Chapter 1.

3 See, for instance, Arnold (1874) which devotes a lengthy chapter to the professional training of schoolmasters for the *gymnasia* and *realschule* in Prussia (Chapter 5).

4 I have analysed developments in this period in detail in Simon (1965).

5 See especially Legge (1929) on Liverpool, and Gosden and Sharp (1978, pp. 77ff.) on the West Riding.

6 Percy Nunn was Principal of the University of London Institute of Education from 1922 to 1936. His textbook went through over 20 reprintings between its publication in 1920 and 1940; it was required reading for many graduates training

as teachers. For an acute critique of Nunn's biologism, see Gordon and White (1979, pp. 207–213).

7 This position is concisely reflected in a statement by Cyril Burt in 1950: 'Obviously in an ideal community, our aim should be to discover what ration of intelligence nature has given to each individual child at birth, then to provide him with an appropriate education, and finally to guide him into the career for which he seems to have been marked out' (Burt, 1950).

8 These points are argued in detail, supported by empirical evidence derived from systematic classroom observation, in Galton, Simon and Croll (1980).

9 For a critique of this approach by a psychologist who has worked closely with Piaget (regarded as the authority for individualisation, for instance, in the Plowden Report), see Duckworth (1979).

10 See Vygotsky, 1963; see also Vygotsky, 1962, 1967. For Vygotsky's views on education, 'Teaching and Development: a Soviet Investigation', Special Issue of *Soviet Education*. Vol. 19, nos. 4–6, 1977.

REFERENCES

Arnold, M. (2nd edn 1874) *High Schools and Universities in Germany*, London, Macmillan.

Bain, A. (1879) *Education as a Science*, London, Kegan Paul.

Bruner, J. S. (1972) *The Relevance of Education*, London, Allen & Unwin.

Burt, C. (1921) *Mental and Scholastic Tests*, London, Staples Press.

Burt, C. (1950) 'Testing intelligence', *The Listener*, 16 November.

Duckworth, E. (1979) 'Either we're too early and they can't learn it or we're too late and they know it already: The dilemma of "applying Piaget" ', *Harvard Educational Review*, 49, 3.

Fletcher, A. E. (ed.) (2nd edn 1889) *Cyclopaedia of Education*, Swan Sonnenschein.

Galton, M., Simon, B. and Croll, P. (1980) *Inside the Primary Classroom*, London, Routledge & Kegan Paul.

Gordon, P. and White, J. (1979) *Philosophers as Educational Reformers*, London, Routledge & Kegan Paul.

Froebel, F. (1912) *The Education of Man*, New York & London, Appleton.

Gosden, P. H. J. H. and Sharp, P. R. (1978) *The Development of an Education Service, the West Riding 1889–1974*, Oxford, Martin Robertson.

Honey, J. R. de S. (1977) *Tom Brown's Universe*, London, Millington.

Isaacs, S. (1932) *The Children We Teach: 7 to 11 Years*, London, University of London Press.

Isaacs, S. (1963) *The Psychological Aspects of Child Development*, London: Evans.

Legge, J. G. (1929) *The Rising Tide*, Oxford, Blackwell.

Luria, A. R. (1962) *Voprosy Psikhologii* 1962, 4.

Murphy, G. (1938) *Historical Introduction to Modern Psychology*, New York, Harcourt, Brace.

Plowden Report, the (1967) *Children and their Primary Schools*, London, HMSO.

Quick, R. H. (1869) *Essays on Educational Reformers*, London, Longmans Green.

Simon, B. (1965) *Education and the Labour Movement, 1870–1920*, London, Lawrence & Wishart.

Spearman, C. (1927) *The Nature of 'Intelligence' and the Principles of Cognition*, London, Macmillan.

Stones, E. (1979) *Psychopedagogy: Psychological Theory and the Practice of Teaching*, London, Methuen.

Storr, F. (ed.) (1889) *Life and Remains of the Rev. R. H. Quick*, Cambridge, Cambridge University Press.

Vygotsky, L. S. (1962) *Thought and Language*, London, Wiley.

—— (1963) 'Learning and mental development at school age', in B. Simon and J. Simon (eds) *Educational Psychology in the USSR*, London, Routledge & Kegan Paul.

—— (1967) Vygotskyan Memorial Issue of *Soviet Psychology and Psychiatry*, 5, 3.

Worsley, T. C. (1967) *Flannelled Fools*, London, Alan Ross.

Part II

Learners

The way teachers view their pupils as learners is a crucial part of the teaching process. This Part looks at a number of different perspectives on learning. The first three chapters, Bourne and Moon, Gardner, and the extract from the London report on *Improving Secondary Schools* explore the concepts of intelligence, ability and achievement and the way these are interpreted in the school context. In different ways each reflects the increased recognition that is now given to *defining pupils' capabilities and abilities in much broader terms than has traditionally been the case.*

Bennett and Dunne look at the current debate about how children learn and the optimal conditions for this learning in a systematic review of recent research. They describe the evidence which points to the *importance of recognising what children already know in building plans for teaching and learning,* and they stress the immensely important role played by the teacher in creating, to use their metaphor, 'a window into the child's mind'. This process, they argue, *demands a sophisticated combination of observation and careful questioning, and talk, therefore, and language are crucially important to the task of teaching and learning.*

Adolescent learners have personal and social characteristics that reflect the society and culture in which they are growing up. John Coleman provides a review of contemporary ideas about the adolescent years and looks in particular at the fundamental transitions that take place in these years and the effects these changes have upon the way the young person functions in the school setting. Sara Delamont points critically to the dangers of books that stress how confused, disturbed, easily led astray and vulnerable adolescents are. This, she argues, is often the way authors project their own anxieties and doubts on the adolescent and there is very little research on how adolescents see their own lives. The literature, however, is clear on the increased importance of the peer group as the child moves into adolescence. *Young people derive many of their values from their homes, but as they move into adolescence their friends' ideas on music, fashion, sexuality and school teachers become increasingly important.* Delamont goes on to explain how research to date on adolescence and schooling has focused mostly on boys.

The way that gender works differently to interpret the mediation between peer group and school remains an unanswered question.

Alec Clegg was one of the most well known of local education authority officers in the middle years of the century. He championed many causes, particularly in the old West Riding area of Yorkshire where he was Director of Education. This short extract from his book, *About Our Schools*, published at the end of his career in 1980 is a succinct polemical statement on the way socio-economic *differences impact on the lives of children and their experience at school*. Tessa Blackstone and Jo Mortimore summarise much of the research evidence that had influenced people such as Clegg, and they *point to the caution with which teachers need to view ideas that imply a causal link between cultural factors and pupils' performance in school*.

The Part continues by looking at the way special needs education could evolve over the next twenty-five years. Klaus Wedell, in a paper that was prepared as part of the build up to the 1993 National Commission on Education, argues that *Special Educational Needs (SEN) merges into the range of diversity of ability identifiable in all pupils*. It follows that *special needs education must be offered more as an extension of education in general . . . Progress in the education of pupils with SENs*, he suggests, *will be inextricably linked with developments in educating all children and young people*, an argument which has ramifications for policy beyond the confines of what has traditionally been seen as the world of special education.

Part II concludes with a survey of secondary school pupils' views on schooling carried out by the National Foundation for Educational Research in 1992. It takes a broad approach to a number of issues, and as the authors point out, raises questions that require further investigation. The findings, however, provide one snapshot of 11- and 14-year-old views with perhaps the most intriguing being the difference between *the overwhelming liking for school and yet, the also clear experience of boredom with much that schools have to offer!* Which brings the focus in again to the activity of learning and the motivation that teachers can bring to that process.

Chapter 3

A question of ability?

Jill Bourne and Bob Moon

Talk in pubs:

'She's got a talent for it'.
'Got the right brains for it'.
'In the family'.

(From Howe, 1990)

Talk in schools:

In this school we try to meet each child's needs according to their age and ability.

(School Booklet)

I teach in a mixed-ability classroom.

(Class teacher)

I want every child to develop their abilities to the full.

(Headmaster)

In this chapter, we want to raise questions about the 'commonsense' concept of 'ability', to trace its origins, and to look at the implications for teachers today. What do we mean when we talk about a child's 'ability'? The dictionary defines 'ability' as cleverness, talent or mental power. When we speak of a child's 'ability' are we describing some kind of inborn 'intelligence', a genetic inheritance? How do teachers know how to assess a child's 'ability'? Can one label a child 'bright' or 'slow'? Why is it that the newer models of assessment avoid the term 'ability' and choose instead to focus on 'attainment'?

Despite decades of research, there is no clear evidence of any single underlying 'intelligence' or generalised 'ability'. Research on people who have been brain damaged suggests the contrary; whilst some areas of activity are impaired, others are not. Gardner (1983), for example, has proposed that there are multiple 'intelligences' (see Chapter 4). Sternberg (1984:312) defines intelligence as 'consisting of purposive selection and shaping of and adaptation to real-world environments relevant to one's life'. The problem with a definition like this is that it leaves one with working out what individuals themselves each perceive as being most relevant to their lives. As Salmon and Bannister (1974:31) have argued: 'People rarely just fail to learn; they leave us with the problem of finding out what it was they were learning while they were not learning what we expected them to learn.'

Of course, the fact that we have such words as 'intelligence' or 'ability', as with the unicorn, does not mean that such things have to exist. But while the terms may not be real 'they can, and do, create barriers to ordinary people's capabilities. That is because they encourage us to believe that we cannot realistically aspire to many accomplishments which we are actually capable of achieving' (Howe, 1990).

As with most 'commonsense' concepts, there is a history behind what has come to be such a natural way of talking about children in the United Kingdom. Yet the concept is historically and culturally specific. Not so long ago, children and their achievements were looked at very differently, as they are in other places in the world today.

When mass schooling was first introduced in the last century, 'ignorance' seems to have been conceived of in moral terms as the result of 'sloth' or laziness (Birchenough, 1914). However, education was not equally open to everyone. There was a different form of differentiation among children, one based not on inborn mental characteristics, but in terms of social hierarchy. Children were educated to take up 'their place' in society. Jacqueline Rose (1984) has shown how, in the nineteenth century, a different form of language education was marked out for different social groups: classics for the wealthy, English literature for the middle classes, basic literacy and 'clear expression' for the poor. Thomas Crabbe wrote of the way education was becoming a social device to mark out social groups and to control the new industrialised society: 'For every class we have a school assigned, rules for all ranks and food for every mind' (cited in Birchenough, 1914, p. 5).

Over this century, however, explicit control over different types of 'knowledges' for different classes, and indeed, gender groups, was gradually relaxed, as intellectual 'ability' or 'intelligences' became naturalised as a biological construct. The influence of Darwin's evolutionary theory, in the context of the heyday of British imperialism, brought about the popularity of 'eugenic' theories of genetically superior types, providing 'scientific' explanations for the dominance of men over women, of the upper and middle classes over the poor, or white over black groups. Poverty was taken as a sign of inferiority, wealth a sign of strength.

These opening paragraphs have been written polemically, and certainly have dealt with this historical period superficially, but what we are trying to bring out is the point that theoretical advances are not divorced from history, but carry with them shadows of old, unstated assumptions, and retain some unsavoury foundations, which can be traced through to the present day.

A SCIENCE FOR SELECTION AND THE START OF 'STREAMING'

In the elementary schools earlier this century, children worked through each 'standard', the majority moving up to the next 'standard' as they passed the annual examinations, others repeating the year (a familiar system today in other parts of the world). But the schools were also given the function of discovering 'individual children who show promise of exceptional capacity', to send them on scholarships to fee-paying 'secondary schools', previously used only by children of the middle class. The concept of 'bright' and 'slow' children seemed an unquestioned assumption, with psychological theories suggesting the direct dependence of attainment on mental abilities.

This was shown strikingly in the 1920s and 1930s when a number of important national reports argued for the introduction of psychological tests to assess a child's suitability for the different types of secondary schooling that were proposed. Harry Torrance (1981) shows how different reports legitimised the notion of general intelligence and fitted this to a form of structurally differentiated school provision very similar to that advanced by Thomas Crabbe. The Spens report, for example, of 1938 was in part based on a memorandum prepared by Professor Cyril Burt, a leading figure of the day whose ideas on general intelligence have been rejected (amid evidence of the falsification of data – see Hearnshaw, 1979) by the large part of the scientific community. Torrance quotes from a section of Spens:

> Intellectual development during childhood appears to progress as if it were governed by a single central factor, usually known as 'general intelligence', which may broadly be described as innate all-round intellectual ability. . . . Our psychological witnesses assured us that it can be measured approximately by means of intelligence tests. . . . We were informed that, with few exceptions, it is possible at a very early age to predict with some degree of accuracy the ultimate level of a child's intellectual powers.
>
> (Torrance, 1981, pp. 123–4)

A large part of the growth in testing, and particularly intelligence testing, can be traced to the national imperative to apportion pupils to schools. This was seen as the progressive direction education should take, and was influenced by ideas that had spread from North America. Individualisation, and the measurement of intelligences, was seen as a crucial feature in the development of the new method and the fair society.

The technology of IQ testing made the new system of selective schools feel 'fair'. There were, after all, only a limited number of places at universities and in higher education yet compulsory, free education was for all. By the 1950s nearly all schools which were big enough were streamed. Children went to secondary schools that matched their innate 'abilities' and were not

Figure 3.1 The pupil becomes an individual

Source: (1922) *American School Board Journal* (reprinted by permission of Department of Special Collections and University Archives, Stanford University Libraries).

only differentiated between schools, but also within them, segregated into different 'streams'. The system spread down into the junior and infant schools. A survey of those junior schools large enough to be able to stream was carried out by Brian Jackson (1964). It showed that 96 per cent were streamed, and that 74 per cent streamed the children by 7 years old. So, children's life chances were usually fixed by 7 years old, as there was very little transfer between streams (Plowden, 1967). Brian Simon (1971) concluded:

the school system appeared to be (as indeed it was) run on the assumption that no child could ever rise above himself, that his level of achievement was fatally determined by an IQ.

EFFECTS OF STREAMING

Brian Jackson's study (1964), highly influential in the 1960s, identified some of the effects of streaming. Taking the quantifiable evidence first, he found that pupils were disadvantaged by streaming on three main counts:

1 *Social background*: children whose fathers were in unskilled jobs had a far greater chance of being placed in a C stream than those with similar IQ scores from the professional classes. Streaming seemed to work as a covert, albeit unconscious, form of social selection. The choice of questions, the design of the test and the process of setting norms and standardising the tests are all ways of differentiating between social groups, by validating the knowledge and experience of some and denying those of the others. Apart from IQ test bias, both Jackson and Barker-Lunn (1970) found a tendency among teachers to underestimate the 'ability' of working-class children, often leading to placement in the lower streams.
2 *Date of birth*: there were also less easily foreseen consequences of streaming. Children with an Autumn birthday, and thus both older and with more experience of school, were found to have a far better chance of entering an 'A' stream.
3 *Teachers*: streaming had led to a concentration of more experienced and qualified teachers in the 'A' streams, with younger and less experienced teachers given the low status 'C' streams.

Case studies of schools, he argued, showed an increase in low expectations for 'B' and 'C' stream children, while the 'A' stream élites appeared to suffer in their turn from dull and repetitive coaching for secondary entrance exams. Brian Jackson describes how, when he began teaching, streaming was so entrenched as a 'commonsense' strategy that he just took for granted that 'A' streams were 'eager, apt and docile' whilst the 'Cs' contained 'the rebellious, the apathetic and the weak'.

Finally, there seemed to be no research evidence suggesting that standards of achievement were significantly better in streamed schools. Barker-Lunn concluded that streaming was less critical to children's achievement than underlying differences in teachers' attitudes and practice.

After visiting newly de-streamed schools, though, Brian Jackson wrote: 'I suspect that there had been no change of values or teaching technique in these schools'. Although Heads 'de-streamed', the change in organisation seemed rarely preceded or followed up with a focus on new teaching strategies to replace old routines. And the underlying concept of innate differences in ability remained stronger than superficial organisational changes, as we shall try to show in the next section.

DE-STREAMING AND MIXED-ABILITY GROUPING

During the 1960s a shift in thinking had taken place with the gradual discrediting of methods of psychometric testing and with public disenchantment with the unfairnesses of the selective system. Throughout the Plowden Report (1967), for example, a major report on the future of primary schooling, the uniqueness of each individual was stressed, the 'enormously wide variability' in maturity, with different mental and physical abilities maturing at different rates within each child, so requiring the individualisation of teaching programmes (see Chapter 2 and Simon's critiques of this perspective). Given this heterogeneity, streaming was no longer thought either possible or desirable, since it merely masked variety. Plowden recommended 'de-streaming' and opposed any fixed forms of grouping by 'ability' within the classroom.

'De-streaming' appears to have taken place very rapidly across the country in the wake of Plowden and, perhaps more importantly, as comprehensive schools were introduced, with the demise of the 11-plus examination. However, as we saw above, not all schools accompanied the organisational change with changes in teaching strategies (HMI, 1978; Galton et al., 1980). Meanwhile, the underlying expectation of different 'abilities' leading to differential achievement remained: 'There will be big and growing differences in children's ability and attainment but they will follow no tidy pattern because interest and motive can make havoc of prediction' (Plowden, para. 824).

Streaming, however, and setting by subject remained, and remains to this day, a major issue of contention within secondary comprehensive schools and internally within the organisational structure of schools that select at the point of admission. The arguments that Jackson had put forward in the context of primary schooling were widely debated. Significant moves were made to de-stream, particularly in the lower forms of the secondary school, and there was a range of publications (Kelly, 1975; Wragg, 1976; HMSO, 1978) which explored the methodology of mixed-ability teaching. There were parallels with the primary experience.

First, a number of major research reports failed to show any particular advantage, in terms of academic attainment, for either streamed or mixed-ability forms of grouping. One well-known study (Newbold, 1977) reported research in a large comprehensive school that had been divided into two 'halls', one streamed and one not. The finding was that:

variations in academic performance which occur at the end of the first two years are generally not attributable to differences in methods of ability grouping . . . with common overall objectives the system of organisation is of less importance for academic standards, if indeed it is important at all, than the other substantial variables which exist.

(Newbold, 1977: 178)

The study, whilst not detecting academic benefits for either form of organisation, did see social effects which could be taken to support the principle of hetero-geneous ability grouping as a means of achieving increased social integration.

Second, although the forms of grouping might have changed, teachers' conceptions of ability had not. Kerry (1984), for example, looked at a range of mixed-ability classes in the early years of the secondary school and concluded that the tasks teachers set took little account of the attainment of pupils in the classroom. The challenge, he suggested, was:

for trainee and experienced teachers to be able to analyze and reflect on the tasks they ask children to undertake, to consider the demands they make on the pupils, and whether these are worthwhile and appropriate as well as exacting and stimulating.

A difference between primary and secondary schooling, however, was the presence in the latter of an examination system which in some senses reflected the selection process of the 11-plus. GCE, CSE and, from the 1980s on, GCSE influenced the form and style of pupil grouping in the prepara-tory years. GCE and CSE covered different types of syllabus, and grouping followed accordingly. GCSE, whilst unified as a system, involves, in many subjects, papers at different levels. The standard assessment tasks associated with the national curriculum at the end of KS3 are also, in a number of subjects, replicating the structured differentiation of the formal examin-ations system. Changes in grouping policy follow accordingly, although as yet there is only anecdotal rather than empirical evidence of the form and extent of this. Grouping is nearly always expressed in ability terms, despite the clear message from the designers of the blueprint for national assessment that makes it clear that the system seeks to measure only attainment rather than anything so problematic as ability.

There have been three recent initiatives within and relevant to the secondary sector that have attempted to change the rules and in some cases challenge the assumptions surrounding the nature of the child's ability. We have already referred to GCSE. Within the planning and organisation of GCSE there has always been the ambition to produce explicit criteria against which pupils could be assessed independently of any comparison with other pupils (a criteria rather than normative approach). Despite the will to achieve this, a principle the national curriculum also attempts to follow, the technical problems of producing meaningful and assessable criteria have proved extremely problematic; see Harlen *et al.*, Chapter 34 of this volume. The examination system at 16, like the 'A' level, still produces something akin to a normative distribution, which internally within schools is often anticipated in advance by different forms of grouping.

In contrast with GCSE, the world of vocational qualifications has gone more directly for a criteria approach. National Vocational Qualifications (NVQs) and their generic equivalents (GNVQs) are organised on five levels against specific criteria. There is, of course, an important difference in use. GCSEs are still used as a selective mechanism for the current minority who go on to advanced academic study, NVQs, as yet, are not. Given this purpose, validity and reliability of the criteria 'cut off' points come under much greater scrutiny than in less socially and politically sensitive areas of the vocational assessment system.

The third initiative has been Records of Achievement, a movement whose origins lay in the attempt to broaden the basis upon which pupils were assessed and reported upon. Many schemes attempted to integrate the dual purpose of providing a reporting form for achievements other than the academic and promoting a more criteria-based approach to subject and topic work within the curriculum. Some progress has been made (Broadfoot *et al.*, 1988), although building the status of abilities other than the scholastic, and finding the technical means of achieving criteria-based assessment, has proved problematic. Within these and other initiatives the commonsense and problematic idea of ability continues to pose pedagogical organisation problems. Ability grouping, where it exists, may lower expectations and, in terms of the process of allocation to groups, may be unfair (see Cecile Wright, Chapter 41 of this volume).

If we challenge ability as an organising framework, however, it hardly seems appropriate to introduce the concept of 'mixed ability'. Both are tainted by the spectre of debilitating determinism and both appear to provide for a sterility in educational and political debate.

RECENT MOVES

In recent years, there has been increased interest from educationalists in social approaches to learning, based on the work of Vygotsky and developed by Jerome Bruner and others. In contrast to Piaget's concept of the isolated individual learner, Vygotsky offered a way of conceptualising the learning process which sees it as essentially arising out of social interaction and dependent on social experience. 'Ability', therefore, has come to be redefined in terms of differences in background experiences and in preferred styles of learning. The focus has shifted from the monitoring of development to the monitoring of attainment. Through observation of the learning process, it is believed that instead of waiting for 'readiness', teachers can build on what children know and can do, challenging their existing knowledge and skills and extending them by working together, co-operatively, before expecting them to achieve new skills on their own.

Taking this perspective, Brian Simon eschews both the psychometric tradition of individualisation which, contrary to the expectations of the cartoonists of the 1920s (see Figure 3.1), has led back to forms of classification reminiscent of the social organisation of the nineteenth century and the more recent pedagogic individualism where the teacher is expected to provide individual support across intellectual, as well as perhaps emotional and physical development. For Simon (Chapter 2, p. 18 of this volume):

> to start from the standpoint of individual differences is to start from the wrong position. To develop effective pedagogy means starting from the opposite standpoint, from what children have in common as members of the human species; to establish the general principles of teaching and, in the light of these, to determine what modifications of practice are necessary to meet specific individual needs. If all children are to be assisted to learn, to master increasingly complex cognitive tasks, to develop increasingly complex skills and abilities or mental operations, then this is an objective that schools must have in common; their task becomes the deliberate development of such skills and abilities in all their children. And this involves importing a definite structure into the teaching, and so into the learning experiences provided for the pupils. Individual differences only become important, in this context, if the pedagogical means elaborated are found not to be appropriate to particular children (or groups of children) because of one or other aspect of their individual development or character.

Of course, this is what many teachers have believed in and tried to do all along. And the possibilities offered by new forms of information technology provide a further range of opportunities by which these may be achieved. However, as it becomes legitimate 'commonsense' practice, it is important to be aware of how new moves may be subverted where a deep and ingrained belief in one general, underlying and fixed 'ability' is still widely accepted in our society.

The teaching profession in the UK is entering into an unprecedented period of public testing, with compulsory national testing in the state school system. It seems vital to look closely at what those tests mean for expectations of pupil potential.

The Task Group on Assessment and Testing (TGAT) Report (1988) remains the only clear statement of the testing strategy underpinning the national curriculum. Its starting point, as we have said, is the assessment of attainment, not of potential: 'The assessment programme depends on a clear view of what children should be being taught and should learn: the curriculum' (para. 140). It warns that 'care should be taken at all reporting ages, but especially at (age 7), to avoid giving the impression that the assessment is a prediction of future performance' (para. 148). It therefore recognises the potency of expectations upon performance. It also recognises differences in 'the pattern of attainment at intake' (para. 18). It argues that 'poor performance against a target should not be seen as a prediction of personal inadequacy; it should usually be regarded as an indication of needs. Such needs must be met' (para. 14).

However, critics of TGAT consider that there are a number of aspects of the TGAT model which are cause for concern. First, learning seems to be presented as taking place in a fixed, hierarchical sequence, thus ten levels of progression are established in each subject area. Goldstein and Noss (1990) point out that it is not at all clear that one particular sequence of learning is either a necessary sequence or the best for everyone.

Second, while TGAT argued that 'To tie the criteria to particular ages only would risk either limiting the very able, or giving the least able no reward, or both' (para. 99), it then suggested that on average, 'a pupil could reasonably be expected to progress by one level in two years of work' (para. 101). An attainment model of testing has been turned into an age-related normative model. We should also note the inbuilt acceptance of the concept of 'the able'. Goldstein and Noss (1990) argue that such 'average' expectations can in practice easily become statements of minimum levels of attainment. However, a child may attain a number of requirements across a range of levels, while at the same time not enough to be deemed to have fully achieved any one of the levels: 'The danger is that such a student will be forced to concentrate on achieving the lowest level not yet attained . . . before being allowed to move on' (Goldstein and Noss, 1990).

Finally, although TGAT claims to be about assessing progress rather than ranking children, the way each child is given a 'level' clearly invites comparison. The edifice of SATs testing begins to carry its own form of validity, a new selection device replacing the old mystique of psychometric testing. It legitimates and even encourages the streaming of children, for emphasis on differences *between* individuals may lead to the overlooking of differences *within* individuals, and thus brings us back to the old notion of ability as common across subjects, a fixed and underlying general intelligence.

At this point one needs to turn to a range of official statements on teaching from government-appointed bodies, to see how the issues of streaming and 'setting' have once more become an issue. Most of the attention has focused on the primary school.

A recent report (Alexander, Rose and Woodhead, 1992), commissioned by government, rejected streaming, however, as 'a crude device which cannot do justice to the different abilities a pupil may show in different subjects and contexts'. Like Plowden, it suggested flexible grouping according to ability 'for a particular purpose' and warned teachers of 'the pitfall of assuming that pupils' ability is fixed' (para. 85).

Soon afterwards, HMI (Ofsted, 1993) recommended 'carefully planned and appropriate groupings of pupils for tasks' and 'teaching specifically targeted to specific individuals or groups' (ibid., p. 22), statements which again suggest flexible and changing groupings for particular tasks.

The National Curriculum Council (NCC, 1993), however, called for attention to be given to 'the setting of pupils according to ability' in different subjects. This statement still clearly recognises that a pupil may have a range of different levels of attainment in different subject areas, but does seem to suggest rather more fixed and less fluid groupings. No explicit indication is given in any of the above reports of how 'ability' in the different subjects is to be assessed.

A DFE circular responding to the reports was soon afterwards sent to all schools, asking them to consider:

> How to achieve a better match of work to children's needs – including the introduction of setting where possible, and of grouping by ability if setting is not possible, taking into account the problem of smaller, rural schools.
>
> (DFE News Circular 16/93, 18 January 1993)

The HMI and NCC recommendations seem slightly re-worked here to introduce into the debate the need to establish more fixed 'sets'. There is no mention of different groupings for different subject areas.

Moving to the broader stage of school organisation, and particularly secondary school organisation, the language of policy has taken an interesting new direction. The White Paper (1992) 'Choice and Diversity' which preceded the 1993 Education Act talked of encouraging school specialisation.

> Other leading industrialised nations combine the attainment of high standards with a measure of specialisation. Such specialisation does not mean selection, which implies choice by the school; instead it means increased choice for parents and pupils. The greater the choice, the greater the opportunity for children to go to schools which cater for their particular interests and aptitudes. That will bring greater commitment to the school by children and their parents – and so lead to a better education.
>
> (para. 10.2)

The word 'ability' is missing, although how 'interests and aptitudes' are to be construed is open to further analysis.

The issue of grouping children or creating new forms of specialist school has thus come back into focus, but based on a different system of testing and assessment. Can this system overcome the problems identified in the past? They seem equally applicable and equally formidable today: lowered expectations through labelling, a widening achievement gap between sets, lowered morale, the production of hierarchies which reproduce themselves, and the possibility of unfair discrimination against certain groups through the assessment norms set and assessment procedures adopted.

While there is a danger that fixed forms of 'ability' grouping could lead back towards the hierarchically structured system of schooling of earlier times, it is clear that the informal limitation of the potential of certain children by theories and practices based on individual 'readiness' cannot provide the alternative. One must distinguish two different strands in the development of assessment: on the one hand, a stronger focus on the process of interaction between teacher, pupil and task in learning and its outcomes; on the other a search for a legitimising technology which could rank children for a differential distribution of resources and access to different kinds of knowledge.

Ensuring equality of opportunity in the classroom will continue to require imaginative solutions, where the best developments of the past years in co-operative teaching and learning strategies, effective communication, and a principled mix of whole-class, flexible groupings, pair and individual work, are supported and improved. But central to the improvement of practice must be the recognition that no child's potential is fixed.

Mortimore and his colleagues (1988), challenging 'common views of intelligence' in a study of primary schools, suggested that the data illustrated that:

> children's performance changes over time. Given an effective school, children make greater progress. Greater progress leads to greater capability and, if handled sensitively, to greater confidence. . . . The responsibility of teachers is to ensure that their pupils do not adopt fixed views of their own abilities but, rather, come to realise that they have considerable potential which, given motivation and good teaching in an effective school, can be realised . . . many parents still regard their children's ability as fixed. We hope our data will persuade both teacher and parents that this is not so and that change is possible. We believe that, in the right circumstances, children can become more intelligent.
>
> (Mortimore *et al.*, p. 264)

Thirty years ago Sir Edward Boyle in the Foreword to a report (Newsom Report, 1963) which looked at the education of the majority of pupils in secondary schools, spoke of:

> The essential point is that all children should have an equal opportunity of acquiring intelligence, and of developing their talents and abilities to the full.

It is salutary that his recognition of the potential for growth and development, one of the enduring characteristics of human behaviour, still requires forceful advocacy in the last decade of the century.

REFERENCES

Alexander, R., Rose, J. and Woodhead, C. (1992) *Curriculum Organisation and Classroom Practice in Primary Schools: A Discussion Paper* ('The Three Wise Men's Report'), London, DES.

Barker-Lunn, J. (1970) *Streaming in the Primary School*, Slough, NFER.

Birchenough, C. (1914) *History of Elementary Education in England and Wales*, London, University Tutorial Press.

Broadfoot, P. *et al.* (1988) *Recorded Achievement*, London, HMSO.

DFE (1993) DFE News 16/93 *Improving Primary Education – Patten*, London, DFE.

Galton, M., Simon, B. and Croll, P. (1980) *Inside the Primary Classroom*, London, Routledge & Kegan Paul.

Gardner, H. (1983) *Frames of Mind: The Theory of Multiple Intelligence*, New York, Basic Books.

Goldstein, H. and Noss, R. (1990) 'Against the stream', *Forum*, 33(1).

Hearnshaw, L.S. (1979) *Cyril Burt. Psychologist*, London, Hodder and Stoughton

HMI (1978) *Primary Education in England: A Survey by HMI*, London, DES.

HMSO (1978) *Mixed Ability Work in Comprehensive Schools*.

HMSO (1992) *Choice and Diversity*.

Howe, M. (1990) 'Children's gifts, talents and natural abilities: an explanatory mythology?', *Education and Child Psychology*, 7(1).

Jackson, B. (1964) *Streaming: An Education System in Miniature*, London, Routledge & Kegan Paul.

Kelly, V. (1975) *Case studies in Mixed Ability Teaching*, London, Harper Row.

Kerry, T. (1984) 'Analysing the cognitive demands made by classroom tasks in mixed ability classes', in Wragg, E. C. (ed.) *Classroom Teaching Skills*, Beckenham, Croom Helm.

Mortimore, P., Sammons, P., Stoll, L., Lewis, D. and Ecob, R. (1988) *School Matters: The Junior Years*, Wells, Open Books.

NCC (1993) *The National Curriculum at Key Stages 1 and 2: Advice to the Secretary of State for Education*, York, NCC.

Newbold, D. (1977) *Ability Grouping: The Banbury Enquiry*, Windsor, NFER/Nelson.

Newsom Report (1963) *Half Our Future*. A report of the Central Advisory Council for Education (England), HMSO.

Ofsted (1993) *Curriculum Organisation and Classroom Practice in Primary Schools: A follow up Report*, London, Ofsted.

Plowden Report (1967) *Children and their Primary Schools*, London, HMSO.

Rose, J. (1984) *The Case of 'Peter Pan' or the Impossibility of Children's Fiction*, London, Macmillan.

Salmon, P. and Bannister, D. (1974) 'Education in the light of personal construct theory', *Education for Teaching*, 94, pp. 25–38.

Simon, B. (1971) *Intelligence Psychology Education*, London, Lawrence & Wishart.

Sternberg, R. (1984) 'A contextualist view of the nature of intelligence', *International Journal of Psychology*, 19, pp. 307–34.

TGAT (1988) *National Curriculum Task Group on Assessment and Testing: A Report*, London, DES/Welsh Office.

Torrance, H. (1981) 'The origins and development of mental testing in England and Wales and the USA', *Journal of Sociology of Education*, 2(1).

Wragg, E. C. (1976) *Teaching Mixed Ability Groups*, Newton Abbot, David & Charles.

Chapter 4

The theory of multiple intelligences[1]

Howard Gardner

CONTRASTING POINTS OF VIEW

Two 11-year-old children are taking a test of 'intelligence'. They sit at their desks labouring over the meanings of different words, the interpretation of graphs, and the solutions to arithmetic problems. They record their answers by filling in small circles on a single piece of paper. Later these completed answer sheets are scored objectively: the number of right answers is converted into a standardised score that compares the individual child with a population of children of similar age.

The teachers of these children review the different scores. They notice that one of the children has performed at a superior level; on all sections of the test, she answered more questions correctly than did her peers. In fact, her score is similar to that of children three to four years older. The other child's performance is 'average' – his scores reflect those of other children his age.

A subtle change in expectations surrounds the review of these test scores. Teachers begin to expect the first child to do quite well during her formal schooling, whereas the second should have only moderate success. Indeed these predictions come true. In other words, the test taken by the 11-year-olds serves as a reliable predictor of their later performance in school.

How does this happen? One explanation involves our free use of the word 'intelligence': the child with the greater 'intelligence' has the ability to solve problems, to find the answers to specific questions, and to learn new material quickly and efficiently. These skills in turn play a central role in school success. In this view, 'intelligence' is a singular faculty that is brought to bear in any problem-solving situation. Since schooling deals largely with solving problems of various sorts, predicting this capacity in young children predicts their future success in school.

'Intelligence', from this point of view, is a general ability that is found in varying degrees in all individuals. It is the key to success in solving problems. This ability can be measured reliably with standardised pencil-and-paper tests that, in turn, predict future success in school.[2]

What happens after school is completed? Consider the two individuals in the example. Looking further down the road, we find that the 'average' student has become a highly successful mechanical engineer who has risen to a position of prominence in both the professional community of engineers as well as in civic groups in his community. His success is no fluke – he is considered by all to be a talented individual. The 'superior' student, on the other hand, has had little success in her chosen career as a writer; after repeated rejections by publishers, she has taken up a middle management position in a bank. While certainly not a 'failure' she is considered by her peers to be quite 'ordinary' in her adult accomplishments. So what happened?

This fabricated example is based on the facts of intelligence testing. IQ tests predict school performance with considerable accuracy, but they are only an indifferent predictor of performance in a profession after formal schooling.[3] Furthermore, even as IQ tests measure only logical or logical-linguistic capacities, in this society we are nearly 'brain-washed' to restrict the notion of intelligence to the capacities used in solving logical and linguistic problems.

To introduce an alternative point of view, undertake the following *Gedanken* experiment. Suspend the usual judgement of what constitutes intelligence and let your thoughts run freely over the capabilities of humans – perhaps those that would be picked out by the proverbial Martian visitor. In this exercise, you are drawn to the brilliant chess player, the world-class violinist, and the champion athlete; such outstanding performers deserve special consideration. Under this experiment, a quite different view of *intelligence* emerges. Are the chess player, violinist, and athlete 'intelligent' in these pursuits? If they are, then why do our tests of 'intelligence' fail to identify them? If they are not 'intelligent', what allows them to achieve such astounding feats? In general, why does the contemporary construct 'intelligence' fail to explain large areas of human endeavour?

In this chapter we approach these problems through the theory of Multiple Intelligences (MI). As the name indicates, we believe that human cognitive competence is better described in terms of a set of abilities, talents, or mental skills, which we call 'Intelligences'. All normal individuals possess each of these skills to some extent; individuals differ in the degree of skill and in the nature of their combination. We believe this theory of intelligence may be more humane and more veridical than alternative views of intelligence and that it more adequately reflects the data of human 'intelligent' behaviour. Such a theory has important educational implications, including ones for curriculum development.

The question of the optimal definition of 'intelligence' looms large in our inquiry. Indeed, it is at the level of this definition that the theory of Multiple Intelligences diverges from more traditional points of view. In a more traditional view, intelligence is defined operationally as the ability to answer items on tests of intelligence. The inference from the test scores to some underlying ability is supported by statistical techniques that compare responses of subjects at different ages; the apparent correlation of these test scores across ages and across different tests corroborates the notion that the general faculty of intelligence, 'g', does not change much with age or with training or experience. It is an inborn attribute or faculty of the individual.[4]

Multiple Intelligences theory, on the other hand, pluralises the traditional concept. An intelligence entails the ability to solve problems or fashion products that are of consequence in a particular cultural setting. The problem-solving skill allows one to approach a situation in which a goal is to be obtained and to locate the appropriate route to that goal. The creation of a *cultural* product is crucial to such functions as capturing and transmitting knowledge or expressing one's views or feelings. The problems to be solved range from creating an end to a story to anticipating a mating move in chess to repairing a quilt. Products range from scientific theories to musical compositions to successful political campaigns.

MI theory is framed in light of the biological origins of each problem-solving skill. Only those skills that are universal to the human species are treated. Even so, the biological proclivity to participate in a particular form of problem solving must also be coupled with the cultural nurturing of that domain. For example, language, a universal skill, may manifest itself particularly as writing in one culture, as oratory in another culture, and as the secret language of anagrams in a third.

Given the desire of selecting intelligences that are rooted in biology, and which are valued in one or more cultural settings, how does one actually identify an 'intelligence'? In coming up with our list, we consulted evidence from several different sources; knowledge about normal development and development in gifted individuals; information about the breakdown of cognitive skills under conditions of brain damage; studies of exceptional populations, including prodigies, *idiots savants*, and autistic children; data about the evolution of cognition over the millennia; cross-cultural accounts of cognition; psychometric studies, including examinations of correlations among tests; and psychological training studies, particularly measures of transfer and generalisation across tasks. Only those candidate intelligences that satisfied all or a majority of the criteria were selected as bona fide intelligences.

In addition to satisfying these criteria, each intelligence must have an identifiable core operation or set of operations. As a neutrally based computational system, each intelligence is activated or 'triggered' by certain kinds of internally or externally presented information.

An intelligence must also be susceptible to encoding in a symbol system – a culturally contrived system of meaning, which captures and conveys important forms of information. Language, picturing, and mathematics are but three nearly worldwide symbol systems that are necessary for human survival and productivity. The relationship of a candidate intelligence to a human symbol system is no accident. In fact, the existence of a core computational capacity anticipates the existence of a symbol system which exploits that capacity. While it may be possible for an intelligence to proceed without an accompanying symbol system, a primary characteristic of human intelligence may well be its gravitation toward such an embodiment.

THE MULTIPLE INTELLIGENCES

Note: This section summarises descriptions and contains quotations from Gardner's book *Frames of Mind*.[5]

This analysis of a wider and more disparate set of data about human intellectual abilities suggests a minimum of seven distinct intelligences; logical-mathematical, linguistic, spatial, bodily-kinaesthetic, musical, inter-personal, and intrapersonal. A brief description of each of these intelligences is now presented.

Logical-mathematical intelligence

This intelligence can be understood as the ability, described in Piaget's theory of intellectual development, which involves the formal operation of symbols according to accepted rules of logic and mathematics. It is this intelligence that has been almost exclusively measured in 'intelligence tests'. Although it has been given pre-eminence in Western societies, there is no reason to believe that it is more fundamental than the other intelligences. There is more than one form of logic and each intelligence has an equally valid logic of its own.

Linguistic intelligence

There is strong neurological evidence for citing the existence of a separate linguistic intelligence. People with brain damage to a specific location in the left hemisphere have grave difficulty in forming grammatical utterances, although other thought processes are apparently unaffected. The linguistic intelligence makes use of rhetoric, for persuasion, allows us to develop semantic storage of information, and also to explain events, including its own operations. It differs from logical-mathematical intelligence in having a strong auditory/oral component and in not being tied to the world of physical objects.

Spatial intelligence

This intelligence enables us to recognise faces, to find our way around a site, and to notice fine details. All these capacities are affected by damage to parts of the right hemisphere of the brain. Spatial intelligence is perhaps seen at its most developed among certain islanders who are able to navigate long distances by the stars.

> Central to spatial intelligence are the capacities to perceive the visual world accurately, to perform transformations and modifications upon one's initial perceptions, and to be able to re-create aspects of one's visual experience, even in the absence of relevant physical stimuli.
>
> (Gardner 1983:173)

Bodily-kinaesthetic intelligence

This intelligence describes the abilities to use the body or parts of the body to solve problems or to produce worthwhile products or displays. It involves at its core the capacities to control bodily motions and to handle objects skilfully. In different forms and combinations it is exemplified by skilled dancers, athletes, surgeons, and instrumentalists. Again it is possible to identify these skills with a specific area of the brain, in this case the motor cortex.

Musical intelligence

It is possible that language and music evolved together as a single auditory–oral intelligence, but in the present day they appear to be separate, with many examples of people with high musical, but low linguistic, intelligences. Musical intelligence involves the capacities for imitation of vocal targets, for sensitivity to relative as well as absolute pitch, and for appreciating various kinds of musical transformations.

Interpersonal intelligence

> The core capacity here is *the ability to notice and make distinctions among other individuals* and, in particular, among their moods, temperaments, motivations, and intentions. . . . Interpersonal knowledge permits a skilled adult to read the intentions and desires – even when these have been hidden – of many other individuals and, potentially, to act upon this knowledge – for example, by influencing a group of disparate individuals to behave along desired lines. We see highly developed forms of interpersonal intelligence in political and religious leaders . . . in skilled parents and teachers, and in individuals enrolled in the helping professions, be they therapists, counsellors, or shamans.
>
> (Gardner 1983:240)

Intrapersonal intelligence

> The core capacity at work here is *access to one's own feeling life* – one's range of affects or emotions: the capacity instantly to effect discriminations among these feelings and, eventually, to label them, to enmesh them in symbolic codes, to draw upon them as a means of understanding and guiding one's behaviour. . . . One finds this form of intelligence in a novelist (like Proust) who can write introspectively about feelings, in the patient (or therapist) who comes to attain a deep knowledge of his own feeling life, in the wise elder who draws upon his own wealth of inner experiences in order to advise members of his community.
>
> (Gardner 1983:239–40)

Of these seven intelligences, spatial, logical-mathematical, and bodily-kinaesthetic are all 'object related': they depend on relationships with the external physical world. Language and music are, in contrast, 'object-free'.

> Finally, the personal forms of intelligence reflect a set of powerful and competing constraints: the existence of one's own person; the existence of other persons; the culture's presentations and interpretations of selves. There will be universal features of any sense of person or self, but also considerable cultural nuances, reflecting a host of historical and individuating factors.
>
> (Gardner 1983:278)

THE UNIQUE CONTRIBUTIONS OF THE THEORY

As human beings, we all have a repertoire of skills for solving different kinds of problems. Our investigation has begun, therefore, with a consideration of these problems, the contexts they are found in, and the culturally significant products that are the outcome. We have not approached 'intelligence' as a reified human faculty that is brought to bear in literally any problem setting; rather, we have begun with the problems that humans *solve* and worked back to the 'intelligences' that must be responsible.

Evidence from brain research, human development, evolution, and cross-cultural comparisons was brought to bear in our search for the relevant human intelligences: a candidate was included only if reasonable evidence to support its membership was found across these diverse fields. Again, this tack differs from the traditional one: since no candidate faculty is *necessarily* an intelligence, we could choose on a motivated basis. In the traditional approach to 'intelligence', there is no opportunity for this type of empirical decision.

We have also determined that these multiple human faculties, the intelligences, are to a significant extent *independent*. For example, research with brain-damaged adults repeatedly demonstrates that particular faculties can be lost while others are spared. This independence of intelligences implies that a particularly high level of ability in one intelligence, say mathematics, does not require a similarly high level in another intelligence, like language or music. This independence of intelligences contrasts sharply with traditional measures of IQ that find high correlations among test scores. We speculate that the usual correlations among subtests of IQ tests come about because all of these tasks in fact measure the ability to respond rapidly to items of a logical-mathematical or linguistic sort; we believe that these correlations would be substantially reduced if one were to survey in a contextually appropriate way the full range of human problem-solving skills.

Until now, we have supported the fiction that adult roles depend largely on the flowering of a single intelligence. In fact, however, nearly every cultural role of any degree of sophistication requires a combination of intelligences. Thus, even an apparently straightforward role like playing the violin transcends a reliance on simple musical intelligence. To become a successful violinist requires bodily-kinaesthetic dexterity, and the interpersonal skills of relating to an audience and, in a different way, choosing a manager; quite possibly it involves an intrapersonal intelligence as well. Dance requires skills in bodily-kinaesthetic, musical, interpersonal, and spatial intelligences in varying degrees. Politics requires an interpersonal skill, a linguistic facility, and perhaps some logical aptitude. Inasmuch as nearly every cultural role requires several intelligences, it becomes important to consider individuals as a collection of aptitudes rather than as having a singular problem-solving faculty that can be measured directly through pencil-and-paper tests. Even given a relatively small number of such intelligences, the diversity of human ability is created through the differences in these profiles. In fact, it may well be that the 'total is greater than the sum of the parts'. An individual may not be particularly gifted in any intelligence; and yet, because of a particular combination or blend of skills, he or she may be able to fill some niche uniquely well. Thus it is of paramount importance to assess the particular combination of skills which may earmark an individual for a certain vocational or avocational niche.[6]

COPING WITH THE PLURALITY OF INTELLIGENCES

Under the Multiple Intelligences theory, an intelligence can serve both as the *content* of instruction and the *means* or medium for communicating that content. This state of affairs has important ramifications for instruction. For example, suppose that a child is learning some mathematical principle but is not skilled in logical-mathematical intelligence. That child will probably experience some difficulty during the learning process. The reason for the difficulty is straightforward: the mathematical principle to be learned (the content) exists only in the logical-mathematical world and it ought to be communicated through mathematics (the medium). That is, the mathematical principle cannot be translated *entirely* into words (which is a linguistic medium) or spatial models (a spatial medium). At some point in the learning process, the mathematics of the principle must 'speak for itself'. In our present case, it is at just this level that the learner experiences difficulty – the learner (who is not especially 'mathematical') and the problem (which is very much 'mathematical') are not in accord. Mathematics, as a *medium*, has failed.

Although this situation is a necessary conundrum in light of the Multiple Intelligences theory, we can propose various solutions. In the present example, the teacher must attempt to find an alternative route to the mathematical content – a metaphor in another medium. Language is perhaps the most obvious alternative, but spatial modelling and even a bodily-kinaesthetic metaphor may prove appropriate in some cases. In this way, the student is given a *secondary* route to the solution to the problem, perhaps through the medium of an intelligence that is relatively strong for that individual.

Two features of this hypothetical scenario must be stressed. First, in such cases, the secondary route – the language, spatial model, or whatever – is at best a metaphor or translation. It is not mathematics itself. And at some point, the learner must translate back into the domain of mathematics. Without this translation, what is learned tends to remain at a relatively superficial level; cookbook-style mathematical performance results from following instructions (linguistic translation) without understanding why (mathematics re-translation).

Second, the alternative route is not guaranteed. There is no *necessary* reason why a problem in one domain *must be translatable* into a metaphorical problem in another domain. Successful teachers find these translations with relative frequency; but as learning becomes more complex, the likelihood of a successful translation diminishes.

While Multiple Intelligences theory is consistent with much empirical evidence, it has not been subjected to strong experimental tests within psychology. Within the area of education, the applications of the theory are even more tentative and speculative. Our hunches will have to be revised many times in the light of actual classroom experience. Still there are important reasons for considering the theory of Multiple Intelligences and its implications for education. First of all, it is clear that many talents, if not intelligences, are overlooked nowadays; individuals with these talents are the chief casualties of the single-minded, single-funnelled approach to the mind. There are many unfilled or poorly filled niches in our society and it would be opportune to guide individuals with the right set of abilities to these billets. Finally, our world is beset with problems; to have any chance of solving them, we must make the very best use of the intelligences we possess.

Perhaps recognising the plurality of intelligences and the manifold ways in which human individuals may exhibit them is an important first step.

NOTES

1 This chapter is based on extracts from an article by J. H. Walters and H. Gardner (1984) published by and reprinted with the permission of the Association for Supervision and Curriculum Development, and on summaries from *Frames of Mind* by Howard Gardner (1983) published by Basic Books (New York).
2 Cooley, W. W. and Lohnes, P. R. (1976) *Evaluation Research in Education*, New York: Irvington Publications Inc.
3 Jencks, C. (1972) *Inequality: A Reassessment of the Effect of Family and Schooling in America*, New York: Basic Books.
4 Eysenck, H. J. (1983) 'The nature of intelligence', in M. P. Friedman, J. P. Das, and N. O'Connor (Eds.) *Intelligence and Learning*, New York: Plenum Press.
5 Gardner, H. (1983) op. cit.
6 Walters, J. M. and Gardner, G. (1985) 'The theory of multiple intelligences: Some issues and answers', in R. Sternberg and R. Wagner (Eds.) *Practical Intelligence: Origins of Competence in the Everyday World*, Cambridge: Cambridge University Press.

Chapter 5

Widening the achievement concept

ILEA Committee on the Curriculum and
Organisation of Secondary Schools

We do not feel that we should be bound by psychologists' measures of achievement, such as tests of numerical or verbal attainment, or by the popular measures of achievement, such as performance in the 16 plus public examinations. By no means do we dismiss such definitions, but we believe it would be unwise to be restricted by them. Most people, and certainly a large majority of those who submitted evidence to us, question the extent to which public examinations are capable of measuring the whole range of knowledge, skills, abilities and qualities which the secondary school seeks to develop in its pupils. The purpose of our inquiry is to find means by which underachievement can be reduced and thus achievement increased. An improvement in the general level of performance in public examinations is undoubtedly one aim of the Authority, but in our view it should not be the only aim. We interpret our terms of reference to be directed at a much broader improvement in the achievements of pupils in comprehensive schools and to that end we distinguish four aspects of achievement. We offer these four aspects in order to clarify our own and our readers' thinking about achievement, and we believe that such a scheme is appropriate to the educational aims of comprehensive schools and secondary school teachers.

ACHIEVEMENT ASPECT I

This aspect of achievement is strongly represented in the current 16 plus public examinations. It involves most of all the capacity to express oneself in a written form. It requires the capacity to retain propositional knowledge, to select from such knowledge appropriately in response to a specified request, and to do so quickly without reference to possible sources of information. The capacity to memorise and organise material is particularly important. Public examinations measure such achievement in that they are mainly written tests, set with strict time limits and with the requirement that pupils have few or no additional resources available to them. The examinations emphasise knowledge rather than skill; memorisation more than problem-solving or investigational capacities; writing rather than speaking or other forms of communication; speed rather than reflection; individual rather than group achievement.

ACHIEVEMENT ASPECT II

This aspect of achievement is concerned with the capacity to apply knowledge rather than knowledge itself, with the practical rather than the theoretical, with the oral rather than the written. Problem solving and investigational skills are more important than the retention of knowledge. This aspect is to some degree measured in public examinations, but it is often seen as secondary and less important than aspect I. It tends to be more difficult, as well as more time-consuming and more expensive, to assess than aspect I.

ACHIEVEMENT ASPECT III

This aspect is concerned with personal and social skills; the capacity to communicate with others in face-to-face relationships; the ability to co-operate with others in the interests of the group as well as of the individual; initiative, self-reliance and the ability to work alone without close super-vision; and the skills of leadership. This aspect of achievement remains virtually untapped by the 16 plus examinations.

ACHIEVEMENT ASPECT IV

This aspect of achievement involves motivation and commitment; the willingness to accept failure without destructive consequences; the readiness to persevere; the self-confidence to learn in spite of the difficulty of the task. Such motivation is often regarded as a prerequisite to achievement, rather than as an achievement in itself. We do not deny that motivation is a prerequisite to the other three aspects of achievement, but we also believe that it can be regarded as an achievement in its own right. For some pupils come to their schools without such motivation, yet the school succeeds in generating it in them and, in such circumstances, both the school and the pupils have made an important achievement. By contrast, some schools actively reduce the motivation and commitment of pupils, thereby causing further underachievement in aspects I–III. In one sense, aspect IV is the most important of all, since without it achievement in the other three aspects is likely to be very limited, both at school and in the future. Working class pupils are particularly vulnerable here, since some of them, because of disadvantaged circumstances, come to school with already low levels of aspect IV achievement, they rely upon teachers, in a way that most middle class pupils do not, for immediate and basic help with aspect IV. If the school does not attend to aspect IV as a central feature of its work, then achievement in the other three aspects becomes improbable. When the school believes it is not within its powers to influence aspect IV, the teachers begin to explain the lack of achievement in terms of the pupils' background, and these low teacher expectations become self-fulfilling. And when pupils experience their schooling as a threat to their aspect IV achievement, it becomes rational for them to play truant or to protect themselves by classroom misbehaviour.

We are conscious that our scheme of four aspects of achievement is crude and open to many criticisms. The distinctions are analytical and cannot readily be distinguished in classrooms. Nor is the scheme exhaustive of all that schools are trying to achieve with their pupils. Nevertheless, we believe that the scheme, albeit rough and ready, has some advantages over the everyday and popular conceptions of achievement and underachievement, which stress aspect I and so often under-emphasise aspects II–IV.

Chapter 6

How children learn
Implications for practice

Neville Bennett and Elisabeth Dunne

The 1990s herald a period of great change in the way we run our schools, and in the curriculum we 'deliver' or enact in our classrooms. The content of the curriculum will, of course, change in line with the requirements of the national curriculum, but not necessarily the ways in which that content is taught. The originators of the national curriculum specifically avoided making prescriptions about teaching styles or strategies, believing that these were areas of professional judgement best left to the teacher. We agree with this but believe it is important that these judgements are informed by current theories, ideas and research findings, particularly at a time when the theories which underpin current practices are seriously being questioned. Central to the current debate is the crucial question of how children learn, and the optimal conditions for their learning. This chapter therefore considers first the question of how children learn, then discusses implications for classroom practice. Finally the material assesses, from recent research, the extent to which current practice is consistent with contemporary conceptions of learning.

HOW CHILDREN LEARN

The topic of how children learn is a complex one, and no attempt is made here to provide a full and critical exposition. The aim of this section is to capture the essence of learning by identifying core issues, and by considering the ideas of the different theorists in the debate.

The first point to note is that what children learn in the classroom will depend to a large extent on what they already know. Irrespective of their age, children will have some knowledge and some conception of the classroom topic they are faced with, which they have acquired from books, television, talking to parents and friends, visits to places of interest, previous work in school, and so on. However, these conceptions, or schemata as they are generally called, are likely to be incomplete, hazy or even plain wrong. They are, nevertheless, the children's current ideas, which they use to make sense of everyday experiences. In other words, children do not come to any lesson empty-headed; they come with partial schemata. For example, a top junior teacher we observed recently asked her class 'What are clouds made of?' The responses were many and varied. Some thought they were made of smoke, some had fuzzy notions about them being made over the sea, but they were unclear of the process. On the other hand, another child, the son of a local meteorologist, was able to talk about evaporation and had a clear schema of the water cycle. There was, then, tremendous variation in the schemas held by the children in that class. The teacher's job there, as in any classroom, was to find effective ways of modifying, extending or elaborating the children's schemata. Indeed, we can define learning in these terms as the extension, modification or elaboration of existing cognitive schemas.

That children have different schemata is, of course, one reason for the stress on individualisation of learning. But this should not be taken too far. Ideas or schemata are often shared, and this is not surprising. Children who come from the same school catchment area will, for example, have shared experiences in their local environment as well as in their school; another powerful shared experience is that of television.

So, children have schemata which are differentially complete or correct, some of which are shared. But how do their schemata change in school? Teachers offer knowledge in the form of telling, demonstrating and explaining, and pupils work on different kinds of tasks or activities designed to allow the practice, development or generation of a wide range of knowledge and understanding. Most importantly, it is the child who makes sense of these inputs, by constructing links with their prior knowledge. It is assumed that the construction of links is an active intellectual process involving the generation, checking and restructuring of ideas in the light of those already held. Construction of meaning is a continuous process and this view of learning is often referred to as 'constructivist'.

There is little argument among theorists that learning involves the construction of knowledge through experience. Arguments occur in relation to the conditions under which such learning is optimised – should learning be individual or social? Bruner and Haste (1987) capture this argument well when contrasting children as 'social beings' and 'lone scientists'.

A quiet revolution has taken place in developmental psychology in the last decade. It is not only that we have begun to think again of the child as a social being – one who plays and talks with others, learns through interactions with parents and teachers – but because we have come once more to appreciate that through such social life, the child acquires a framework for interpreting experience, and learning how to negotiate meaning in a manner congruent with the requirements of the culture. 'Making sense' is a social process; it is an activity that is always situated within a cultural and historical context.

Before that, we had fallen into the habit of thinking of the child as an 'active scientist', constructing hypotheses about the world, reflecting upon experience, interacting with the physical environment and formulating increasingly complex structures of thought. But this active, constructing child had been conceived as a rather isolated being, working alone at her problem-solving. Increasingly, we see now that, given an appropriate, shared social context, the child seems more competent as an intelligent social operator than she is as a 'lone scientist' coping with a world of unknowns.

This support for the child as a social being rather than as a lone scientist constitutes an attack on Piaget's views of learning, which assume that genuine intellectual competence is a manifestation of a child's largely unassisted activities. Bruner (1986) stresses far more the importance of the social setting in learning. 'I have come increasingly to recognise that most learning in most settings is a communal activity, a sharing of the culture. It is not just that the child must make his knowledge his own, but that he must make it his own in a community of those who share his sense of belonging to a culture.' This leads him to emphasise the role of negotiating and sharing in children's classroom learning, and in this he has been influenced by the work of Vygotsky. Vygotsky (1978) assigned a much greater significance to the social environment than Piaget: 'Learning awakens a variety of internal developmental processes that are able to operate only when the child is interacting with people in his environment and in co-operation with his peers.' Social interaction is thus assigned a central role in facilitating learning. For Vygotsky, a child's potential for learning is revealed and indeed is often realised in interactions with more knowledgeable others. These 'more knowledgeable others' can be anybody – peers, siblings, the teacher, parents, grandparents, and so on.

One of Vygotsky's main contributions to our understanding of learning is his concept of the 'zone of proximal development', which refers to the gap between what an individual can do alone and unaided, and what can be achieved with the help of more knowledgeable others – 'What a child can do today in co-operation, tomorrow he will be able to do on his own' (Vygotsky, 1962). For him, the foundation of learning and development is co-operatively achieved success, and the basis of that success is language and communication. 'Children solve practical tasks with the help of their speech, as well as with their eyes and their hands' (Vygotsky, 1962). Through speech to themselves (inner speech) and others, children begin to organise their experiences into thought.

The belief that talk is central to learning is not new. In 1972 Britton wrote: 'We have seen that talk is a major instrument of learning in infancy; that the infant *learns by talking* and that *he learns to talk by talking* . . . they must practise language in the sense in which a doctor "practises" . . . and not in the sense in which a juggler "practises" a new trick before he performs it'. The

Bullock Report (1975) devoted itself entirely to language, and welcomed the growth of interest in oral language, 'for we cannot emphasise too strongly our conviction of its importance in the education of the child.' It was argued that all schools ought to have, as a priority objective, a commitment to the speech needs of their pupils.

The National Association for the Teachers of English (NATE) neatly encapsulated the argument when stating that, 'One of the major functions of language that concerns teachers is its use for learning: for trying to put new ideas into words, for testing out one's thinking on other people, for fitting together new ideas with old ones and so on, which all need to be done to bring about new understanding. These functions suggest active uses of language by the pupil, as opposed to passive reception.'

The status of talk in the classroom was reinforced in the 1980s through the focus on oracy by the Assessment of Performance Unit (APU). From their survey of 11-year-olds they reported that gains in mastery of spoken language may have beneficial effects on pupils' learning capabilities. 'The experience of expressing and shaping ideas through talk as well as writing, and of collaborating to discuss problems or topics, help to develop a critical and exploratory attitude towards knowledge and concepts.' They concluded that 'Pupils' performances could be substantially improved if they were given regular opportunities in the classroom to use their speaking and listening skills over a range of purposes, in a relaxed atmosphere' (APU, 1986).

Following this, the authors of the English national curriculum recommended a separate language component for speaking and listening, thus demonstrating their belief in oracy. 'Our inclusion of speaking and listening as a separate profile component in our recommendations is a reflection of our conviction that these skills are of central importance to children's development' (National Curriculum Council, 1989).

Hence, a constructivist view of learning perceives children as intellectually active learners already holding ideas or schema which they use to make sense of their everyday experiences. Learning in classrooms involves the extension, elaboration or modification of their schemata. This process is one by which learners actively make sense of the world by constructing meanings. Learning is optimised in settings where social interaction, particularly between a learner and more knowledgeable others, is encouraged, and where co-operatively achieved success is a major aim. The medium for this success is talk, which is now widely accepted as a means of promoting pupils' understandings and of evaluating their progress.

IMPLICATIONS FOR PRACTICE

That pupils bring schemas of their own to bear on any given topic, and that some of these will be shared and others idiosyncratic, has to be taken into account by teachers in their planning of classroom tasks. To take these schemas adequately into account necessitates a clear understanding of what they are, that is, it requires the teacher to take on the role of diagnostician (Bennett *et al.*, 1984). A useful metaphor for gaining access to children's conceptions is that of creating 'a window into the child's mind'. To open the curtains of that window often needs far more than a rudimentary look at a child's work. It demands a sophisticated combination of observation and careful questioning and this is likely to need a great deal of time.

Judging an appropriate level for a task or activity is clearly critical to the development of learning. In this context, the notion of the 'zone of proximal development' is again important; Vygotsky believed that optimal learning is that which involves the acquisition of cognitive skills slightly beyond the child's independent grasp. A similar concept is that of 'match' between task and child, about which Her Majesty's Inspectorate (HMI) have been much concerned over the past decade. Their definition, put crudely, is that tasks should be planned which are neither too difficult nor too easy for the child (HMI, 1978, 1983, 1985; see also, Bennett and Desforges, 1988). Despite 'match' or 'appropriateness' being differently defined by Vygotsky and HMI, their relationship to diagnosis is the same. Without adequate diagnosis of children's competences or understandings, it is unlikely that teacher judgements of appropriate tasks will be accurate.

Having made decisions about content, teachers then present tasks to pupils. In whatever mode this is done (demonstration, discussion, experiment, etc.), pupils' construction of meanings will be facilitated by clear statements of purpose, and information about how the task fits into work previously done and its relation to that which will be tackled in the future.

The view that learning is optimised through talk in co-operative settings has implications for presentation, as well as for classroom management. The nature of the teacher's talk needs to be carefully considered, as does the kind of classroom setting which allows for peer tutoring and co-operative working between pupils.

The most explicit advice on this aspect of classroom practice is to be found in the NCC guidance on the English curriculum, particularly that on speaking and listening (NCC, 1989). Here the guidance prescribes classrooms where children feel sufficiently encouraged and secure to be able to express and explore their thoughts, feelings and emotions; where teachers encourage talk which is genuinely tentative and explanatory, while demonstrating that talk is a rigorous activity. Drawing clearly from constructivist ideas, the guidance argues that children should be able to make connections between what they already know and new experiences and ideas, and that the main vehicle for this will be their own talk. Teachers are also asked to reflect on their own questioning strategies. For example, in talking with children the teacher should ensure that questions are genuinely open-ended, that children have problems to solve without a subtly indicated, expected

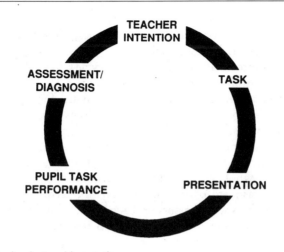

Figure 6.1 A simple teaching cycle

answer, and that they are encouraged to speculate, hypothesise, predict and test out ideas with each other and with the teacher. The emphasis should be on language being used, not to communicate what is known, but as an instrument of learning. 'It is time for children to think aloud, to grapple with ideas and to clarify thoughts.' The guidance argues that once children have developed new understandings they will need to reflect and exchange ideas and views with other pupils and the teacher in order to consolidate their learning. Such talk does, of course, also indicate to the teacher the state of the child's understanding; that is, it is an aid to diagnosis.

This guidance appears to be attempting to create what Edwards and Mercer (1987) describe as a framework for shared understanding with children, based on joint knowledge and action. This framework acts as a 'scaffold' 'for children's mental explanations, a cognitive climbing-frame – built by children with their Vygotskyan teacher – which structures activity more systematically than the discovery sand-pit of the Piagetian classroom. Talk between teachers and children helps build the scaffolding. Children's activity, even "discovery", in the absence of such a communicative framework may, in cognitive terms, lead nowhere.'

CURRENT PRACTICE

Having considered current perspectives on how children learn, and the implications of these perspectives for classroom practice, the critical question now to be considered is 'how does current teaching measure up?' The aim here is not to provide a complete description of present-day primary practice and analyse its strengths and weaknesses – that would need a book in itself. Rather, we will concentrate on those aspects of teaching identified in the last section: eliciting and diagnosing children's conceptions, provision and presentation of appropriate learning activities, co-operation and grouping, and the nature of classroom talk.

The use of a simple diagram of a teaching cycle allows these aspects, and their inter-relationships, to be examined. In Figure 6.1, the cycle begins with the teacher planning and preparing tasks and activities for children which are then presented in some way (e.g. through discussion, an experiment, a television programme, etc.) The children then engage with their work within a classroom management system set up by the teacher (e.g. individuals working on individual tasks; mixed ability groups in an integrated day arrangement; the whole class working in small co-operative groups on the same technology task, etc.). Once this work has been completed, it would be expected that teachers would assess or diagnose it, using that information to feed back to pupils, and to feed forward to inform their next round of planning.

REFERENCES

Assessment and Performance Unit (1986) *Speaking and Listening, Assessment at Age 11*. Windsor. NFER-Nelson.

Bennett, N. and Desforges, C. (1988) 'Matching classroom tasks to students' attainments'. *Elementary School Journal*, 88, 221–34.

Bennett, N., Desforges, C., Cockburn, A. and Wilkinson, B. (1984) *The Quality of Pupil Learning Experiences*. London. Erlbaum.

Britton, J. (1970) *Language and Learning* (1972 edition). Harmondsworth. Penguin Books.

Bruner, J. (1986) *Actual Minds, Possible Worlds*. Cambridge (MA). Harvard University Press.

Bruner, J. and Haste, H. (1987) *Making Sense*. London. Methuen.

Bullock Report (1975) *A Language for Life*. London. HMSO.

Edwards, D. and Mercer, N. (1987) *Common Knowledge: The Development of Understanding in the Classroom*. London. Methuen.

Her Majesty's Inspectorate (1978) *Primary Education in England*. London. HMSO.

Her Majesty's Inspectorate (1983) *9–13 Middle Schools: An Illustrative Survey*. London. HMSO.

Her Majesty's Inspectorate (1985) *Education 8–12 in Combined and Middle Schools*. London. HMSO.

National Curriculum Council (1989) *English in the National Curriculum Key Stage One*. York. NCC.

Vygotsky, L. S. (1962) *Thought and Language*. Cambridge (MA). MIT Press.

Vygotsky, L. S. (1978) *Mind and Society: The Development of Higher Psychological Processes*. Cambridge (MA). Harvard University Press.

Chapter 7

Adolescence

John C. Coleman

INTRODUCTION

Adolescence is a complex stage of human development, for the years 12 to 18 involve a wide range of major life changes. In fact it is unlikely that the individual undergoes greater changes at any other stage in the life cycle apart from infancy. During the teenage years the young person experiences puberty, which has an impact on physical, physiological and psychological systems. He or she undergoes a significant maturation of cognitive function. Major changes in the self-concept are likely to occur, and there are radical alterations in all social relationships to be negotiated. How can we understand such fundamental transitions in human development, and make sense of the effects which they have upon the individual? Especially important in the context of the present book are the effects which these changes have upon the way the young person functions in the school setting, and it is primarily to this question that I shall address myself in what follows.

Broadly speaking there are two ways in which we can attempt to make sense of adolescent development. On the one hand we can look to theory. We can study theoretical notions of adolescence, and determine for ourselves the validity or logic of the different approaches. On the other hand we can turn to the research evidence. This will provide us with a factual base upon which to make an assessment of this period of the life cycle, but will inevitably leave a wide range of questions unanswered. It is my view that neither theory nor research can at present provide a complete answer. Both have limitations, and yet both have valuable insights to offer.

Clearly the scope of the present chapter must be limited. It seems important, however, to provide some form of introduction to the educational issues raised by adolescent development, and to offer a framework for those who wish to pursue further their study of adolescence, aided no doubt by the chapters that follow. I shall therefore review briefly two major theoretical views of adolescent development, and then turn to one or two of the issues which appear most pertinent to the school context. I have chosen to cover

puberty, cognition and some aspects of social development, but have deliberately excluded the topic of the peer group.

TRADITIONAL THEORIES

There is general agreement by all who have written about adolescence that it
makes sense to describe the stage as being one of transition. The transition, it
is believed, results from the operation of a number of pressures. Some of
these, in particular the physiological and emotional pressures, are internal;
while other pressures, which originate from peers, parents, teachers, and
society at large, are external to the young person. Sometimes these external
pressures carry the individual towards maturity at a faster rate than he or she
would prefer, while on other occasions they act as a brake, holding the
adolescent back from the freedom and independence which he or she
believes to be a legitimate right. It is the interplay of these forces which, in
the final analysis, contributes more than anything to the success or failure of
the transition from childhood to maturity.

So far two classical types of explanation concerning the transitional
process have been advanced. The psychoanalytic approach concentrates on
the psychosexual development of the individual, and looks particularly at
the psychological factors which underlie the young person's movement
away from childhood behaviour and emotional involvement. The second
type of explanation, the sociological, represents a very different perspective.
While it has never been as coherently expressed as the psychoanalytic view,
it is none the less of equal importance. In brief, this explanation sees the
causes of adolescent transition as lying primarily in the social setting of
the individual and concentrates on the nature of roles and role conflict, the
pressures of social expectations, and on the relative influence of different
agents of socialisation.

PUBERTY

Puberty, and the physical growth that accompanies it, is important to those
involved in education for a number of reasons. In the first place puberty has
a range of physiological effects which are not always outwardly apparent to
observers, but which can none the less have a considerable impact on the
individual. Second, rates of maturation vary enormously, leading inevitably
to questions of normality and comparability between young people.
Furthermore, especially early or unusually late developers have particular
difficulties to face, which again have marked implications for classroom
performance and behaviour. Third, physical development cannot fail to have
psychological consequences, often affecting self-concept and self-esteem,
factors which themselves play a major part in motivation and learning. Thus
it can be seen that an understanding of puberty is essential in making sense of

adolescent development as a whole. I shall deal with each of these areas in turn.

Adults often fail to appreciate that puberty is accompanied by changes not only in the reproductive system and in the secondary sexual characteristics of the individual, but in the functioning of the heart and thus of the cardiovascular system, in the lungs, which in turn affect the respiratory system, in the size and the strength of many of the muscles of the body, and so on. One of the many physical changes associated with puberty is the 'growth spurt'. This term is usually taken to refer to the accelerated rate of increase in height and weight that occurs during early adolescence. It is essential to bear in mind, however, that there are very considerable individual differences in the age of onset and duration of the growth spurt, even among perfectly normal children. This is a fact which parents and adolescents themselves frequently fail to appreciate, thus causing a great deal of unnecessary anxiety. In boys the growth spurt may begin as early as 10 years of age, or as late as 16, while in girls the same process can begin at 7 or 8, or not until 12, 13 or even 14. For the average boy, though, rapid growth begins at about 13, and reaches a peak somewhere during the fourteenth year. Comparable ages for girls are 11 for the onset of the growth spurt and 12 for the peak age of increase in height and weight. Other phenomena associated with the growth spurt are a rapid increase in the size and weight of the heart (the weight of the heart nearly doubles at puberty), accelerated growth of the lungs and a decline in basal metabolism. Noticeable to children themselves, especially boys, is a marked increase in physical strength and endurance (see Tanner 1978 for a full description).

Sexual maturation is closely linked with the physical changes described above. Again the sequence of events is approximately eighteen to twenty-four months later for boys than it is for girls. Since individuals mature at very different rates, one girl at the age of 14 may be small, have no bust and look very much as she did during childhood, while another of the same age may look like a fully developed adult woman, who could easily be taken for someone four or five years in advance of her actual chronological age. Such marked physical differences will have particular consequences for the individual's psychological adjustment.

COGNITION

Those involved in education will no doubt be more aware than others of the significance of cognitive development during adolescence. In a short review such as this it is possible only to draw attention to the major themes, and to highlight one or two of the most significant areas of recent work in this field. For those wishing to read further, good general discussions of cognition in adolescence are to be found in Coleman and Hendry (1990), Serafica (1982) and Conger and Petersen (1984).

Changes in intellectual functioning during the teenage years have implications for a wide range of behaviours and attitudes. Such changes render possible the move towards independence of both thought and action; they enable the young person to develop a time perspective which includes the future; they facilitate progress towards maturity in relationships; and finally they underline the individual's ability to participate in society as worker, voter, responsible group member and so on. We cannot consider these changes without looking first at the work of Piaget, for it is he who has laid the foundation for almost all subsequent work on cognitive development. It will be worthwhile also to discuss briefly some work on adolescent reasoning and to review ideas on both moral and political thought in adolescence.

The work of Jean Piaget, the Swiss psychologist, is the most obvious starting place for a consideration of cognitive development during the teenage years. It was he who first pointed out that a qualitative change in the nature of mental ability, rather than any simple increase in cognitive skill, is to be expected at or around puberty, and he has argued that it is at this point in development that formal operational thought finally becomes possible (Inhelder and Piaget 1958).

Another area of interest to researchers in the field of cognitive development is that of moral and political thought. How is this changed by formal operations? Do young people pass through different stages of thinking where morals and politics are concerned, and if so, what is the nature of such stages? As far as moral thinking is concerned it is once again Piaget's notions which have formed the springboard for later thinking on this subject, and although a number of different theories have been put forward to explain the development of concepts of morality in young people, the 'cognitive-developmental' approach of Piaget and Kohlberg has undoubtedly been the most influential. In his work on the moral judgement of the child, Piaget described two major stages of moral thinking. The first, which he called 'moral realism', refers to a period during which young children make judgements on an objective basis, for example by estimating the amount of damage which has been caused in an accident. Thus a child who breaks twelve cups is considered more blameworthy than one who only breaks one cup, regardless of the circumstances. The second stage, applying usually to those between the ages of 8 and 12, has been described as that of the 'morality of co-operation', or the 'morality of reciprocity'. During this stage, Piaget believed, decisions concerning morality were usually made on a subjective basis, and often depended on an estimate of intention rather than consequence.

Kohlberg (1969) has elaborated Piaget's scheme into one which has six different stages. His method has been to present hypothetical situations concerning moral dilemmas to young people of different ages, and to classify their responses according to a stage theory of moral development. Some of Kohlberg's most interesting work has involved the study of moral development in different cultures. He has shown that an almost identical sequence appears to occur in widely different cultures, the variation between cultures being found in the rate of development, and the fact that in more primitive societies later stages of thinking are rarely used.

SOCIAL RELATIONSHIPS

I intend in this section to concentrate particularly on the role of adults, and on the nature and significance of relationships between young people and parents, teachers and important others. In selecting issues which will be of relevance to the educational context, I have chosen the development of independence, since out of the many available this seemed to me to be one of the most obviously pertinent.

One of the central themes of adolescent development is the attainment of independence, often represented symbolically in art and literature by the moment of departure from home. However, for most young people today independence is not gained at one specific moment by the grand gesture of saying goodbye to one's parents and setting off to seek one's fortune in the wide world. Independence is much more likely to mean the freedom to make new relationships, and personal freedom to take responsibility for oneself in such things as education, work, political beliefs and future career choice.

There are many forces which interact in propelling an individual towards a state of maturity. Naturally both physical and intellectual maturation encourage the adolescent towards greater autonomy. In addition to these factors there are, undoubtedly, psychological forces within the individual as well as social forces within the environment which have the same goal. In the psychoanalytic view, mentioned earlier, the process of seeking independence represents the need to break off the infantile ties with the parents, thus making new mature sexual relationships possible. From the perspective of the sociologist, more emphasis is placed on the changes in role and status which lead to a redefinition of the individual's place in the social structure. Whatever the explanation, it is certainly true that the achievement of independence is an integral feature of adolescent development, and that the role of the adults involved is an especially important one.

In understanding this process it is necessary to appreciate that the young person's movement towards adulthood is far from straightforward. While independence at times appears to be a rewarding goal, there are moments when it is a worrying, even frightening, prospect. Childlike dependence can be safe and comforting at no matter what age, if, for example, one is facing problems or difficulties alone, and it is essential to realise that no individual achieves adult independence without a number of backward glances. It is this ambivalence which underlies the typically contradictory behaviour of adolescence, behaviour which is so often the despair of adults. Thus there is nothing more frustrating than having to deal with a teenager who is at one moment complaining about adults who are always interfering, and the next bitterly protesting that no one takes any interest. However, it is equally important to acknowledge that adults themselves usually hold conflicting attitudes towards young people. On the one hand they may wish them to be independent, to make their own decisions, and to cease making childish demands, while on the other they may be anxious about the consequences of independence, and sometimes jealous of the opportunities and idealism of youth. In addition it should not be forgotten that the adolescent years often coincide with the difficulties of middle age for parents in particular. Adjusting to unfulfilled hopes, the possibility of retirement, declining physical health, marital difficulties and so on may all increase family stress, and add further to the problems faced by young people in finding a satisfactory route to independence.

Research evidence has not provided much support for the notion that wide-ranging conflict between adults and young people is the order of the day. Noller and Callan (1991), in reviewing the data available, come to the conclusion that the general picture that emerges from experimental studies is that of relatively harmonious relationships with adults for the majority of young people. Of course adolescents do seek independence, of that there is no dispute, and so the question arises as to how common sense and research evidence can be fitted together. In the first place it is clear that some adolescents do, temporarily at least, come into conflict with or become critical of adults. In addition there is no doubt that some adults do become restrictive, attempting to slow down the pace of change. Research has shown that there are a number of factors which affect the extent of the conflict occurring between the generations. Cultural background, adult behaviour, age and social class all need to be taken into account.

REFERENCES

Coleman, J. C. and Hendry, L. (1990) *The Nature of Adolescence*, 2nd edn, London: Routledge.

Conger, J. and Petersen, A. (1984) *Adolescence and Youth*, 3rd edn, New York: Harper & Row.

Inhelder, B. and Piaget, J. (1958) *The Growth of Logical Thinking*, London: Routledge & Kegan Paul.

Kohlberg, L. (1969) *States in the Development of Moral Thought and Action*, New York: Holt, Rinehart & Winston.

Noller, P. and Callan, V. (1991) *The Adolescent in the Family*, London: Routledge.

Serafica, F. C. (ed.) (1982) *Social-cognitive Development in Context*, London: Methuen.

Tanner, J. M. (1978) *Foetus into Man*, London: Open Books.

Chapter 8

Sex roles and the school

Sara Delamont

'A friend wants to come over to do some recording on my cassette player,' said my teenage son. 'Tim's into heavy metal.' Oh dear, I thought what am I letting myself in for? Well, the music which boomed out wasn't my cup of tea but when I walked into the room, there was no wild, headbanging orgy taking place, just a quiet young lad sitting on the settee doing embroidery! Not a traycloth nor a cushion cover, I hasten to add, but a denim jacket with an intricate design of a pop group's logo. I learned later that he is doing three A-levels, including higher maths and physics. Perhaps our teenagers are not the stereotypes we often think them, and I, for one, will try to look beyond the labels in future.

This was the Star Letter in *Woman* on 16 January 1988. Again the pressures of the conventional view of appropriate male and female behaviour are apparent. Why a young man interested in heavy metal should not embroider a traycloth if he wished to is not specified, but it is clear that designing stage clothes for a rock group is permissible where cushion covers would not be.

THE ADOLESCENT SOCIETY?

There is a very large literature on adolescence from which it is clear that many adult social scientists are extremely anxious about people between 12 and 21. The majority of authors project their anxieties and doubts on to adolescents, and there are dozens of books which stress how confused, disturbed, easily led astray and vulnerable adolescents are. There is not, however, very much research on how adolescents see their own lives, not much sociology, and the literature has some very clear biases and omissions. Adolescents are researched if they are deviant or delinquent, and not if they are normal or conformist. Adolescent boys are researched if they are working class but not otherwise. Adolescent girls are researched if they are promiscuous or pregnant, but not otherwise. Hell's Angels are studied but not Boy Scouts; Children of God but not members of the Methodist Youth

Club and so on. Researchers on adolescence have been tempted by the bizarre and exciting, not the respectable and conventional.

Researchers and commentators have generally been extremely ambivalent about young people. In their introduction to *Working Class Youth Culture*, Mungham and Pearson (1976:1) pointed out that adolescents were portrayed either as 'rebellious, ill-fitting members of a well-ordered world; or glorified as potential rebels . . . who will overturn a world which is sick, lifeless and dull'. Attempting to bring some order to the confused debate, Mungham and Pearson emphasised the sloppiness of most writing about young people, which talks loosely of 'generation gaps' and 'problems'. They preferred to see 'youth culture', not as a unitary phenomenon, but as something differentiated by class, occupation, education, ethnic identity and sex. In this they shared the opinion of most of the level-headed commentators on adolescence. However, their own collection and the volume from Hall and Jefferson (1975) which appeared at about the same time both perpetuated one of the worst flaws in the literature on adolescents: its neglect of gender divisions. Mungham and Pearson claimed (1976:4) that they could not find anyone to write about the lives of working-class adolescent girls; while Hall and Jefferson included one theoretical note and a short article which drew on data collected in a youth club.

Those two collections date from the early 1970s. Since then there have been some studies of young women (e.g. McRobbie 1990; Smith 1978; Wilson 1978; Lees 1986; Coffield *et al.* 1986; Wallace 1987) and of female school pupils (notably Griffin 1985 and Davies 1984). However, it is noticeable that much of the work on females appears only in scattered articles rather than books (see Delamont (1989: 273) for the details of this). It is also striking that many authors ignore gender despite the existence of recent research on females. Marsland (1983) has written a review of the literature on 'youth' which deals only with men. Only research on males is reviewed, only male authors cited, yet Marsland never explains his focus.

The lack of attention to gender distinctions in the research on adolescence is one of the major flaws in it. Apart from the attention paid to deviant or delinquent youth the methods used in nearly all the studies are biased by the conscious or unconscious preconceptions of their devisors. Detailed attention to nearly every study published reveals such in-built sexism in the methods. For example, Irene Jones (1974) scrutinised *Mass Media and the Secondary School* by Murdock and Phelps (1973), and raised considerable doubts about their conclusions. One particular aspect of the research struck Jones because of its implicit assumptions. The researchers offered a sample of 322 girls and 299 boys a series of teenage role models with which to identify themselves or not as they chose. Some of these role models were common to both sexes, but some were only offered to either the boys or the girls.

Jones argues that by offering certain roles only to one sex and not the other, Murdock and Phelps were creating polarised results and forcing the two sexes into different, stereotyped roles, rather than undertaking a study without preconceptions. The roles offered to both sexes were good pupil, rebel, ritualist, good bloke/good friend, and pop fan. Boys were also offered street peer, sports fan, boyfriend, and natural leader; while girls were given homemaker, tomboy, girlfriend, and fashion follower. While the girlfriend/boyfriend pairs were matched, the other roles offered only to one sex or the other reinforce crude stereotyping. There is no role of natural leader in the girls' list nor any equivalent of it. Thus no data are available on what proportion of girls saw themselves as leaders. Equally stereotyped is the existence of roles as homemaker and fashion follower for girls (while denying them the option of street peer or sports fan) yet not offering boys any home-centred role (model builder, carpenter, etc.) or any interest in fashion and clothes. Effectively, therefore, Murdock and Phelps pre-ordained that girls would come out home centred and sheep-like, boys street centred and aggressive. Much research on teenagers has suffered from having preconceptions built into it, and has to be read with scepticism.

There is one finding from the literature on adolescence that is particularly important for schooling: the role of the peer group as a source of influence on young people. Young people derive many of their values from their homes, but as they move into adolescence their friends' ideas on music, fashion, sexuality and schoolteachers become increasingly important. When pupils face transfer to secondary school, they fear the loss of friends made in the lower school and an absence of friendship in the new one. Peer groups, or cliques, are a major factor in adolescents' school lives.

PEER GROUPS AND PRESSURES

The importance of friendship groups among boys in school has certainly been widely documented (e.g. Hargreaves 1967; Lacey 1970; Willis 1977; Beynon 1985). Membership of, and adherence to the norms and values of, a particular peer group can make a difference to the school attainment and involvement of boys. A boy whose friends work hard and share the teachers' values is likely to work hard and be tuned in to the teachers' values himself. He and his friends are likely to dress in clothes the school approves of, be ambitious for academic success, and enjoy different kinds of leisure activity and pop music from other groups. In contrast, groups like Willis's 'lads' will avoid schoolwork, reject teachers' standards, dress in unapproved styles, do not want academic success, and choose other kinds of leisure. And, as Hargreaves (1967) and others have pointed out, adherence to peer group norms, if they are anti-school, will be stronger than any pressure the school can exert.

Much of this research focused on anti-school or deviant pupils. More recently Aggleton and Whitty (1985) have discussed middle-class adolescents and John Abraham (1989a, b) has produced an account of two different anti-school groups in the late 1980s – one the same type of rebel as Hargreaves's from the 1960s and Willis's from the 1970s, the other (gothic punks) very different in style and philosophy. The gothic punks were disliked by some staff for having female friends, disliking football, and enjoying art – in short for being 'effeminate'.

Whether peer groups have functioned in the same ways among girls over the past 30 years is not known. Furlong (1976, 1984) argued that the whole idea of a group was too static, and analysed the classroom behaviour of West Indian girls in London via the more fluid notion of the *interaction set*, which changed from one context to another. However, Lambart (1977, 1980), Meyenn (1980), Llewellyn (1980), Fuller (1980) and Delamont (1976, 1984a, b) all found girls' peer groups in schools during the 1960s and 1970s which did function as important parts of their members' lives and did mediate school experience through group attitudes.

Meyenn (1980) found that the 12 and 13 year old girls in an English middle school did have groups of friends rather than one best friend, and their groups were important to them. One girl, Diane, is quoted as saying 'if we had to say somebody who was our best friend you wouldn't say one person. It would be all this lot'. Meyenn found that the sixteen girls were in four groups, which he called 'P.E.', 'nice', 'quiet', and 'science lab.'. The quiet girls saw themselves as 'dunces' and were in bottom groups for lessons. Yet they were not anti-school, but accepted their low status and co-operated to have fun. The 'nice' girls were apparently concerned to go through school unnoticed, neither excelling nor failing. The two more visible groups were the 'P.E.' and 'science lab.' girls. Both these groups wore fashionable clothes and make up, but differed in the relationship to the school. The P.E. girls were noisy and aggressive, and helped each other with schoolwork. The science lab. girls were regarded by the teachers as mature and had interna-lised the idea that schoolwork was competitive and individual. Their 'matur-ity' meant they were allotted the task of caring for the animals in the science lab. and recognised the value of their privilege. The science lab. and P.E. girls did not get on very well together, for as Diane (a science lab. girl) says 'When we get good marks they all say "teacher's pet" and things like that' while a P.E. girl, Betty, told Meyenn about the science lab. group 'They're always trying to get round the teachers and everything. They're always teachers' pets, them four.'

Meyenn found that none of these girls was a real discipline problem for the staff, because even anti-school cliques of girls are not, apparently, actively disruptive or aggressive to teachers as boys are. Hargreaves *et al.* (1975:31) in a study of school deviance actually say that 'teachers very rarely talked to us about "difficult" girls'. Meyenn's data are very similar to Ball's (1981) from Sussex and mine on upper-middle-class 14 year olds collected in Scotland (Delamont 1984a, 1989). At St Luke's there were similar distinctions between girls who had adopted fashion and make up and those who had not, and between those who accepted the school's ideas about intellectual effort and those who saw schoolwork as a task to be completed by fair means or foul (e.g. copying). Data are needed on far more girls in many more kinds of schools from all over Britain to establish if girls too have strong peer groups which function to mediate between the individual and the school. (Better data on boys would also be useful and illuminating!)

REFERENCES

Abraham, J. (1989a) 'Teacher ideology and sex roles in curriculum texts', *British Journal of Sociology of Education* 10 (1): 33–52.

Abraham, J. (1989b) 'Gender differences and anti-school boys', *Sociological Review* 37 (1): 65–88.

Aggleton, P. and Whitty, G. (1985) 'Rebels without a cause?', *Sociology of Education* 58 (1): 60–72.

Ball, S. (1981) *Beachside Comprehensive*, Cambridge: Cambridge University Press.

Beynon, J. (1985) *Initial Encounters in the Secondary School*, London: Falmer.

Coffield, F. *et al.* (1986) *Growing up at the Margins*, Milton Keynes: Open University Press.

Davies, L. (1984) *Pupil Power*, London: Falmer.

Delamont, S. (1976) 'The girls most likely to: cultural reproduction and Scottish elites', *Scottish Journal of Sociology* 1 (1): 29–43.

Delamont, S. (1984a) 'The old girl network', in R. G. Burgess (ed.) *The Research Process in Educational Settings*, London: Falmer.

Delamont, S. (1984b) 'Lessons from St. Luke's', in W. B. Dockrell (ed.) *An Attitude of Mind*, Edinburgh: SCRE.

Delamont, S. (1989) *Knowledgeable Women*, London: Routledge.

Fuller, M. (1980) 'Black girls in a London comprehensive', in R. Deem (ed.) *Schooling for Women's Work*, London: Routledge & Kegan Paul.

Furlong, V. J. (1976) 'Interaction sets in the classroom', in M. Stubbs and S. Delamont (eds) *Explorations in Classroom Observation*, Chichester: Wiley.

Furlong, V. J. (1984) 'Black resistance in the liberal comprehensive', in S. Delamont (ed.) *Readings on Interaction in the Classroom*, London: Methuen.

Griffin, C. (1985) *Typical Girls?*, London: Routledge & Kegan Paul.

Hall, S. and Jefferson, T. (eds) (1975) *Resistance through Rituals*, London: Hutchinson.

Hargreaves, D. (1967) *Social Relations in a Secondary School*, London: Routledge & Kegan Paul.

Hargreaves, D., Hester, S. K. and Mellor, F. J. (1975) *Deviance in Classrooms*, London: Routledge & Kegan Paul.

Jones, I. (1974) Unpublished dissertation, University of Leicester.

Lacey, C. (1970) *Hightown Grammar; The School as Social System*, Manchester: The University Press.

Lambart, A. (1977) 'The sisterhood', in M. Hammersley and P. Woods (eds) *Process of Schooling*, London: Routledge & Kegan Paul.

Lambart, A. (1980) 'Expulsion in context', in R. Frankenberg (ed.) *Custom and Conflict in British Society*, Manchester: Manchester University Press.

Lees, S. (1986) *Losing Out*, London: Heinemann.

Llewellyn, M. (1980) 'Studying girls at school', in R. Deem (ed.) *Schooling for Women's Work*, London: Routledge & Kegan Paul.

McRobbie, A. (1990) *Feminism and Youth Culture*, London: Macmillan.

Marsland, D. (1983) 'Youth', in A. Hartnett (ed.) *The Social Sciences in Educational Studies*, London: Heinemann.

Meyenn, R. J. (1980) 'School girls' peer groups', in P. Woods (ed.) *Pupil Strategies*, London: Croom Helm.

Mungham, G. and Pearson, G. (eds) (1976) *Working Class Youth Culture*, London: Routledge & Kegan Paul.

Murdock, G. and Phelps, G. (1973) *Mass Media and the Secondary School*, London: Macmillan.

Smith, L. S. (1978) 'Sexist assumptions and female delinquency', in C. Smart and B. Smart (eds) *Women, Sexuality and Social Control*, London: Routledge & Kegan Paul.

Wallace, C. (1987) *For Richer, For Poorer*, London: Methuen.

Willis, P. (1977) *Learning to Labour*, Farnborough: Saxon House.

Wilson, D. (1978) 'Sexual codes and conduct', in C. Smart and B. Smart (eds) *Women, Sexuality and Social Control*, London: Routledge & Kegan Paul.

Chapter 9

Acknowledging disadvantages

Alec Clegg

When I first began to work in education administration, those of us on the inside of the service held a number of fairly simple beliefs about the children in our schools. They were born with a certain ability and this we could measure with an intelligence test. We could then with reasonable certainty pick out the ablest children and give them an education which accorded with their age, aptitude and ability. So we tested them all at the age of eleven, we put the clever ones in the grammar schools, the next layer in many areas found their way into junior technical or junior art schools, and the rest went to such all-age schools as still remained, or into modern schools.

I was in Birmingham at the time, and we accepted the fact that there would be far fewer clever children from the poorer areas of Rae Street and Steward Street than from Harborne where those who were clever and wealthy lived. It was as simple as that, and we made the assumption, even if we did not state it, that the shortcomings of the Steward Street children were inherited, and to some extent this was true.

But in those days, few of us realised, as now we do, how long is the list of impediments which can contribute to the insecurity and lack of confidence and of achievement of those children who live in the grey areas of the country, where housing is dismal and amenities are poor. As teachers in training we had learned academically about horme and mneme, about routine and ritual, about the play way and so on. As teachers in employment we had made a profound study of examination questions and how to coach our pupils in the art and science of answering them. We were not anything like as fully aware, as we now are, of the long list of differences between education in 'Smogville' and the education in 'Cheltenmouth'.

Today however, because of the researches of the National Children's Bureau and of many other individuals and bodies, as well as discoveries of several Central Advisory Councils, we know much more about these differences. We know, for instance, that in the grey areas:

more children die young
more children suffer ill health

more have sick parents
more live in areas where doctors are scarce
more have parents who depend to some extent on their children's earnings
more live in overcrowded homes
more live in homes which lack the basic amenities
more have parents who are school shy
more have parents who left school as soon as they were able
more are dependent on the social services
more have come into contact with the probation service and with detention
more live in an area where there is dirt and pollution
more live in ugly derelict areas
more attend old and ill-kept schools which are awaiting closure
more come from homes where books are few
more are taught by teachers who do not live in the area
more are from impoverished families
more are from families dependent on school meals
more lack the facilities necessary to keep themselves clean
fewer have parents who know their way about the education service
fewer hear school English spoken in their homes
fewer talk often with adults
fewer read to their parents
fewer have parents who read to them
fewer have articulate parents
fewer receive extra-curricular help
fewer take enriching holidays
fewer are taken to galleries or concerts by their parents
fewer question their parents about school matters
fewer have parents who could answer questions about school matters if
    asked
fewer become prefects
fewer are members of school teams
fewer join youth clubs
fewer stay at school beyond the leaving age
fewer experience success at school
fewer take external examinations
fewer succeed in those examinations when they take them
fewer obtain jobs immediately on leaving school.

The National Children's Bureau has shown us how potent these social impediments to learning can be. Children from large families are likely to be twelve months behind in their reading at the age of seven, children from homes with poor amenities eight months behind, children of parents who left school as soon as they legally could six months per parent behind, and the difference between the children of unskilled workers and those of the top professionals is a gap of seventeen months. It is curious that for so long we have failed to assess the full effect of environment, yet it is probably true to say that however stupid, no farmer on earth who had ten cows on scrub land and ten cows on good pasture would attribute the difference in milk yield to inheritance. There is of course no doubt about the factor of inheritance, but it is significant that when the performance of seriously deprived children was looked at, the illegitimate group were found to have risen from a position well below average to a position above it once they had been taken into caring homes.

Fortunately most children are resilient and most can survive combinations of most damaging circumstances. But the heads and teachers of schools which serve the more dismal social areas are fully aware of the symptoms and effects of domestic deprivation on the less resilient of their pupils. There are children who are denied attention at home and overtly crave it in school, children who have learned cruelty and viciousness at home and are cruel and vicious in school; children who, because they are repellent, are rejected by their peers and crave the constant support of the teacher, or who are defiant and aggressive in order to secure in one way the attention they do not easily get in another, children who are fearful and withdrawn, and the list could be greatly extended.

There are those who claim that such children are exceptional, but in fact they are to be found in every classroom in existence, for in any group of children there will be one who is the least happy, one who is the least loved, one who is the least likeable, one who is the least articulate and so on. It should not of course be thought that children born into affluence and comfort do not from time to time also suffer. Indeed one of the worst fates that can befall a pupil of modest ability is to be the offspring of ambitious parents whose pressures are such that they are likely to give the child a loathing of the whole school learning process. And of course there are now many homes where children are given such lavish attention that they are insulated against the school's endeavours to stimulate, they become blasé, and what the teacher does to enliven learning is no more than tolerated.

Chapter 10

Cultural factors in child-rearing and attitudes to education

Tessa Blackstone and Jo Mortimore

THE 'CULTURAL DEPRIVATION' THESIS

In America during the 1960s a widely accepted explanation for the school failure of disadvantaged children was embodied in the concept of 'cultural deprivation'. The term was widely used after the publication of *The Culturally Deprived Child* (Riessman, 1962). The development of the concept of cultural deprivation has been traced by Friedman (1967) and Becker (1963). Adherents of this notion maintained that low achievement could be attributed to early environmental experiences and different child-rearing practices which resulted in cognitive and linguistic deficits (Krugman, 1956, Wrightstone, 1958 and Brooks, 1966). Interest grew after 1963 because of the Federal Government's 'War on Poverty'. Education was seen as a means of countering these deficits, thereby improving the conditions and life chances of poor people and ethnic minority groups.

'Culturally deprived' children were considered to come from homes which were both materially and intellectually inadequate. These were often graphically described. For example, Brooks writes of a culturally deprived child as having 'taken few trips, perhaps his only one the cramped, uncomfortable trip from the lonely shack on the tenant farm to the teeming, filthy slum dwelling and he probably knows nothing of poetry, music, painting or even indoor plumbing'. Psychologists such as Hunt (1964) went so far as to state that 'the difference between the culturally deprived and the culturally privileged is, for children, analogous to the difference between cage-reared and pet-reared rats and dogs'. Deutsch (1964) stressed the importance of the pre-school years as the most effective age at which to administer 'compensatory' enrichment programmes. There arose a plethora of such programmes, many of them aimed at alleviating material, as well as supposed cultural disadvantage. Some were aimed at helping pre-school children (Operation Head Start) others were aimed at the older age groups (Higher Horizons Program, Project Upward Bound).

In Britain the notion of cultural deprivation was accepted by the Plowden

Committee, who wrote, 'Cultural deprivation can also have disastrous results . . . a child brought up in a family which, because of poverty, missing parents or the low intelligence of parents, cannot provide security or sufficient emotional or intellectual stimulation, may miss a significant stage in his early social development.' Whilst acknowledging that a child from an impoverished background may have a normal, satisfactory emotional life, the committee considered that 'what he often lacks is the opportunity to develop intellectual interests. This shows in his poor command of language.' The lack of intellectual stimulation, and inadequately developed language skills were seen as contributing to the cultural deprivation which undermined the disadvantaged child's chances of educational achievement. The root of these failings was considered to lie in poor motivation; in the quality of mother–child interactions during the formative years, which were crucial for intellectual development; in the lack of language skills and literary experiences offered by parents who possessed few books and rarely read to their children and in the lack of parental interest in and knowledge of the child's education. The evidence in support of these views and some of the counter arguments will be considered next.

MOTHER–CHILD INTERACTIONS

During the 1950s and 1960s the belief in the importance of the first five years of life for intellectual development was strengthened by research findings. Early mother–child interactions were said to bear directly on later mental health (Bowlby, 1953). Animal research suggested that imprinting had permanent effects (Connolly, 1974) and studies of the development of IQ indicated that, although IQ varies in the early years, by the age of four it has stabilised (Bloom, 1964). However, research findings on social class differences in parenting during early childhood are not consistent. It has been claimed that in the early months of a baby's life the amount of physical contact and stimulation received by the child is related to his mental development (Lewis and Goldberg, 1969, Yarrow, 1963, cited in Pilling and Pringle, 1978). There is evidence to suggest that, if anything, working-class children, particularly girls, are at an advantage at this time (Moss et al., 1969). Lewis and Wilson (1972) found that there were no social class differences in the mother's verbal contacts with the child but women from lower social class groups had more physical contact with their infant. During these early months infants whose parents came from the lower socioeconomic groups tended to be ahead in mental development. However, Tulkin and Kagan (1972) claim that their sample of middle-class mothers of ten-month-old, first-born girls spent less time in physical contact but more time in verbal interaction and cognitive stimulation with their children. These differences are considered to be important since it is thought that verbal, not physical, stimulation and the mother's involvement in the child's play, rather than the number of toys, fosters mental development during the child's second year of life (Clarke-Stewart, 1973, cited in Pilling and Pringle).

Active, as opposed to passive, learning and goal-directed behaviour has been the subject of much research by psychologists (Held and Hein, 1958, Piaget, 1955). It will not be discussed in detail here. However, some of the research findings have implications for the discussion of disadvantage and under-achievement. Greenfield (1969, cited in Bruner, 1974) has noted the importance of the environment and the sequence of goals set for the child by the parent in the development of cognitive growth. Schoggen (1969, cited in Bruner) found social class differences in the emphasis on goal-directed behaviour which adults attempted to elicit from the children in the two groups. Middle-class children received more stimulation towards attaining a goal than did working-class children. Similar trends emerged from studies on how mothers from upper and lower socio-economic groups teach their children. Hess and Shipman (1965) and Bee (1969) found that the middle-class mothers paid more attention to goal-directed action, they allowed their children to set their own pace and to make more decisions, they used questioning as a strategy for structuring problem-solving and praised successful efforts rather than criticising failure.

Research based on observations and/or interviews with the mothers of slightly older children of four to seven years, has shown social class differences in control techniques (Hess and Shipman, 1965 and 1967, Newson and Newson, 1972 and 1976). In a study carried out by Cook-Gumperz (1973) it was found that in a hypothetical social control situation, middle-class mothers used strategies which included more information about consequences of an action, whilst working-class mothers used more imperatives. Follow-up data from Hess and Bear (1968) and Hess et al. (1969) showed that the more a mother felt externally controlled and less in command of her everyday life, when her child was four years old, the more likely the child was to have a low IQ and poor academic achievement at the age of six or seven. This view is supported by Greenfield (1969) who asks, 'If a mother believes her fate is controlled by external forces, that she does not control the means necessary to achieve her goals, what does this mean for her children?' One possible answer is suggested by Robinson and Robinson (1968), who concluded that 'children with a high degree of achievement motivation tend to become brighter as they grow older, those with a more passive outlook tend to fall behind . . . the degree of achievement motivation is related to the socio-cultural background of the child; middle-class children are more strongly motivated towards achievement than are lower-class children.'

The incidence of depression and neurotic disorder is higher among working-class women. They are, however, less likely than middle-class women to seek medical help (Rutter, 1976). Furthermore, Brown et al.

(1975) showed that working-class women with young children experienced far more acute stress than middle-class women with young children. Phillips (1968) also found that stress was more frequent in the lowest social groups and that disturbance was more likely if there was a lack of positive experience. He suggests that the balance between positive and negative experiences is important. Rutter *et al.* (1970), in their study on the Isle of Wight and in an Inner London Borough, found that emotional disorders were more common in London, both in ten-year-old children and their parents. In both areas child psychiatric disorder was associated with family disruption, parental illness or criminality and social disadvantage (measured by family size, overcrowding and type of accommodation). On the Isle of Wight depression in women was strongly associated with personal and family problems and in London with low social status. It should be recognised, however, that many of the studies cited in this section have not examined the relationship of these factors to educational outcomes.

Few specifically educational policies would do much to alleviate depression and neuroticism among mothers in situations of social disadvantage. Broader changes in social and economic policies would be needed. However, improved day-care and pre-school provision and parental and community involvement programmes would help some women. It is argued that such programmes may also help *children* from disadvantaged backgrounds with problems of poor motivation. When Zigler and Butterfield (1968) administered the Stanford Binet Intelligence Test in a way which was intended to increase the child's motivation by giving him or her a feeling of success then disadvantaged pre-school children increased their test competence.

LANGUAGE

A series of experiments by Kirk, Hunt and others found that four-year-old children enrolled on a Headstart Programme, whose parents were mainly unskilled or unemployed, were less competent at a series of naming tasks than middle-class children (Hunt *et al.*, 1975, Kirk and Hunt, 1975). Kirk and Hunt suggest that if the children do not know some of the words that are used during their early years in school, the resulting confusion may contribute to their cognitive disadvantage. As Pilling and Pringle point out, this may not mean that socially disadvantaged children have smaller vocabularies. They may know as many words as middle-class children but some of them may be from their own culture and not incorporated in any cognitive demands. Pilling and Pringle have reviewed the evidence suggesting that language is a major contributor to differences in intellectual performance between middle-class and working-class children. They conclude that there is evidence of social class differences in the *mastery* of language. Social class differences in *understanding* are not always found (Bruck and Tucker, 1974) and where they are found, Nurss and Day (1971) and Labov (1973) consider that they may be due to dialect difficulties. However, there have been claims that middle-class children are better at using syntactic knowledge (Frasure and Entwisle, 1973), using more complex speech at infant school age (Tough, 1970, Hawkins, 1969, Brandis and Henderson, 1970) and at secondary-school age (Bernstein, 1962; Lawton, 1968).

While socially and educationally disadvantaged children tend to score low on psychometric tests it has not been established that this failure is *caused* by linguistic and intellectual deficits as supporters of the notion of cultural deprivation maintain. Advocates of the 'cultural difference' theory argue that most socially disadvantaged children do not have language or cognitive defects and that they come to school with the same ability to reason and the same language structure as middle-class children (Labov, 1973, Baratz and Baratz, 1969 and 1970, Ginsburg, 1972). It is argued that every human society provides experiences sufficient for normal cognitive and linguistic development and that lower working-class and ethnic minority children come from cultures which are different, rather than deficient.

There may, however, be differences in the ease with which children from different social class backgrounds approach school demands. Cole and Bruner (1972), Bruner (1974) and Blank (1973) consider that, although working-class and middle-class children have the same range and distribution of linguistic and cognitive ability, working-class children fail to use their ability in the classroom, partly because they are not sufficiently motivated and partly because they have difficulty in transferring skills acquired elsewhere to the classroom. Whereas the middle-class child uses his intellectual skills in a variety of situations, the working-class child might only use his when specifically required to do so.

Bernstein has suggested that differences in early childhood socialisation and in ways of communicating have implications for how children from different backgrounds respond to school. Bernstein maintains that the middle-class child learns to use an 'elaborated' communication code which 'orientates the child early towards the significance of relatively context independent meanings' (Bernstein, 1977). The middle-class mother is a 'powerful and crucial agent of reproduction who provides access to symbolic forms and who shapes the disposition of her children so that they are better able to exploit the possibilities of education'. Disadvantaged children are often said to arrive at school with poorly developed language and lacking basic concepts (AMMA Report, 1979). Tough (1974, 1977) maintains that disadvantaged children are not linguistically deficient but that lack of practice, opportunities and encouragement contribute to their apparent unwillingness to use language in a manner appropriate to the educational environment. However, there is some evidence that the great majority of working-class children both talk and are talked to a good deal at home, and only a small minority may suffer deprivation in this respect (Wootton,

1974). A study by Tizard *et al.* (1980) of children's language at home and at school suggests that both middle-class and working-class children talked and were talked to a good deal at home but that school provided fewer occasions for adult–child conversations than is normally supposed. In addition, research by Francis (1975) with children with reading difficulties suggests that they have sufficient knowledge of the language structure and vocabulary to master reading. Poor test scores or reading failure in the socially disadvantaged may not be due to language or cognitive defects but to the lack of motivation or interest discussed earlier.

Ginsburg (1972) considers that the lower-class environment *may* be deficient in that the parents provide fewer reading experiences for the pre-school child but he maintains that this does not warrant compensatory education, but rather an adaptation by the school to the language and ways of thinking of disadvantaged children. Similarly, in their Report, the Plowden Committee accepted the recommendation by the National Association for the Teaching of English that research be carried out into the types of reading schemes and library books which would be most effective with children of different backgrounds and abilities. (Research commissioned by the Plowden Committee (Morton-Williams, 1967) found that 60 per cent of unskilled workers had five books or less in the home apart from children's books and magazines compared with 5 per cent of professional workers and that the children of unskilled workers borrowed fewer library books.)

There are no clear-cut conclusions on the linguistic competence of disadvantaged children. The position is complicated by claims about dialect or cultural differences. However, it seems likely that certain children may experience difficulty in responding to school demands. Teachers and policymakers need to be aware of this and attempt to develop strategies for eliciting in the classroom the language skills learned outside school.

PARENTAL ATTITUDES

The importance of parents' attitudes for children's achievement emerged some years ago in studies by Fraser (1959), and Floud, Halsey and Martin (1956). In Douglas' study (1964) the level of parental interest in their children's work was based on reports made by the class teachers and on records of parents' visits to school. This 'second-hand' reported information may have biased the results in favour of middle-class parents. However, on the face of it, the evidence supported the view that the working-class child was disadvantaged at school largely because of his parents' lack of interest in his educational progress. Parental interest and attitudes to education outweighed the effects of social class, size of family, quality of housing and academic record of the school. The effect of parental interest was partly explained by social class, a larger proportion of middle-class than working-class children having interested parents. But within each social class those children whose parents were interested in their education scored higher on achievement tests than those with uninterested parents.

The Plowden Committee commissioned their own survey of primary-school children, teachers and parents and found, like Douglas, that parental attitudes to school were more strongly associated with educational achievement than any other factor. As measures of parental interest in and attitude towards their child's education the Plowden researchers took parents' answers to questions about the age at which they wanted their children to leave school and the secondary school they preferred. (A selective system still operated in many areas in 1967.) Account was taken of parental initiative in visiting the school and making contact with the head and teachers and in asking for work for the children to do at home. Questions were asked about the amount of time parents spent with children at home in the evening and whether they helped them with school work. The 'literacy' of the home was assessed by what the parents and children read, whether they belonged to a library and how many books there were in the home (Morton-Williams, 1967).

The survey found evidence of an association between social class and the responsibility and initiative taken by parents over the children's education, in the interest and support shown by fathers over education and upbringing, in the time and attention devoted to children's development and their interest in and knowledge of their children's school work. For all of these factors the situation was likely to be more favourable the better the social circumstances of the home. There were, however, noticeable differences in the part played by the father in the child's education. Over 40 per cent of manual workers but only 25 per cent of non-manual workers had left the choice of school to their wives. Almost half of the manual, but less than a quarter of the non-manual workers, had not been to their child's present school. There was little class difference in the parents wanting the school to give their child work to do at home in the evenings, yet far fewer children of manual workers were, in fact, given work to do. More recently Newson and Newson (1977) found that in their study in Nottingham 82 per cent of working-class parents of seven year olds helped their child with reading. The Plowden Committee concluded that 'a strengthening of parental encourage-ment may produce better performance in school'. However, Bernstein and Davies (1969) argue that the Plowden measures of parental interest and attitudes were, in fact, measures of strongly class-linked behaviour patterns and it was these behaviour patterns that were associated with school achieve-ment. Encouraging schools to increase their parent contacts would not necessarily, by itself, raise the achievements of working-class children.

Acland (1980) has criticised the way the findings of the national survey commissioned by the Plowden Committee were arrived at and used to support the key policy recommendations relating to parental involvement and Educational Priority Areas. He re-analysed the raw data obtained in the course of the national survey and maintains 'the independent effect of attitudes on achievement is weak and uncertain and so gives little support for the view that improved attitudes will lead to improved performance levels'. Acland claims that in the original analysis data for some subgroups showed attitudes to be considerably less important than circumstances or school variables and that sometimes attitude variables had been incorrectly identified as circumstance variables and vice versa. His re-calculations suggest that circumstances were of almost equal importance to attitudes. He also points out there there is an element of judgement in the classification of the variables. For example, one variable which the Plowden researchers identified as an 'attitude' variable was based on a question about whether or not the parents took their children on outings. Yet it can be argued that this is just as much a reflection of the families' financial resources and should have been included in the list of 'circumstance' variables. Acland regrouped the home background variables selection items which were 'intuitively most interesting and most clearly relevant to the parent involvement policy'. These were, the level of contact between home and school; parents' feelings of exclusion from school; level of parental help given at home; child's response to school; and measures of literacy of the home and parental aspiration. The findings indicate the importance of the variables measuring parental aspirations (no doubt affected by the 11+ examination) and literacy of the home. The variables most closely identified with parental involvement (for example, parental contact with the school) were only weakly related to achievement. Acland's re-analysis also included an examination of the association between variations in the school environment of the kind described in the parent involvement policy and the measures of parents' supportive behaviour and attitudes. The results showed firstly a relatively strong association between school factors and parental contact which suggest that the more schools provide opportunities for meetings with teachers the more parents will take up these opportunities although the direction of influence is uncertain. Acland suggests that it could be the more parents pressed for such provision the more likely the school would be to respond. Secondly, there was only a weak association between school provision and parents' attitudes. Though schools may make more provision, parents may still feel excluded or discouraged. It is possible that seeing what does go on in schools (for example, 'Fletcher' (Maths), 'Breakthrough' (reading) and 'Projects') will make them feel even less able to help their children.

Davie et al. (1972) used three measures of parental interest: the teacher's rating; whether or not the parents had visited the school to discuss their child; and the parents' aspirations for the child. Using these criteria it was found that social class differences on all three were large. For example, 76 per cent of children in social class I had parents who had initiated discussions with a member of staff, compared with 43 per cent of children in social class V. What social class differences do exist are likely to be greatest between disadvantaged and more privileged families. Thus, Wedge and Prosser (1973) found that neither parent of three out of every five of the children in the disadvantaged group had visited the school compared with one in three of the other group.

There is other research, however, which suggests that working-class and/or disadvantaged parents, do not lack interest in their child's education. For example, Halsey's research in Educational Priority Areas found considerable concern and interest in education (Halsey, 1972).

Although there may be some working-class parents uninterested in their children's education, possible explanations for what is sometimes assumed to be lack of support, need to be explored. One explanation may be the opportunities or lack of opportunities offered for parent–teacher contact. Davie et al. found that middle-class children were more likely to be at a school which had established parent–school contacts (89 per cent) than were working-class children (75 per cent). A second possibility may be that working-class parents feel ill at ease or the subject of criticism when they visit school. Teachers represent authority and parents who have had unhappy experiences at school or with authority figures may be reluctant to meet them (Halsey, 1972). Moreover, interviews with parents have consistently shown that working-class parents tend to have less knowledge of the education system and of school practices. Midwinter (1977) asserts that the disadvantage of many working-class children at school is due to their parents' lack of educational knowledge. Jackson and Marsden (1962) found middle-class parents knew how to set about choosing a primary and secondary school with good academic records, whilst working-class parents often made the choice on quite trivial grounds. Many are ill-informed about the curriculum and even the smallest change in methods can be a source of confusion to working-class parents. Young and McGeeney (1968) wrote 'they could see the massive walls; they did not understand what went on behind them'. The difficulties of overcoming the communication gap between parents and nursery teachers are discussed by Tizard et al. (1981). They suggest the gap is not due to lack of interest nor just to differences in knowledge but also to differences in parents' and nursery teachers' respective interpretation of 'play', 'reading' and 'learning' and the values attached to such activities.

The evidence on parental interest, or lack of it, needs to be treated with caution. Sometimes at least part of the evidence is based on teachers' assessments which may tilt the balance in favour of more advantaged groups. Other evidence is based on indicators which may not be the most sensitive or even the most appropriate and which may be measuring something other than parental interest. For example, frequency of visits to their child's school may indicate more about the relatively flexible working hours of fathers in non-manual occupations than about their level of interest in their child's education. It seems likely that there are several possible explanations for behaviour which is often interpreted as lack of interest. Teachers need to be aware of the alternative possibilities.

REFERENCES

Acland, H. (1980), 'Research as stage management: the case of the Plowden Committee' in M. I. A. Bulmer (ed.), *Social Research and Royal Commissions*, George Allen & Unwin.

Assistant Master and Mistress Association (AMMA) (1979), 'Report of the primary and preparatory Education Committee on Nursery Education', *Report*, 2, 4, January 1980.

Baratz, J. C. and Baratz, J. (1969), 'A bi-dialectal task for determining language proficiency in economically disadvantaged Negro children', *Child Dev*, 40, 3.

Baratz, J. C. and Baratz, J. (1970), 'Teaching reading in an urban negro school system' in F. Williams (ed.), *Language and Poverty*, Markham, Chicago.

Becker, H. S. (1963), 'Education and the lower-class child' in A. W. Gouldner and H. P. Gouldner (eds), *Modern Sociology*, Harcourt Brace.

Bee, H. L. (1969), 'Social class difference in maternal teaching strategies and speech patterns', *Developmental Psychology*, 1, 6.

Bernstein, B. (1962) 'Social class, linguistic codes and grammatical elements', *Language and Speech*, 5.

Bernstein, B. (1977), 'Class and pedagogies: visible and invisible' in J. Karabel and A. H. Halsey (eds), *Power and Ideology in Education*, Oxford University Press. Also in *Class, Codes and Control*, Vol. III (1975), Routledge & Kegan Paul.

Bernstein, B. and Davies, B. (1969), *Perspectives on Plowden*, Penguin.

Blank, M. (1973), *Teaching and Learning in the Pre-school*, Columbus Merrill.

Bloom, B.S. (1964), *Stability and Change in Human Characteristics*, John Wiley.

Bowlby, J. (1953), *Child Care and the Growth of Love*, Pelican.

Brandis, W. and Henderson, D. (1970), *Social Class, Language and Communication*', Routledge & Kegan Paul.

Brooks, C. (1966), 'Some approaches to teaching English as a second language' in S.W. Webster (ed.), *The Disadvantaged Learner*, Chandler Publishing Company.

Brown, G.W., Bhrolchain M.N. and Harris, T. (1975), 'Social class and psychiatric disturbance among women in an urban population', *Sociology*, 9.

Bruck, M. and Tucker, C.R. (1974), Social class differences in the acquisition of school language', *Merrill-Palmer Quarterly*, 20.

Bruner, J.S. (1974), *Relevance of Education*, Penguin.

Clarke-Stewart, K.A. (1973), 'Interaction between mothers and their young children: characteristics and consequences', *Monograph for the Society for Research in Child Development*, Series No. 153.

Cole, M. and Bruner, J.S. (1972), 'Preliminaries to a theory of cultural differences', 71st *Nat. Soc. Educ. Yearbook*, part 2 cited in J. Bruner, (1974), *The Relevance of Education*, Penguin.

Connolly, K. in Connolly, K. and Bruner, J. (eds) (1974), *The Growth of Competence*, Academic Press.

Cook-Gumperz, J. (1973), *Social Control and Socialisation*, Routledge & Kegan Paul.

Davie, R., Butler, N. and Goldstein, H. (1972), *From Birth to Seven*, a report of the National Child Development Study, Longman.

Deutsch M. (1964), 'Facilitating development in the pre-school child: social and psychological perspectives', *Merrill-Palmer Quarterly*, 10, April.

Douglas, J. W. B. (1964), *The Home and the School*, MacGibbon and Kee.

Floud, J. E., Halsey, A. H., and Martin, F. M. (1956), *Social Class and Educational Opportunity*, Heinemann.

Francis, H. (1975), *Language in Childhood*, Elek Press.

Fraser, E. D. (1959), *Home Environment and the School*, University of London Press.

Frasure, N. E. and Entwisle, D. R. (1973), 'Semantic and syntactic development in children', *Developmental Psychology*, **9**.

Friedman, N. L. (1967), 'Cultural deprivation: a commentary on the sociology of knowledge', *Journal of Educational Thought*, **1**, 2.

Ginsburg, H. (1972), *The Myth of the Deprived Child: Poor Children's Intellect and Education*, Prentice-Hall.

Greenfield, P. M. (1969), 'Goal as environmental variable in the development of intelligence', Paper presented at conference on Contributions to Intelligence, University of Illinois, Urbana, cited in J. Bruner (1974), *The Relevance of Education*.

Halsey, A. H. (1972), *Educational Priority. EPA Problems and Policies*, Vol. I, HMSO.

Hawkins, P. (1969), 'Social class, the nominal group and reference', *Language and Speech* 12 February, reprinted in B. Bernstein, *Class, Codes and Control*, Vol. II, Routledge & Kegan Paul, 1973.

Held, R. and Hein, A. V. (1958), 'Adaptation of disarranged hand/eye coordination contingent upon reafferent stimulation', *Percept. and Motor Skills*, **8**.

Hess, R. D. and Shipman, V. C. (1965), 'Early experience and the socialisation of cognitive modes in children', *Child Dev.*, **36**, 4.

Hess, R. D. and Shipman, V. C. (1967), 'Cognitive elements in maternal behaviour' in J. P. Hill (ed.), *Minnesota Symposia on Child Psychology*, Vol. I, University of Minnesota Press, Minneapolis.

Hess, R. D. and Bear, R. M. (1968), *Early Education: Current Theory, Research and Action*, Aldine.

Hess, R. D. *et al.* (1969), *The Cognitive Environments of Urban Pre-school Children*, Graduate School of Education, University of Chicago.

Hunt, J. McV. (1964), 'The psychological basis for using pre-school enrichment as an antidote for cultural deprivation', *Merrill-Palmer Quarterly*, **10**, July.

Hunt, J. McV., Kirk, G. H. and Lieberman, C. (1975), 'Social class and pre-school language skill: IV semantic mastery of shapes', *Genetic Psychol. Monographs*, **91**, pp. 317–37.

Jackson, B. and Marsden, D. (1962), *Education and the Working Class*, Routledge & Kegan Paul.

Kirk, G. F. and Hunt, J. McV. (1975), 'Social class and pre-school language skill I', *Intro. Gen. Psych. Monograph* 91.

Krugman, J. L. (1956), 'Cultural deprivation and child development', *High Points*, **38**, November.

Labov, W. (1973), 'The logic of non-standard English' in N. Keddie (ed.), *Tinker, Tailor . . . the Myth of Cultural Deprivation*, Penguin Education.

Lawton, D. (1968), *Social Class, Language and Education*, Routledge & Kegan Paul.

Lewis, M. and Goldberg, S. (1969), 'Perceptual-cognitive development in infancy: a generalised expectancy model as a function of mother/infant interaction', *Merrill-Palmer Quarterly*, **15**.

Lewis, M. and Wilson, C. D. (1972), 'Infant development in lower-class American families', *Human Development*, **15**.

Midwinter, E. (1977), *Education for Sale*, Allen & Unwin.

Morton-Williams, R. (1967), 'The 1964 Nat. Survey among Parents of Primary

School Children' in Central Advisory Council for Education, *Children and their Primary Schools, 2, Research and Surveys*, HMSO.

Moss, H. A., Robson, K. S. and Pederson, F. (1969), 'Determinants of maternal stimulation of infants and consequences of treatment for later reactions to strangers', *Developmental Psychology*, **1**, 3.

Newson, J. and Newson, E. (1972), *Patterns of Infant Care*, Penguin.

Newson, J. and Newson, E. (1976), *Seven Years Old in the Home Environment*, Allen & Unwin.

Newson, J. and Newson, E. (1977), *Perspectives on School at Seven Years Old*, Allen & Unwin.

Nurss, J. E. and Day, D. E. (1971), 'Imitation, comprehension and production of grammatical structures', *Journal of Verbal Behaviour*, **10**.

Phillips, D. L. (1968), 'Social class and psychiatric disturbance: the influence of positive and negative experiences', *Social Psychiatry*, **3**.

Piaget, J. (1955), *The Construction of Reality in the Child*, trans. M. Cook, Routledge & Kegan Paul.

Pilling, D. and Pringle, M. K. (1978), *Controversial Issues in Child Development*, Paul Elek.

Riessman, F. (1962), *The Culturally Deprived Child*, Harper and Row.

Robinson, H. B. and Robinson, N. M. (1968), 'The problem of timing in pre-school education' in R. D. Hess and R. M. Bear (eds), *Early Education*, Aldine.

Rutter, M. L. (1976), 'Prospective studies to investigate behavioural change' in J. S. Strauss, H. M. Batigian and M. Ross (eds), *Methods of Longitudinal Research in Psychopathology*, Plenum.

Rutter, M. L., Tizard, J. and Whitmore, K. (eds) (1970), *Education, Health and Behaviour*, Longman.

Schoggen, M. (1969), 'An ecological study of three year olds at home', George Peabody College for Teachers, Nashville, cited in J. Bruner (1974), *The Relevance of Education*.

Tizard, B., Mortimore, J., and Burchell, B. (1981), *Involving Parents in Nursery and Infant School: A Sourcebook for Teachers*, Grant McIntyre.

Tizard, J., Schofield, W. and Hewison, J. (1980), 'The Haringey Reading Project', Unpublished report to the DES.

Tough, J. (1970), Language and Environment: An Interim Report on a Longitudinal Study, University of Leeds Institute of Education (unpublished).

Tough, J. (1974), *Focus on Meaning: Talking to Some Purpose with Young Children*, Allen & Unwin.

Tough, J. (1977), *Development of Meaning*, Allen & Unwin.

Tulkin, S. R. and Kagan, J. (1972), 'Mother/child interaction in the first year of life', *Child Dev.*, **43**.

Wedge, P. and Prosser, N. (1973), *Born to Fail?*, Arrow Books.

Wootton, A. J. (1974), 'Talk in the homes of young children', *Sociology*, **82**.

Wrightstone, J. W. (1958), 'Discovering and stimulating culturally deprived talented youth', *Teachers College Record*, **60**.

Yarrow, L. J. (1963), 'Research in dimensions of early maternal care', *Merrill-Palmer Quarterly*, **9**.

Young, M. and McGeeney, P. (1968), *Learning Begins at Home: A Study of a Junior School and its Parents*, Routledge & Kegan Paul.

Zigler, E. and Butterfield, E. C. (1968), 'Motivational aspects of changes in IQ test performance of culturally deprived nursery school children', *Child Dev.*, **39**.

Chapter 11

Special needs education
The next 25 years

Klaus Wedell

SUMMARY

1 During the 1970s and up to the late 1980s there was remarkably rapid development both in understanding children and young people's special educational needs (SENs) and in their education.

2 The role of environmental factors in contributing to SENs was recognised. It became evident that SENs occurred in a continuum from the most severe to those less so, many experienced by pupils in ordinary schools; about 20% of pupils were involved at some point in their schooling.

3 The 1981 Act asserted the right of children and young people with SENs to be educated as far as possible with their peers in ordinary schools; it remains a challenge for all schools to extend their flexibility so as to respond to pupils' learning needs in the future.

4 Recent educational legislation has, in conjunction with fiscal constraint, increased the difficulties that LEAs and schools face in meeting their obligations to pupils with SENs and has fragmented responsibility for ensuring that SENs are met.

5 Examples are cited of good practice which point to potential future developments:
   - making better use of available resources through collaboration between teachers, schools and authorities;
   - improved practice in schools, such as collaborative learning groups for pupils with different learning needs, 'teacher support teams', realising the potential of computer-aided learning, better partnership with parents;
   - more effective teaching through emphasising curriculum-based teacher assessment for monitoring pupil achievement and planning progress.

INTRODUCTION

How can one gauge the potential scale of development of special needs education over the next 25 years? One way is to look back over a similar period to see what has been achieved. This shows that principles and practice relating to the education of children and young people with special educational needs (SENs) have developed more during this period than have those in most areas of education. Unfortunately, recent education legislation has put some achievements of the past at risk and legislation currently proposed could possibly jeopardise future development. One should none the less consider the means of making progress in this field. This Briefing aims to cover three areas, with coverage confined to the school years:
– the development of special needs education over the last 25 years;
– the implications of recent and proposed legislation; and
– the scope for future development.

THE DEVELOPMENT OF SPECIAL NEEDS EDUCATION OVER THE LAST 25 YEARS

It is easy to forget that, in the UK, the right to education of all those with SENs was not recognised until the 1970 Act. This legislation brought pupils with the most severe learning difficulties, who had been termed 'ineducable' and had therefore been cared for and educated within the NHS, under the responsibility of the Local Education Authority (LEA). The Act reflected developments in thinking in other countries as well as in the UK about the role of education in providing access to equal opportunities. In 1978, the Warnock Committee summarised thinking about SENs up to that time, and made the points shown in Panel 1 (DES, 1978).

The concept of the 'continuum' of SENs was derived from studies which showed that, in addition to the 2% of pupils who received their education largely in special schools and units, a further 18% of pupils might require some form of special needs education at some time in their schooling. Education in general therefore had to take account of pupils' diversity of learning ability. The interactive causation of SENs, the recognition of the right to integration, and the rights of parents in decision-making were included in the first Act to be concerned specifically with SENs, which was passed in 1981 and implemented in 1983. The Act defines SENs as those which require additional or different provision from that 'made generally' within an LEA. The LEA also has to identify those children whose needs require provision which it can only offer on an individual basis, whether in the child's school or in a special school or with other support. For such a decision, a multiprofessional assessment of the child has to be carried out by LEA-designated personnel, with the needs and provision to be set out in a 'Statement' to be reviewed annually. Parents must be given an opportunity

---

PANEL 1: The Warnock Committee's views

1 The aims of education are the same for all children. The means needed to achieve these might be different for pupils with SENs, as might the extent to which the aims can be reached.
2 SENs are not caused solely by deficiencies *within* the child. They result from interaction between the strengths and weaknesses of the child, and the resources and deficiencies of the environment. SENs occur in a continuum of degree of severity, and so it is not meaningful to attempt to draw a hard and fast line between the 'handicapped' and the 'non-handicapped'.
3 All schools have a responsibility to identify and meet pupils' SENs and all children and young people with SENs should be educated alongside their peers as long as their needs can be met and it is practicable to do so.
4 Parents, and as far as possible the children and young people with SENs themselves, have the right to share in the decisions about how their needs are met.

---

to comment on any provision the LEA proposes and can appeal if they disagree. The current Education Bill proposes that appeals be considered by Tribunals, which would replace the existing variety of arrangements.

In the light of the Warnock Committee's rejection of the label of 'handicap', the then Department of Education and Science (DES) subsequently ceased to collect data on pupils by category of handicap. In order to plan provision for SENs as they occur, it is of course still important to have information on the prevalence of hearing, visual or motor impairment, problems in language development, emotional and behavioural difficulties, difficulty in learning ranging from specific difficulties with reading for example, to severe and general learning difficulties, and combinations of any of these. The last 25 years have seen changes in the incidence of disabling conditions as the result of advances in preventive medicine and in obstetric practice. The former has drastically reduced the incidence of, for example, hearing impairment; the latter has, to varying extents, led to the survival of children with more severe and multiple disabilities.

The Warnock Committee made a number of crucial recommendations which were not incorporated in the 1981 Act, and have still not been instituted. The Committee recommended that parents of children should be offered a 'named person', who could guide them in planning appropriate provision for their children. Another recommendation was that *all* teachers with designated responsibility for special needs education should have a recognised qualification appropriate to their work. In the years following the 1981 Act, a small number of research projects was commissioned to study how special needs education had changed from the publication of the Warnock Report onwards. The following are some of the changes reported up to the middle or late 1980s in studies of samples of LEAs:

- 66% of LEAs increased staff supporting pupils with SENs in ordinary schools between 1978 and 1983 (Gipps *et al.*, 1987).
- 54% of LEAs increased expenditure on special needs relative to inflation between 1983 and 1987, a reflection of the fact that the 1981 Act had been introduced without additional funding (Goacher *et al.*, 1988).
- 76% of LEAs reported an increase of pupils with SENs taught in nursery, primary and secondary schools between 1983 and 1985. There was a general shift from segregated to less segregated provision for pupils with all forms of SEN except for emotional and behaviour problems (ibid.).
- Data from LEA returns to the DES showed that, between 1982 and 1987 there was an overall drop from 1.53% to 1.41% in the percentage of pupils aged 5–15 in special schools in England. This study also revealed wide variations between different LEAs, with some showing significant increases (Swann, 1987).[20]

The above findings show that most LEAs responded to concern about meeting the SENs of pupils in ordinary schools. There was, overall, a move to reducing the extent to which pupils with SENs were segregated. However, it has to be remembered that these general trends smooth over significant variations between different LEAs.

THE IMPLICATIONS OF RECENT LEGISLATION

When introduced as a Bill, the 1988 'Education Reform Act' made barely any reference to how special needs education was to be furthered or even maintained. Schools' funding was to depend predominantly on the number of their pupils and they would compete for pupils through their position in league tables of aggregate achievement in the national curriculum. Both these provisions constituted a potential disincentive for schools to admit pupils with SENs and to allocate resources to support them. At the same time, LEAs were required to delegate increasing proportions of their funds to schools, thus reducing the amount available for central services to support pupils with SENs. Community Charge-capping and the loss of funds allocated to 'opted-out' grant maintained schools further reduced LEA budgets. A number of studies illustrated the effect of these problems on schools and LEAs:

- the National Foundation for Educational Research (NFER) found that, already in late 1991, 15% of a sample of 81 LEAs reported that schools had made cuts in special needs co-ordinator posts and in learning support departments (Fletcher-Campbell and Hall, 1993).
- an unpublished study for the Economic and Social Research Council found that 85% of a sample of 946 secondary teachers in 4 LEAs were concerned about the resource implications for pupils with SENs (Wrigley and Clough, 1992).[23]
- the Audit Commission and HMI found that, in a small sample of

headteachers interviewed, 52% judged that the resources to meet pupils' SENs were insufficient, although 69% claimed that they were not limiting their admission of pupils with SENs (Audit Commission/HMI, 1992).

There is a considerable body of anecdotal evidence suggesting that both ordinary and special schools are finding it difficult to meet pupils' SENs. The trend is reflected in increases in the percentage of pupils with statements of special needs in LEAs. If schools cannot fund the resources they need to meet pupils' SENs, the Statement procedure offers a way of obtaining additional resources from the LEA. Thus:

- it was reported that between 1990 and 1992, the average percentage of pupils who had been 'statemented' rose from 2.0% to 2.4%, despite the fact that most LEAs had policies intended to limit increases (Evans and Lunt, 1992);
- a study of Department for Education (DFE) data on the percentage of children in special schools showed that there was a new rise from 1.02% to 1.04% between 1988 and 1991 among primary school children, while the trend for secondary school children continued downwards from 2.09% to 2.05% (Swann, 1992);
- a survey carried out at the end of 1991 found that 50% of LEAs reported an overall increase in pupils placed in special schools (Lunt and Evans, 1991);
- a DFE report expresses concern about the number of pupils excluded from schools. This matches other reports of a marked increase in exclusions (DFE, 1992). It is important to distinguish among these those pupils who are regarded as having SENs, usually those with emotional or behaviour disturbances. But it is significant that data obtained over a two year period showed that 12.5% of excluded pupils had Statements, indicating that even the designated resources were not proving sufficient for these pupils.

The Bill published in November 1992 poses further problems for meeting pupils' SENs. It envisages a progressive limitation of the LEA's scope to co-ordinate support in its area for pupils' SENs, as the proportion of its 'opted-out' schools increases. If and when the proportion reaches 75%, the LEA's responsibility for SENs will be limited to pupils with Statements. At this point, the Bill would also stop provision for SENs being administered as a continuum. It would also make it impossible for LEAs to submit to the Secretary of State their plans for meeting the full range of pupils' SENs in their area, as required in Circular 7/91. The crucial need for LEAs to co-ordinate provision was stressed by the House of Commons Select Committee on Education in its 1987 report on the functioning of the 1981 Act. The Committee concluded that special needs provision was too complex to be left to the responsibility of individual schools.

Under the Bill, Grant Maintained schools would come under a national Funding Agency for Schools (FAS), which would presumably share responsibility for pupils with SENs with the LEA. This would add to the already existing difficulty in achieving co-ordination of responsibility for meeting SENs between education and non-education agencies serving different geographical areas (Goacher *et al.*, 1988). A further agency, the Office for Standards in Education (OFSTED), now has the general responsibility for supervising the quality of education offered. It will delegate this responsibility to inspection teams whose tenders it accepts. Although the procedures to be adopted by these teams include inspection of special needs provision, there are no assurances that the teams will have the necessary level of expertise. The teams will not be responsible for ensuring that any required improvements are achieved.

The Bill and the 1988 Act thus fragment responsibility for ensuring that the range of pupils' SENs are met. In response to representations made to it, the government has amended the Bill to require that all schools supply information about how they meet their pupils' SENs, and has also permitted LEAs to continue to offer some specialist services for pupils with SENs. Many of the detailed requirements regarding provision for pupils' SENs will be covered in a 'Code of Practice' yet to be agreed. It remains to be seen what this will contain and how its requirements will be funded. It is paradoxical that, while the Bill increases the uncertainties about how pupils' SENs can be met effectively, its main specific provisions on SENs focus on revising procedures to enable parents to appeal if they are dissatisfied with the provision made for their children.

THE FUTURE

The Audit Commission and HMI showed that there has been much to criticise as well as to praise in the past and present education of pupils with SENs (Audit Commission/HMI, 1992). In general, however, the evidence indicates that following the Warnock Report there was a period of considerable advance, but since the time of the 1988 Act there has been a deterioration in provision for pupils with SENs. The current Bill, as it stands at the time this chapter is being written, might well continue this trend. The provisions of the recent legislation have been termed 'reforms', and so one would have expected them at least to promote the good which has been achieved. Referring to the proposals for special needs education in the Bill, the Chairman of the Select Committee on Education (Sir Malcolm Thornton) is quoted (TES December 11th 1992) as saying 'If we really believe that SENs are going to be given a better deal under the new legislation than under the old system, then this is the biggest triumph of hope over experience that I have ever encountered'.

It is paradoxical that a number of the aims espoused by the recent legislation are ones which would be regarded as reasonable, were it not that the means chosen to implement them are potentially counter-productive and potentially harmful to pupils with SENs. The following are some examples:

1 The aim of giving schools flexibility by allowing them to manage their own budgets is to be commended. However, if the cost of meeting pupils' SENs is included, then under present circumstances the integration of pupils with SENs may be hindered. When funds are short and schools' budgets depend on competition for pupil numbers, a school's commitment towards 'expensive' and potentially 'popularity reducing' pupils is put under strain, and at worst becomes incompatible with practicalities of funding.

2 Greater regard for the cost-effectiveness of services could lead to more considered use. However, this does not imply that special needs services can be operated on market-economy principles. Forcing specialist services to depend on purchaser-provider relationships with individual schools makes them too sensitive to the ability of schools to afford them. Quality services for pupils' SENs can be quickly lost, but would take long to rebuild. This will need to be considered in guidance about the amendment to the Bill allowing LEAs to continue to offer specialist services.

3 The promotion of parental involvement in democratic decision-making about the education of their children should be encouraged. There must, however, be safeguards for parents of children with SENs who are by definition in a minority. With pupil-led funding in times of constrained finances, schools wishing to maximise their resources may favour policies supporting the interests of the majority of parents, thus jeopardising the rights of the few.

4 The aim of making funding formulae for schools 'transparent' and 'easily understood' might seem desirable, but not if the formulae are *educationally* meaningless. For example, a recent consultation paper on funding GM schools proposes that the cost of meeting their pupils' SENs should be based on the proportion of pupils who obtain free meals in any given school, because this is an easily derivable figure. The Audit Commission and HMI showed that many LEAs have developed collaborative audit procedures which offer not only a direct means of assessing the various levels of support schools provide for pupils' SENs, but which also form an essential part of the development of whole school policies on meeting SENs (Audit Commission/HMI, 1992). These procedures may not be 'transparent', but they can make a direct contribution to raising school effectiveness.

From the point of view of special needs education, perhaps the main paradox

PANEL 2: A flexible response

1 Making better use of available resources

- The Audit Commission and HMI (1992) reported how schools in some LEAs participate in decisions about the equitable sharing of resources for pupils with and without Statements. As a result, schools are led to consider their own needs in relation to the needs of other schools.
- Schools which group themselves into partnerships to share resources for their pupils' SENs have been the subject of a recent study (Evans *et al.*, in press). Such schools have increased their capacity to meet pupils' SENs through mutual support in developing whole-school policies and through sharing the expertise available both in their own schools and from specialist support services. The partnerships often span the phases of schooling, and so ensure continuity in the way in which individual pupils' needs are met.
- Ordinary schools have set up links with special schools to exchange pedagogic and subject expertise between staff, and to allow flexible movement of pupils between the schools (Jowett *et al.*, 1988). This flexibility can counter the potential segregation of pupils in special schools, and widen the interpersonal experience of mainstream pupils.
- In-service materials have been developed to enable Education, Health and Social Services staff to collaborate in organising special needs provision, in order to meet pupils' needs more effectively and also to avoid wasteful overlapping and interference (Evans *et al.*, in press).

2 Matching pedagogical practice to the needs of pupils and the demands of a broad and balanced curriculum

- 'Teacher support teams' have been formed in schools to mobilise the varied expertise of staff in schools to help individual teachers facing problems in meeting their pupils' needs (Norwich and Daniels, 1992).
- The contributions of teachers and classroom assistants have been made more effective through systematic planning of their respective roles to maximise support for pupils in the classroom (Balshaw, 1991).
- In many curriculum areas children with different learning needs have been shown to learn more effectively if they are grouped to collaborate in each other's learning (Slavin, 1989).
- Parents have made a major contribution to their children's learning through collaboration with teachers. This has been demonstrated in a variety of studies including some of children learning to read and others concerned with the development of personal competence in children with severe learning difficulties (Wolfendale, 1989).
- The contribution of computer-aided learning for pupils with SENs has been amply demonstrated across a range of curriculum areas (Hawkridge and Vincent, 1992). Flexible 'shell' programmes have made it simpler for teachers to match programmes to individual pupils' learning needs, and 'talking' computers have extended scope for responsiveness. Micro-processors have also revolutionised methods of helping children with motor or sensory disabilities to overcome communication barriers.

3 Effective teaching depends ultimately on teachers being able to respond flexibly to pupils' learning

- Teachers need a clear framework of curricular progression against which to monitor pupil progress, and efficient ways of recording what pupils have achieved.
- Pedagogic practice in the education of pupils throughout the range of SENs has long been grounded in curriculum-based assessment, and a variety of user-friendly means of record-keeping has been devised. The introduction of the national curriculum has offered a so-far unrealised opportunity to build a relevant and realistic framework of progression in the curricular areas covered, and this could contribute to improved curriculum-based assessment.

is that the current legislation proposes means which do not further its aims to provide for pupils' diverse educational needs. Seen from 25 years hence, it will seem inexplicable that, although we recognised our failure to meet diversity, we did not recognise the reasons for this failure.

It is not the task of this chapter to prognosticate on the future of education in general. However, from the point of view of the education of pupils with SENs two points emerge. First, many writers on special needs education in this country (Ainscow, in press) and in the USA (Stainback and Stainback, 1984) have pointed out that the continuum of pupils' SENs merges into the range of diversity of ability identifiable in all pupils, and consequently special needs education must be offered more as an extension of education in general. Second, special needs education has for long been organised to achieve flexibility of response to pupils' diversity *within* schools, both ordinary and special schools. The extent to which flexibility has been achieved in ordinary schools is illustrated in the Danish concept of the 'school for all' (Hansen, 1992). It is significant that, in Denmark, only about 0.5% of pupils have to be offered education in segregated provision.

Progress in the education of pupils with SENs in the next 25 years will be inextricably linked with developments in educating all children and young people. These developments will start from the recognition that schools cannot meet the diversity of their pupils' needs with the rigidity of preordained classes of standard size, each staffed by a teacher required to provide standard pedagogical approaches to an over-detailed curriculum. Seen from 25 years on, it will seem incredible that we did not use the scope for organisational and pedagogical flexibility which already exists to respond to the particular demands both of the various aspects of a broad and balanced curriculum and of pupils' learning needs. These varied demands call for flexibility in using the range of teacher expertise, non-teaching support, size of pupil grouping, and instructional media including micro-processors. They also call for the participation of pupils, parents and the community, and the involvement of supporting specialist education, health and social services personnel.

Educational approaches for pupils with SENs offer many indications about how these kinds of flexible response to pupil needs and curricular demands can be achieved. Panel 2 shows three areas.

CONCLUSIONS

The examples in the panel show that practices in the education of pupils with SENs already indicate how an educational context could be created which could respond to pupil diversity. A further crucial requirement is that the requisite spectrum of teacher expertise is available to match pupils' SENs. This in turn demands that opportunities are assured for teachers to acquire appropriate forms and levels of professional qualification, one of the aims of the Warnock Report which has not yet been achieved.

Progress in education for the next 25 years has to start with a recognition of children and young people as they are. From this a context can be created which meets the full range of pupils' SENs along the lines of the principles originally stated in the Warnock Report. It is clear that effectiveness cannot be achieved without a commitment to providing the necessary means, but the examples given show that concern for the efficient use of resources does not have to be neglected. Perhaps the most significant finding of all is that many of the necessary developments depend on creating a climate which encourages the collaborative sharing of responsibility. Will it be possible to pursue the vision of these developments through the present turbulence in education?

REFERENCES

Ainscow, M. (in press) *Towards effective schools for all*. National Association for SENs.

Audit Commission/HMI (1992) *Getting in on the Act/Getting the Act together*. HMSO.

Balshaw, M. (1991) *Help in the classroom*. Fulton

DES (1978) *Special educational needs, the 'Warnock report'*. HMSO.

DFE (1992) *Exclusions – a discussion paper*.

DFE (1992) *A common funding formula for grant-maintained schools*.

Evans *et al.* (1989) *Decision-making for SENs*. Institute of Education.

Evans et al. (in press) Clusters, the collaborative approach to meeting SENs, in Riddell, S. and Brown, S. (eds) *Children with SENs: Policies and practice into the 1990s*. Routledge.

Evans, J. and Lunt, I. (1992) *Developments in special education under LMS*. Institute of Education.

Fletcher-Campbell, F. with Hall, C. (1993) *LEA support for special needs*. NFER-Nelson.

Gipps, C. *et al.* (1987) *Warnock's eighteen percent*. Falmer Press.

Goacher, B. *et al.* (1988) *Policy and provision for SENs*. Cassell.

Jowett, S. *et al.* (1988) *Joining forces: a study of links between special and ordinary schools*. NFER-Nelson.

Hansen, J. (1992) The development of the Danish Folkeskole, towards a school for all, *European Journal of Special Needs Education*. 7.

Hawkridge, D. and Vincent T. (1992) *Learning difficulties and computers*. Jessica King.

Lunt, I. and Evans, J. (1991) *SENs under LMS*. Institute of Education.

Norwich, B. and Daniels, H. (1992) Support from the team. *Managing Schools Today* 1 (6) 30–31.

Slavin, R. E. (1989) Co-operative learning and student achievement, in: Slavin, R. E. (ed.) *School and classroom organisation*, Erlbaum.

Stainback W. and Stainback S. (1984) A rationale for the merger of special and regular education. *Exceptional Children* 51 (2).

Swann, W. (1987) *Integration statistics*. Centre for Studies on Integration in Education.

Swann, W. (1992) *Segregation statistics*. Centre for Studies on Integration in Education.

Wolfendale, S. (ed.) (1989) *Parental involvement*. Cassell.

Wrigley, V. and Clough, P. (1992) Personal communication.

Chapter 12

What *do* students think about school?

Wendy Keys and Cres Fernandes

The research described in this report was undertaken by the National Foundation for Educational Research on behalf of the Working Group on Schools, Society and Citizenship of the National Commission on Education.

The main aims of the study were to investigate the experiences and attitudes of 11- and 13-year-old students (Year 7 and 9) to their schools in order to:

- test the hypothesis that students' levels of motivation towards schooling are lower in Year 9 than in Year 7;
- identify the factors associated with motivation towards school and learning and hypothesise causes for hostility towards school;
- highlight those results which are most likely to assist the Commission's Working Party on Schools, Society and Citizenship in the formulation of its recommendations.

COMPARISONS BETWEEN THE LEVELS OF MOTIVATION TOWARDS SCHOOL AND LEARNING OF STUDENTS IN YEAR 7 AND YEAR 9

In general, the findings of this study support the hypothesis that students' levels of motivation towards schooling are lower in Year 9 than in Year 7. It is possible, of course, that some of the differences between the two age groups, especially where there appears to have been a shift from an extreme response by Year 7 students to a less extreme response by those in Year 9 (for example from 'strongly agree' to 'agree'), could have arisen from the fact that the older students have become more discerning and worldly wise and less willing to express extreme levels of enthusiasm. This caveat should be borne in mind when considering the following results. The most striking differences between the two age groups are given below.

Compared with Year 7 students, those in Year 9 were:

- less likely to say that their school work was interesting and more likely to say that their lessons were boring;
- less likely to say that they liked all or most of their teachers;
- less likely to agree that their teachers tried hard to make them work as well as they were able;
- less likely to agree that their teachers were making efforts to maintain discipline;
- less likely to agree that their teachers could keep order in class and that their school had sensible rules;
- more likely to have played truant (23 per cent compared with only 9 per cent of those in Year 7).

There was very little or no difference between the Year 7 and Year 9 samples of students in:

- their perceptions of their own ability, which were quite positive;
- their strong belief that schools should help them to do well in exams, teach them things which would be useful when they got jobs and to be independent;
- their perceptions of their parents' aspirations for their future.

THE FACTORS ASSOCIATED WITH MOTIVATION TOWARDS SCHOOL AND LEARNING

The correlation and regression analyses reported showed that the following factors were associated with positive attitudes towards school amongst Year 9 and Year 7 students:

- interest in school work (and lack of boredom);
- liking for teachers;
- a belief in the value of school and school work;
- positive perceptions of the school's ethos;
- positive views of their own ability and perseverance;
- good behaviour in school;
- a high level of perceived parental support.

These findings suggest that students who dislike school are more likely than those expressing more positive attitudes to:

- find school boring;
- dislike their teachers;
- place low values on school and schoolwork;
- have negative perceptions of the ethos of their school;
- have negative views of their own ability and perseverance;
- behave badly in school;
- perceive lower levels of support from their parents.

The following factors were found to be unassociated, or only weakly associated, with motivation towards school and learning:

- type of catchment area; type of school, the percentage of students receiving free school meals; reading age of intake, GCSE results; and retention rates;
- the cultural level of the home (although this finding should be regarded with caution since only one surrogate measure was included in the analysis).

Most of the conclusions of this study have been based on students' perceptions of their schools and their teachers, which may not, of course, always accurately reflect life in school. However, it should be borne in mind that students' perceptions of school and teachers are of paramount importance and are likely to be a major influence on their behaviour in school and attitudes towards education.

OTHER IMPORTANT FINDINGS OF THE RESEARCH

There were a number of findings of the research which, although not directly related to the hypotheses set out at the beginning of this chapter, may well have implications for the work of the Commission.

It is important to bear in mind that:

- in spite of the age-related differences identified above the majority of students in both age groups expressed favourable attitudes on most of the aspects of school covered in the questionnaire.

However, some of the other findings of the research give cause for concern.

- A fairly substantial minority of students said they found their school work boring (about 9 per cent indicated they were bored in all or most lessons and a further 40–55 per cent said that they were bored in some lessons).
- Many teachers did not praise their students for good work (only about half of the students said that all or most of their teachers praised them when they did good work).
- A substantial minority (nearly a quarter) of students perceived their teachers to be 'fairly easily satisfied' with their students' work.
- Many students (about 40 per cent) said they had not discussed their work individually with their teachers during this school year.
- Students in both age groups expressed the greatest preference for lessons where they could work with their friends and the least preference for lessons where they worked alone.
- The majority of students perceived a high level of parental interest and

support and both age groups reported talking about their career plans more frequently with their parents than with their teachers.

– The reported incidence of bullying appeared quite high, particularly amongst the Year 7 students. More than half of the Year 7 students and about a third of those in Year 9 reported being bullied in school during the current school year, although usually only 'once or twice'. However, 15 per cent of Year 7 students and 8 per cent of those in Year 9 reported being bullied 'often or quite often'. Nevertheless, it must be stressed that students were not provided with, or asked for, a definition of bullying and that it seems inevitable that the definitions they used would have varied. For this reason, our findings with regard to bullying should be regarded with caution. It seems clear that further research into the incidence of bullying is needed.

– More than half the students in both age groups said that they spent three hours or more each day watching television or videos.

THE MAIN IMPLICATIONS OF THE RESEARCH

This research has shown that students' attitudes towards school and learning tend to deteriorate to some extent as they progress from Year 7 to Year 9 in their secondary schools. Our findings also suggest that, although the majority of students expressed positive views about school and education, a minority appears to be disaffected.

Our regression analyses, however, identified a number of factors which were associated with positive attitudes towards school. Many of these have implications for teachers, school managers and the education system. The main implications of our study are, therefore, discussed under the following headings:

– Teaching and learning practices
– School management
– The education system as a whole
– Further research.

Teaching and learning practices

The study identified quite strong associations between students' attitudes and a range of aspects of teaching behaviour. High expectations on the part of the teacher, regular feedback, praise for good work and effective class-room discipline were shown to be associated with students' positive attitudes towards school and education. This finding is not new. Most educationalists are aware of the importance of these factors. However, the results of our research suggest that many teachers were not lavish with praise, that a minority of teachers were 'fairly easily satisfied' and that many pupils did not talk individually with their teachers about their work. It seems clear that there is a need for action which will encourage and enable teachers to make more use of strategies, such as high expectations, regular feedback, and praise for good work, which this and other research has shown to be associated with students' positive attitudes towards school.

The research showed that substantial minorities of students found school work boring. It also found that students liked lessons where they could work with their friends and lessons where they could make things, and much preferred lessons where they had discussions to lessons where they worked alone. Strategies which involve students in their own learning and build upon their preferences for co-operative and practical work and discussions could well help to remotivate bored and disaffected students.

School management

Other factors found to be associated with positive attitudes on the part of students were related to the way their schools were managed: effective discipline; well-maintained premises; a good reputation; and well-behaved students. This result is also consistent with previous research. However, the results of our study on the extent of truancy and bullying, for example, suggest that a minority, at least, of schools may need to take action on these issues.

The results of this research also suggest that students believe strongly that schools should help them to pass examinations, teach them things that will help them when they get jobs and help them to become independent. Those involved in developing new curricula could well bear this finding in mind.

Beyond the school

The study found that parental interest and support were associated with positive attitudes towards education. Interestingly, most of the students taking part in this study believed that their parents were interested in their progress, supportive and held high aspirations. Yet there is a great deal of anecdotal evidence on the low level of parental involvement in secondary education. It may be that this results from parents' lack of confidence (Wedge and Prosser, 1973) and understanding of the educational process, rather than from a lack of interest. It seems clear that secondary schools in all types of catchment areas could, with advantage, consider the development or expansion of strategies designed to capitalise on the parental interest perceived by the students taking part in this study. Further investigation of some of the schemes developed in disadvantaged areas may provide useful ideas of ways in which parents could be involved more fully in their children's schooling. However, it should not be forgotten that such schemes, which could well involve home visiting and other out-of-school hours activities, are likely to require additional resources (not least in terms of staff time).

Further research

The results of this study have raised a number of questions, many of which can only be answered by further research. It is particularly important to investigate the following issues more fully.

– As indicated above, we found that students' perceptions of parental interest and support were associated with positive attitudes towards school, and previous research has identified links between parental involvement and their children's achievement. Furthermore, one of the stated purposes of the Parents' Charter is to help parents become more effective partners in their children's education. As far as we are aware, no baseline data exist on the current level of interest and involvement in their children's education amongst the totality of parents in England and Wales. Although the reforms initiated by the Education (No. 2) Act 1986 and the Education Reform Act 1988, giving parents greater power in the management of schools, have resulted in the greater involvement of some parents, there is anecdotal evidence from secondary school teachers that large numbers of parents show little interest or involvement in their children's education. The findings of our research, however, suggest that most Year 7 and Year 9 students believed that their parents were interested in their schooling. This suggests that there may be a pool of parental interest waiting to be tapped. The purpose of further research in this area would be to map the extent and type of parental involvement in their children's secondary schooling; identify parents' reasons for becoming or not becoming involved; identify those aspects of schooling which parents consider to be most important for their children's future; describe examples of good practice and make recommendations on ways in which secondary schools could involve parents more fully and effectively.
– Our study has provided a broad brush picture of the associations between certain teaching approaches (such as holding and expressing high expectations, regular feedback and ample praise) and students' positive attitudes towards school and learning. An in-depth research study designed to identify and describe examples of good classroom practice and incorporate these into staff development materials would be of great value to the education profession.
– A substantial minority of the students taking part in the study indicated that they believed they had been the subject of bullying. This study did not provide or ask for any definitions of bullying, and it could well be that many students included less serious behaviour under the general

category of bullying. However, we cannot be sure that this is the case. Clearly, there is a need for further research to find out the true extent and type of bullying in secondary schools, to identify the main causes and ways in which bullying could best be prevented.

- Similarly, substantial minorities of students (especially in Year 9) indicated that they had played truant, albeit usually for a day or a lesson at a time. Further research, designed to go beyond the information to be published in league tables, which would map the extent and type of truancy in secondary schools, identify the main causes of truancy and provide examples of good practice in its prevention would clearly be of value to school managers, classroom teachers and educational administrators.

- The main purpose of this study was to provide information on students' motivation towards education and learning which would aid the National Commission on Education in the development of their recommendations. In order to meet the Commission's time scale, it was necessary to carry out a cross-sectional study comparing the responses of Year 7 and Year 9 students. A longitudinal study, following up the same cohort of students annually from Year 7 to the end of compulsory schooling (or even beyond), complemented by a more in-depth interview programme, would throw far more light on to the way students' motivation towards school and education develops throughout the secondary years by identifying the key stages and/or events which affected students' attitudes. Such a study would clearly be of great value to all concerned with the education of young people.

REFERENCE

Wedge, P. and Prosser, H. (1973) *Born to Fail?*, London, Arrow Books.

Part III

Teachers

In Part III the focus moves to teachers. The first chapter is a short article by the head of a Midlands School. He asks the question *'What Makes a Good Teacher?'* and in the context of the move towards appraising teachers comes up with a personal view of the good and the bad in teaching.

The three contributions by Berliner, by Wragg and Wood, and by Shulman, describe some of the most recent ideas about teaching expertise. Berliner's research provides some reassurance to new teachers who watch with some envy the apparently effortless skills of their more experienced colleagues. He points out, using a range of examples, that *individuals at different levels of experience in classroom teaching differ in their interpretative abilities, their use of routines, and the emotional investment that they make in their work*. Hence the sort of experience of first encounters with classes described by Wood and Wragg. And Shulman, with a discussion that can be usefully related to Simon's question 'Why no Pedagogy in England?', asks how a student's content knowledge or subject expertise can be developed into what he terms *pedagogical content knowledge*, a crucial part of the professional development of teachers.

The professional role of teachers has generated a wealth of opinion and comment. Shulman has no hesitation in according the teacher the title of 'professional'. *The professional* holds knowledge, not only of how – the capacity for skilled performance – *but also of what and why* – and this, he suggests, is an awareness that distinguishes the draftsman from architect or book-keeper from auditor. This is a theme that James Calderhead takes up, in defining what the key characteristics of the teacher's professional role are. He reflects the ideas put forward by Shulman and also Berliner in pointing to the way *teachers through repeated practice develop various specialist skills which replicate the 'knowledge-in-action' of the professional*.

The extracts from a much-quoted account of research in London primary schools are relevant to teachers in both primary and secondary schools. This chapter looks at the issue of teachers' expectations according to pupil age, social class, sex, ability and behaviour and, as well as providing a useful survey of research, points to the significant impact, both positive and negative, that expectations can have on pupils' achievements.

Finally, Jon Nixon in an extract from a book on multi-cultural education illustrates the knowledge-in-action dimension by looking at the teachers' counselling role. In this extract he explores cross-cultural counselling; an issue which he believes has received scant attention within educational circles.

Chapter 13

What makes a good teacher?

Roger Smith

What happens in schools is now more open to public scrutiny than ever before. Open doors, parental help and constant media debate has meant that all kinds of people can begin to interpret and understand something of what is happening.

This openness will become more formal as the search for effective schools and effective teaching becomes intense. Governors, including parent governors, will have much more say in the running of schools and teachers would be wise to regard this as an invasion of allies rather than try to hide behind classroom doors.

As the national curriculum is implemented, testing at seven, eleven and fourteen begins, and test results are published, more and more people will turn their interest to what goes on inside classrooms. What was once a debate amongst professionals will have a much wider audience.

Teacher appraisal

The appraisal of teachers will eventually become a 'normal' part of life in schools and, despite conflict over the best way to do this, it is generally agreed that the observation of teachers 'teaching' will play a key role.

This assumes, of course, that those appraising and those publicly opening up the effective schools debate know, and can recognise, what is 'good' practice. Many of those commenting on this issue appear to think that this is easy and that there is an accepted list of criteria which everyone agrees with. In reality, classroom observation is difficult, and views on what is 'good' and 'bad' teaching can vary widely.

What happens in classrooms is complex and, whilst the national curriculum will provide us with ideas about the content of what is taught, it will not help to 'nationalise' the styles and processes necessary to deliver the curriculum. But why should it? After all, teaching is a creative act rather than a set of prescribed events. Even so, it does help to have some way of defining what is or is not effective teaching.

DEVELOPING CRITERIA

It is important that schools should begin to formalise what they mean when they debate and explain what is 'good' about their educational practice. Schedules and criteria need to be worked out during whole-school INSET that will develop and refine what happens to children in classrooms. School staffs will then be able to justify in a cohesive way what they are doing.

The ideas I have developed through my own experience and research can best be shared in the form of lists. These may find general agreement but, if not, it will mean that the concept of what is good and what should happen in classrooms is very difficult to pin down.

EFFECTIVE TEACHING

The first list tries to define what should happen in an effective classroom – the learning processes that every teacher has to manage. It will be interesting to see how much agreement you can reach with your colleagues.

In an effective classroom

- the children should be involved in the work they are doing and 'own' part of it because they have helped to plan it;
- what the child brings to the task has been noted and taken into account thus helping to match the task to the child;
- there is an emphasis on framing and solving problems;
- each child is helped to make sense of the world they live in;
- there is lots of working co-operatively in groups, organised to take into account continuity and progression;
- concrete experiences are used as starting points;
- when the content of the work is organised, targets and outcomes are built into the programme. There will be flexibility so that children can go off at tangents within the first hand practical experiences;
- the teacher's role is as a facilitator so that the child does not rely on adult supervision all the time;
- each child is encouraged to collect data and given time to analyse it and translate it into appropriate end products;
- there is evidence of a blend of integrated activities where areas of experience merge;
- record-keeping is thorough and realistic;
- all areas of the curriculum are dealt with during each term.

The 12 points outline areas of 'good' classroom management. What they don't do is tell us what kinds of style and approach an effective teacher uses. I would argue that there are certain processes that children go through which have positive and negative results. The positive first:

A good teacher

- always recognises and minimises worry and tension;
- makes children feel good about themselves, recognising that they are individuals and need individual attention;
- believes strongly in a work ethos and on-task behaviour, but does this without negative pressure;
- views children and parents in a positive way and understands that there should be a working partnership;
- avoids shouting and bullying but is a quiet, firm disciplinarian who sees positive control as a means to exciting learning;
- emphasises praise rather than criticism;
- recognises and uses children's enthusiasm, talent and individuality;
- sees outcomes as varying and interesting;
- sees a wide-ranging curriculum as the best way to incorporate basic skills;
- sees creativity and curiosity as the key to learning experiences;
- sees change as positive and necessary in any inspired institution;
- varies teaching styles to suit the content and the children.

A class managed by such a teacher should be full of lively, interested and positive children who achieve high standards. There will be low stress and little tension. There will be a lot of group co-operation and tolerance. The children should live up to the teacher's high expectations and behave accordingly. They will be trusted and have lots of self-discipline and self-confidence. The work they do and the attitudes they develop should be seen as effective in the sense that they are educationally valid.

INEFFECTIVE TEACHING

There are, however, teachers who are the opposite of those described above.

A bad teacher

- quite often frightens children and acts as a kind of adult bully;
- creates tension based on the pressure of unrealistic goals and deadlines;
- sees children and parents as threats and views parental help in a negative light;
- emphasises punishment rather than praise, stress rather than calm, and hardly ever smiles or laughs;
- has a style of control that builds up petty incidents out of proportion and has a similar level of punishment for all incidents, big and small;
- often stifles enthusiasm and sees lively and curious children as a threat;
- frowns on a wide curriculum and sees education in terms of a narrow range of basic skills;

- sees outcomes as standard and stereotyped and develops a restrictive timetable that dominates every routine;
- defines self-expression, the 'arts' and most forms of spontaneous creativity as not being 'work';
- has a suspicious attitude towards change rather than an informed opinion;
- demands passive learning and has a single dominating teaching style;
- often insults children and yet expects good manners and tolerance.

If most of these attributes are present, children will often produce less and of a lower standard because they are working at the pace of the slowest and what they do is teacher-controlled. The stress of such a regime might be such that many children become cowed and submissive. There would be little peer group co-operation and tolerance. A teaching style dominated by criticism rather than praise would lead to fear rather than good behaviour. Such children might well be 'high' when out of the classroom and have little self-control. Typically they would be frightened of making mistakes and lack self-esteem.

CONCLUSION

If at least some of my points about effective management are accepted or even recognised, it must follow that classrooms are complex social organisms. There are many more ways of defining what happens in schools and we should beware of casually accepting the idea that teachers' roles and the teaching process are simple and easy to come to terms with.

Heads and teachers in every school need to get together and, within any local and national guidelines, define clearly what they mean by 'good' and 'effective' teaching. The criteria they list should be ones which can be observed, and used to demonstrate to those who express an interest that every child receives a full and rich curriculum.

Chapter 14

Teacher expertise

David Berliner

Experts in areas as divergent as chess, bridge, radiology, nursing, air-traffic control, physics, racehorse handicapping, and pedagogy show certain kinds of similarities. Despite their apparent diversity, experts in these fields seem to posses similar sets of skills and attitudes and to use common modes of perceiving and processing information (Chi, Glaser, and Farr, 1986; Berliner, 1986). These abilities are not found among novices. Experience allows experts to apply their extensive knowledge to the solution of problems in the domain in which they work. To the novice, the expert appears to have uncanny abilities to notice things, an 'instinct' for making the right moves, an ineffable ability to get things done and to perform in an almost effortless manner.

Although we have gained some insight into the differences between experts and novices in various fields, we have only the scantiest knowledge about the ways that one progresses from novice to expert within a field. In part, this is because scientific knowledge about expertise is relatively new. But such research also requires longitudinal studies, and these studies are among the most difficult for which to get support.

Despite the shortage of scientific research in this area, some thoughtful speculation about the ways in which one becomes expert in a particular field is needed, because the planning of instruction for novices and the evaluation of others in a field are inherently related to theories of the development of expertise within the field. If we focus on the field of teaching, then answers to questions about what to teach novices, when to teach it, and how to teach it depend in part on implicit theories about the role of experience in the ability to learn the pedagogical skills, attitudes, and ways of thinking that teacher educators believe to be desirable. The evaluation of teachers also depends on such implicit theories of development. What one chooses to observe or test for, when one expects to see it, how it should be measured, and the criteria by which successful performance is judged all depend on some notions, perhaps fragmentary, about the development of ability in pedagogy. To make these often implicit and incomplete theories more explicit and complete, I report here on a general theory about the development of expertise.

A THEORY OF SKILL LEARNING

There are five stages to consider in the journey one takes from novice to expert teacher. We begin with the greenhorn, the raw recruit, the *novice*. Student teachers and many first-year teachers may be considered novices. As experience is gained, the novice becomes an *advanced beginner*. Many second- and third-year teachers are likely to be in this developmental stage. With further experience and some motivation to succeed, the advanced beginner becomes a *competent* performer. It is likely that many third- and fourth-year teachers, as well as some more-experienced teachers, are at this level. At about the fifth year, a modest number of teachers may move into the *proficient* stage. Finally, a small number of these will move on to the last stage of development – that of *expert* teacher. Each of these stages of development is characterised by some distinctive features.

Stage 1: Novice

This is the stage at which the commonplace must be discerned, the elements of the tasks to be performed must be labelled and learned, and a set of context-free rules must be acquired. In learning to teach, the novice is taught the meaning of terms such as 'higher-order questions,' 'reinforcement,' and 'learning disabled.' Novices are taught context-free rules such as 'Give praise for right answers,' 'Wait at least three seconds after asking a higher-order question,' 'Never criticise a student,' and that old standby, 'Never smile until Christmas.' The novice must be able to identify the context-free elements and rules in order to begin to teach. The behaviour of the novice, whether that person is an automobile driver, chess player, or teacher, is very rational, relatively inflexible, and tends to conform to whatever rules and procedures the person was told to follow. Only minimal skill should really be expected. This is a stage for learning the objective facts and features of situations and for gaining experience. And it is the stage at which real-world experience appears to be far more important than verbal information, as generations of drivers, chess players, and student teachers have demonstrated.

Stage 2: Advanced beginner

This is when experience can meld with verbal knowledge. Similarities across contexts are recognised, and episodic knowledge is built up. Strategic knowledge – when to ignore or break rules and when to follow them – is developed. Context begins to guide behaviour. For example, advanced beginners may learn that praise doesn't always have the desired effect, such as when a low-ability child interprets it as communicating low expectations. The teacher may also learn that criticism after a bad performance can be quite motivating to a usually good student. Experience is affecting behaviour, but the advanced beginner may still have no sense of what is important. Benner (1984, pp. 23–24) makes this point in describing the difference between novice and advanced beginner nurses on the one hand and competent nurses on the other:

> I give instructions to the new graduate, very detailed and explicit instructions: When you come in and first see the baby, you take the baby's vital signs and make the physical examination, and you check the I.V. sites and the ventilator and make sure that it works, and you check the monitors and alarms. When I would say this to them, they would do exactly what I told them to do, no matter what else was going on. . . . They couldn't choose one to leave out. They couldn't choose which was the most important. . . . They couldn't do for one baby the things that were most important and then go on to the other baby and do the things that were most important, and leave the things that weren't as important until later on. . . . If I said, you have to do these eight things . . . they did those things, and they didn't care if their other kid was screaming its head off. When they did realize, they would be like a mule between two piles of hay.

The novice and the advanced beginner, though intensely involved in the learning process, may also lack a certain responsibility for their actions. This occurs because they are labelling and describing events, following rules, and recognising and classifying contexts, but not actively determining through personal action what is happening. The acceptance of personal responsibility for classroom instruction occurs when personal decision making, wilfully choosing what to do, takes place. This occurs in the next stage of development.

Stage 3: Competent

There are two distinguishing characteristics of competent performers. First, they make conscious choices about what they are going to do. They set priorities and decide on plans. They have rational goals and choose sensible means for reaching the ends they have in mind. In addition, they can determine what is and what is not important – from their experience they know what to attend to and what to ignore. At this stage, teachers learn not to make timing and targeting errors. They also learn to make curriculum and instruction decisions, such as when to stay with a topic and when to move on, on the basis of a particular teaching context and a particular group of students.

Because they are more personally in control of the events around them, following their own plans, and responding only to the information that they choose to, teachers at this stage tend to feel more responsibility for what happens. They are not detached. Thus they often feel emotional about success and failure in a way that is different and more intense than that of novices or advanced beginners. And they have more vivid memories of their successes and failures as well. But the competent performer is not yet very fast, fluid, or flexible in his or her behaviour. These are characteristics of the last two stages in the development of expertise.

Stage 4: Proficient

This is the stage at which intuition and know-how become prominent. Nothing mysterious is meant by these terms. Consider the microadjustments made in learning to ride a bicycle – at some point, individuals no longer think about these things. They develop an 'intuitive' sense of the situation. Furthermore, out of the wealth of experience that the proficient individual has accumulated comes a holistic recognition of similarities. At this stage, a teacher may notice without conscious effort that today's mathematics lesson is bogging down for the same reason that last week's spelling lesson bombed. At some higher level of categorisation, the similarities between disparate events are understood. This holistic recognition of similarities allows the proficient individual to predict events more precisely, since he or she sees more things as alike and therefore as having been experienced before. Chess masters, bridge masters, expert air-traffic controllers, and expert radiologists rely on this ability. The proficient performer, however, while intuitive in pattern recognition and in ways of knowing, is still analytic and deliberative in deciding what to do. The proficient stage is the stage of most tournament chess and bridge players. But the grand masters are those few who move to a higher stage, to the expert level.

Stage 5: Expert

If the novice, advanced beginner, and competent performer are rational and the proficient performer is intuitive, we might categorise the experts as often arational. They have both an intuitive grasp of the situation and a nonanalytic and nondeliberative sense of the appropriate response to be made. They show fluid performance, as we all do when we no longer have to choose our words when speaking or think about where to place our feet when walking. We simply talk and walk in an apparently effortless manner. The expert striker in football, the expert martial artist in combat, the expert chess master, and the expert teacher in classroom recitations all seem to know where to be or what to do at the right time. They engage in their performance in a qualitatively different way than does the novice or the competent performer, like the race-car driver who talks of becoming one with her machine or the science teacher who reports that the lesson just moved along so beautifully today that he never really had to teach. The experts are not consciously choosing what to attend to and what to do. They are acting effortlessly, fluidly, and in a sense this is arational, because it is not easily described as deductive or analytic behaviour. Though beyond the usual meaning of rational, since neither calculation nor deliberative thought is involved, the behaviour of the expert is certainly not irrational. The writings of Schon (1983) about knowledge in action characterise the behaviour of the expert practitioner.

Experts do things that usually work, and thus, when things are proceeding without a hitch, experts are not solving problems or making decisions in the usual sense of those terms. They 'go with the flow,' as it is sometimes described. When anomalies occur, things do not work out as planned, or something atypical happens, they bring deliberate analytic processes to bear on the situation. But when things are going smoothly, experts rarely appear to be reflective about their performance.

FINDINGS AND IMPLICATIONS

1 *There are differences in the ways that teachers at various levels of experi-ence and expertise interpret classroom phenomena.* Because of a lack of experience, those near the novice end of the developmental continuum can be expected to have trouble interpreting events. Until episodic knowledge is built up and similarities can be recognised across contexts, confusion may characterise the interpretations of classroom phenomena made by novices and advanced beginners. Experts are more likely than those with less ability to discern what is important from what is not when interpreting classroom phenomena. And we should also expect that experts will show more effortless performance and rely more on experi-ence for interpreting information. We obtained data supportive of these ideas in some of our studies.

2 *There are differences in the use of classroom routines by teachers at various levels of expertise and experience.* The effortless and fluid performance that often characterises the experts' performance may be due, in part, to their use of routines. Adherence to routines by teachers and students makes classrooms appear to function smoothly. In studying elementary-school mathematics lessons, Leinhardt and Greeno (1986) compared an expert's opening homework review with that of a novice. The expert teacher was found to be quite brief, taking about one-third less time than the novice did. This expert was able to pick up information about attendance, about who did or did not do the homework, and was also able to identify who was going to need help later in the lesson. She elicited

correct answers most of the time throughout the activity and also managed to get all the homework corrected. Moreover, she did so at a brisk pace and never lost control of the lesson. She also had developed routines to record attendance and to handle choral responding during the homework checks and hand-raising to get attention. This expert also used clear signals to start and finish the lesson segments. In contrast, when the novice was enacting an opening homework review as part of a mathematics lesson, she was not able to get a fix on who did and did not do the homework, she had problems taking attendance, and she asked ambiguous questions that led her to misunderstand the difficulty of the homework. At one time the novice lost control of the pace. She never did learn which students were going to have more difficulty later in the lesson. It is important to note that the novice showed lack of familiarity with well-practised routines. She seemed not to act in habitual ways.

3 *There are differences in the emotionality displayed by teachers at various levels of expertise and experience.* When the developmental stage of competence is reached, it is said to be accompanied by a qualitatively different kind of emotionality and sense of responsibility for the work of the performer. We have some evidence for that, obtained in a curious way, in the study in which experts, advanced beginners, and novices planned and then taught a lesson [in a University-based laboratory context] (Berliner, 1988). The novices in that study were quite happy about their performance, although we did not rate it highly. Advanced beginners were generally affectless in describing their experience. They had a task to do and they did it. The experts, however, were quite angry about their participation in the task and disappointed about their performance.

In retrospect, and on the basis of our interviews, it appears that we had inadvertently taken away some of the experts' edge. First, we had created an artificial teaching situation. Second, according to their standards, they did not have enough time to prepare the lesson. Third, the students were not trained in the routines that make the experts' classrooms hum. One expert expressed his anger by walking out of the study. Another stopped in the middle of the lesson and had to be coaxed to continue. One started crying during the playback of her videotape. All were upset. Two weeks after the study, one expert, when asked what she remembered of her experience, said:

> I just remember it as the worst experience in my entire life, and I was depressed. . . . The things that stick out in my mind are the negative things. I remember just being frustrated the whole time I taught the lesson. . . . I don't like what happened. I've been real depressed and down [since then].

Other comments by experts were about their feelings of uncomfortableness, stress, terror, and so forth. In this situation, advanced beginners and novices were virtually untouched at any deep emotional level, but our experts were affected deeply. In addition, they felt that in some way they had let us down – their sense of responsibility played a part in their feelings. Expert teachers, apparently like other experts, show more emotionality about the successes and failures of their work.

Summary

A growing body of literature is documenting the ways in which individuals at different levels of experience in classroom teaching and other fields differ in their interpretive abilities, their use of routines, and the emotional investment that they make in their work. From this one can extract a general principle, namely, that very important qualitative differences exist in the thinking and the performance of novices, experts, and all those who fall between these two points on the continuum. The developmental sequence involved in the acquisition of expertise, however, is not yet as clearly described. The five-stage theory of the development of expertise presented above is intended to help us think more about that issue and is well supported by data that were collected for other purposes.

REFERENCES

Benner, P. (1984), *From Novice to Expert*, Reading, MA, Addison-Wesley.

Berliner, D. C. (1986) 'In pursuit of the expert pedagogue', *Educational Researcher*, 15, pp. 5–13.

Berliner, D. C. (1988) 'Memory for teaching as a function of expertise', paper presented at meetings of the American Educational Research Association, New Orleans, April.

Chi, M. T. H., Glaser, R. and Farr, M. (eds) (1986) *The Nature of Expertise*, Hillsdale, NJ, Erlbaum.

Leinhardt, G. and Greeno, J. (1986) 'The cognitive skill of teaching', *Journal of Educational Psychology*, 78, pp. 75–95.

Schon, D. (1983) *The Reflective Practitioner*, New York, Basic Books.

Chapter 15

Teachers' first encounters with their classes

E. C. Wragg and E. K. Wood

Student teachers usually begin their school experience or teaching practice part way through the school year. By the time they arrive routines have been established which, for better or worse, will persist through the school year.

A chemistry graduate once arrived at his teaching practice school in January. Before commencing his own teaching he watched a third-year class's regular chemistry teacher take a double period of practical work. After a brief exposition delivered whilst seated on the front bench, one or two shared jokes and asides, the experienced chemistry teacher signalled the start of the practical phase with, 'Right 3C, you know what to do, so get the gear out and make a start.' The class dispersed briskly to hidden cupboards and far recesses for various pieces of equipment, and an hour of earnest and purposeful experimental work ensued.

The following week the chemistry graduate took the class himself, and began by lolling on the front bench in imitation of the apparently effortless and casual manner he had witnessed only seven days earlier. After a few minutes of introduction he delivered an almost identical instruction to the one given by the experienced man the week before, 'Right 3C, get the gear out and do the experiment.' Within seconds pupils were elbowing their fellows out of the way, wrestling each other for bunsen burners, slamming cupboard doors. He spent most of the practical phase calling for less noise and reprimanding the many pupils who misbehaved.

This true story illustrates the problems facing student teachers. What they have not seen is experienced teachers' first encounters with their classes in early September at the beginning of the school year, when rules and relationships are established. There are few studies available of teachers during their first phase of the year. Indeed a common response to a request to be allowed to watch lessons in early September is for the teacher to say, 'Would you mind coming in a fortnight when things have settled down?'

FIRST ENCOUNTERS WITH A CLASS

A number of social psychologists have looked at first encounters between human beings in a variety of social settings. Goffman (1971) has described the process of impression management which commences at first meetings and continues through subsequent encounters:

> The individual's initial projection commits him to what he is proposing to be and requires him to drop all pretences of being other things. As the interaction among the participants progresses, additions and modifications in this informational state will of course occur, but it is essential that these later developments be related without contradiction to, and even built up from the initial positions taken by the several participants.
>
> (pp. 21–2)

Argyle (1967) has described the rapidity with which people reach conclusions about those they meet, the difference in sensitivity of acute observers, like Sherlock Holmes, and mental patients whose perceptions appear distorted, and the growth of relationships in the early period of acquaintance.

> A will categorize B in terms of social class, race, age, intelligence or whatever dimensions of people are most important to him, and this will activate the appropriate set of social techniques on the part of A. It is found that people vary widely in what they look for first in others.
>
> (p. 46)

It is not merely the individual personalities which are important when people meet. The social setting is also a powerful influence on events: whether one person meets another as a colleague, employer, supplicant, whether someone holds a certain rank or status, wears a uniform, whether the encounter is in private or in public, between two people or several, takes place informally on the street, in a home, or formally at a gathering, in an institution or work-place.

When teachers meet a new class of pupils, a variety of social, environmental and institutional factors are at work in addition to the effects of the several individual personalities involved. Teachers, whatever their individual style, are known to be legally *in loco parentis*. They are inescapably part of a national, local and professional culture, even if they personally reject a number of aspects of it.

When teachers have been in a school for some time their reputation will precede them, and pupil folklore will have told their new classes a great deal about what to expect. Experienced teachers who have moved to another school frequently express surprise during their first few weeks about the difficulty of establishing their identity in a new location after their previous school in which so much could be taken for granted. Supply teachers in particular have to become adept at managing first encounters in new and varying locations because they have so many of them.

It is not too surprising, therefore, that there has been relatively little research into these intimate first moments of contact between teacher and pupils. The success or failure of a whole year may rest on the impressions created, the ethos, rules and relationships established during the first two or three weeks in September, and that is one reason why many teachers see it as a private matter rather than something to be observed and analysed.

Information prior to meeting a class

There was a marked difference between experienced teachers and trainees about the information they would need prior to meeting a class. The experienced teachers almost all stressed that, other than essential medical information over deafness, epilepsy or the like, they preferred to find out for themselves rather than take on the prejudices of others. Several said they might look up pupils' records later in the year. This experienced art teacher's was typical of most replies:

> I don't deliberately read anything that might be about their characters and background which might prejudice my judgement. Later on reading about them [the pupils] might throw light on some of my experiences with them.

Some teachers described how they had learned this the hard way and reflected back on their first year, like this experienced English teacher:

> I like to meet them without any preconceived ideas. I like to teach them first and then look up information about them after. Otherwise I think that they tend to live up to their reputations. I wasn't like that to begin with. Once I wanted to know all about them before I met them.

An experienced maths teacher described how she had been given information in her first year that turned out to be incorrect. She was told that one of her classes was an especially bright group:

> I assumed that this was a correct statement of their abilities and I taught at top speed. They weren't that good and I had to lower my sights with them. You've got to do the assessing yourself.

There were only one or two exceptions to this general tone. An experienced French teacher said he wanted to know who were the 'bad eggs' so that he could think about where to seat them, and one drama teacher was quite precise about his need to be able to observe a future class beforehand if possible to assess the likely atmosphere:

> I'd like to see whether there are any noticeable problems, like isolation or

over-exhibitionism . . . I'd like to see how far they can concentrate and how far they are inhibited with movement. This finding-out process is very important, especially if they have previously been taught by untrained drama teachers.

Student teachers, in sharp contrast, are extremely anxious about their relative lack of knowledge about children generally, and the classes they will take in particular. Almost all expressed their needs quite differently from the experienced teachers, and most were predictably anxious about potential discipline problems. There were only 4 out of 40 students who, like the experienced teachers, wanted to know little in advance. The great majority echoed this PGCE geography student:

> I'd like to know if they are a disruptive class. If they do mess about a lot, I expect that the experienced teachers will know why and I'll be able to avoid it when it does occur.

The PGCE students also showed special concern over individual needs, typified by this science graduate: 'I'd ask the last teacher to talk to me about every individual pupil for a few minutes. I'd be more interested in the individual than his capability in the subject.'

The BEd. students, presumably because of their experience of their previous block practice, made much more reference to needing information about materials, resources and facilities. They also wished to know about school organisation, standards of work, punishment, discipline and the predominant system of routines and established signals used by the staff.

Thoughts on first lessons

When asked to reflect on the day before, an hour before, during the walk down the corridor and upon first entry to a new class, there were again predictable differences between experienced and novice teachers. The experienced teachers were able to describe events with considerable precision and certainty. For them these first lessons were part of a taken-for-granted set of routines during which they established varying degrees of dominance by restricting pupils' movement, taking up a central position, clearly being 'in charge', and making use of their eyes, a feature mentioned by several:

> I'd make a point of not turning my back on them or taking my eyes off them. I would say that eyes are the greatest controlling factor.
>
> (French teacher, male)

> The amount of looking you do is important.
>
> (Science teacher, male)

I keep alert. It's very tiring, but I keep an eye on them all the time. I can keep this attention by staring a bit rudely for the first two or three weeks.

(French teacher, female)

There was a larger-than-life quality as teachers spoke of how they exaggerated themselves, established rules by being more pernickety than normal, defined territory:

I walk up and down the gangways. I don't hide behind the furniture. If they ask to leave the room I try to discourage them by umm-ing and ah-ing. I take their names and the time they left the classroom. I don't allow queuing. I don't allow standing by the teacher's desk. They only come out when I tell them to. You [the teacher] give the directions. They don't touch windows or blinds.

(French teacher, male)

It was very much a personal matter, what an English teacher called 'my rules, for my room, for my area'. Almost all the teachers stressed that they would stand by the door and see the class into the room at the beginning of the first lesson and supervise their exit at the end.

By contrast the students were much more jelly-like in their apprehension and uncertainty. Far from using their eyes to establish presence, they were self-conscious about themselves being looked at. They spoke of thudding hearts and excitement, especially the PGCE students:

I think I'd just be a mass of nerves. I don't really know how I'll react in a class situation, but . . . deep breath, plunge straight in.

(History PGCE, female)

I'd briefly look over my notes, limber up my mind, feeling of 'help!' brush hair back, compose features, steady the nerves.

(German PGCE, male)

I'll be a bit apprehensive, what they'll be like. Will they be noisy? Will I be able to control them? Will they give me a hard time? I'll wonder if they'll compare me with their usual teacher. I wonder how they'll measure me up. I'll wonder how they'll react as I go through the door. Will they all be making a great noise whooping around, or will they be sitting down waiting?

(Geography PGCE, male)

BEd. students tended to show more uncertainty about subject matter and whether they were master of it than PGCE students who, so soon after graduation, claimed a degree of confidence in their subject knowledge.

First-lesson content

Both experienced teachers and BEd. students described how they would outline work for the term. Postgraduates, surprisingly perhaps in view of their strong subject concern, hardly mentioned explaining their overall plan.

The most striking contrast between experienced and novice teachers was that for the former first-lesson content was almost irrelevant. They perceived this opening encounter largely in terms of management rituals: 'The lesson would be concentrating on establishing standards. The work wouldn't be the most important thing. It would be secondary. I would be setting up expectations of behaviour' (geography teacher, female).

Even with those teachers who had more firm intentions to make a start on their subject there was a need to establish some predominant image, as in the lesson of this male science teacher:

> Right at the start of the lesson there must be something for them to do: games, workcards, anything, because they rarely arrive at the same time. I try to create an atmosphere in which they start science as soon as they come in through the door.

The work itself would be simple and unexacting, 'nothing too earth-shattering' in the words of one teacher, simply a means of keeping children busy whilst teachers gained some perception both of individual pupils and the likely chemistry of the class mix.

Student teachers gave a great deal of thought to lesson content and little to managerial aspects. About half were desperate to make an impact with 'something interesting', 'a game', 'something dramatic like a fountain', 'quite exciting', 'interesting and active', 'a magic poetry machine that would make them look forward to the next time'. They spoke of their eagerness to sell themselves, to get introductions over quickly by writing their name on the board, and then give a performance that would sell themselves and their subject for the rest of term.

The other half were much more cautious, would adopt a lower profile, choose a topic that was 'safe' not risky, conservative rather than radical. One PGCE geography student described his approach to Australian grasslands:

> I'll introduce it and talk about it for a while, quite a conventional type of lesson, not flashy because it might go wrong and the kids will remember, quite a safe lesson, a good conventional approach. I'd leave the flashy things to later on when I knew them better.

The BEd. students, more aware from their previous practice of the possibility of topic and tone being determined in some cases by the supervising teacher, and also, in some cases, having tried without success the spectacular opener, were more cautious than PGCE students. One remarked ruefully that she wished 'someone had said use something very set like cards, a textbook or worksheets, so that they know where they are going'.

Mood and image

The presentation of self in the first lesson was described graphically by all the experienced teachers in the sample. All stressed the projection of some larger-than-life image, though the nature of that image differed from teacher to teacher. The importance of what, for most respondents, was described in terms analogous to an opening-night theatre performance, was summed up by an experienced English teacher when she said: 'I think the first lesson is vitally important. If you don't make your mark in the first lesson in the way you want to, you will never make it again.'

The varying kinds of image which teachers sought to project are shown by the responses of people from different subject areas. A drama teacher, even more prone than most, perhaps, to an opening theatrical style, described how he quite consciously generated a sense of mystery about himself:

> The first impression I try to give is of tight purposeful nervous energy. The children learn to expect this. I try to create a feeling that something's going to happen, even if I don't know what I'm going to do. . . . It's important to be hard in the first lesson. By 'hard' I mean a body thing, creating a shroud of mystery. I don't allow the kids to pierce it thoroughly until later.

In their reflections on the type of image they sought to project, several teachers described an element of self-caricature, even a deliberate cultivation of the crackpot in some cases:

> I'm well known for being mad. I do daft things, but they cannot do as they like.
>
> (English teacher, male)
>
> They consider me weird. . . . Everyone at school thinks of me as being a bit eccentric, a mad scientist. I play on this.
>
> (Science teacher, male)

For experienced teachers the first lesson with a new class is a time when they are acutely conscious of the need to reinforce and indeed exaggerate whatever they see as the predominant features of their reputation in the schools. In some cases this reputation was thought to be fearsome:

> I have a reputation before they arrive here. They come in fear and trembling because they think I am severe. . . . It's important to put on a bit of a front at the beginning.
>
> (French teacher, male)

I'm very stern and very hard. I am consciously being a little harder than I am.

(PE teacher, male)

The reactions of the student teachers on mood and change in first lessons were different from each other. The BEd. students' responses were much closer to those of experienced teachers, with emphasis on performance, the establishment of dominance, and even the exaggeration of eccentricity and 'character': 'I'd keep control in my hands by constantly stopping them' (BEd. drama, female).

Next time I'm going to be just as rough and aggressive as I was last time, scare the hell out of them at the beginning, it'll be alright afterwards. I shall say, 'I'm the new teacher. If you treat me fairly, I'll treat you fairly.'

(BEd. PE, male)

I'd say, 'I'm going to be teaching you for the next x weeks. I've got a very funny name so we're all going to have a good laugh'. . . . I'd ham this up completely. . . . 'Everyone get ready to laugh'. The kids ask what it is. I say, 'You don't look ready to laugh.'

(BEd. drama, female)

By contrast the PGCE students were quite different. Their emphasis was on being friendly and approachable. They identified much more with the pupils, saw themselves as reluctant to be socialised into the 'hard teacher' stereotype, regarded their class as a collection of thirty individuals, and spoke much more in terms of negotiation, 'appealing to common sense', not seeing them 'as a class to be lectured at', reluctant to alienate by coming on too strong or setting too much homework. Most had given little precise thought to the matter beyond recognising in general terms what they guessed might be appropriate:

Ideally I'd like a fairly intimate relationship with the class, but I realise that requires drawing a line between intimacy and cheek, a fine balance I'd like to achieve. I don't know how. I haven't given it a lot of thought. It's important. I need to think about it.

(PGCE English, male)

Establishing rules

There were two major differences between experienced and novice teachers about the establishment of rules. The first was that experienced teachers were quite clear about which rules were important and how they would secure compliance. The second difference lay in the nature of the classroom rules by which each group would seek to live.

The most common rule mentioned by all groups was 'no talking when the teacher is talking' in public sessions rather than during private conversations with individual children. Everyone mentioned this in interview, though subsequently when teachers and students were observed there was considerable variation in the extent to which the rule materialised.

Apart from this universal rule there was a very noticeable distinction in the tone of rules mentioned by teachers and students. Experienced teachers frequently cited rules that governed territory (entering and leaving the room, who could move where and when), respect for property, work ethic (having the 'right' attitude to learning, homework, etc.) and safety. Teachers' responses made frequent use of words with a strong moral component, like 'right', 'proper', 'correct', 'suitable', a dimension that was rarely present in the interviews with students.

It was a moral tone that was set by the teacher, but most spoke of transferring responsibility to the pupil, in the class of the science teacher below through a little handing-over ritual. 'They understand the course cost . . . All books are numbered and I check them. I say I hope they've got lots of pocket money for bills if they damage things' (business studies teacher, female).

> I give out exercise books and textbooks calling them out to fetch their books so as to identify them further, and also to stress that *I* have given them the book and it is *their* responsibility . . . for homework after the first lesson I tell them to cover books and look after them. I reinforce that the books are in *their* care.
>
> (Science teacher, male)

This greater moral certainty which distinguished so clearly between experienced and beginning teachers came out very clearly when interviewees responded to the four photographs of classroom scenes described above. Most experienced teachers took an immediate stance on each issue, and declared immediately who was right or wrong and what the teacher would do:

> She has got to be made to do it [move to another seat] because of the audience. If she has the 'why?' look, I'd not give her a reason, I'd become very authoritarian.
>
> (English teacher, male)

> I'd go over to the group and say . . . 'the rules say you shouldn't do this'.
>
> (Science teacher, male)

> Shout at them, particularly if I'm talking. It would be something short and sweet like, 'shut up!' You need a mental sledgehammer.
>
> (Science teacher, male)

Student teachers on the other hand usually spoke of treating the incident lightly, often identifying with the pupils and recalling times when they had behaved in a similar way: 'I'd treat it fairly lightly – "Oh yes, very funny, ha ha. Can we get on with some work now." Then they'd realise that it's a bit stupid' (BEd. drama, female).

Some teachers were extremely precise about their classroom rules, and one maths teacher listed ten rules immediately he was asked, without any hesitation. He was one of 7 out of the 20 in the sample who said he announced his rules in the first lesson. Other teachers 'discussed' the rules, though no-one claimed the pupils had any right to change them. 'Discussion' was really an alternative and more memorable way of communicating what were principally determined by the school authorities or the teacher, as one science specialist explained: 'I know what the rules are, but we establish them through discussion. I believe that they remember them better if they have helped formulate them.'

Almost all teachers said they made use of case law. Whether they announced or discussed rules, they would assume that pupils were likely to make an inference from the way the teacher behaved in particular instances. It was common to hear statements like 'you have to make an example of someone early on' (maths teacher) or 'I stop the song if they aren't joining in' (music teacher).

There was a sharp contrast between experienced teachers and students on the question of rules, especially, though not exclusively, in the case of PGCE students, many of whom were reluctant to speculate and felt that an intuitive approach was better:

> I'd make up rules as appropriate when I see them doing something wrong. It's difficult to see what this would be.
>
> (PGCE geography, female)

> I'd bring the rules out gradually and naturally. I'd offer explanations because I think it is simpler to understand.
>
> (PGCE history, female)

> I'd establish the rules as the problem arises.
>
> (BEd. English, female)

Most students were anxious not to hazard personal relationships by giving prominence to rules of behaviour: 'The Art Room should have a happy atmosphere, and if you start telling them they mustn't do this and they mustn't do that, it ruins the atmosphere' (PGCE art, female).

Personal relationships

Almost everyone in the sample, teacher or student, declared in interview that personal relationships were important. It is a concept in teaching which it is, of course, hard to be against. Experienced teachers showed more awareness of contact outside the classroom than did trainees.

A lot of understanding occurs outside the classroom, walking down the corridor. . . . I play the clarinet. I have just started to learn. I play with the fourth year and am not very good . . . I put myself in a learning situation, and they can see that I also make silly errors.

(English teacher, male)

I try to go on school hikes and camps. I get the kids away from the classroom. I always take my own kids along so that they [the pupils] see me in a different context.

(Science teacher, male)

Student teachers spoke mainly of relationships within the classroom and were again aware of the, to them, thin line between friendliness and over familiarity. This geography PGCE student's fear of loss of control was echoed by many: 'I'm in favour of developing personal relationships as long as I don't get down to the "friend" level. I don't want to get too familiar, otherwise they will take advantage of me.'

REFERENCES

Argyle, M. (1967) *The Psychology of Interpersonal Behaviour*, Penguin, Harmondsworth

Goffman, E. (1971) *The Presentation of Self in Everyday Life*, Penguin, Harmondsworth

Chapter 16

Those who understand
Knowledge growth in teaching

Lee S. Shulman

He who can, does.
He who cannot, teaches.
   (George Bernard Shaw)

I don't know in what fit of pique George Bernard Shaw wrote that infamous aphorism, words that have plagued members of the teaching profession for nearly a century. They are found in 'Maxims for revolutionists,' an appendix to his play *Man and Superman*. 'He who can, does. He who cannot, teaches' is a calamitous insult to our profession, yet one readily repeated even by teachers. More worrisome, its philosophy often appears to underlie the policies concerning the occupation and activities of teaching.

Where did such a demeaning image of the teacher's capacities originate? How long have we been burdened by assumptions of ignorance and ineptitude within the teaching corps? Is Shaw to be treated as the last word on what teachers know and don't know, or do and can't do?

My colleagues and I refer to the absence of focus on subject matter among the various research paradigms for the study of teaching as the 'missing paradigm' problem. The consequences of this missing paradigm are serious, both for policy and for research.

CONTENT AND PEDAGOGY IN THE HISTORY OF THE ACADEMY

Why this sharp distinction between content and pedagogical process? Whether in the spirit of the 1870s, when pedagogy was essentially ignored, or in the 1980s, when content is conspicuously absent, has there always been a cleavage between the two? Has it always been asserted that either one knows content and pedagogy is secondary and unimportant, or one knows pedagogy and is not held accountable for content?

I propose that we look back even further for teachers and examine the history of the university as an institution to discern the sources for this distinction between content knowledge and pedagogical method.

In *Ramus, method and the decay of dialogue*, Father Walter Ong (1958) presents an account of teaching in the medieval university in a chapter with the captivating title 'The pedagogical juggernaut.' He describes a world of teaching and learning in those universities, where instead of separating content and pedagogy (what is known from how to teach it), no such distinction was made at all. Content and pedagogy were part of one indistinguishable body of understanding.

To this day, the names we give our university degrees and the rituals we attach to them reflect those fundamental connections between knowing and teaching. For example, the highest degrees awarded in any university are those of 'master' or 'doctor,' which were traditionally interchangeable. Both words have the same definition; they mean 'teacher.' 'Doctor' or 'dottore' means teacher; it has the same root as 'doctrine,' or teaching. Master, as in school master, also means teacher. Thus, the highest university degree enabled its recipient to be called a teacher.

Ong's (1958) account of these matters is enlightening:

> The universities were, in principle, normal schools, not institutions of general education. This was true of all faculties: arts, medicine, law, and theology; and it was most true at Paris and at universities modeled on Paris (rather than on Bologna), such as Oxford and Cambridge and, later, the German universities. Such universities were in brief, medieval guilds, or were composed of four teachers' guilds or faculties with their associated pupils. The degree of master or doctor (the terms were equivalents, varying from university to university or from faculty to faculty) was the formal admission to the guild, just as the bachelorship which preceded it was admission to the body of apprentice teachers.

The universities were, therefore, much like normal schools: institutions for preparing that most prestigious of professionals, the highest level of scholar, the teacher. The tradition of treating teaching as the highest demonstration of scholarship was derived from the writings of a far greater authority than George Bernard Shaw on the nature of knowledge. Aristotle, whose works formed the heart of the medieval curriculum, made these observations in *Metaphysics* (cited in Wheelwright, 1951).

> We regard master-craftsmen as superior not merely because they have a grasp of theory and *know* the reasons for acting as they do. Broadly speaking, what distinguishes the man who knows from the ignorant man is an ability to teach, and this is why we hold that art and not experience has the character of genuine knowledge (episteme) – namely, that artists can teach and others (i.e., those who have not acquired an art by study but have merely picked up some skill empirically) cannot. (p. 69)

We thus find in Aristotle a very different view of the relationship between knowing and teaching than we find in either Shaw or in the criteria for certification and licensure in some of our sovereign states.

THE MISSING PARADIGM

We have thus seen that the sharp distinction between knowledge and pedagogy does not represent a tradition dating back centuries, but rather, a more recent development. Moreover, identification of teaching competence with pedagogy alone was not even commonplace during Shaw's time. A century ago the defining characteristic of pedagogical accomplishment was knowledge of content.

The pendulum has now swung, both in research and in policy circles. The missing paradigm refers to a blind spot with respect to content that now characterises most research on teaching and, as a consequence, most of our state-level programmes of teacher evaluation and teacher certification.

In reading the literature of research on teaching, it is clear that central questions are unasked. The emphasis is on how teachers manage their classrooms, organise activities, allocate time and turns, structure assignments, ascribe praise and blame, formulate the levels of their questions, plan lessons, and judge general student understanding.

What we miss are questions about the *content* of the lessons taught, the questions aked, and the explanations offered. From the perspectives of teacher development and teacher education, a host of questions arise. Where do teacher explanations come from? How do teachers decide what to teach, how to represent it, how to question students about it and how to deal with problems of misunderstanding? The cognitive psychology of *learning* has focused almost exclusively on such questions in recent years, but strictly from the perspective of learners. Research on teaching has tended to ignore those issues with respect to teachers. My colleagues and I are attempting to redress this imbalance through our research program, 'Knowledge Growth in Teaching.'

What are the sources of teacher knowledge? What does a teacher know and when did he or she come to know it? How is new knowledge acquired, old knowledge retrieved, and both combined to form a new knowledge base?

We assume that most teachers begin with some expertise in the content they teach. (This may be an unfounded assumption, and the consequences of varying degrees of subject matter competence and incompetence have become a serious topic of our research as well.) Secondary teaching candidates, in particular, have typically completed a major in their subject speciality.

Our central question concerns the transition from expert student to novice teacher. How does the successful college student transform his or her expertise in the subject matter into a form that high school students can comprehend? When this novice teacher confronts flawed or muddled textbook chapters or befuddled students, how does he or she employ content expertise to generate new explanations, representations, or clarifications? What are the sources of analogies, metaphors, examples, demonstrations, and rephrasings? How does the novice teacher (or even the seasoned veteran) draw on expertise in the subject matter in the process of teaching? What pedagogical prices are paid when the teacher's subject matter competence is itself compromised by deficiencies of prior education or ability?

Our work does not intend to denigrate the importance of pedagogical understanding or skill in the development of a teacher or in enhancing the effectiveness of instruction. Mere content knowledge is likely to be as useless pedagogically as content-free skill. But to blend properly the two aspects of a teacher's capacities requires that we pay as much attention to the content aspects of teaching as we have recently devoted to the elements of teaching process.

In our research, we have focused on the development of secondary teachers in English, biology, mathematics, and social studies.

A number of strategic research sites and key events are particularly illuminating for our understanding of how knowledge grows in teaching. Often a young teacher will be expected to teach a topic that he or she has never previously learned. For example, the biology major encounters a unit on levers and simple machines in a general science course. The English major must teach a novel or play never previously encountered. The political science major with strong preparation in Central America confronts a unit on India or the Middle East. Even the math major encounters such occasions, as when teaching introductory topics in algebra or geometry, topics he or she has not encountered since high school or even earlier. How does the teacher prepare to teach something never previously learned? How does learning *for* teaching occur?

Another strategic site occurs in conjunction with sections of textbooks that the teacher finds problematic, flawed in their conception of the topic, incomplete in their treatment, or inadequate in explanation or use of examples. How are these deficiencies in curriculum materials (which appear to be commonplace) apprehended and dealt with by teachers? How do teachers take a piece of text and transform their understanding of it into instruction that their students can comprehend?

A PERSPECTIVE ON TEACHER KNOWLEDGE

As we have begun to probe the complexities of teacher understanding and transmission of content knowledge, the need for a more coherent theoretical framework has become rapidly apparent. What are the domains and categories of content knowledge in the minds of teachers? How, for example, are content knowledge and general pedagogical knowledge related? In which forms are the domains and categories of knowledge represented in the minds of teachers? What are promising ways of enhancing acquisition and development of such knowledge? Because I see these as among the central questions for disciplined inquiry into teacher education, I will now turn to a discussion of some ways of thinking about one particular domain – content knowledge in teaching – and some of the categories within it.

How might we think about the knowledge that grows in the minds of teachers, with special emphasis on content? I suggest we distinguish among three categories of content knowledge: (a) subject matter content knowledge, (b) pedagogical content knowledge, and (c) curricular knowledge.

Content knowledge

This refers to the amount and organisation of knowledge per se in the mind of the teacher.

In the different subject matter areas, the ways of discussing the content structure of knowledge differ. To think properly about content knowledge requires going beyond knowledge of the facts or concepts of a domain. It requires understanding the structures of the subject matter in the manner defined by such scholars as Joseph Schwab. (See his collected essays, 1978.)

For Schwab, the structures of a subject include both the substantive and the syntactic structures. The substantive structures are the variety of ways in which the basic concepts and principles of the discipline are organised to incorporate its facts. The syntactic structure of a discipline is the set of ways in which truth or falsehood, validity or invalidity, are established. When there exist competing claims regarding a given phenomenon, the syntax of a discipline provides the rules for determining which claim has greater warrant. A syntax is like a grammar. It is the set of rules for determining what is legitimate to say in a disciplinary domain and what 'breaks' the rules.

Teachers must not only be capable of defining for students the accepted truths in a domain. They must also be able to explain why a particular proposition is deemed warranted, why it is worth knowing, and how it relates to other propositions, both within the discipline and without, both in theory and in practice.

Thus, the biology teacher must understand that there are a variety of ways of organising the discipline. Depending on the preferred color of one's BSCS text, biology may be formulated as (a) a science of molecules from which one aggregates up to the rest of the field, explaining living phenomena in terms of the principles of their constituent parts; (b) a science of ecological systems from which one disaggregates down to the smaller units, explaining the activities of individual units by virtue of the larger systems of which they are a part; or (c) a science of biological organisms, those most familiar of analytic units, from whose familiar structures, functions, and interactions one weaves a theory of adaptation. The well-prepared biology teacher will recognise these and alternative forms of organisation and the pedagogical grounds for selecting one under some circumstances and others under different circumstances.

The same teacher will also understand the syntax of biology. When competing claims are offered regarding the same biological phenomenon, how has the controversy been adjudicated? How might similar controversies be adjudicated in our own day?

We expect that the subject matter content understanding of the teacher be at least equal to that of his or her lay colleague, the mere subject matter major. The teacher need not only understand *that* something is so; the teacher must further understand *why* it is so, on what grounds its warrant can be asserted, and under what circumstances our belief in its justification can be weakened and even denied. Moreover, we expect the teacher to understand why a given topic is particularly central to a discipline whereas another may be somewhat peripheral. This will be important in subsequent pedagogical judgments regarding relative curricular emphasis.

Pedagogical content knowledge

A second kind of content knowledge is pedagogical knowledge, which goes beyond knowledge of subject matter per se to the dimension of subject matter knowledge *for teaching*. I still speak of content knowledge here, but of the particular form of content knowledge that embodies the aspects of content most germane to its teachability.[1]

Within the category of pedagogical content knowledge I include, for the most regularly taught topics in one's subject area, the most useful forms of representation of those ideas, the most powerful analogies, illustrations, examples, explanations, and demonstrations – in a word, the ways of representing and formulating the subject that make it comprehensible to others. Since there are no single most powerful forms of representation, the teacher must have at hand a veritable armamentarium of alternative forms of representation, some of which derive from research whereas others originate in the wisdom of practice.

Pedagogical content knowledge also includes an understanding of what makes the learning of specific topics easy or difficult: the conceptions and preconceptions that students of different ages and backgrounds bring with them to the learning of those most frequently taught topics and lessons. If those preconceptions are misconceptions, which they so often are, teachers need knowledge of the strategies most likely to be fruitful in reorganizing the understanding of learners, because those learners are unlikely to appear before them as blank slates.

Curricular knowledge

If we are regularly remiss in not teaching pedagogical knowledge to our students in teacher education programmes, we are even more delinquent with respect to the third category of content knowledge, *curricular knowledge*. The curriculum is represented by the full range of programmes designed for the teaching of particular subjects and topics at a given level, the variety of instructional materials available in relation to those programmes, and the set of characteristics that serve as both the indications and contraindications for the use of particular curriculum or programme materials in particular circumstances.

The curriculum and its associated materials are the *materia medica* of pedagogy, the pharmacopoeia from which the teacher draws those tools of teaching that present or exemplify particular content and remediate or evaluate the adequacy of student accomplishments. We expect the mature physician to understand the full range of treatments available to ameliorate a given disorder, as well as the range of alternatives for particular circumstances of sensitivity, cost, interaction with other interventions, convenience, safety, or comfort. Similarly, we ought to expect that the mature teacher possesses such understandings about the curricular alternatives available for instruction.[2]

Forms of knowledge

A conceptual analysis of knowledge for teachers would necessarily be based on a framework for classifying both the domains and categories of teacher knowledge, on the one hand, and the forms for representing that knowledge, on the other. I would like to suggest three forms of teacher knowledge: *propositional knowledge, case knowledge*, and *strategic knowledge*.

Recall that these are 'forms' in which each of the general domains or particular categories of knowledge previously discussed – content, pedagogy, and curriculum – may be organised. (There are clearly other important domains of knowledge as well, for example, of individual differences among students, of generic methods of classroom organisation and management, of the history and philosophy of education, and of school finance and administration, to name but a few. Each of these domains is subdivided into categories and will be expressible in the forms of knowledge to be discussed here.)

Much of what is taught to teachers is in the form of propositions. When we examine the research on teaching and learning and explore its implications for practice, we are typically (and properly) examining propositions. When we ask about the wisdom of practice, the accumulated lore of teaching experience, we tend to find such knowledge stored in the form of propositions as well.

The research-based principles of active teaching, reading for comprehension, and effective schools are stated as lists of propositions. The experience-based recommendations of planning five-step lesson plans, never smiling until Christmas, and organising three reading groups are posed as sets of propositions. In fact, although we often present propositions one at a time, we recognise that they are better understood if they are organised in some coherent form, lodged in a conceptual or theoretical framework that is generative or regenerative. Otherwise they become terribly difficult to recall or retrieve.

The roots of the 'case method' in the teaching of law in this country, certainly the best known approach to employing cases as vehicles for professional education, lie in their value for teaching theory, not practice.

Case knowledge is knowledge of specific, well-documented, and richly described events. Whereas cases themselves are reports of events or sequences of events, the knowledge they represent is what makes them cases. The cases may be examples of specific instances of practice – detailed descriptions of how an instructional event occurred – complete with particulars of contexts, thoughts, and feelings. On the other hand, they may be exemplars of principles, exemplifying in their detail a more abstract proposition or theoretical claim.

I have referred to *strategic knowledge* as the third 'form' of teacher knowledge. Both propositions and cases share the burden of unilaterality, the deficiency of turning the reader or user toward a single, particular rule or practical way of seeing. Strategic knowledge comes into play as the teacher confronts particular situations or problems, whether theoretical, practical, or moral, where principles collide and no simple solution is possible.

Strategic knowledge must be generated to extend understanding beyond principle to the wisdom of practice. We generally attribute wisdom to those who can transcend the limitations of particular principles or specific experiences when confronted by situations in which each of the alternative choices appears equally 'principled.' Novice bridge players rapidly learn the principles of the game, embodied in such maxims as 'Lead fourth highest from your longest and strongest suit,' and 'Never lead away from a king.' But when you must lead away from a king to lead fourth highest, then propositional knowledge alone becomes limited in value. Strategic knowledge (or judgement) is then invoked.[3]

When strategic understanding is brought to bear in the examination of rules and cases, professional judgement, the hallmark of any learned profession, is called into play. What distinguishes mere craft from profession is the indeterminacy of rules when applied to particular cases. The professional holds knowledge, not only of how – the capacity for skilled performance – but of what and why. The teacher is not only a master of procedure but also of content and rationale, and capable of explaining why something is done. The teacher is capable of reflection leading to self-knowledge, the metacognitive awareness that distinguishes draftsman from architect, bookkeeper from auditor. A professional is capable not only of practising and understanding his or her craft, but of communicating the reasons for professional decisions and actions to others (see Shulman, 1983).

NOTES

1 There is also pedagogical knowledge of teaching – as distinct from subject matter – which is also terribly important, but not the object of discussion in this paper. This is the knowledge of generic principles of classroom organisation and management and the like that has quite appropriately been the focus of study in most recent research on teaching. I have no desire to diminish its importance. I am simply attempting to place needed emphasis on the hitherto ignored facets of content knowledge.

2 Although in this paper I discuss aspects of content knowledge (including content-specific pedagogical knowledge and curricular knowledge) exclusively, a proper professional board examination would include other equally important sections as well. These would assess knowledge of general pedagogy, knowledge of learners and their backgrounds, principles of school organisation, finance and management, and the historical, social, and cultural foundations of education among many more. Exams would also tap teaching performance and other capabilities unlikely to be adequately assessed using conventional paper-and-pencil instruments. Discussion of the character of a professional board for teachers and its desirability, however, is appropriate for another paper.

3 It may well be that what I am calling strategic *knowledge* in this paper is not knowledge in the same sense as propositional and case knowledge. Strategic 'knowing' or judgment may simply be a process of analysis, of comparing and contrasting principles, cases, and their implications for practice. Once such strategic processing has been employed, the results are either stored in terms of a new proposition (e.g., 'Smiling before Christmas may be permissible when . . .') or a new case. These then enter the repertoire of cases and principles to be used like any others. In that sense, it is possible that strategic analysis occurs in the presence of the other forms of knowledge and is the primary means for testing, extending, and amending them.

REFERENCES

Ong, W. J. (1958) *Ramus, method and the decay of dialogue.* Cambridge, MA: Harvard University Press.

Schwab, J. J. (1978) *Science, curriculum and liberal education.* Chicago: University of Chicago Press.

Shulman, L. S. (1983) 'Autonomy and obligation: the remote control of teaching', in L. S. Shulman and G. Sykes (eds) *Handbook of teaching and policy.* New York: Longman.

Wheelwright, P. (ed.) (1951) *Aristotle.* New York: Odyssey.

Chapter 17

Teaching as a 'professional' activity

James Calderhead

Teaching is a complex process that can be conceptualised in many different ways, using alternative models, metaphors, and analogies. One metaphor that acknowledges the intentional, problem-solving aspects of teachers' work is that of teaching as a reflective, thinking activity. This highlights several key characteristics of teaching, which it shares with many other professions such as medicine, law, architecture, and business management. Consequently, the metaphor sometimes used is that of teaching as a professional activity.

According to this metaphor, teachers possess a body of specialised knowledge acquired through training and experience. Just as a doctor possesses formal knowledge of physiology and pathology, together with knowledge acquired from experience about patient behaviour and the various combinations of symptoms that complicate the task of diagnosis, the teacher has acquired knowledge about the curriculum, teaching methods, subject matter, and child behaviour together with a wealth of other particular information resulting from the experience of working with children in numerous contexts and with different materials. Like other professionals, teachers rely upon this specialist knowledge in their daily work.

A second feature of professional activity is its goal-orientation in relation to its clients. Doctors aim to cure their patients, lawyers to defend their clients' interests, architects to design buildings to suit their clients' specifications. In the case of teaching, who the clients are is a little more ambiguous. Although much of teachers' activity may be oriented to the education of their pupils, teachers, more so than many professionals, are also answerable to a number of others, including parents, administrators, advisers, inspectors, employers, curriculum development agencies, and politicians. These individuals and agencies are in a position to influence what teachers do by controlling the provision of materials, curriculum guidelines, and finance, and in the determination of the conditions in which teachers work. Influence might also be exerted at an ideological level through the perpetuation of beliefs and ideologies of good classroom practice. There is rarely any consensus amongst teachers' 'clients' on what constitutes good practice.

Consequently, teachers may encounter numerous expectations that can be in conflict with each other as well as with the beliefs of the individual teacher. The fact that there are no agreed goals for education and that there are several interest groups to whom teachers may be held accountable frequently results in teachers facing impossible dilemmas. Consider, for instance, the recently popular call for the school curriculum to return to basics, coupled with the equally popular demand for schools to prepare children for a future, technological, computer-oriented society!

A third characteristic is that the problems professionals deal with are often complex and ambiguous, and professionals must use their expert knowledge to analyse and interpret them, making judgements and decisions as they formulate a course of action intended to benefit their client. A lawyer, for instance, may encounter an array of conflicting evidence. His knowledge of court practice and legal procedures, together with his previous experience and knowledge of how witnesses and juries typically respond, enable him to make judgements about the plausibility of alternative lines of argument. He can decide how best to interpret and present evidence in court, which features to emphasise, and when doubts might be implied about particular points of fact in order to advantage his client.

Teachers similarly face complex situations, and this is well described by Doyle (1986), who concisely summarises the complexity of the classroom environment in terms of six general features: *multidimensionality, simultaneity, immediacy, unpredictability, publicness*, and *history*. Classrooms are busy places. At any one time, teachers may be faced with a series of incidents to manage – keeping the class working quietly, for instance, while dealing with one particular child's difficulty and postponing or redirecting other children's requests for attention. As a result, teachers face competing demands and often teaching decisions are a compromise amongst multiple costs and benefits. For instance, in deciding whether to carry out a particular activity in groups or as a class, teachers may have to weigh the possible benefits of encouraging co-operative work and perhaps obtaining greater pupil satisfaction against the costs of more preparation, the risk of some pupils opting out and leaving others to do the work, and greater demands on teachers' managerial skill. The pace of teachers' activity in the classroom is necessarily rapid. There is also considerable uncertainty in the teachers' world. Unexpected events, distractions, and interruptions threaten to disturb the normal course of events. Lessons don't always go as expected, and children's behaviour is sometimes unpredictable. In addition, teachers, for much of the day, are 'on show'. How they are seen to cope with classroom situations can influence how individual children assess them and respond to them in the future. And as a result of classroom interactions, particularly those occurring early in the year when teachers and children are first assessing one another, each class develops its own norms, its own ethos, its own work routines, a history that shapes the ways in which it copes and responds to activities in the present.

Given this complexity of the teaching task, it indeed seems a remarkable achievement that teaching and learning occur in schools at all! The school and classroom environment clearly place a heavy burden upon teachers to attend to and process a large volume of information and continually to juggle conflicting and competing interests. Teachers must use their knowledge to cope with a constant barrage of complex situations.

In classroom teaching, however, there is often little opportunity to reflect upon problems and to bring one's knowledge to bear upon their analysis and interpretation. Teachers must often respond immediately and intuitively. This relates to a fourth feature of professional activity, namely that it involves skilful action that is adapted to its context. Through repeated practice and reflection on practice, the professional has developed various specialist and 'knowledgeable' skills. The lawyer, for instance, in his skills of cross-examination demonstrates a keen knowledge of human behaviour in a legal context and an awareness of alternative questioning strategies. The professionals' expert knowledge enables them to perceive significant features in their work and to respond to them. Teachers have extensive knowledge about children, curriculum materials, classroom organisation, and approaches to instruction. This knowledge helps them to establish relationships with children, manage the class, decide how best to teach a particular topic, maintain the children's interest, and instruct them. The teachers' knowledge and experience of children in a classroom context has in some cases become so closely tied to their practice that they can, for instance, notice a child's inattention to work and readily identify it as a case of difficulty in understanding, attention-seeking, lack of interest, tiredness, or the child having an 'off-day', and respond appropriately, when to an outsider the same cues may be lost in a blur of classroom noise and activity.

Schon (1983) uses the term 'knowledge-in-action' to describe the knowledge that is embedded in the skilled action of the professional. Knowledge-in-action is sometimes inaccessible directly to professionals themselves in the sense that, although they can demonstrate it in action, they are unable to disclose it verbally. Just as expert tennis players, who might return shots in rapid succession, intuitively calculated to land at particular spots on the court, often cannot describe the knowledge of ball control that lies in their skilled performance, neither can lawyers in their skills of cross-examination or teachers in their classroom interaction.

In some respects, teaching sits uneasily alongside professions such as medicine, law, or architecture. Teachers, for instance, are not self-employed, in most countries they do not have their own professional association that oversees a standard of good practice, nor generally do they have high status or high salaries. In fact, it has sometimes been suggested that teachers' claims to professionalism can be viewed as status-enhancing strategies or as a means of defending competence, autonomy, and individualism from outside inter-ference (Hargreaves 1980; Lortie 1975). Nevertheless, in terms of the types of activities in which professionals engage, there seem to be some enlighten-ing similarities, and the metaphor may be a valuable one in helping us to conceptualise and explore further the nature of teachers' practice. Such a metaphor illuminates crucial aspects of teaching by guiding us towards an exploration of the nature of teachers' knowledge and the influences on its formation, how it is applied to the analysis of teaching situations, and how it has come to be embedded in teachers' action.

REFERENCES

Doyle, W. (1986) 'Classroom Organization and Management'. In Wittrock, M. C. (ed.) *Handbook of Research on Teaching*. 3rd edition, New York: Macmillan.
Hargreaves, D. H. (1980) 'The Occupational Culture of Teachers'. In Woods, P. (ed.) *Teacher Strategies*. London: Croom Helm.
Lortie, D. C. (1975) *Schoolteacher*, Chicago, IL: University of Chicago Press.
Schon, D. A. (1983) *The Reflective Practitioner*. London: Temple Smith.

Chapter 18

Teacher expectations

*Peter Mortimore, Pamela Sammons, Louise Stoll,
David Lewis and Russel Ecob*

In this chapter we will discuss the phenomenon of teacher expectations and examine our data for evidence of differential expectations for any of these groups.

Every class room inevitably contains pupils of differing personalities, abilities and backgrounds. Previous research findings demonstrate that, for some teachers at least, the expectations they have for their pupils can influence the children's future academic performance and self-perception (see, for example, Pilling and Kellmer Pringle, 1978; and Meyer, 1982). Nash (1973) suggests that the teachers' behaviour is affected by their expectations, and somehow the teacher's mental attitudes to the child are . . . being communicated . . .' (p. 12). Thus, different pupils may be presented with quite different psychological environments by their teachers.

Inevitably, many predictions about pupil achievement are based on past experience and may well reflect accurate teacher expectations. Furthermore, as Brophy and Good (1974) pointed out, not all teachers will allow their expectations to interfere with their ability to treat pupils appropriately. Some studies, however, have shown that certain teachers do treat children differently according to differential beliefs about them (see Pilling and Kellmer Pringle, 1978). We have been able to consider whether teacher behaviour, particularly in terms of individual contacts with pupils, varied towards different groups of children. These groups are defined by age, sex, social class, ethnic background, perceived ability and behaviour.

AGE DIFFERENCES

The attainment of younger pupils within a year group was generally poorer than that of their older peers, although there was no difference in their progress in cognitive skills. Teachers, however, were found consistently to have judged pupils born in the summer months as being of lower ability and having more behaviour difficulties. Younger pupils themselves also were found to have a less positive view of school than their older peers.

SOCIAL CLASS DIFFERENCES

The influence of pupils' background upon teacher behaviour in the class-room has concerned researchers for some time (see Pilling and Kellmer Pringle, 1978, for a review). Opinion is divided. Some studies have found no social class effect (Nash, 1973; Murphy, 1974; Croll, 1981). Others, how-ever, indicate that social class is one of the major sources of expectations teachers hold for their pupils (Goodacre, 1968: Barker Lunn, 1971; Dusek and Joseph, 1983) and that teachers' behaviour can vary according to a child's background. For example, Sharp and Green (1975) found that pupils whom teachers regarded as more 'successful' were given greater attention than other children. These pupils invariably came from a 'good area'. The influence of social class may not always be relevant, particularly if teachers know little about a child's home circumstances. Nonetheless, other cues such as speech, physical appearance and eligibility for free school meals, may also be indicators of social class.

The fact that pupils from non-manual backgrounds had higher attainments in most of the cognitive assessments and made more progress in reading and writing has already been pointed out. They were also rated by their teachers as of higher ability, even after account had been taken of their attainment. Those from unskilled manual backgrounds and from homes where the father was absent were perceived by their teachers as having a greater incidence of behaviour problems. Thus, it appears that some teachers have different expectations of pupils from different social class backgrounds, irrespective of the children's performance on cognitive assessments.

SEX DIFFERENCES

There is already considerable evidence of differences in teacher action towards, and judgements of, girls and boys (Palardy, 1969; Good and Brophy, 1971; Whyte, 1983). The reinforcement of sex-stereotyping in the classroom has also been referred to as part of the 'hidden curriculum' (Serbin, 1983). Thus, teachers may well be completely unaware of their own behaviours that encourage and sustain stereotyping and that, subsequently, may have an effect upon the academic progress, and behavioural development of girls and boys.

It will also be seen that girls had higher attainments in reading and writing throughout their junior schooling and slightly higher attainment in mathematics by the third year. There were few other sex differences in pupil performance or progress. Although it did not reach statistical significance, teachers tended to rate boys' ability slightly higher than that of girls, when account was taken of their attainments in cognitive areas. This was surprising, because boys were consistently assessed as having more behaviour difficulties, and were also found to be less positive in their attitude to school.

They were also observed to be less involved with their work by the field officers.

The I.L.E.A's Primary Record Summary, completed by teachers at the end of infant school, and at the end of the first and second junior years, was examined for all children individually. Significantly more girls than boys were rated as demonstrating marked ability in the four areas of written language: personal statements; factual statements; imaginative writing; and using information from various sources of reference. Conversely, more boys were rated as showing serious and persistent difficulties in these areas. For mathematics, the only difference was noted at the end of the second year, when more girls were rated at the later stages of development in work involving operations with whole numbers. This is in line with our finding of better progress by girls in mathematics.

Differences, once again in favour of girls, were also found in the stage of reading development reached, particularly at the end of the second year. By this year, significantly more girls could, in the opinion of their class teachers, follow a narrative, appraise material critically, and skim and scan material. They also showed more proficiency in the use of dictionaries, indexes and other reference sources.

A similar difference was noted in favour of girls in records of pupils' creative abilities, particularly in dance, drama and music. For art and craft work, there was a slight variation. More boys at the end of infant schooling had difficulties, but there were also more boys showing a particular flair in two and three-dimensional work. In the junior years, differences in teachers' records of boys' and girls' art work were not significant.

Analyses show that teachers communicated more at an individual level with boys than with girls. This was found to be true for both female and male teachers. Differences were greatest in the third year when it was found that female teachers gave boys relatively even more attention.

The major difference concerned a greater use of criticism and neutral remarks to individual boys about their behaviour. This difference was not related to the sex of the teacher. Teachers also communicated more with boys on a non-verbal level, using both facial gestures and physical contact, and teased them more frequently. The extra behaviour control comments to boys are not surprising, given the teachers' lower assessments of boys' behaviour and the boys' tendency to be distracted more often from their work, as seen in the classroom observations. Another possibility is that the boys' poorer behaviour and attitudes to school may be related to, and exacerbated by, their treatment by teachers in the classroom. Thus, perhaps, pupils are reacting to the way they are treated by their teachers, as well as teachers responding to pupils' behaviour.

There were also differences between the sexes in their contact with teachers on work-related issues. Boys were given more work supervision, particularly in the form of extra feedback. Girls, however, received significantly more praise from teachers. Although there was no consistent pattern, there was some suggestion that teachers discussed the factual content of the work more frequently with the boys. There was no difference, however, in the frequency with which teachers heard girls and boys read throughout the day, although in sessions specifically designated for quiet reading, teachers heard more boys than girls read.

Overall, it appears that the main difference in teachers' classroom contact with girls and boys was in the greater number of negative comments, referring to their behaviour, made to boys. Boys also received more communication in general, and work feedback in particular, from their teachers. Given their poorer performance in cognitive areas this is perhaps not surprising. As far as positive work feedback was concerned, however, girls received more. It is interesting that teachers tended to rate the boys slightly more favourably than the girls in terms of ability, when account was taken of individual pupils' performance. Perhaps teachers were being influenced by the generally livelier behaviour of boys.

ETHNIC DIFFERENCES

It has also been suggested that teachers' expectations for pupils may be influenced by pupils' ethnic background. Thus, the Rampton Report (1981) proposed that the performance of ethnic minority children might be affected by low teacher expectations due to negative stereotypes about the abilities of such groups. The Swann Report (1985), whilst not rejecting the conclusions of the interim Rampton Report, suggested that the issues involved are complex and merit considerably more research. Eggleston et al. (1985) reached similar conclusions to those of Rampton about the educational and vocational experiences of young people of different ethnic groups in the secondary school context. However, an alternative interpretation was offered by Short (1985), who suggested that teachers' expectations might have been influenced by their experience of ethnic minority groups in the classroom.

The Junior School Project found no relationship between teachers' ratings of pupils' ability and the children's ethnic background, once account had been taken of other background factors and attainment. Ability ratings, however, were strongly related to pupil attainments. These attainments were lower in reading, writing and mathematics for Caribbean and some Asian pupils than for other pupils. This suggests, as indicated at the beginning of this section, that for pupils from all ethnic backgrounds, teacher expectations appear to be tied to specific knowledge of previous attainment and performance in the classroom.

The data supply no evidence to support the view that teachers were withholding attention from any ethnic group. In fact they appeared to go out of their way to attend to black and ethnic minority pupils. This evidence is positive though, quite clearly, it is not definitive. Expectations can be transmitted in subtle ways and it is possible that it was precisely through such differences in teacher attention that teachers were signalling differential expectations.

ABILITY DIFFERENCES

Most studies of teacher expectations, and the ways in which these may be mediated within the classroom, have concerned the effects of such expectations upon pupils of different abilities (see, for example, Rosenthal and Jacobson, 1968; and Barker Lunn, 1971). Burstall (1968) found that pupils taught by teachers who believed that low ability children were able to learn French achieved better results than those whose teachers thought that such children would not be able to do so.

More recently, attention has focused on teacher behaviour in the classroom. Studies have varied in the extent to which differences in the behaviour of teachers towards high and low ability pupils have been observed. Some researchers have noted higher rates of contact with children of above average ability, more praise for correct responses, less criticism for incorrect responses, and greater opportunities to contribute in class (see the reviews by Brophy, 1983; and Galton and Delafield, 1981). Others, however, reported no differences. Alpert (1974), for example, found as much 'good' teaching with the least able reading group as with the most able. Previous research, therefore, has produced no firm conclusions on the extent to which teacher behaviour varies towards different groups of pupils.

We found that pupils of below average ability had a higher number of individual contacts with their class teachers. This contrasts with the findings of other research quoted above. Teachers were also found to talk with the low ability pupils significantly more often about their work and to listen to them read more frequently. The less able pupils were also given more feedback on their work than more able children.

When eight teachers' contacts with a sub-sample of 80 pupils were examined in some detail, it was discovered that they criticised the higher ability pupils' work significantly more often than they criticised that of the lower ability children. Conversely, they praised the less able pupils' work more frequently than they praised that of more able children. These results are contrary to the findings of most other studies (see the review by Brophy, 1983). It is possible that teachers are less prepared to accept poor work from pupils they believe are capable of producing a high standard.

On average, teachers made significantly more non-work comments to low ability pupils. These included both extra routine instructions and more neutral and negative remarks related to their behaviour. This is likely to reflect the significant relationship between teachers' ratings of pupils' behaviour and their ability, even after pupils' attainment had been taken into account. Furthermore, as a group, lower ability pupils spent less time involved in work activities. The relationship between ability and behaviour will be explored in more detail later in this section.

It is possible that teachers' expectations may be influenced, at least in part, by the judgements of previous teachers. An examination of teachers' records of the progress of individual pupils showed that pupils rated as above average ability, at the beginning of the second year, were significantly more likely to have reached a further stage of development in their reading work. For example, by the end of the first year 59 per cent of the high ability pupils knew how to use a dictionary whereas the same was true for only 18 per cent of low ability pupils.

BEHAVIOUR DIFFERENCES

Teachers make judgements about not only the ability and work habits of pupils, but also about their behaviour. In teachers' statements of aims, intellectual objectives are seen as no more important than those concerning pupils' personal and social development. Behaviour control is also seen to be an important aspect of classroom management. Much previous research has, generally, neglected the importance of behaviour when studying differences in teacher action towards various groups of children. It was decided, therefore, to examine whether teachers' behaviour varied towards pupils perceived by them as well or poorly behaved.

Teachers devoted significantly more individual attention to pupils they had rated as poorly behaved. In contrast, well-behaved pupils received more teacher contact in groups than predicted. The teachers also initiated fewer of their discussions with poorly-behaved children and more with well-behaved pupils. Calling across the room occurred more frequently with children perceived as naughtier. Either the teachers called across to pupils who were not getting on with their work, or these pupils called out to get teacher attention, rather than going up to their teachers or putting their hands up.

Teachers spent significantly more time on management and other non-work matters with poorly-behaved pupils. This included criticising their behaviour more frequently. Observations of the poorly-behaved pupils showed them to be more frequently distracted from their work than were their better-behaved peers. The extra non-work feedback given by the teachers, therefore, is likely to relate directly to pupils' behaviour in class. However, it was also found that teachers tended to praise the good behaviour of those pupils who were generally poorly-behaved significantly more often than that of their well-behaved peers.

Well-behaved pupils were much less likely to receive negative comments on their work than poorly-behaved pupils, although the amount of praise for good work did not differ between the two groups. In work discussions, teachers also tended to joke with and tease naughtier pupils more than other children. There was no difference between these groups of pupils in the frequency with which teachers heard them read, or in the amount of communication connected with the more detailed content of their work.

Overall, therefore, teachers' interactions with pupils they perceived to be different in terms of behaviour, tended to relate most closely to keeping the pupils 'on task'. It appears that teachers tried to achieve this end by using both positive, and negative control comments.

THE LINK BETWEEN ABILITY AND BEHAVIOUR

A link between teachers' assessments of pupil ability and pupil behaviour has already been noted. The findings also indicate that teachers differentiate children in respect of their behaviour as well as their ability. Galton and Delafield (1981) suggest that, if teachers are forced to make judgements about the ability of pupils who have similar attainment levels, they do so largely on the basis of pupils' classroom behaviour. Thus, it has been argued that those nominated as of the highest ability are the quietest, most obedient pupils, and those of the lowest ability are the noisiest, most disruptive children. We were able to compare teachers' ability and behaviour ratings for individual pupils. It became apparent that teachers could separate out their judgements of pupils' ability from those of behaviour. (This accords with the conclusions of Murphy, 1974.) Amongst pupils perceived as of high or of low ability, both poor and good behaviour ratings were recorded.

For pupils of lower ability who also have behaviour difficulties, a greater emphasis on work rather than routine discussions may improve their performance, and also the way that they feel they are perceived by teachers. It was encouraging to see that teachers were supportive of pupils with learning and behaviour difficulties when they had made a particular effort. Nonetheless, praise was not commonly observed in classrooms for any group of children.

Two final points need to be made in relation to teachers' expectations of, and behaviour towards, different groups of pupils. First, a particular pupil may appear in a number of different groups. This has been illustrated in the analysis of pupils categorised according to behaviour and ability. It is also true for social class, sex, race and, as pointed out earlier, for age. Any pupil appearing in the less positive category of all or most of these dimensions may be more likely to be treated differentially. Even though the teacher may go out of her or his way to give individual attention to such a pupil, the effect of such interactions may be negative. If this is the case, the message transmitted by the interactions is likely to reinforce still further the lower expectations.

The second point is that much of this process may be subconscious. Teachers may feel they are doing all they can to divide their time between all their pupils in as fair a way as possible. They may be quite unaware of the different meanings that their behaviour could convey to pupils. Some may try to give particular attention to, or be especially nice to, specific groups (girls or black pupils) without realising that, by this very action, they may be indicating lower academic expectations. The work of Dweck and Repucci (1973) provides some illustrations of the paradoxical nature of teachers' praise for the inadequate work of some groups of pupils. In considering the effects of differential expectations transmitted in the classroom it must be remembered that, for children interacting daily over a period of a year with a teacher who has a low perception of their abilities, the inhibiting effect may be stultifying. In the same way, for one of the pupils about whom the teacher holds positive views, the effect will be stimulating.

REFERENCES

Alpert, J. (1974) Teacher Behaviour Across Ability Groups: A Consideration of the Mediation of Pygmalion Effects. *Journal of Educational Psychology*. Vol. 66, No. 3, pp. 348–53.

Barker Lunn, J. (1971) *Social Class, Attitudes and Achievement*. Slough, NFER.

Barker Lunn, J. (1982) Junior Schools and their Organizational Policies. *Educational Research*. Vol. 24, No. 4, pp. 259–60.

Brophy, J. (1983) Research on the Self Fulfilling Prophecy and Teacher Expectations. *Journal of Educational Psychology*. Vol. 75, No. 5, pp. 631–661.

Brophy, J. and Good, T. (1974) *Teacher–Student Relationships: Causes and Consequences*. New York, Holt, Rinehart & Winston.

Burstall, C. (1968) *French National Experiment*. Occasional Publication Series, No. 18, Slough, NFER.

Croll, P. (1981) Social Class, Pupil Achievement and Classroom Interaction. In B. Simon, and J. Willcocks (eds) *Research and Practice in the Primary Classroom*. London, Routledge & Kegan Paul.

Dusek, J. and Joseph, G. (1983) The Bases of Teacher Expectancies: A Meta-Analysis. *Journal of Educational Psychology*. Vol. 75, No. 3, pp. 327–346.

Dweck, C. W. and Repucci, N. D. (1973) Learned Helplessness and Reinforcement Responsibility in Children. *Journal of Personality and Social Psychology*. Vol. 25, pp. 109–116.

Eggleston, S. J., Dunn, D. K., and Ajjali, M. (1985) *The Educational and Vocational Experiences of 15–18 Year Old Young People of Ethnic Minority Groups*. Department of Education, University of Keele.

Galton, M. and Delafield, A. (1981) Expectancy Effects in Primary Classrooms. In B. Simon and J. Willcocks (eds) *Research and Practice in the Primary Classroom*. London, Routledge & Kegan Paul.

Good, T. and Brophy, J. (1971) Questioned Equality for Grade One Boys and Girls. *Reading Teacher*, Vol. 25, No. 3, pp. 247–252.

Goodacre, E. (1968) *Teachers and Their Pupils' Home Background*. Slough, NFER.

Meyer, W. U. (1982) Indirect Communications about Perceived Ability Estimates. *Journal of Educational Psychology*. Vol. 74, No. 6, pp. 888–897.

Murphy, J. (1974) Teacher Expectations and Working-Class Underachievement. *British Journal of Sociology*. Vol. 25, No. 3, pp. 326–44.

Nash, R. (1973) *Classrooms Observed: The Teacher's Perception and Pupil's Performance*. London, Routledge & Kegan Paul.

Palardy, J. (1969) What Teachers Believe – What Children Achieve. *Elementary School Journal*. Vol. 69, pp. 370–374.

Pilling, D. and Kellmer Pringle, M. (1978) *Controversial Issues in Child Development*. National Children's Bureau. London, Paul Elek.

Rampton Report (1981) *West Indian Children in Our Schools: Interim Report of the Committee from Ethnic Minority Groups*. London, HMSO.

Rosenthal, R. & Jacobson, L. (1968) *Pygmalion in the Classroom: Teacher Expectation and Pupils' Intellectual Development*. Holt, Rinehart Winston, New York.

Serbin, L. A. (1983) The Hidden Curriculum: Academic Consequences of Teacher Expectations, In M. Marland (ed.) *Sex Differentiation and Schooling*. London, Heinemann.

Sharp, R. and Green, A. (1975) *Education and Social Control – A Study in Progressive Primary Education*. London, Routledge & Kegan Paul

Short, G. (1985) Teacher Expectation and West Indian Underachievement. *Educational Research*. Vol. 27, No. 2, pp. 95–101.

Swann Report (1985) *Education for All: The Report of the Committee of Inquiry into the Education of Children from Ethnic Minority Groups*, London, HMSO.

Whyte, J. (1983) *Beyond the Wendy House: Sex Role Stereotyping in Primary Schools*. York, Longman Schools Council Resources Unit.

Chapter 19

Teachers and cross-cultural counselling

Jon Nixon

PUPILS AND TEACHERS

The quality of the relationships between pupils and teachers, and between the pupils themselves, is a further factor determining, within the social environment of the school, the impact of the teachers' attempts to educate for a multicultural society. Pupils have a vital part to play in the process of collaboration. Indeed, if this process is not extended to include the pupils themselves, then whatever innovations are attempted in the name of multi-cultural education are likely to be severely limited. Anyone concerned with establishing within a school the conditions necessary for change should pay particular attention to the ways in which pupils and teachers can begin to learn together.

One way is for teachers always to make explicit to pupils the point and purpose of any task that is set. Pupils' own perceptions of innovation are rarely monitored, or even acknowledged, when developmental work is attempted in schools. Yet, these perceptions affect quite profoundly the value of the work undertaken. No matter how clearly thought out a scheme of work may be, it will fail if the pupils have no frame of reference by which to grasp its significance. The first task of the innovator is, therefore, to explain to the class why they are doing what they are doing and to discuss with them their own feelings about the task.

Without this degree of openness it is impossible to create an atmosphere of trust in which pupils are able to talk freely to one another, and to the teacher, about their own attitudes and assumptions. Such trust is essential in the area of multicultural education which touches on highly controversial isues, about which pupils are likely to be confused and perhaps troubled. Any discussion of racism, for example, is bound to involve sooner or later some consideration of our own attitudes and how these attitudes are related to discriminatory practices within society. Such discussion will remain hopelessly superficial unless pupils and teachers can exchange their views frankly and honestly.

This is not to say that teachers should condone racist views, but that they should respect their pupils sufficiently to challenge such views, when they arise, by recourse to reason rather than dogmatic assertion. There is, on the other hand, little point in the teacher adopting a position of academic, or what is sometimes referred to as 'procedural' (Stenhouse, 1983, 133–9), neutrality when confronted with views of this kind. By adopting such a stance teachers risk confusing pupils as to their real intentions. What is needed is a clear statement of principle, backed up by rational argument and relevant information. If these fail to convince, the right to differ should be upheld.

Above all, teachers need to show that they are listening and that they are willing, if necessary, to rethink their own attitudes in the light of the pupils' own insights. In that way dialogue becomes a vehicle for change. There is, after all, no point in asking pupils for their opinions if one is unwilling to respond to what they are saying. Pupils see through such a ploy. They realise that it has little, if anything, to do with genuine collaboration and quickly write it off as a waste of time. Only when honest dialogue is accompanied by a willingness to change does it enable both pupils and teachers to learn together.

CROSS-CULTURAL COUNSELLING

An aspect of the teacher's pastoral role that has received scant attention within educational circles is cross-cultural counselling. In examining this aspect of the teacher's role I shall, inevitably, be narrowing the focus of attention onto the concerns of those teachers who work in a multiracial context. For those who work in other settings, however, this section may still have some relevance, since the problem it poses is common to a wide range of situations. The estrangement of teachers from the cultural world of their pupils is by no means limited to the multiracial school.

The problem of estrangement is particularly acute in counselling, the core of which, according to Colin Lago, is the attempt 'to understand the client as if one were the client' (Lago, 1981, 62). From the client's', or in our case the pupil's, point of view this process offers what the British Association for Counselling (BAC) refers to as an 'opportunity to explore, discover and clarify ways of living more resourcefully and towards greater well-being' (British Association for Counselling, 1979). Counselling, so conceived, is the art of listening.

Disciplined listening of this kind is never an easy matter. When conducted in a multiracial context it may present the teacher with what has been described as an 'almost impossible task' (Lago and Ball, 1983, 39). The disparity of experience between the counsellor and pupil in certain cross-cultural encounters poses a crucial question: How, as a white teacher, can I begin to understand the black pupil 'as if' I were that pupil, when I have had no experience of what it is to be a victim of racial prejudice and discrimination?

One answer to that question is simply 'You can't!': 'no matter how well-founded the intentions, there's no way a white man can ever know what it's like to live in a black skin' (Rack, 1978, 133). For the practising teacher any such denial will seem somewhat academic. The white teacher attempting to counsel the black pupil must, in practice, cling to the possibility that a wary, sympathetic imagination will win through. This is not to deny the importance of the black British person's self-determination, but simply to acknowledge the demands of the teacher's many-sided role. A more pragmatic response, then, is to admit that any attempt at cross-cultural counselling is fraught with difficulties, and to go on from there to try to understand more clearly what these difficulties are.

A large part of the problem in any cross-cultural encounter is ensuring that you are hearing what the pupil intends you to hear. The cultural differences between people of differing ethnic backgrounds may stretch the counsellor's skill in active, interpretive listening to its limit. These cultural differences include distinct patterns, not only of verbal and non-verbal behaviour, but of the social conventions governing each:

Verbal behaviour. Difficulties may arise over the meaning of particular words and phrases; as in the case of the Creole speaker, for whom the expression, 'Mind you don't go home,' means the exact opposite of what it means to the speaker of standard English. Other difficulties may centre on the intonation patterns employed by various speakers. By placing the emphasis on different parts of the sentence, the speaker for whom English is a second language may, for example, communicate to an 'English as mother tongue' speaker a tone or attitude that is quite unintended.

Non-verbal behaviour. An example which illustrates the extent to which apparently minor aspects of non-verbal behaviour can affect our assessment of individuals comes from a recent report which found that half of the Asian student doctors taking an important Royal College examination were failing it because of their pattern of eye contact. Their avoidance of eye contact with their examiners throughout the examination was misinterpreted as diffidence, or even shiftiness, by those for whom it was intended as a mark of respect. The consequences of this misinterpretation, as far as the teachers' career prospects were concerned, were disastrous (Ezard, 1983).

Social conventions. Difficulties may also centre on what is felt to be appropriate within the counselling situation. Colin Lago has suggested, for example, that 'whereas for an Englishman it may be appropriate to ask reasonably direct questions early in an interview, such directness, to an Asian interviewee, would be interpreted as most impolite' (Lago, 1981, 61).

The point was made more strongly by a group of third-year Bengali girls in an east London comprehensive school. When asked, in the course of a class discussion, where they might go for help and advice if they needed it, one of the pupils replied: 'We wouldn't. We don't want our inside problems to go out.'

A crucial step towards overcoming the kinds of difficulties mentioned above is simply to acknowledge that, in cross-cultural counselling, there will almost certainly be aspects of each person's style of communication that the other is unaware of; to be sensitive, in other words, to the fact that 'we don't know what we don't know' about the other person's communicative intent. To discover what these areas of ignorance are, and how they affect the counselling task, requires a willingness on behalf of the counsellor to learn something of the child's cultural background. It is not, however, an abstract or academic knowledge that is needed – although books may help – but a personal knowledge that comes from genuine dialogue.

In cross-cultural counselling, as in any other kind of counselling, teachers must feel their way, acquiring the necessary skills and expertise as they proceed. There is a danger in prespecifying, as Douglas Hamblin (after Rogers, 1951, and Truax and Carkhuff, 1967) has done, 'the personality of the counsellor' (Hamblin, 1974, 11–14). Julian Wohl (1976) has suggested, for example, that the qualities of genuineness, warmth and empathy, as initially defined by Rogers (1951), are inappropriate in counselling situations involving people of Burmese origin, who might rate them as evidence of weakness and incompetence on the part of the counsellor. Insofar as the notion of 'the personality of the counsellor' is a useful one, it should be seen as denoting a product as well as a prerequisite of effective pastoral work in schools.

There is an equal danger, however, of oversensitivity. The teacher who, as Paul Zec put it, 'approaches cultural differences as something "given" and not to be, as it were, tampered with . . . provides logical support for just that which people most concerned with multicultural education abhor – stereotyping of pupils by teachers' (Zec, 1981, 42–3). To be effective pastorally, teachers need to be sure about the general principles – such as that of respect for persons – which guide their work. Without a keen awareness of their own cultural framework and a sense of confidence in the educational values to which they adhere, teachers are unlikely to be of much use to their pupils. For it is only possible to understand a pupil 'as if' one were that pupil, by first finding out what it is in oneself that has to be bracketed in order to achieve that understanding. Counselling has nothing to do with self-surrender.

Nor does it have to do with imposing one's own preconceptions on the pupil. Only by approaching the other person with great tact and circumspection can the counsellor avoid stereotyping the pupil. Although the identity of minority ethnic groups in Britain is shaped by their members' common experience of racial discrimination and prejudice, each such group contains within it great diversity of attitude and opinion. Counsellors who rely on the traditional culture of a particular group as their only reference point will be unaware of the adaptations which many immigrant groups have already made. They will also be insensitive to the situation of those born in Britain who are forming a distinct culture of their own, different from both that of their parents and that of white society. For counsellors who want to see beyond the stereotypes, the most authoritative primary source must be the case in front of them.

In an article to which I have already referred, Colin Lago and Russell Ball offer what they describe as 'some tentative guidelines for those involved in cross-cultural counselling'. These sum up many of the points mentioned in this section. The following items from their checklist are essential starting points for any teachers trying to develop their counselling skills within a multicultural context:

- To have a genuine interest in and knowledge of the client's culture.
- To develop awareness of one's own cultural framework and how this may differ from that of the client.
- To attempt to gain knowledge of the moral values of the other culture.
- To be aware of our own cultural norms about verbal and non-verbal communication.
- The counsellor needs to have security within his own cultural identity and personality to risk exploring in the client's cultural framework and yet not get lost in it.
- The counsellor needs to consider carefully many ethical concepts, including confidentiality, his role in the situation, his underlying philosophy, all of which may have very different connotations for the client.
- In some complex situations a model of minimum intervention may be appropriate.
- To develop knowledge of when it may be appropriate to refer people to other forms of help, possibly from their own cultures, and try to build a network of such provision.

(Lago and Ball, 1983, 48)

REFERENCES

British Association for Counselling (1979), *Counselling: Definition of Terms*

Ezard, J. (1983), *The Guardian*, 7 January

Hamblin, D. (1974), *The Teacher and Counselling*, Blackwell

Lago, C. (1981), 'Cross-cultural Counselling: Some Developments, Thoughts and Hypotheses', *New Community*, 9, 1 (Spring–Summer), pp. 59–63

Lago, C. and Ball, R. (1983), 'The Almost Impossible Task: Helping in a Multicultural Context', *Multiracial Education*, 11, 2 (Spring), pp. 39–50

Rack, P. (1978), *In Working With Asian Young People*, National Association for Asian Youth

Rogers, C. (1951), *Client Centred Therapy*, Houghton Mifflin

Stenhouse, L. (1983), *Authority, Education and Emancipation*, Heinemann

Truax, C. and Carkhuff, R. (1967), *Towards Effective Counselling and Psychotherapy*, Aldine

Wohl, J. (1976), 'Interactional Psychotherapy Issues: Questions and Reflections', in P. Pederson, W. Loner and J. Dragnus, *Counselling Across Cultures*, University of Hawaii, Honolulu

Zec, P. (1981), 'Multicultural Education: What Kind of Relativism is Possible?', in A. James and R. Jeffcoate (eds), pp. 29–44

Part IV

Classrooms

This Part opens with an extract from a much-quoted book on *Life in Classrooms* by Philip Jackson. The context is the USA but the message is universal, *in three major ways, as members of crowds, as potential recipients of praise or reproof and as pawns of institutional authorities, pupils are confronted with aspects of reality that, at least during their childhood years, are relatively confined to the hours spent in classrooms.*

The chapters that follow review a range of research and writing which focuses on the classroom. Taylor reviews a number of classroom variables that have attracted both political interest and research attention. He points to the importance of the research but also argues that *detailed study and analysis cannot generate comprehensive and situationally specific procedural rules that teachers can learn and then apply in order to consistently obtain a desired outcome.* Bennett and Dunne, who in Part II were arguing for the significance that should be attached to co-operative forms of learning, quote Kagan's assertion that *the most neglected topic in co-operative learning is classroom management.* And they then explore a number of management factors that teachers ought to take into account when setting up groupwork. Neil Mercer's chapter explains how *language is at the heart of education. It is,* he argues, *the principal means of communication between teachers and learners. It is also,* he suggests, *the vital means by which we represent our own thoughts to ourselves and it is mainly through the medium of spoken and written language that successive generations of society benefit from their forebears.* The form that communication takes in the classroom is, therefore, a crucial variable. The interactions that take place in classrooms are, however, influenced by gender. Delamont, in a second contribution, uses data from several studies of schools to illustrate ways in which sexual differentiation and discrimination take place. She suggests, using a range of examples, *that some of the ways in which classroom practice is sexually divisive can seem 'trivial' or even 'natural' but that both labels prevent change.* McManus addresses squarely an issue of overriding concern to new teachers: how to avoid pupil disruption or misbehaviour in class. He looks at a range of research evidence, much of which focuses on the experience of the student or new teacher. The reading ranges across a range of classroom variables to show how different processes interact to allow for effective management.

The Part concludes with two chapters that look at the ways information technology is, and will be increasingly, changing the learning environment of the classroom. Noel Thompson describes the different ways in which *computers will break down school walls (metaphorically!). Improved communications through electronic mail, electronic conferencing and the potential for tutoring at a distance will, he argues, make it possible to be much more flexible about classwork in schools and formalised learning in college.* Finally, an OECD report provides a detailed analysis of the trends in the development of information technology that have the potential to revolutionise classrooms, schools and the whole concept of the learning process.

Chapter 20

Life in classrooms

Philip Jackson

School is a place where tests are failed and passed, where amusing things happen, where new insights are stumbled upon, and skills acquired. But it is also a place in which people sit, and listen, and wait, and raise their hands, and pass out paper, and stand in line, and sharpen pencils. School is where we encounter both friends and foes, where imagination is unleashed and misunderstanding brought to ground. But it is also a place in which yawns are stifled and initials scratched on desktops, where milk money is collected and recess lines are formed. Both aspects of school life, the celebrated and the unnoticed, are familiar to all of us, but the latter, if only because of its characteristic neglect, seems to deserve more attention than it has received to date from those who are interested in education.

In order to appreciate the significance of trivial classroom events it is necessary to consider the frequency of their occurrence, the standardisation of the school environment, and the compulsory quality of daily attendance. We must recognise, in other words, that children are in school for a long time, that the settings in which they perform are highly uniform, and that they are there whether they want to be or not. Each of these three facts, although seemingly obvious, deserves some elaboration, for each contributes to our understanding of how students feel about and cope with their school experience.

The amount of time children spend in school can be described with a fair amount of quantitative precision, although the psychological significance of the numbers involved is another matter entirely. In most states the school year legally comprises 180 days. A full session on each of those days usually lasts about six hours (with a break for lunch), beginning somewhere around nine o'clock in the morning and ending about three o'clock in the afternoon. Thus, if a student never misses a day during the year, he spends a little more than 1,000 hours under the care and tutelage of teachers. If he has attended kindergarten and was reasonably regular in his attendance during the grades, he will have logged a little more than 7,000 classroom hours by the time he is ready for junior high school.

The magnitude of 7,000 hours spread over six or seven years of a child's life is difficult to comprehend. On the one hand, when placed beside the total number of hours the child has lived during those years it is not very great – slightly more than one-tenth of his life during the time in question, about one-third of his hours of sleep during that period. On the other hand, aside from sleeping, and perhaps playing, there is no other activity that occupies as much of the child's time as that involved in attending school. Apart from the bedroom (where he has his eyes closed most of the time) there is no single enclosure in which he spends a longer time than he does in the classroom. From the age of six onward he is a more familiar sight to his teacher than to his father, and possibly even to his mother.

A classroom, like a church auditorium, is rarely seen as being anything other than that which it is. No one entering either place is likely to think that he is in a living room, or a grocery store, or a train station. Even if he entered at midnight or at some other time when the activities of the people would not give the function away, he would have no difficulty understanding what was *supposed* to go on there. Even devoid of people, a church is a church and a classroom, a classroom.

This is not to say, of course, that all classrooms are identical, anymore than all churches are. Clearly there are differences, and sometimes very extreme ones, between any two settings. One has only to think of the wooden benches and planked floor of the early American classroom as compared with the plastic chairs and tile flooring in today's suburban schools. But the resemblance is still there despite the differences, and, more important, during any particular historical period the differences are not that great. Also, whether the student moves from first to sixth grade on floors of vinyl tile or oiled wood, whether he spends his days in front of a black, blackboard or a green one, is not as important as the fact that the environment in which he spends these six or seven years is highly stable.

In their efforts to make their classrooms more homelike, elementary school teachers often spend considerable time fussing with the room's decorations. Bulletin boards are changed, new pictures are hung, and the seating arrangement is altered from circles to rows and back again. But these are surface adjustments at best, resembling the work of the inspired housewife who rearranges the living room furniture and changes the colour of the drapes in order to make the room more 'interesting'. School bulletin boards may be changed but they are never discarded, the seats may be rearranged but thirty of them are there to stay, the teacher's desk may have a new plant on it but there it sits, as ubiquitous as the roll-down maps, the olive drab wastebasket, and the pencil sharpener on the window ledge.

Even the odors of the classroom are fairly standardised. Schools may use different brands of wax and cleaning fluid, but they all seem to contain similar ingredients, a sort of universal smell which creates an aromatic background that permeates the entire building. Added to this, in each classroom, is the slightly acrid scent of chalk dust and the faint hint of fresh wood from the pencil shavings. In some rooms, especially at lunch time, there is the familiar odour of orange peels and peanut butter sandwiches, a blend that mingles in the late afternoon (following recess) with the delicate pungency of children's perspiration. If a person stumbled into a classroom blindfolded, his nose alone, if he used it carefully, would tell him where he was.

All of these sights and smells become so familiar to students and teachers alike that they exist dimly, on the periphery of awareness. Only when the classroom is encountered under somewhat unusual circumstances, does it appear, for a moment, a strange place filled with objects that command our attention. On these rare occasions when, for example, students return to school in the evening, or in the summer when the halls ring with the hammers of workmen, many features of the school environment that have merged into an undifferentiated background for its daily inhabitants suddenly stand out in sharp relief. This experience, which obviously occurs in contexts other than the classroom, can only happen in settings to which the viewer has become uncommonly habituated.

Not only is the classroom a relatively stable physical environment, it also provides a fairly constant social context. Behind the same old desks sit the same old students, in front of the familiar blackboard stands the familiar teacher. There are changes, to be sure – some students come and go during the year and on a few mornings the children are greeted at the door by a strange adult. But in most cases these events are sufficiently uncommon to create a flurry of excitement in the room. Moreover, in most elementary classrooms the social composition is not only stable, it is also physically arranged with considerable regularity. Each student has an assigned seat and, under normal circumstances, that is where he is to be found. The practice of assigning seats makes it possible for the teacher or a student to take attendance at a glance. A quick visual sweep is usually sufficient to determine who is there and who is not. The ease with which this procedure is accomplished reveals more eloquently than do words how accustomed each member of the class is to the presence of every other member.

An additional feature of the social atmosphere of elementary classrooms deserves at least passing comment. There is a social intimacy in schools that is unmatched elsewhere in our society. Buses and movie theatres may be more crowded than classrooms, but people rarely stay in such densely populated settings for extended periods of time and while there, they usually are not expected to concentrate on work or to interact with each other. Even factory workers are not clustered as close together as students in a standard classroom. Indeed, imagine what would happen if a factory the size of a typical elementary school contained three or four hundred adult workers. In all likelihood the unions would not allow it. Only in schools do thirty or more people spend several hours each day literally side by side. Once we leave the classroom we seldom again are required to have contact with so many people for so long a time.

A final aspect of the constancy experienced by young students involves the ritualistic and cyclic quality of the activities carried on in the classroom. The daily schedule, as an instance, is commonly divided into definite periods during which specific subjects are to be studied or specific activities engaged in. The content of the work surely changes from day to day and from week to week, and in this sense there is considerable variety amid the constancy. But spelling still comes after arithmetic on Tuesday morning, and when the teacher says, 'All right class, now take out your spellers', his announcement comes as no surprise to the students. Further, as they search in their desks for their spelling textbooks, the children may not know what new words will be included in the day's assignment, but they have a fairly clear idea of what the next twenty minutes of class time will entail.

Despite the diversity of subject matter content, the identifiable forms of classroom activity are not great in number. The labels: 'seatwork', 'group discussion', 'teacher demonstration', and 'question-and-answer period' (which would include work 'at the board'), are sufficient to categorise most of the things that happen when class is in session. 'Audio-visual display', 'testing session', and 'games' might be added to the list, but in most elementary classrooms they occur rarely.

Each of these major activities is performed according to rather well-defined rules which the students are expected to understand and obey – for example, no loud talking during seatwork, do not interrupt someone else during discussion, keep your eyes on your own paper during tests, raise your hand if you have a question. Even in the early grades these rules are so well understood by the students (if not completely internalised) that the teacher has only to give very abbreviated signals ('Voices, class'. 'Hands, please'.) when violations are perceived. In many classrooms a weekly time schedule is permanently posted so that everyone can tell at a glance what will happen next.

Thus, when our young student enters school in the morning he is entering an environment with which he has become exceptionally familiar through prolonged exposure. Moreover, it is a fairly stable environment – one in which the physical objects, social relations, and major activities remain much the same from day to day, week to week, and even, in certain respects, from year to year. Life there resembles life in other contexts in some ways, but not all. There is, in other words, a uniqueness to the student's world. School, like church and home, is someplace special. Look where you may, you will not find another place quite like it.

There is an important fact about a student's life that teachers and parents often prefer not to talk about, at least not in front of students. This is the fact that young people have to be in school, whether they want to be or not. In this regard students have something in common with the members of two other of our social institutions that have involuntary attendance: prisons and mental hospitals. The analogy, though dramatic, is not intended to be shocking, and certainly there is no comparison between the unpleasantness of life for inmates of our prisons and mental institutions, on the one hand, and the daily travails of a first or second grader, on the other. Yet the school child, like the incarcerated adult, is, in a sense, a prisoner. He too must come to grips with the inevitability of his experience. He too must develop strategies for dealing with the conflict that frequently arises between his natural desires and interests on the one hand and institutional expectations on the other. The thousands of hours spent in the highly stylised environment of the elementary classroom are not, in an ultimate sense, a matter of choice, even though some children might prefer school to play. Many seven-year-olds skip happily to school, and as parents and teachers we are glad they do, but we stand ready to enforce the attendance of those who are more reluctant. And our vigilance does not go unnoticed by children.

In sum, classrooms are special places. The things that happen there and the ways in which they happen combines to make these settings different from all others. This is not to say, of course, that there is no similarity between what goes on in school and the students' experiences elsewhere. Classrooms are indeed like homes and churches and hospital wards in many important respects. But not in all.

The things that make schools different from other places are not only the paraphernalia of learning and teaching and the educational content of the dialogues that take place there, although these are the features that are usually singled out when we try to portray what life in school is really like. It is true that nowhere else do we find blackboards and teachers and textbooks in such abundance and nowhere else is so much time spent on reading, writing, and arithmetic. But these obvious characteristics do not constitute all that is unique about this environment. There are other features, much less obvious though equally omnipresent, that help to make up 'the facts of life', as it were, to which students must adapt. From the standpoint of understanding the impact of school life on the student some features of the classroom that are not immediately visible are fully as important as those that are.

The characteristics of school life to which we now turn our attention are not commonly mentioned by students, at least not directly, nor are they apparent to the casual observer. Yet they are as real, in a sense, as the unfinished portrait of Washington that hangs above the cloakroom door. They comprise three facts of life with which even the youngest student must learn to deal and may be introduced by the key words: *crowds*, *praise*, and *power*.

Learning to live in a classroom involves, among other things, learning to live in a crowd. This simple truth has already been mentioned, but it requires greater elaboration. Most of the things that are done in school are done with others, or at least in the presence of others, and this fact has profound implications for determining the quality of a student's life.

Of equal importance is the fact that schools are basically evaluative settings. The very young student may be temporarily fooled by tests that are presented as games, but it doesn't take long before he begins to see through the subterfuge and comes to realise that school, after all, is a serious business. It is not only what you do there but what others think of what you do that is important. Adaptation to school life requires the student to become used to living under the constant condition of having his words and deeds evaluated by others.

School is also a place in which the division between the weak and the powerful is clearly drawn. This may sound like a harsh way to describe the separation between teachers and students, but it serves to emphasise a fact that is often overlooked, or touched upon gingerly at best. Teachers are indeed more powerful than students, in the sense of having greater responsibility for giving shape to classroom events, and this sharp difference in authority is another feature of school life with which students must learn how to deal.

In three major ways then – as members of crowds, as potential recipients of praise or reproof, and as pawns of institutional authorities – students are confronted with aspects of reality that at least during their childhood years are relatively confined to the hours spent in classrooms. Admittedly, similar conditions are encountered in other environments. Students, when they are not performing as such, must often find themselves lodged within larger groups, serving as targets of praise or reproof, and being bossed around or guided by persons in positions of higher authority. But these kinds of experience are particularly frequent while school is in session and it is likely during this time that adaptive strategies having relevance for other contexts and other life periods are developed.

Chapter 21

Classroom variables

William Taylor

The volume of research on school-level variables that influence effectiveness is matched, or even exceeded, by that on classroom factors. What *does* make for better teaching? It helps to know, even if we are still left with the problem of how best practice is made more general and consistent.

Several things are obvious from the start. Teaching is an art, not a technology. Detailed study and analysis, however careful, cannot generate comprehensive and situationally specific procedural rules which teachers can learn and then apply in order consistently to obtain a desired outcome. There is no single route to classroom effectiveness. Teachers know this. It is one of the reasons that makes them wary of proposals for evaluation and appraisal which do not recognise the complexity of the teaching/learning relationship. It is here that detailed studies in the ethnographic tradition of how teachers work have been so valuable.

Regularities revealed by even the most carefully designed survey cannot of their nature do justice to the uniqueness of each successful teacher's art. This does not mean that lists of effective practices derived from surveys are useless. But we have to recognise that such schedules are in themselves only of *limited* use; it is only when translated into coherent programmes of initial and in-service training and experience, mediated by skilled and sensitive practitioners through precept, principle and practice, that they begin to influence what you and I do in classroom, laboratory, lecture room or administrative office.

One set of classroom variables that receives a lot of attention in the literature is the quality of teachers' management and organisation for learning. One early study, much quoted in subsequent reviews, (Brophy 1979, 1983) identifies five characteristics of effective classroom management behaviour.

First, 'withitness' – awareness of what is going on everywhere in the classroom, being able to interpret and act upon the meaning of verbal and visual cues.

Second, 'overlapping' – the ability to handle a number of different tasks simultaneously without, as it were, the edges showing.

Third, momentum and pacing – pursuing the objects of a lesson in a brisk but smooth manner, taking potentially disruptive interruptions in one's stride.

Fourth, maintaining a high level of group alertness and accountability – by random questioning, and by keeping students 'attentive to presentations because something new or exciting could happen at any time, and to keep them accountable for learning the content by making them aware that they might be called on at any time'.

Finally, variety and challenge in what Americans call 'seatwork'. Much work has been done on this last point. It has produced interesting findings about the success rate that students need to achieve in order to maintain motivation and understanding when working individually. Success rates of 70–80 per cent are effective when a teacher is present to provide immediate feedback and to monitor responses. But in the case of homework and individual assignments, higher rates are needed if progress is to be maintained. Much more massive reinforcement of success is required than intuition indicates. Thus teachers' choice of questions and material in relation to the ability and responses of particular groups and individuals can be crucial to subsequent success. All this has implications for the quality of initial and in-service training.

In writing about these matters Gage (1984) refers not to the *science* of teaching, but the *scientific basis of the art of teaching*. He says:

> If teaching is an art in large degree, it cannot be taught in the same way that we use to train assembly-line workers, aircraft mechanics, or medical technicians. Teachers need more autonomy and more freedom to use their judgement than any workers of that kind. But teaching is an art with obligations to the society, with moral imperatives relating to the welfare of students and the body politic. So teachers cannot have the complete autonomy of the creative artist who can choose to be a surrealist, an atonalist, or a dadaist. Thus we need approaches to teacher education that will walk the path between unacceptable regimentation and unacceptable anarchy.

CLASSIFYING TEACHING STYLES

A lesson learned from studies of teaching styles is the difficulty of categorising teaching behaviour in terms such as progressive, traditional or formal. Some recent work on teaching styles, about to be published in a report from the National Foundation for Educational Research (NFER), and involving both longitudinal and cross-sectional studies, supports earlier findings that, depending upon circumstances, class teaching, group work and individualised approaches can all be equally successful (see Boydell 1980). The NFER researchers show that within particular teaching styles there are a number of specific characteristics and practices which make for less or more effective teaching. These they classify under the headings of discipline and control, classroom organisation and management, and instructional technique.

Aspects of instructional technique that made for success were: giving clear instructions and checking they had been understood; achieving an appropriate balance between instruction and classwork (in which connection an interesting non-linear relationship between academic interaction and pupil performance was shown); striking a balance between whole class teaching and attending to individual pupils; skilful use of questioning for purposes of recapitulation, to check that instructions have been understood, for exposition and to maintain order; and the application of immediate feedback – not only prompt marking, but also 'public praise and private criticism'.

The longitudinal aspect of the NFER study complicates the issue of style by suggesting that consistency in teacher effectiveness and teacher performance over two successive years was only 'moderate'. Much depends on the setting. Before any particular style can be recommended as 'effective' there needs to be a full appraisal of the nature and requirements of the subjects to be taught and of student characteristics, as well as of the attributes and preferences, strengths and weaknesses of teachers themselves.

As emphasised earlier, there is no simple technology of teaching. Teachers have to be flexible enough to adapt methods and styles to circumstances generated by the interaction between the characteristics of particular student groups and what it is intended should be acquired by way of information, understanding and skill. We are back to the need for a holistic approach. Comprehensive analyses of the teacher's task, thorough disaggregation of the elements that enter into particular teaching performances, and efforts to relate these to outcomes can all be valuable, especially in offering a more systematic structure for the professional aspects of initial training and INSET. Teachers need, however, the confidence, perceptiveness and flexibility that enable them to respond to circumstances that vary not just from year to year, but from day to day and period to period.

ACTIVE LEARNING TIME

One classroom variable with consistent positive relationships with achievement is the *time* available and used for learning. Studies have been made of the formal length of the school year, the school day and subject allocated time in relation to outcomes. Others have looked in somewhat more detail at students' actual involvement in instruction, as measured by attendance and engagement in learning activities. A number of studies have employed the measure of 'time on task', that is, the amount of time an average student is actively engaged in or attending to academic instruction or tasks. (Caldwell *et al.* 1982). Researchers have refined this measure as 'academic learning time', the amount of time a student spends attending to relevant academic tasks *while performing with a high rate of success*. Such a measure takes into account findings referred to earlier on rates of success needed to ensure progress. Academic learning time has been found to be strongly associated with achievement. All this makes it important that time available for learning is used to the full, and distribution of teacher and student effort during available time is such as to maximise 'time on task' and 'academic learning time' (Leach and Tunnicliffe 1984).

Some years ago, the NFER reported on studies of how primary and secondary teachers spend their day. Forty-three per cent of the teaching session time available to primary teachers was used for actual lesson instruction to a class, a group or an individual pupil. The corresponding figure for secondary teachers was 33 per cent. A further 16 per cent of primary teachers' time and 12 per cent of their secondary counterparts' time went on organising pupils, and the remainder on a variety of other tasks, including supervision, mechanical chores, lesson planning and so on.

Given the general tendency for time-related variables to correlate significantly with achievement, sharp variations in 'academic learning time' between schools and teachers, and over time in the same school and with the same teacher, are matters of some concern. Hilsum and Strong (1978) found large variations across the period of their study in the time devoted to various activities. In a single day, the amount of direct teaching undertaken might vary from $1^{1}/_{2}$ to $3^{1}/_{4}$ hours. US studies report time actually allocated for second-grade mathematics ranging from 24 minutes at one extreme to 61 minutes at another, and for second grade reading from 32 minutes to 131 minutes. This research has also shown considerable variations within classes on the amount of time that individual pupils spend on a particular subject – an example is quoted of a fifth-grade student spending 39 minutes on maths, while another in the same class spent 75 minutes (Caldwell *et al.* 1982).

PRAISING AND BLAMING

To conclude these few illustrative examples of variables, associated with achievement that have been the subject of systematic research, a word about praise.

Technically, we can regard praise as an aspect of the more general process of feedback. Psychologists have long been concerned with the role of praise in reinforcing behaviour. Some theories of teaching depend heavily on its use for the purposes of motivation and control. We do not have to be behaviourists, however, to recognise the importance of the part played by praise in almost every aspect of social life, including life in classrooms. Whether expressed in terms of the lapel button or teeshirt emblazoned 'Smile!', or in terms of behaviour reinforcement through positive feedback, we all recognise the importance of this aspect of handling relationships among individuals and in groups.

The choice of praise as the last of my examples of classroom variables that have been studied in connection with improving teaching is not, of course, accidental. The feelings aroused by formal appraisal and evaluation procedures are intimately connected with our personal response to praise and to blame. Very few observations we make about the behaviour of others, or which we hear or interpret about our own, are neutral.

According to that combination of nature and nurture that has made us what we are, there is great variation in need for and response to praise. At one end of the spectrum, excessive sensitivity can seriously inhibit action and create crippling anxiety. At the other, indifference to the judgements of others produces behaviour we label psychopathic.

There is no evidence that effective teaching is the prerogative of particular personality types. One reason why appraisal and evaluation need to be undertaken as close as possible to the actual work setting is the need to take fully into account the personality characteristics of those assessed or evaluated. What is water-off-a-duck's-back to one person can be a crushing rebuke to another. To depersonalise appraisal and evaluation is to destroy much of its purpose, but there is need nonetheless to ensure that the assessment dialogue is task-oriented.

REFERENCES

Boydell, D. (1980) 'The organisation of junior school classrooms: a follow-up survey', *Educational Research*, 23, 1, November.

Brophy, J. E. (1979) 'Teacher behaviour and its effects', *Journal of Educational Psychology*, 71, 6.

Brophy, J. E. (1983) 'Classroom organisation and management', *The Elementary School Journal*, 83, 4.

Caldwell, H. J., Huitt, W. G. and Graeber, A. O. (1982) 'Time spent in learning: implications from research', *The Elementary School Journal*, 82, 5.

Gage, N. (1984) *Hard Gains in the Soft Sciences: the Case of Pedagogy*, Bloomington, IN, Phi Delta Kappan.

Hilsum, S. and Cane, B. (1971) *The Teacher's Day*, Slough, National Foundation for Educational Research.

Hilsum, S. and Strong, B. (1978) *The Secondary Teacher's Day*, Slough, National Foundation for Educational Research.

Leach, D. J. and Tunnicliffe, M. R. (1984) 'The relative influence of time variables on primary mathematics achievement', *Australian Journal of Education*, 28, 2.

Chapter 22

Managing groupwork

Neville Bennett and Elisabeth Dunne

In this chapter, two major features in the management of groupwork are discussed: first, general classroom management, which provides the context for effective ways of working and, second, the choosing of groups that are likely to co-operate successfully.

CLASSROOM MANAGEMENT

> If the institution of cooperative learning is not accompanied with an effective classroom management system, serious problems are likely to occur. In my experience the single most important but most neglected topic in cooperative learning is classroom management.
>
> (Kagan, 1988)

The national curriculum asks that teachers should set up different groups for different tasks and purposes. Our concern in this section is thus to shed some light on management factors that teachers ought to take into account when setting up groups for co-operative work. Since one of our major interests lies in the ways that teachers can reorganise their time, particularly so that assessment demands can be met, we generally recommend that all groups work on the same task at the same time, at least when resources allow. . . . When teachers use this organisational strategy, their management burden is eased, and demands and pressures on their time become fewer. There are two major reasons for this. First, when all children work on the same task, it is easier for the teacher to predict the kinds of problem that will emerge and to concentrate on their solution – rather than responding to the wide range of both procedural and cognitive demands that occur with individualised work, or when each group has a different task. Second, co-operative groupwork encourages children to take on more responsibility for their own work and the management of their own groups.

A management system which allows for a whole class to be working in groups at the same time and on the same task is one that we would want to encourage and develop. This does not mean that it is the only way in which groups should function, nor does it mean that it is the only management system that should be adopted. However, for that part of the curriculum which lends itself to co-operative groupwork, it is a system which enables teachers to focus clearly on the content of a task, and to be specifically prepared for the kinds of materials, questions, problems, and so on which emerge from that one task. This, in turn, means that they are likely to be better prepared to cope with pupil demands. It is also a system which is designed to ease the complexities of management and is most likely to give teachers time for observation or assessment.

Kagan (1988), an American, stresses the importance of managing the structure and sequence of groupwork lessons, especially since he believes that teachers will have to rethink their management strategies.

> There are two major topics to cover with regard to managing the cooperative classroom: (1) managing student behaviour and (2) managing the structure and sequence of the lesson. In both areas, classroom management differs radically from classroom management in the traditional classroom.

The changes demanded of American teachers may be more drastic than those needed in British classrooms. Kagan describes a scene to summarise the situation as he perceives it.

> It has become second nature to most teachers to exert energy keeping students quiet and attending only to the teacher or text. Teachers forget that they are demanding that students not do what they most want to do – interact with their peers. It is no wonder that teachers maintaining a traditional classroom end up so exhausted. They are bucking the basic nature of the student. Students want to question, discuss, argue and share. It is the great strength of cooperative learning that it channels this natural intelligence toward positive academic and social outcomes. In the process, however, great energy is released among students and the effective cooperative learning teacher must know how to manage a classroom of teams.

In British primary classrooms, however, teachers are well used to children being seated in groups and rearrangement of furniture for co-operative work will seldom be necessary. In addition, teachers have allowed and encouraged talking for many years, so that noise level is unlikely to be a feature of concern. In other areas of management, changes will need to be similar on both sides of the Atlantic, particularly with regard to the teacher's role. Kagan emphasises how, in more traditional lessons, teachers provide an input which is followed by individual practice or application; for co-operative learning, the lessons may become structurally more complex – with both pupils and teacher assuming different roles in different parts of the lesson.

Although our own research suggests that teachers rarely set up group-

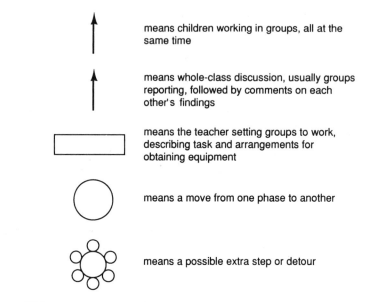

means children working in groups, all at the same time

means whole-class discussion, usually groups reporting, followed by comments on each other's findings

means the teacher setting groups to work, describing task and arrangements for obtaining equipment

means a move from one phase to another

means a possible extra step or detour

Figure 22.1

work in which all children tackle the same task at the same time, as is automatically assumed by Kagan, it is not actually a new idea. For example, Wynne Harlen (1985) provides a schematic way for thinking through flexible approaches to co-operative groupwork in science. She examines both teacher and pupil roles at different 'stages' of a lesson or topic, and shows how groupwork is just one of several kinds of learning context which needs support from other contributions. During each stage, the nature of interactions will be different and children will be involved in different kinds of activity.

Harlen provides a set of symbols to describe management possibilities (Figure 22.1). Harlen applies these symbols to four different kinds of 'topic' in science; one example is given below to demonstrate how co-operative groupwork is part of a whole system of management. The particular sequence is one that she sees as appropriate for questions such as: 'Which detergent washes the clothes best?'; 'Which polish is best for shining shoes?' and so on, but could be adapted to many other circumstances. A useful sequence for these topics allows children to work out how to decide which is 'best' during an initial period of free interaction with the materials (Figure 22.2).

This system of planning for the requirements of individual tasks is useful when thinking through the general organisation and management of lessons. Surprisingly, this kind of overall planning, even at its most simple level, may not frequently occur. For example, the use of class follow-up or reporting back sessions may not be widespread. In Kerry and Sands (1982), it is stated:

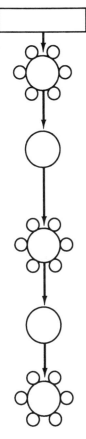

Teacher sets the scene, briefly describes problem of deciding 'which is best?'

Groups have equipment to explore and use while defining what 'best' means, what they have to do to decide it and what tests are necessary. A group record of their suggestions is drawn up.

Suggestions are collected from groups on the blackboard or large sheets of paper. Comments are invited about whether the suggested tests will show what they are intended to show, whether one test will be enough to decide 'best', etc. In some cases tests may already have been carried out roughly; suggestions should be made for improvement. Ways of recording results discussed.

Children carry out tests (probably different ones by each group or similar ones carried out in different ways). Teacher reminds them about recording; helps by showing techniques where necessary.

Groups' results reported to others, possibly by demonstrating what was done and showing results already drawn up in a table, graph or chart. Discussion of meaning of results, whether enough testing done to justify selection of 'best', etc. Critical review leading to suggestions for improvement.

Groups act on suggestions for extending and improving tests. May modify results and conclusions. Possible preparation of classroom display of results.

Figure 22.2

I did not see one lesson where there was a follow-up so that children could pool experience. I felt that this was one of the major weaknesses of the group work I saw. A follow-up would have been useful and helpful for the children for two important reasons:

1 to pool experience of work which had gone well or badly.
2 to revise and link together aspects of the whole topic when each group had been working on slightly different activities.

The power of a system which is dependent on reporting back, sharing activities, knowledge, ideas and so on, both with the teacher and other class members, is inevitably lost if different groups are working in different curriculum areas or on completely different subject content. However, co-operative groupwork is likely to be most effective when used as part of a whole series of activities and part of a co-operative process involving the whole class.

CHOOSING GROUPS

For myself, as the teacher, the major difficulty was the initial choosing of the groups. It was necessary to take into account the children's ability, sex and personality.

Eggleston and Kerry (1988) suggest that setting up groups needs serious attention; a learning tool which has great potential may not be effectively utilised, they say, since teachers do not have efficient knowledge of group dynamics. They are, however, fully aware of a central problem:

in a typical class of top juniors there may be six years difference between the reading ages of the ablest and least able readers; and other abilities will be similarly disparate. For this reason, and because the whole philosophy of the mixed-ability class seems to run counter to grouping by ability, teachers are often at a loss to know how to assign pupils to working groups.

When setting up groupwork, one of the major questions to be addressed has to be: 'What is the best way to arrange the groups?' This is a question for which it is not easy to provide a cut-and-dried response since few studies have directly investigated the problem. Indeed Biott (1984) concluded that it is impossible to opt for any one best composition for groups, since 'decisions about grouping a class will have to be made in a specific context. No generalised strategy is appropriate.'

There is, however, a growing body of research which has highlighted more appropriate or less appropriate features in terms of group size and composition, and details of these are outlined below.

Group size

In Britain, teachers tend to seat their pupils in groups of between four and six children (HMI, 1978; Bennett *et al.*, 1984); this pattern no doubt reflecting attempts to make the best use of space and furnishing constraints as well as curriculum resources. So far as co-operative groupwork is concerned, it remains difficult to give hard-and-fast rules about optimal size.

Biott (1984) suggests that there should be no fixed rules, with groups of three, four or five being satisfactory, since any decisions made will need to be dependent on the classroom context. In contrast to this, Kagan (1988) is very clear about group size, since it will have a marked impact on the opportunity for, and the nature of, children's interactions. He points out that the number of children in a group will determine the number of lines of communication and hence states: 'Teams of four are ideal. A team of three is often a dyad and an outsider; in a team of three there are three possible lines of communication; in a team of four there are six. Doubling the lines of

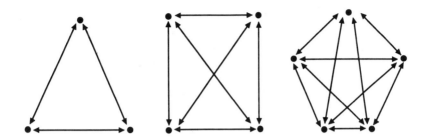

Figure 22.3 Lines of communication in groups of three to five pupils

communication increases learning potential. . . . Teams of five often leave an odd man out and leave less time for individual participation.'

When this is shown in diagrammatic form (Figure 22.3), it becomes instantly clear that the impact of group size is inevitably great and that a group of four will allow for a range of possibilities without making the 'lines of communication' too complex. For our own research, a team of teachers in one school spent the best part of a year experimenting with group size and reported that, in their experience, teams of four did seem to be the most effective. The National Oracy Project (1990) also suggest that groups of four can be used as a strategy for developing co-operation:

> As a generalization, younger and quieter children seem to do better in pairs than in larger groups. A useful strategy is to start children off in friendship pairs and then put two pairs together to share what they have done. This means that each pair has a contribution to make.

There is a good deal of evidence that pairs of children will work well together (see the ever-increasing literature on peer-tutoring; for example, Topping (1988)) but in our own research we have not used pairs.

As a generalisation, it does seem that groups of three and four are the most likely to co-operate to good purpose; that groups of five may divide into a dyad and a trio, or may allow individuals to opt out; and that larger groups will certainly split up into smaller groupings, with the possibility of opting out made far more likely.

REFERENCES

Bennett, N., Desforges, C., Cockburn, A. and Wilkinson, B. (1984) *The Quality of Pupil Learning Experiences*, London, Erlbaum.

Biott, C. (1984) *Getting on Without the Teacher*, Sunderland Polytechnic, Centre for Educational Research and Development.

Eggleston, J. and Kerry, T. (1988) *Topic Work in the Primary School*, London, Routledge.

Harlen, W. (1985) *Taking the Plunge*, London, Heinemann.

Her Majesty's Inspectorate (1978) *Primary Education in England*, London, HMSO.

Kagan, S. (1988) *Cooperative Learning: Resources for Teachers*, Riverside, University of California.

Kerry, T. and Sands, M. (1982) *Handling Classroom Groups: a Teaching Skills Workbook*, Basingstoke and London, Macmillan Educational.

National Oracy Project (1990) *Teaching, Talking and Learning in Key Stage One*, York, NCC.

Topping, K. (1988) *The Peer Tutoring Handbook*, London, Croom Helm.

Chapter 23

Classrooms, language and communication

Neil Mercer

In English, we have the words 'teaching' and 'learning', but no single word for the process of 'teaching-and-learning'. (The term 'education' usually refers to something more general, and at an institutional level.) Perhaps this is why in Britain there is less discussion of the quality of the process as a whole, than of its supposed constituent parts. For example, explanations of why individual children succeed or fail in school are commonly couched in terms of individual intelligence, motivation or aptitudes for learning; while critical comments by politicians on the quality of British education seem to focus inexorably on the attributes and competences of teachers.

For anyone interested in what really goes on in schools or homes or any other educational settings, there are very good reasons for rejecting such partial perspectives on teaching-and-learning. The most obvious is that people do most of their learning by talking and interacting with other people. Another is that children's responses to tests of their aptitudes and competences have been found to be strongly influenced by the particular social, interpersonal circumstances in which the tests are carried out. Education at the classroom level needs to be recognised as a communicative process, in which the outcomes in terms of learning are jointly determined by the efforts of teachers and learners. It also needs to be recognised that this is a process for sharing knowledge, not simply acquiring it or transmitting it, and the prime medium for that sharing is language.

Language is at the heart of education not only because it is the principal means of communication between teachers and learners, but also for at least two other reasons. One is that language is a vital means by which we represent our own thoughts to ourselves. The Russian psychologist Vygotsky (1978) described language as a *psychological tool*, something each of us uses to make sense of experience. The second reason is that language is also our prime *cultural tool*. It is mainly through the medium of spoken and written language that successive generations of a society benefit from the experience of their forebears, and it is also through language that each new generation shares, disputes, resolves and refines its own experience.

Education is – or should be – a process for developing the effective use of both these language functions, psychological and cultural.

Becoming 'educated' essentially involves gaining entrance to an intellectual community. It is not simply a matter of acquiring a body of knowledge, and it certainly cannot be achieved through personal, unaided discovery. An educated person not only has access to a certain body of knowledge, but also has acquired a set of procedures for solving problems and a set of language practices for describing and discussing ideas, problems and the relationships between them. Becoming a 'scientist', for example, is not really about becoming more independent, detached, or abstract in one's manner of analysis and representation, but instead is largely a matter of learning to think, talk and write like other members of the scientific community. Of course, fields of knowledge are not static, and emergent scientists may use their entry into the discourse of the community to challenge and change established theories and practices. But education is always primarily a matter of social and linguistic enculturation.

IN THE CLASSROOM

To move from generalities to classroom events, consider the following piece of classroom discourse (Sequence 1, below). It was recorded in a primary school in the West Midlands in 1989. Two children, one 11 and one 5, were working together without their teacher. They were doing an activity of a kind which is increasingly common in British primary schools, in which an older and younger child work together as 'talk partners' on some specific task – see Madeley and Lautman (1991), and Meyer (1991), for fuller accounts of such activities: Sequence 1 can be heard on the audiocassette of the Open University INSET pack which contains these two articles. On this occasion (at which I was present), the older child (a girl called Michelle) and the younger (a boy called Ashley) were engaged in the retelling of his favourite picture-book story, *The Very Hungry Caterpillar* by Eric Carle (1986). Both Ashley and Michelle had read the book, but they did not have a copy of it with them during the activity. (Note: pauses of more than three seconds are indicated by //.)

Sequence 1: *The Very Hungry Caterpillar*

ASHLEY	MICHELLE
	1 Right what's your favourite book Ashley?
2 The Very Hungry Caterpillar	
	3 Is it a good book?
4 Yea	
	5 Can you tell me the story please?

6 Yea//in the light of the moon a egg lay on a leaf//

7 What happened next?

8 Um//8 Um//

9 Did he wake up?

10 No

11 He didn't? What happened then? Was it on a Sunday morning?

12 Yea

13 Right, can you carry on then? On a Sunday morning//did he pop out of the little egg?//

14 Yea

15 And what happened after that, then?

16 He started to look for food// and on Monday, he ate through two pears, and //on Wednesday he ate through three plums

17 He was greedy, weren't he? What did he eat on Thursday?

18 Four strawberries

19 Friday?

20 Four//five oranges

21 What else did he eat?

22 //Don't know

23 On Saturday what did he eat?

24 On Saturday he ate a slice of cherry chocolate cake, one ice cream, one pickle, one Swiss cheese, one//one slice of salami

25 Did he eat anything else?

26 One lollipop//

27 Any pie?

28 Some cherry pie//one cup cake//and a sausage

29 And a sausage. He was greedy wasn't he? What else happened?

30 And the next and that night he had a belly ache and the next day was Monday again and he ate through one nice green leaf and after that he felt much better.

Now he wasn't small any more he
was a big fat caterpillar. He built a
house round himself called a
cocoon//and he stayed in there for
more than two weeks and he
nibbled an 'ole and he pushed his
way out and he was a beautiful
butterfly

31 Lovely

In this episode we see Michelle helping Ashley to reconstruct the text of a book. This is accomplished through a conversation. We can infer some interesting things about Ashley's education from this conversation. In his re-telling, he reproduces not only the plot of the story, but also much of the actual written language of the book. He shows that he has learned the story as a piece of literature, an item of contemporary literary culture. And by providing this kind of re-telling he also shows that he is aware of what can be called an *educational ground rule*, namely that when asked to re-tell the story of a book you do so by keeping as closely as possible to the original text. Although he is not working here with a teacher, Ashley recognises the key contextual features of the situation, and so is able to act accordingly. It is important to note that developing this kind of awareness is not necessarily unproblematic for children. For example, the anthropologist Shirley Brice Heath (1982, 1983) has shown that differences between what counts as 'storytelling' in school and in their home community can be an important and enduring source of educational problems for children of some cultural backgrounds. I will say more about 'educational ground rules' later.

Sequence I also shows that both Ashley and Michelle have learned the discourse requirements for doing one kind of educational activity: they seem to have few problems in making a 'talk partners' activity happen as a joint enterprise. It is also very apparent that Michelle has developed the ability to engage in some other educational language practices: she has learned how to take a teacher's role. We see her 'setting up' the activity through her initial remarks. She asks questions in order to stimulate Ashley's recall (e.g. lines 7, 15, 21) rather than to elicit information of which she is truly ignorant. She gives him a series of 'prompts', switching from general questions to providing more specific clues from the story when she feels he is struggling (lines 7–13; 21–27). She reiterates what he has said (line 29) and provides supportive, evaluative feedback (lines 17, 29, 31). One way in which she perhaps behaves differently from most adult teachers is that she tolerates very long pauses before offering him further prompts (Edwards, 1992; Wood, 1992).

'Scaffolding' learning

In her role as surrogate teacher, Michelle elicits the whole story from Ashley: she demonstrates that he really knew it all himself. But his realisation of his knowledge for the purpose of this activity is achieved by her careful management and support of what could have been for Ashley too difficult and too daunting a task. A useful concept for describing what she does is that of *'scaffolding'*, of which Jerome Bruner says 'it refers to the steps taken to reduce the degrees of freedom in carrying out some task so that the child can concentrate on the difficult skill she is in the process of acquiring' (Bruner, 1978: 19). It represents the kind and quality of cognitive support which an adult or more competent peer can provide for a child's learning – a form of 'vicarious consciousness' (as Bruner also put it) which anticipates the child's own internalisation of mental function. (See Maybin, Mercer and Stierer, 1992, for a fuller discussion of 'scaffolding' in the classroom.)

Michelle and Ashley's activity is dependent on a great deal of prior, shared educational knowledge and experience. That knowledge and experience provides a *contextual framework* for their conversation and the task in hand. Although no teacher is directly involved, the sequence illustrates well how activity, and hence learning, in the classroom is accomplished through dialogue which is heavily context-dependent, with the context being constructed by speakers from their current and past shared experience. A person's education proceeds by the extension and revision of such contextual frameworks. The way in which Michelle highlights aspects of the structure and content of the story for Ashley may help him learn more about story-telling and books, and so guide his future literary, and literate, experience. He will almost certainly come away with his assumptions about educationally appropriate modes of story-telling confirmed. An activity of this kind, successfully completed, could also be expected to increase Ashley's confidence and fluency in demonstrating his knowledge and understanding through talk (a field of competence now formally included in the English national curriculum).

TEACHERS' COMMUNICATIONS WITH PUPILS

Vygotsky proposed that 'the very essence of cultural development is in the collision between mature cultural forms of behaviour with the primitive forms which characterise the child's behaviour' (Vygotsky, 1981: 151). If this is true, then the quality of interactions between adults and children is a crucial issue for any society. More specifically, the quality of communication between teachers and pupils is crucial for the quality of education.

Try asking someone why teachers need to talk to children. They will probably say because teachers must tell children what to do, how to do it, when to start and when to stop. Teachers certainly do those things, but they do much more. They assess children's learning through talking to children and listening to what they say, they provide children with educational experiences which would be hard to provide by any other means than talk (e.g. telling stories, reading poetry, describing events, supplying factual information at the right time and in an accessible form). And, of course, one very important function of talk for teachers is to control the behaviour of children. There has been a good deal of educational research on classroom talk as a medium for 'social control'. But only quite recently has there been much research into its function as a medium for sharing knowledge, and one through which adults influence the representations of reality, the interpretations of experience, which children eventually adopt.

At the classroom level, education proceeds by *the development of shared understanding*. Through talk and joint action, participants in the process of teaching and learning can build a body of common knowledge which provides a contextual basis for further educational activity. This applies to activities in which a teacher is talking with pupils, and to those in which pupils are working together. The extent to which educational knowledge becomes 'common' to teachers and pupils is one measure of the effectiveness of the educational process. One important and problematic aspect of the 'common knowledge' of classroom education is what I referred to earlier as *educational ground rules* (Edwards and Mercer, 1987; Sheeran and Barnes, 1991). By this is meant the implicit norms and expectations that it is necessary to take account of to participate successfully in educational discourse. Ground rules of this kind govern the language practices we observed Michelle and Ashley following in Sequence 1. Becoming educated means becoming able to follow the ground rules: but having acquired these rules, people then tend to assume that what is involved is no more than 'common sense'. As Sheeran and Barnes say, 'In spite of their importance, these tacit expectations or ground rules are seldom discussed with pupils, because the teachers themselves are largely unaware of them.' (1991: 2). They go on to show how many of the requirements for providing satisfactory essays and other written work in different school subjects are never made explicit to pupils. And even when some of those requirements are made clear, teachers hardly provide justifications which will help children understand *why* they should write in particular ways. Classroom research has provided many examples of how children's interpretations of the ground rules may differ in important ways from those of their classmates and/or their teachers. For example, while some children may see 'discussion group' activities as an opportunity for airing problems and misunderstandings, others in the same group may see them only as occasions on which you must try to demonstrate that you know the 'right answers'. Yet other children may think that that real imperative is to talk fluently and without hesitation, rather like in the radio programme *Just a Minute!* (Mercer, Edwards and Maybin, 1988). Research on GCSE oral English examinations has suggested that children sometimes graft the ground rules of TV 'chat shows' on to their discussions (Hewitt, 1989). There is evidence that when teachers bring ground rules for discussion out into the open for consideration with their classes, this can lead to improved motivation and levels of performance amongst the children. (Prentice, 1991; Steel, 1991; Dawes, Fisher and Mercer, 1992).

One striking feature of the language behaviour of teachers is that they ask a great many questions. Teachers use questions to monitor children's knowledge and understanding, so that they can evaluate their teaching, assess the learning of their pupils, and so plan ahead. However, teachers also use questions to try to shape the course of children's learning, and there is some controversy about how useful questions are as a strategy for doing so. (See chapters by Wood, Mercer, Edwards, Wells and Brierley *et al.* in Norman, 1992.) For example, Dillon (1982) and Wood (1992) argue that teachers' questions often constrain and limit the directions of classroom discussion in quite unfortunate ways. By requiring short, factual answers, teachers may actually inhibit pupils' intellectual activity. Wood (1992) shows that when teachers use other kinds of conversational strategies, such as offering their own reflective observations, this can encourage pupils to do likewise and can generate longer and more animated responses from pupils. However, while Wood provides a good example of a nursery teacher generating animated and extended responses from two four-year-old children (1992: 211–12), it is not clear that the talk in the example is related to a curriculum! The amount of lively talk which goes on during teaching-and-learning is not, in itself, a measure of its quality. The crucial issue for primary and secondary teachers is maintaining a suitable balance between, on the one hand, offering children opportunities for open-ended exploration and discussion and, on the other, fulfilling a responsibility for achieving established curriculum goals. It is generally accepted that this is a difficult balance to achieve.

There are some interesting examples of teachers' questions in Sequence 2 (below), which was videorecorded for an Open University course in a secondary school in Derbyshire. As part of their English studies, a class of fourteen-year-olds were engaged in an extended computer-based communication with children in a nearby primary school. In a 'fantasy adventure' setting, the secondary students were (in groups of three) pretending to be a group of characters stranded in time and space. Explanations of their predicaments and requests for solutions were e-mailed to the primary children, whose responses were considered and developed by each group of students. Sequence 2 is one small part of a recorded session in which their English teacher was questioning them about the most recent interaction and their future plans. (*Note*: *T* = teacher: *P1, P2* and *P3* are the girls in one group. Simultaneous speech is indicated by [and [] indicates that some speech has been omitted.)

Sequence 2: *guidance through questions*

    T: What about the word 'dimension', because you were going to include that in your message, weren't you?

    P1: Yeh. And there's going to be – if they go in the right room, then they'll find a letter in the floor and that'll spell 'dimension'.[]

    T: What happens if they do go in the wrong room?

    P2: Well, there's no letter in the bottom, in the floor.

    T: Oh God! So they've got to get it right, or that's it! (*everyone laughs*) for ever. And Cath can't get back to her own time. What do you mean the letters are in the room, I don't quite [follow that?

    P2: On the floor, like a tile or something.

    T: Oh I see. [] Why did you choose the word 'dimension'?

    P1: Don't know. (*pupils looking to each other, seeming uncertain*)

    P2: It just came up. Just said, you know, 'dimension' and everyone agreed.

    P3: Don't know.

    T: Right, because it seemed to fit in with, what, the [fantasy flow, flavour?

    P3:   [Yeh.

    T: OK. Why do they go through the maze rather than go back? I mean what motivation do they have for going through it in the first place?

    P: Um, I think that it was the king told them that Joe would be in the maze or at the end of the maze, and they didn't go back because of Joe, think it was. I'm not sure about that.

    T: You've really got to sort that out. [It's got to be *very, very* clear.

    P1:   [Yeh.

    P2: Joe went through this secret passage, you see, round the edge. [And we couldn't go through there it was like a different door.

    T: [OK.

    P2: Yeh and that was like the only way we could meet Joe.

    T: OK. Do remember that anything that you don't explain adequately, the primary school children are going to pick up on, and so it's got to make sense. Particularly at this end of the project, because they're not going to have much time to reply to your messages.

                    (From Videocassette 2, EH232 *Computers and Learning*)

In Sequence 2 the teacher uses questions to draw out from the students the content of their recent e-mail message, and also some justifications for what they included in it. At one level, she is simply monitoring their activity and assessing the adequacy of their attempt to continue the communication with the younger children. But her questions are not merely assessment, they are *part of her teaching*. Like many effective teachers, she is using questions not only to monitor children's activity, but also to guide it. Through questions like 'Why did you choose the word "dimension"?' and 'Why do they go through the maze rather than go back?' she directs their attention to matters requiring more thought and clarification. In much of her talk, and particularly her imperative conclusions ('You've really got to sort that out.' and 'Do remember . . .') we can see her 'scaffolding' her students' endeavours. Children can learn a lot from working together on computer-based activities, as they can from practical science activities, individual study pursuits and so on. But teachers need to highlight key points and to create continuities between past, present and future events in children's classroom experience if they are to make educational sense of it all.

Through observational research in primary schools, Derek Edwards and I (Edwards and Mercer, 1987) set out to describe how teaching and learning, as a process of sharing and constructing knowledge, was carried out. Amongst other things, we identified various kinds of discourse strategies used by teachers to control the representation of educational knowledge through their talk with pupils. These were basically of two kinds: *elicitations* and *knowledge markers*.

Elicitations

One obvious thing that teachers do is to *directly elicit* information from children, in order to see what the children know already. But teachers often avoid direct elicitations, and instead try to draw out the information they want – the 'right' answers to their questions – by *cued elicitations* in which they give children strong visual clues and verbal hints as to what answer is required. (I will use Sequence 3 below to illustrate some of these strategies.)

Knowledge markers

Teachers also use talk to mark particular things which are said and done as important for pupils' learning. To be more precise, they mark some items of knowledge as *significant and joint*. There are a number of features of teachers' discourse which can operate in this way: *confirmations* (as, for example, a teacher's 'Yes, that's right' to a pupil's answer) are one of the most obvious and straightforward of such features. *Repetitions* of 'correct' answers or other utterances made by children and judged by the teacher to have educational significance are another. Teachers may paraphrase or *reformulate* a pupil's remark, so as to offer the class a revised, tidied-up version of what was said. The term *elaborations* can be used to describe instances when a teacher picks up on a cryptic statement made by a pupil and expands and/or explains its significance to the rest of the class.

'*We*' *statements* (as in a teacher saying to a class 'last week we learned how to measure angles') are another interesting procedure for representing knowledge or experience as significant. They show how teachers represent their classes, *to* their classes, as small intellectual communities which have significant past experience in common and so have gained shared knowledge and collective understanding. Teachers also frequently *literally recap* for the benefit of the class what has gone on earlier in a lesson, and in previous lessons. More problematically, they also sometimes *reconstructively recap* what has been said and done by themselves and the children on earlier occasions, 'rewriting history' so as to make events fit better into their pedagogic framework. (For, example, a science teacher might remind pupils of 'the lesson in which we made a vacuum', even though the lesson saw more failed attempts than successes!)

We can see some of these features, in Sequence 3 (below), which was recorded in 1991 as part of the *SLANT* research project (see Mercer, Phillips and Somekh, 1989; Mercer and Fisher, 1992; Dawes, Fisher and Mercer, 1992 for more information about this project). *SLANT* (which stands for Spoken Language and New Technology) was concerned with the quality of talk in computer-based activities in primary school classrooms. In Sequence 3, the computer-based activity in question had been devised by the class teacher as part of a larger scheme of work on traditional fairy tales. From discussions with the teacher, we know that she had three main aims for this activity. She wanted her pupils (aged 6 and 7) to learn about the structure of such stories and how characters in them are typically represented. She wanted to develop her pupils' understanding of the 'language level' of young children who read such stories. And she intended this computer-based activity also to fulfil the aim of developing the computing skills of her pupils.

She therefore asked them to design and use an 'overlay' for the keyboard, transforming it into a 'concept keyboard' which the children in the nursery class of their school could use to select a limited set of words to make sentences and so create their own fairy stories. Eight pupils in the class were working on this task in pairs, and the teacher supported their activity by going round to each pair in turn. With each pair, she would observe the current state of their progress, draw attention to certain features and use them to raise issues related to the successful completion of the activity. In the sequence, she is talking with one such pair, Carol and Lesley. (*Note: T =* teacher. Simultaneous speech is marked by [.)

Sequence 3: *designing a concept keyboard*

> T: (*Standing behind the pair of pupils*) So what are you going to put in this one? (*points to a blank square on their overlay*)
> CAROL: [(*inaudible mutters*)
> LESLEY: [(*inaudible mutters*)
> T: Come on, think about it.
> LESLEY: A dragon?
> T: A dragon. Right. Have you got some words to describe a dragon?

CAROL: [No
LESLEY: [No
T: (*Reading from their overlay and pointing to the words as she does so*) 'There is a little amazing dragon'. They could say that, couldn't they?
CAROL: [Yes.
LESLEY: [Yes.
(*Carol and Lesley continue working for a short while, with the teacher making occasional comments*)
T: Now let's pretend it's working on the computer. You press a sentence and read it out for me, Lesley.
LESLEY: (*pointing to the overlay as she reads*) 'Here . . . is . . . a . . . wonderful . . .'.
T: Wait a minute
LESLEY: 'Princess . . .'
T: (*turning to Carol*) Right, now you do one. You read your sentence.
CAROL: (*pointing to overlay*) 'Here . . . is . . . a little . . . princess'.
T: Good. What do you need at the end of the sentence, so that the children learn about – [how
LESLEY: [Full stop
T: Full stop. We really should have allowed some space for a full stop. I wonder if we could arrange . . . When you actually draw the finished one up . . . we'll include a full stop. You couldn't actually do it. We'll put it there. (*She writes in a full stop on the overlay*) so that when you, can you remember to put one in? So what are the children going to learn? That a sentence starts with a . . .?
LESLEY: Capital letter
T: And finishes with?
LESLEY: A full stop.
T: And it's showing them? (*She moves her hand across the overlay from left to right*) What else is it showing them about sentences? That you start? On the?
LESLEY: On the left.
T: And go across the page (*She again passes her hand from left to right across the page*).

(Mercer and Fisher, 1992: xx)

Sequence 3 includes good examples of some of the teachers' discourse strategies described above. Selecting particular themes; the teacher elicits responses from the pupils which draw them along a particular line of reasoning on that theme (a line of reasoning consonant with her own goals for the activity). Moreover she provides *cued elicitations* for some of those responses through the form of her questions (e.g. 'That a sentence starts with a . . .?') and through her gestures (as when she moves her hand across the overlay, indicating the way text is laid out). By her *repetition* of Carol's answer 'a full stop' she marks a 'right answer'. In her final remark, she also *elaborates* Lesley's brief, cryptic response to make the point more clearly. At a number of points in the sequence, she defines the learning experience as one which is shared by her and the children through her use of 'we' and 'let's'.

In the sequence, we can see how a teacher uses talk, gesture and the shared experience of the piece of work in progress to draw the children's attention to salient points – the things she wishes them to do, and the things she wishes them to learn. She reminds pupils of some specific requirements of the task in hand, clarifies some of those requirements, and so guides their activity along a path which is in accord with her pre-defined curriculum goals for the activity. She 'scaffolds' their participation in the activity so as to try to ensure (a) that its demands do not exceed the capabilities of the children and (b) that the activity keeps 'on track' for the specific curriculum goals she had set. (For the record, Lesley and Carol did produce a satisfactory overlay, and went on to teach the nursery children how to use it.)

CONCLUSIONS

In this chapter I have tried to describe some important educational functions of language in the classroom. I hope that some of the practical implications of my discussion of classroom language are clear: that children need to be helped to acquire certain educational language practices and – crucially – to see the point and purpose of them; and that teachers need to be aware of how, and how well, they teach through talk. However, I should say that I am very aware that I have only dealt superficially with some important matters, and left some others out entirely. For example, the issue of 'educational ground rules' leads into a cluster of thorny educational language problems, including such controversial matters as how and when children should be introduced to the technical vocabularies of school subjects and how children's competence and confidence with language should be taken into account in making assessments of their understanding of subject knowledge. (Interested readers might turn to Maclure, Phillips and Wilkinson, 1988; Sheeran and Barnes, 1991; Norman, 1992.)

Early in the chapter I suggested that the essence of 'becoming educated' is gaining admission to an intellectual community and to a universe of discourse. I hope that I have shown some of the ways that this process of gaining admission takes place. The talk and writing which goes on in any particular classroom only has meaning if it is embedded in a wider, less tangible but potentially very powerful discourse which links schools and other cultural institutions across time and space. It is in that broad context that the communicative process of teaching-and-learning should be studied and evaluated. I have not addressed some of the most problematic features of that process: many people who go to school do not gain proper entry to an intellectual community, or they have no good reasons to value membership of such a community, or their entry to it does not lead to any significant improvement to the quality of their lives. (See, for example, Edwards, 1979; Heath, 1982; Carraher, Carraher and Schliemann, 1985; Martin, 1986; Edwards, V., and Sienkewitcz, T., 1990.) My own view is that we can only begin to address those problems seriously at a practical level when education is given the political and economic priority it deserves, as a communicative process at the heart of the cultural development of any society.

REFERENCES

Bruner, J. (1978) 'The role of dialogue in language acquisition' in Sinclair, A., Jarvella, R. and Levelt, W. J. M. (eds) *The Child's Conception of Language*, New York, Springer-Verlag.

Carle, E. (1986) *The Very Hungry Caterpillar*; London, Hamish Hamilton.

Carraher, T. N., Carraher, D. W. and Schliemann, A. D. (1985) 'Mathematics in the streets and in schools', *British Journal of Developmental Psychology*, 3, pp. 21–9.

Dawes, L., Fisher, E. and Mercer, N. (1992) 'The quality of talk at the computer', *Language and Learning*, October 1992, pp. 22–5.

Dillon, J. T. (1982) 'The effects of questions in education and other enterprises', *Journal of Curriculum Studies*, 14(2), pp. 127–52.

Edwards, A. D. (1992) 'Teacher talk and pupil competence' in Norman, K. (ed.) *Thinking Voices: the Work of the National Curriculum Project*, London, Hodder & Stoughton for the National Curriculum Council.

Edwards, D. and Mercer, N. (1987) *Common Knowledge: the Development of Understanding in the Classroom*, London, Methuen.

Edwards, J. R. (1979) *Language and Disadvantage*, London, Edward Arnold.

Edwards, V. and Sienkewitcz, T. (1990) *Oral Cultures Past and Present: Rappin' and Homer*, Oxford, Basil Blackwell.

Heath, S. B. (1982) 'What no bedtime story means: narrative skills at home and school', *Language and Society*, 11, pp. 49–76.

Heath, S. B. (1983) *Ways with Words*, Cambridge, Cambridge University Press

Hewitt, R. (1989) 'Oral assessment and the new oracy'. Paper presented at the CLIE Symposium on Oracy and Assessment, Birkbeck College, University of London, November 1989.

Maclure, M., Phillips, T. and Wilkinson, A. (1988) *Oracy Matters*, Milton Keynes, Open University Press.

Madeley, B. and Lautman, A. (1991) 'I like the way we learn' in *P535 Talk and Learning 5–16: an In-service Pack on Oracy for Teachers*, Milton Keynes, The Open University.

Martin, T. (1986) 'Leslie: a reading failure talks about failing', *Reading*, 20, pp. 43–52.

Maybin, J., Mercer, N. and Stierer, B. (1992) ' "Scaffolding" learning in the classroom' in Norman, K. (ed.) *Thinking Voices: the Work of the National Curriculum Project*, London, Hodder & Stoughton for the National Curriculum Council.

Mercer, N., Edwards, D. and Maybin, J. (1988) 'Putting context into oracy' in Maclure, M., Phillips, T. and Wilkinson, A. (1988) *Oracy Matters*, Milton Keynes, Open University Press.

Mercer, N., Phillips, T. and Somekh, B. (1989) 'Research note: spoken language and new technology', *Journal of Computer Assisted Learning*, 7, pp. 195–202.

Mercer, N. and Fisher, E. (1992) 'How do teachers help children to learn? An analysis of teachers' interventions in computer-based activities', *Learning and Instruction*, 2(4), pp. 339–55.

Meyer, B. (1991) 'Talk partners in the infant classroom' in *P535 Talk and Learning 5–16: an In-service Pack on Oracy for Teachers*, Milton Keynes, The Open University.

Norman, K. (ed.) (1992) *Thinking Voices: the Work of the National Curriculum Project*, London, Hodder & Stoughton for the National Curriculum Council.

Prentice, M. (1991) 'A community of enquiry' in *P535 Talk and Learning 5–16: an In-service Pack on Oracy for Teachers*, Milton Keynes, The Open University.

Sheeran, N. and Barnes, D. (1991) *School Writing: Discovering the Ground Rules*, Milton Keynes, Open University Press.

Steel, D. (1991) 'Granny's garden' in *P535 Talk and Learning 5–16: an In-service Pack on Oracy for Teachers*, Milton Keynes, The Open University.

Vygotsky, L. S. (1981) 'The genesis of higher mental functions' in Wertsch, J. (ed.) *The Concept of Activity in Soviet Psychology*, Amonk NY, Sharpe.

Vygotsky, L. S. (1978) *Mind in Society: the Development of Higher Psychological Processes*, London, Harvard University Press.

Wood, D. (1992) 'Teaching talk' in Norman, K. (ed.) *Thinking Voices: the Work of the National Curriculum Project*, London, Hodder & Stoughton for the National Curriculum Council.

Chapter 24

Sex stereotyping in the classroom

Sara Delamont

It is very hard to recognise all the ways in which perfectly ordinary schools segregate, differentiate and even discriminate against some pupils on the basis of their sex. We all grew up in schools that divided us by sex, and we are all liable to perpetuate sexual divisions because we simply do not notice them. When some of the ways in which schools are sexually divisive are mentioned they seem trivial; others are seen as 'natural' and both labels prevent change. This section uses data from several studies of schools to illustrate ways in which sexual differentiation and discrimination take place.

MOTIVATION AND CONTROL

The ORACLE team found teachers using gender differentiation as a way of motivating and controlling pupils. Using ridicule to enforce discipline was also common. For example, when Miss Wordsworth at Melin Court told the girls in her form to line up for Assembly and a boy, Wayne, stood up, she said 'Oh Wayne thinks he's a girl'. Wayne sat down again immediately. Abraham's (1989) fieldwork in a comprehensive in the south of England in 1986 says:

> Disruptive boys would be made to sit with the girls on the assumption that that would keep the boys quiet.

> (p. 70)

Attempting to motivate boys to work by comparing them to girls was frequently seen. For example:

> At Waverly Miss Southey had a class in the school library and when she saw most of the girls had borrowed books but none of the boys she said 'All the girls are taking out books but not one boy yet. Can't the boys read in this class?'

A few boys then borrowed books but most did not, despite the teacher's comment. Similar teacher strategies were common in nine Welsh schools in 1985/6 both to maintain order or organise activities for which no educational reason existed. For example at Gwaelod-y-Garth the fourth-year remedial and statemented group had a rural studies lesson in which the boys were sent out, unsupervised, to wheel some barrow loads of earth to a new flower bed while the master interviewed the girls and filled in their assessment profiles with them. As only one girl could be seen at once, and the others were left to chat, they could have been moving the earth with the boys. The sex segregation served no educational purpose, only an organisational one. A common teacher control strategy was to allow one sex to leave the room before the other. Thus, in Mrs Leithen's class at Gwaelod-y-Garth:

> It is 3.30. Mrs. Leithen says 'Nobody is going from here till you are all quiet'. When they are quiet they are allowed to leave a small number at a time, girls first, then the boys in small groups.

This may work as a control strategy, but at the cost of emphasising that boys and girls are different, and reinforcing their own prejudices. At Derllwyn when the Senior Mistress of the Lower School was doing a history lesson on Pompeii with the remedial and statemented first years she found that Royden was doing nearly all the answering, so she suggested, 'Let's ask the girls for a change'. When the class moved on to RE Royden again volunteered answers to most of the questions and this teacher too suggested that, 'Now the girls in front are sitting awful quiet'. Here again the reasonable teacher strategy – getting other pupils to share in the progress of the lesson – is realised in a sex-segregating way. Other pupils are 'girls' – not individuals – and the other boys in the class were equally unresponsive to the teacher's questions and needed to be encouraged to answer. Singling out 'girls' serves only to reinforce their difference from Royden and other boys, 'shows them up' and does nothing to encourage all the other pupils to participate in the discourse.

TEACHING STRATEGIES AND LESSON CONTENT

The content of much of the curriculum, and the ways in which teachers taught the material is also full of sex stereotyping. Carol Buswell (1981) analysed the lower-school humanities materials. There were 326 pages of text, including 169 pictures of men and only 21 of women, and 102 individual men were described as against 14 women. Among the tasks for pupils were the following:

1 Look at the pictures of the clothes the Romans wore. Would they be easy for your mother to wash if you were a Roman?
2 Find the name of this make of car. Your father or brother will probably know, ask them.
3 Make up a poem about a very rich man or a very poor man.

Winter (1983) has highlighted the restricted number of female characters in reading materials for slow learners in the secondary age range, and the limited range of occupations and low ambitions the women characters have. Frances James, a remedial teacher, made the same point in a letter to the *Guardian* (17 February 1987).

Sexual stereotyping was also common in the textbooks, worksheets and teaching in the Welsh schools. So for example at Ffynnon Frenhines when the second year were doing an exercise on healthy eating with Mrs Barralty, she discovered that none of the children knew what stock was.

> Mrs. Barralty asked 'What's in a stock? Come on, girls, you do cookery . . .'
>
> Vaughan replies 'OXO'.

This interaction was doubly interesting. It confirmed for the observer that all the staff knew boys did not do cookery at Ffynnon Frenhines, and stereotyped the girls. As a boy (Vaughan) was the only child in the room to have any idea how gravy was made, so the teacher's expectation was confounded. At Heol y Crynwyr, a school where most activities were integrated, stereotyped curriculum materials were in use. For example, in Mr Arcoll's laboratory the walls were decorated with posters. One faded set featured boys and girls doing dangerous things in the lab and being reprimanded by an adult. Another series, published by the Royal Society of Chemistry, on 'Achievements in Chemistry', included five posters, four of males, one the Curies. The Equal Opportunities Commission (EOC) posters of women scientists (see Smail 1984:38) were *not* displayed.

Abraham (1989) has provided a detailed analysis of the textbooks and materials used in English, French and maths in 1986 in one comprehensive. He concluded that the textbooks in maths and French were male dominated, with men in the powerful and active roles and females in stereotyped 'feminine' ones. One maths book defines 'a mathematician' as male, and another includes the inaccurately sexist claim that:

> If the government says that the unemployment rate is 6% they mean that averaged over the whole country six out of every 100 *men* are unemployed.

Such bias in teaching materials is carried through into exams. The Fawcett Society (see Hendry 1987) studied all the 1985 GCE papers in maths, physical sciences, computing, languages, history and social sciences. Maths papers were replete with 'workmen', 'foremen' and men investing money as well as problems about engines and football. The science and computing papers were 'impersonal', but across 250 papers 22 different, famous male scientists were named but only one woman (Marie Curie's death). English literature exams focus on male characters in plays, poems and novels written by men as do the literature papers in French and German. Home economics exams provide the most blatant examples – especially the practical test:

Your brother has a Saturday job at a local farm. (a) Prepare and pack a substantial midday meal for him to take and make a family supper dish. (b) Launder his shirt and trousers, clean and press his jacket and clean his shoes ready for a disco in the evening.

(Hendry 1987:37)

As the researcher concludes, boys are 'rigorously excluded' from the home economics papers, except as recipients of women's labour.

The stereotyping in texts and materials is particularly damaging because pupils have a 'blind spot' concerning the use of the words 'man' and 'men' to mean human beings rather than just males. This is a common flaw in teaching materials and in the oral parts of lessons. There is ample research evidence that pupils and students hear 'man' to mean 'males' unless they are explicitly told that it covers people of both sexes. There are forty-four articles on this point in Thorne et al. (1983), including Schneider and Hacker (1973) who found undergraduates studying social science interpreted 'men' in that way and Harrison (1975) who reports adolescents making the same mistake studying 'the evolution of man'. Teachers need to explain to pupils, especially those who are low-achievers, that 'man's evolution' means human evolution, and 'great men of science' includes Marie Curie, Rosalind Franklin and Barbara McClintock, but few currently do so.

There are authors who claim that teachers allow boys to dominate the talk in classrooms, taking three-quarters of all the teacher's attention and making three-quarters of the pupil contributions (e.g. Spender 1982; see also Delamont 1984). Such claims do not stand up to close scrutiny because there are too few data to make them. However, studies do show differences in the ways teachers respond to male and female pupils. Shuy's (1986) analysis of a high school civics lesson taught by William Bennett (at the time Reagan's Secretary of State for Education) showed he regularly challenged things his male pupils said ('why did you say that?') but never the responses from his female pupils. The girls got positive or neutral feedback ('Okay', 'Alright', 'Very nice', 'Terrific'). (See also Delamont (1986) on this lesson.) A great deal more research is needed on this area, but all teachers can tape themselves and examine whether they are treating the boys and girls in their rooms differently and, if so, in what ways.

Sometimes teachers try to avoid sexism but are frustrated by others. At Ffynnon Frenhines we saw the girls from the 'remedial and statemented' class join one of the 'B' band forms for PE. The teacher, Mrs Varrinder, sent those girls who had forgotten their kit down from the upstairs gym to the downstairs one, where the boys were having PE, to fetch back the benches that were normally kept there which had been 'borrowed' before half term. They returned empty handed, followed by boys carrying the benches, detailed by the PE master, who had been teaching male PE in the main hall. Mrs Varrinder's attempt to get some girls to carry benches was frustrated by the PE master, who chivalrously assigned boys to do it for them, stressing female dependence. Some of the boys assigned were smaller than the girls they were 'helping'!

REFERENCES

Abraham, J. (1989) 'Teacher ideology and sex roles in curriculum texts', *British Journal of Sociology of Education* 10 (1): 33–52.

Buswell, C. (1981) 'Sexism in school routines and classroom practice', *Durham and Newcastle Research Review* 946: 195–200.

Delamont, S. (1984) 'Sex roles and schooling: or, "See Janet suffer, see John suffer too" ', *Journal of Adolescence* 7: 329–35.

Delamont, S. (1986) 'Discussion: a view from a quadruple outsider', *Teaching and Teacher Education* 2 (4): 329–32.

Harrison, L. (1975) 'Cro-Magnon woman – in eclipse', *Science Teacher* 42 (4): 9–11.

Hendry, E. (1987) *Exams for the Boys*, London: The Fawcett Society.

Schneider, J. and Hacker, S. (1973) 'Sex-role imagery in the use of the generic "man" in introductory texts', *American Sociologist* 8: 12–18.

Shuy, R. (1986) 'Secretary Bennett's teaching', *Teaching and Teacher Education* 2 (4): 315–24.

Smail, B. (1984) *Girl Friendly Science*, London: Longman.

Spender, D. (1982) *Invisible Women*, London: Writers & Readers Publishing Cooperative.

Thorne, B., Kramarae, C. and Henley, N. (eds) (1983) *Language, Gender and Society*, Rowley, MA: Newberry House.

Winter, M. (1983) 'Remedial education', in J. Whyld (ed.) *Sexism in the Secondary Curriculum*, London: Harper & Row.

Chapter 25

Managing classes

Mick McManus

The aim of this chapter is to describe and discuss the teacher skills that have been observed to be associated with freedom from pupil disruption in expert teachers' classrooms.

Lessons conducted in the traditional style often fall into phases to which varying rules and expectations are attached. Hargreaves *et al.* (1975) noted an entry phase, settling down, the lesson proper which included teachers' exposition and pupils' work, clearing up and finally exit. The amount of movement and pupil talk varies from phase to phase and some pupils seem to have more difficulty than others in adjusting to this. It is therefore necessary to give explicit directions and clear warnings when a change of phase is imminent. These warnings have been called 'flags' (Marland, 1975) and 'switch signals' (Hargreaves *et al.*, 1975). Some of the signals and cues observed by Evertson and Emmer (1982) included a real switch signal: 'moving to a specific area of the room, ringing a bell, or turning on the overhead projector'. If the lesson is planned, or the teacher can see its unfolding form if it is extempore, then it is relatively easy to make changes within the lesson clear and to prepare the pupils for them. For example: 'In two minutes we will stop and read the first paragraph.' The amount of class time occupied by transitions has been estimated at up to 15 per cent with the associated finding that these are peak times for misbehaviour to occur. Despite the common belief, external interruptions from visitors are responsible for only 10 per cent of classroom distractions (Wittrock, 1986: 406).

The traditional form of lesson, the recitation or question and answer type, is by its very nature vulnerable to disruption. Ironically, it is a form of teaching that was intended to put voice and life in place of the deadness of print. Stowe, an early teacher trainer of the 1840s, called it 'picturing out': he described how the teacher was to engage the attention of the class by interrogation, suggestion and ellipsis – which would nowadays be called the cloze procedure (see Curtis, 1963: 216). A basically similar style of teaching in America appears to have evolved from a different activity: having individuals recite lessons privately to the teacher (Hamilton quoted in Wittrock, 1986: 403). The teacher conducts an inquisition, attempting to involve the whole class and keep silent the non-attending parts of it. Observations of such lessons, for example Barnes *et al.* (1969), indicate that questions are typically closed, that is admitting only of the answers in the teacher's mind, thus limiting and constraining the range of contributions from pupils. Although recitation has the appearance of a joint teacher and pupil search for understanding, in reality the teachers hold most of the cards and the pupils are reduced to guessing them. What masquerades as an inquiry after meaning and truth may become a game of 'guess the word I'm thinking of.' An example of learning degenerating into a guessing game in a primary school is analysed in MacLure and French (1980). Teachers give information, elicit answers, direct who shall speak, decide whether an answer is acceptable or not, and evaluate publicly both the answer and the pupil's effort. Pupils are limited to seeking permission to speak and reacting or replying if called upon. Perhaps some procedure of this sort is inevitable in crowded class-rooms where teachers' knowledge has to be shared in some sort of inter-active way: few school teachers consider straightforward lecturing to be appropriate or possible.

Approximately one third of classroom time is said to be occupied in this way and in general observers note a high degree of pupil involvement as compared with other classroom activities. Where the questions are closed and admit of only limited answers, participation is limited to the more able pupils; where the emphasis is on ideas and opinions, and almost all answers are acceptable, lower ability pupils take a greater part and some of the more able tend to withdraw (see Doyle's review in Wittrock, 1986: 402–5). Class discussion sessions in which all answers are apparently accepted have been noted in infant schools (MacLure and French, in Woods, 1980a). However, although teachers seemed to accept all answers, this was only a surface feature of their remarks to the class, and the authors show that pupils' logically derived responses were in fact rejected in favour of the single answer in the teacher's mind. There is no doubt that the whole-class recitation method generates a considerable number of easily breakable rules. A pupil need only speak to a neighbour upon the topic under inquiry to create a disruptive event. Mehan (1979) notes that the rules of turn-taking, and the ways of displaying knowledge which are appropriate to the class-room community, may remain implicit. Some pupils need these rules and expectations made explicit.

The traditional teacher control of the classroom does not necessarily evaporate in open, resource-based environments. Whatever the limitations and difficulties of recitation as a classroom strategy the traditional teacher presence is still necessary from time to time. Edwards and Furlong (1978) reported on a school organised along open, resource-based lines where pupils had fewer restraints and more opportunity to follow their own learning paths. To some extent they were able to create their own 'local' curriculum, to work at their own pace, and to have a wider range of their knowledge and interests valued. Nevertheless, the authors observed no marked reduction in teacher control of knowledge – booklets were a substitute for teacher talk – and teachers retained some of their directive role, though in response to pupils' demands rather than on their own initiative. Where possible, therefore, it may be strategically appropriate to avoid the recitation (or teacher versus the class) style. To use a varied menu of learning and teaching styles is the first step towards pre-empting control problems in the classroom.

EARLY ENCOUNTERS

Control is normally easier to establish if the teacher is in position ready to receive the class. It is not an auspicious start to have to calm an already disorderly group. Rutter *et al.* (1979) reported that where teachers were waiting for classes and able to supervise their entry there was less school disorder. Research reported in Wragg (1984) showed that experienced teachers, when compared with students, were more likely to greet the pupils, occupy a central position in the room, wait for silence before speaking, issue directions authoritatively and use eye contact. They did not rely on voice alone to convey their requirements: posture and expression were relaxed and confident. Goffman (1968) has observed that impressions given off, as distinct from those deliberately given, are normally taken as a more accurate guide to a person's inner state. Naturally, if a troublesome class is expected there is a temptation to cut short an unpleasant encounter by arriving late. Similarly, one is more likely to find oneself shouting and less confident about taking a position forward of the desk while looking pupils in the eye. Many years ago a teachers' newspaper published a cartoon showing a teacher standing in front of a class, arms folded, impassive. The pupils are depicted in a state of disorder: paper aircraft and chair legs fill the air; cobwebs stretch from the teacher to the walls and ceiling and the caption is: 'I'm still waiting.' It takes courage to try non-verbal control skills and few teachers are completely free of the fear that they too may find themselves still waiting.

Laslett and Smith (1984) convey the briskness associated with effective teachers in their summary of the entry rules as greeting, seating, starting. They and Marland (1975) point out that a straightforward start to lessons, with something that occupies pupils in their desks, allows the teacher to cope with interruptions and late-comers. Where this advice seems uncongenial or inappropriate, perhaps where pupils are engaged in group projects, interruptions can still be prevented from becoming disruptions. For example, late arrivals can be briskly and amiably greeted and directed to the topic, without shifting one's attention from the rest of the class. There is no need to express annoyance or begin an interrogation: any necessary enquiries can be conducted later.

One way of proceeding with classes that are already out of hand is to draw up a short list of rules and make some sort of bargain with the class. This is especially effective with primary age pupils. When asked to suggest three rules for the class, both teachers and pupils tend to express them in negative terms. For example: no shouting; no wandering about; no spoiling other people's work. It is more effective to express the rules positively so that the pupils know what they have to do rather than not do. The three rules mentioned would therefore be written up on the board as follows: we must talk in quiet voices; we must stay in our own places; we must be helpful and polite to each other. Having established some simple and achievable rules in this way the teacher may then offer a reward. This can be tangible or not according to the particular circumstances: some classes are happy just to show they can keep bargains. In a primary school, a teacher might say something like this: 'I will look around the class every few minutes – that will be about twenty times this lesson. If everyone is obeying our rules on at least half of those occasions then there will be extra story time this afternoon.' The required success rate must be set at a realistic level that is likely to be achieved: the target can always be raised on future occasions – it is a bad idea to be too ambitious and begin with failure. Bull and Solity (1987) note the importance of stressing to the class the natural consequences of keeping the rules; this makes it easier to gradually withdraw the artificial system when a co-operative and productive atmosphere is established. A similar procedure was found to reduce disruptive behaviour in a study of two secondary school classes (McNamara, in Johnstone and Munn, 1987).

It may be the case, difficult to prove, that some populations of pupils are more amenable to these techniques than others. Rutter remarked that it was very difficult to be a good teacher in some schools. Calderhead (1987) reports on an experiment to discover the influence of the class on teachers – in this case two trainees. One who appeared to have established order of a precarious kind through a good deal of shouting and threatening was exchanged with another who kept control using a quiet voice and positive, rewarding behaviour. The students altered their behaviour so that the former became quieter and the latter began to coerce and shout. This is, however, no reason to surrender a skills approach: if pupils are such powerful constraints upon teacher behaviour then it can never be too early to begin re-educating them.

Wragg's team reported that experienced teachers tried to present a brisk, hard image on first meeting a new class: they would be resistant to enquiries, keep their 'mystery' or perhaps play on their eccentricities if these were known, respected or feared. Many used their first lessons to explain their rules which related to territory, property, work, talking and safety. However, Fontana (1985) warns that teachers should limit their continuous talk to no more than one-and-a-half minutes for each year of the average class age. Many teachers convey their extensive ownership of the classroom by specifying how pupils must use and keep neat their books, materials and desks (Evertson and Emmer, 1982). Rules were precisely stated and continually reiterated.

Students often intended to begin their encounters with something interesting and active, though many chose a less risky start on the day. In one class a student chose to demonstrate a chemical reaction which simulated a volcano: an event which came to symbolise the lesson. In contrast, effective classroom managers tend to begin with activities that have 'a simple, whole-class instructional structure, and the work was familiar, enjoyable and easy to accomplish' (Evertson and Emmer, summarised in Wittrock, 1986). Often, the teaching of the rules and procedures was the substantive lesson.

Evertson and Emmer found significant differences between more and less effective teachers in their behaviour at the start of the school year. They conclude, as others have (Ball, in Woods 1980b; Doyle in Wittrock, 1986) that the beginning of the year is crucial for establishing effective classroom procedures and advise that planning should be done before school starts. Effective teachers had 'a better behavioural map of the classroom and what was required for students to function within it'. This map would not omit the basic precautions mentioned by Fontana (1985): no dead tape-decks, illegible visual aids or stiff glue. The teachers of younger pupils placed more emphasis on teaching their rules and for all teachers the time spent on this activity varied from a few minutes to over forty minutes. Time did not appear as significant, however: effective teachers were more explicit and more likely to give copies of the rules or have pupils write them in their books. In addition: 'More effective managers tended to have more workable systems of rules, and they taught their rules and procedures systematically and thoroughly' (Evertson and Emmer, 1982: 486). This seems to be stating the obvious and in some respects all observational studies are vulnerable to this charge: effective teachers are found to do the things that effective teachers do. In this study they were more vigilant, tended to use more eye contact, responded quickly to inappropriate behaviour, checked and gave feedback on work, maintained contact with the full class and set appropriate tasks which were clearly explained. They kept better track of progress and had 'stronger and more detailed accountability systems'. They were better predictors of pupils' concerns and difficulties and were able to see the classroom 'through the eyes of their students'. Doyle too reported that effective teachers maintained vigilance over the whole class and kept individual contacts brief (Wittrock, 1986: 402).

THE MAIN PART OF THE LESSON

Giving the pupils an outline of the lesson's planned form helps to minimise interruptions and expressions of surprise at a later and possibly more vulnerable time. Similarly, to start with some deskwork ensures that all the pupils have the books and materials they will need for the lesson. This is particularly important with disorderly and forgetful groups. It is sometimes difficult to maintain a fresh and vigorous demeanour with topics repeated from year to year but some extra reading, or re-sequencing the material can help. Laslett and Smith (1984) refer to the Henson and Higgins view that pupil motivation can be engendered by taking an interest in pupils, knowing their names and treating them courteously. This involves being generous with praise and Laslett and Smith suggest preparing a number of synonyms for such tired words as good and nice. Bull and Solity (1987) advise 'full praise statements': gain attention, show approval, specify the progress, point out its benefits, and challenge them to do better. Balson (1982), however, distinguishes between praise and encouragement: certainly, older pupils do not always respond gratefully to praise and this advice must be used with discretion. It is equally important to convey enthusiasm for the lesson topic and thereby communicate to the class that it is something worth taking an interest in.

Partington and Hinchcliffe (1979) noted that effective class managers prepared effectively and extensively: as well as the content, they planned for organisational matters such as movement, time, and the tasks of particular pupils. To make a brisk beginning, explaining the relationship of the lesson's work to the course or to pupils' present concerns and future interests, is preferable to wrangles about the last lesson's leftovers or missing home-work. These can be attended to later when they do not keep uninvolved pupils waiting.

Attempts to introduce new learning methods and groupings sometimes collapse into disorder because pupils are unused to autonomy and unclear about what is expected of them. They may pester the teacher with ques-tions or occupy their time in unwanted activities, hoping that some other group will come up with an answer that they can reproduce. Where pupils are set to solve problems in pairs or groups it is necessary for the task to be explicit. It may even be necessary to specify a number of words, or the headings for lists under which appropriate results may fall. Pupils sometimes fail to co-operate in open-ended paired work because the teachers' evaluation criteria have previously indicated that only some results are valued. This repeats one of the problems encountered with whole class question and answer sessions where questions which appear to be open to several answers are in fact closed and admit of only one answer which is decided by the teacher. Where the task set is open and therefore to some extent ambiguous it is necessary for teachers to reduce the risk of pupils incurring negative evaluations, that is low marks and criticism. Failure to take account of pupils' perception of the teacher's evaluation criteria may result in pupils declining to co-operate: they may pester the teacher for the answers or turn their attention to something safer. Wrong answers may be pupils' attempts to transform tasks into something they can achieve or they may be a clue to the pupils' perception of the teacher's requirements (Posner, 1980).

One of the most widely applied studies of teacher behaviour in orderly classrooms was carried out by Kounin (1970). A particularly valuable skill, which he termed 'withitness', consisted in giving the pupils the impression that the teacher had 'eyes in the back of her head'. Some years earlier, Dreikurs wrote: 'One requirement of all good group leaders – including teachers – is the ability to see everything that goes on in the group at any given time' (1957: 50). Brophy and Evertson (1976) use the term monitoring; Marland (1975) calls it the lighthouse effect. Successful teachers, in respect of classroom order, frequently scan the class and regularly make remarks, which Kounin said must be timely and accurate, to show that they are missing nothing, even when they do not otherwise intervene in inattentive behaviour.

Specifically, teachers watch the behaviour of groups in order to keep the momentum of activities moving. It is necessary to remain vigilant when the pupils have been set a piece of deskwork: in some classes, distracted pupils may look up to find the teacher apparently counting them. Regular marking and giving feedback have the same effect. Copeland had some success with a computer system designed to stimulate the attentiveness to overlapping demands of the classroom. The trainee was required to 'conduct a question-answer session . . . while monitoring the order of turn talking, the accuracy of answers, and another student who is supposed to be engaged in a seatwork task' (Wittrock, 1986: 425). Teachers need to maintain this class-room awareness when dealing with one individual or a group. This may be done by speaking to one pupil while looking at another or by helping an individual using a 'public' voice if the help or directions are appropriate. An expert class manager can question, explain, organise, mark, discipline, listen all at the same time – and while attending to a note from the headteacher. A teacher's day may be short in hours, but long in minutes.

Kounin indicated other teacher skills to which he gave idiosyncratic terms. 'Thrusts and dangles' contributed to classroom disorder: teachers should not interrupt pupil work precipitously and neither should they leave issues incomplete and unresolved. Teachers who stayed on one issue long after they had lost pupil attention were 'overdwelling'. Those whose fore-sight was so hazy as to produce confusion in the pupils were sometimes engaging in 'flip-flops'. This involved starting a new activity and then returning without warning to the one just abandoned: for example, 'maths books away, take out your readers, how many people got number fifteen right?' All these sorts of teacher behaviour interrupted the smooth flow of the lesson: the resulting loss of momentum contributed to a disorderly atmosphere.

Physical location in the classroom is a part of the teacher's non-verbal communication with the class and may also influence attention and behaviour. If possible, pupil desks should be arranged across the narrow length: a closer relationship is created with fewer opportunities for disengagement to develop, out of range and out ot sight, into distraction (Grunsell, 1985).

RESPONDING TO TROUBLE

The first response to incipient disturbance need not to be a verbal rebuke or comment. A stare, averting eyes sideways (not submissively down) if the stare is returned in an uncomfortable or defiant manner by the pupil, can sometimes prevent an escalation of the unwanted activity. Adopting an authoritative stance, for example folding one's arms, or moving closer to a disruptive pupil, invading his or her territory, are other possible ways of regaining control without drawing public attention. Sometimes an invitation to respond to a question serves a similar low key purpose and, with younger pupils, a touch on the shoulder perhaps. For the same reason (avoiding too public a profile early in a potential conflict) it is best to make corrective statements short: nagging, threats, interrogation and recitation of past misdemeanours should be avoided.

It is easy to underestimate the need to make requirements explicit and to target remarks by using names, specifying both the unwanted behaviour and the desired activity.

Loud public rebukes can be effective when they are rare and unexpected; but they communicate weakness where they are a regular feature of a teacher's classroom. Soft and private reprimands, preferably in the absence of an audience, are more likely to be effective: 'a soft answer turneth away wrath'. Numerous public rebukes can disturb the class to the extent that the teacher increases the disruption that he or she seeks to diminish. An effective intervention is 'abrupt, short and does not invite further comment or discussion from the student' (Wittrock, 1986: 421). A relaxed posture, a voice pitched low, an absence of gesticulation or poking help to keep confrontational situations calm. A teacher in a unit for excluded pupils, who happened to be addicted to chocolate, sometimes contrived to unwrap and eat a bar when faced with particularly violent and dangerous situations. Eating is something we do when feeling unstressed, this helped define the situation as unthreatening, and helped to soothe troubled feelings. An unwanted confrontation can sometimes be halted by simply stating the conditions under which co-operative relations can be resumed: explicitly state the peace terms and withdraw from the interaction. Where a pupil has to be removed from the room, it helps persuade the pupil that the teacher is rejecting the behaviour and not the person if the pupil is led to the door rather than ordered out. At the same time some simple condition that must be satisfied for re-entry can be repeatedly emphasised: the rejoining of the group, on what may be privileged terms, is thus uppermost in the exchange – rejection, and the reason for it, is minimised. This style of control helps maintain a cool demeanour and avoids alarming and exciting other pupils, whose continued need for attention must not be neglected. If, in the course of dealing with an incident, the teacher falsely accuses the pupil, a generous or even extravagant apology can be both calming and evidence of the teacher's invulnerability and confidence.

CLEARING UP AND EXIT

The completion stages of a lesson or individual learning session sometimes require planning and preparation in their own right. Often the most difficult pupils are the first to finish work (to their own satisfaction) and this should be planned for. With disaffected groups, an orderly and coherent end to a lesson can leave a general impression of having achieved something worthwhile: this feeling is not confined to the pupils. More effective schools in Rutter et al. (1979) tended not to have lessons finishing too early. Laslett and Smith (1984) note that 'hard-won control is most frequently lost and learning wasted at the end of lessons'. In so far as one lesson's end is another lesson's start, professional responsibility and staffroom harmony depend upon good management in the concluding phase. As the end of a lesson approaches and release for both parties is at hand, the teacher may find less difficulty in gaining attention. It is unwise to use this period for a recitation of the errors of the past session, perhaps mixed with demands for silence, backed by threats of instant detention. The opportunity is best used to summarise and draw together the themes of the lesson's work and perhaps relate them to the intended programme for the next meeting. Review what has been achieved as if all had achieved it: experience shows that even in the most disorderly and chaotic classes, a majority of the pupils are engaged on task for most of the time. It does not depart so far from reality therefore for the teacher to take a positive view and to define the situation as a success. An orderly dismissal, with a relaxed and smiling teacher, helps to minimise problems and is a better prelude to the next meeting than an atmosphere of recrimination and threats. Particularly uncooperative pupils may be held back for a brief word as the class leaves.

Sockett, discussing a possible professional code for teachers in Gordon (1983) lists six items relating to classroom practice. He suggests that teachers should always be properly prepared before classes begin; they should ensure that pupils are always productively engaged; they should not frequently discipline any particular individual during teaching; they should concentrate on their pupils' successes and praise them generously; they should set and mark work regularly and speedily; they should have high expectations of their pupils and manifest them constantly; and they should be punctual. These are, as Sockett himself says, conventional and common-sense prescriptions. As with much classroom management advice, some of this may seem to be too trivial to require specifying and as likely to lower the status of teaching as to raise it. One does not suppose the BMA includes punctuality in the professional code of doctors – perhaps it is as well, for they seldom are. The impression of simplicity and triviality is a false one. Rules and prescriptions vary in their significance according to the context: for example, punctuality does have a juvenile and trivial aspect in everyday life, perhaps reviving childhood memories of reluctant compliance. In teaching, however, it is part of a professional relationship with colleagues as well as pupils: this context makes imperatives of many seeming trivialities.

REFERENCES

Balson, M. (1982) *Understanding Classroom Behaviour*, London, A.C.E.R.

Barnes, D., Britton, J. and Rosen, H. (1969) *Language, the Learner and the School*, Harmondsworth, Penguin.

Brophy, J. E. and Evertson, C. M. (1976) *Learning from Teaching*, Boston, Allyn & Bacon.

Bull, S. J. and Solity, J. E. (1987) *Classroom Management: Principles to Practice*, London, Croom Helm.

Calderhead, J. (1987) *Exploring Teachers' Thinking*, London, Cassell.

Caspari, I. (1976) *Troublesome Children in Class*, London, Routledge & Kegan Paul.

Curtis, S. J. (1963) *History of Education in Great Britain*, Foxton, Cambridge University Tutorial Press.

Dreikurs, R. (1957) *Psychology in the Classroom*, London, Staples Press.

Edwards, D. A. and Furlong, V. J. (1978) *The Language of Teaching*, London, Heinemann.

Evertson, C. M. and Emmer, E. T. (1982) 'Effective management at the beginning of the school year in junior high classes', *Educational Psychology*, 74, 2, pp. 485–98.

Fontana, D. (1985) *Classroom Control*, London, Methuen.

Goffman, E. (1968) *Asylums*, Harmondsworth, Penguin.

Grunsell, R. (1985) *Finding Answers to Disruption*, London, SCDC.

Hargreaves, D. H., Hestor, K. H. and Mellor, J. M. (1975) *Deviance in Classrooms*, London, Routledge & Kegan Paul.

Johnstone, M. and Munn, P. (1987) *Discipline in Schools: a Review of the Literature*, Edinburgh, Scottish Council for Research in Education.

Kounin, J. (1970) Discipline and Group Management in Classrooms, New York, Holt, Rinehart & Winston.

Laslett, R. and Smith, C. (1984) *Effective Classroom Management*, London, Croom Helm.

MacLure, M. and French, P. (1980) 'Routes to right answers: pupils' strategies for answering teachers' questions' in Woods, P. (1980a).

Marland, M. (1975) *The Craft of the Classroom*, London, Heinemann.

Mehan, H. (1979) *Learning Lessons: Social Organisation in Classrooms*, Cambridge, MA, Harvard University Press.

Partington, J. A. and Hinchcliffe, G. (1979) 'Some aspect of classroom management', *British Journal of Teacher Education*, 5, 3, pp. 231–41.

Posner, G. J. (1980) 'Promising developments in curriculum knowledge', paper presented to American Education Research Association, quoted in Sheeran, Y. C. (1988) 'A sociocultural approach to children's writing', M. Phil. thesis, University of Leeds.

Rutter, M., Maughan, B., Mortimore, P., Ouston, J. and Smith, A. (1979) *Fifteen Thousand Hours*, London, Open Books.

Sockett, H. (1983) 'Towards a professional code in teaching', in Gordon, P. (ed.) *Is Teaching a Profession?*, Bedford Way Paper 15, University of London.

Wittrock, M. C. (1986) (ed.) *Third Handbook of Research on Teaching*, New York, American Education Research Association/Macmillan.

Woods, P. (1980a) (ed.) *Pupil Strategies*, London, Croom Helm.

Woods, P. (1980b) (ed.) *Teacher Strategies*, London, Croom Helm.

Wragg, E. C. (1984) *Classroom Teaching Skills*, London, Croom Helm.

Chapter 26

Computers, curriculum and the learning environment

Noel Thompson

Anyone who is planning to use computers in a school, a college or for industrial training should make an effort to understand their capabilities and limitations; and – at least as important – the implications for the way in which tutors, teachers and lecturers need to operate in order to get the best out of them. The easy part – and even the cheap part – is to buy and install the equipment. Much higher costs are involved in providing the in-service training of teachers which is essential if the computer or more recent technologies are to be used effectively. This is not to say that training in computer science, let alone programming is required, but rather how to manage learning in partnership with the technology. Long and sad experience shows that if this dimension is neglected, the learning process under a computer regime can be more costly and less effective than by traditional methods.

If, however, we apply accumulated knowledge and understanding, we can achieve the exact opposite result: a more effective and flexible learning system and a better return on both the initial outlay and the continuing costs.

Computers can enhance the learning environment in a variety of different ways which I will now attempt to outline.

(a) By making learning more PRACTICAL

There is great potential in computer simulations, control activities, word processing and DTP exercises (such as a generation of a newspaper) for enabling the tutor to catalyse student interest and activity. From this, discussion and concept building can follow, based on the actions of pupils themselves and the discoveries which pupils themselves have made. This quality of the microcomputer used to be concentrated in science departments, because it was seen to be a way in which practical science could be made less like the traditional laboratory experiment and more like the real processes of science, involving genuine experimentation and open-ended investigation. More recently it is being recognised that this characteristic is relevant to work in many other subjects across the curriculum. No wonder that computer work has promoted group activities and language development, for these are the natural consequences of the computer's ability to make learning more practical and more relevant.

(b) By making learning more PROVISIONAL

I need not labour the educational potential of the *flexibility* of the computer and the ease with which computer-generated material can be changed – whether it is based on a spreadsheet, a word processor or a database – or otherwise. There has been a major change in the way students now approach the generation of written material, for it is no longer a punishment to ask a student to redraft a word-processed document. It is a natural process which encourages experimentation and the generation of self-critical standards. It is now a natural process based on the recognition that students' work should be seen as developmental, a series of steps from getting something reasonably right, then improving it and refining it until satisfaction is achieved. It is difficult to underestimate the importance of this new freedom which unleashes creativity and develops critical faculties. And it is just as relevant to children in the early years of schooling as it is to continuing education and adult training.

(c) By improving the learners' ACCESS to learning

The most dramatic example of this is seen when a computer enables communication difficulties to have a new window on the world, to socialise, to hold down a job in a community of people who are not, in general, similarly handicapped. But there are many other examples where the power of the computer can provide a totally new access to skills and experiences – e.g. high levels of musical experience can be achieved without the need to learn all the specialist skills required to become proficient on a particular instrument. Or it can bring achievement in Art which can capitalise on creativity when technical skill has not been developed to a sufficient level to exploit it. Art which for many was a frustrating experience because of the barrier of technical skill now becomes truly creative for the first time.

But even more important is the capability of the computer to be used with sophisticated learning systems which provide guidance to the potential student on career choices and the selection of appropriate courses of study. The importance of matching education and training provision to students' needs cannot be overstated – either in social terms and the rights of individuals or in national economic terms where failure and drop-out represent a gross waste of resource. The latest developments in North America and the U.K., amongst other countries, show that for the first time we have affordable computing power to tackle this sensitive and sophisticated need effectively, especially when the machine-based system is working in partnership with the professionally trained counsellor. In many countries the number of the latter is small compared with the call on their services. The computer can provide the solution.

(d) By increasing the focus on HIGHER ORDER skills

An early achievement of the first generation of microcomputers in schools and colleges was based on its fundamental ability to tackle low level, manipulative tasks and calculations which freed the learner for higher order activities, such as decision making, forecasting and planning; for 'what if' speculation, analysis, inference and so on. More recently, the more powerful generations of microcomputers and much more sophisticated software have themselves greatly enhanced the possibilities of the learner engaging in these higher level skills. To quote a rather banal example, 'what if' capabilities of spreadsheets are now accepted without question and used in routine ways which would not have been possible only a few years ago. The newer technologies involving interactive systems and mass storage are extending these capabilities dramatically, raising the premium on skills of searching and organising information, though some might say at the expense of certain levels of fundamental comprehension. The battle for the use of calculators in examinations was not easily won in Britain nor, I imagine, in other countries also. Similar battles may be expected as computers make possible higher level comprehension and manipulation.

(e) By making it possible to adapt learning programmes more nearly to the NEEDS OF THE INDIVIDUAL

This is often these days referred to as *Open and Flexible Learning*. The force behind it has been the need of individuals to have education and training courses tailored to their particular needs and sensitive to the constraints to which they are subject. Indeed, it could easily be argued that the main objective of education and training is to provide learning regimes tailored to the needs, attainment levels and abilities of the individuals: and available so that the learner can progress at the speed which he or she is capable of; and at times and places accessible to the learner. This, you will have noticed, is an aspiration which is not specifically related to machine-based systems. Indeed, machines are important only to the extent that they can help achieve the fundamental conditions for effective learning. I have already mentioned a number of rather important ways in which machines can contribute materially or indeed uniquely to achieving those conditions. But they also make it possible for people to study at times and places that are convenient to them and at the pace with which they are capable of learning. Machines can be switched on and off, and learning can be terminated and resumed in ways which are simply not possible or affordable by traditional methods. They

can not only purvey information across distance, but they can select information that is relevant to the individual from huge databases; they can
mobilise and organise materials in many different media to enhance the
learning process. Computers also have armed the teacher with more tools for
CUSTOMISING the resources that are provided for the learner. Desk top
publishing, word processing, authoring systems, hyper text systems all
improve our ability to construct flexible materials and learning materials
appropriate to the needs of the individual learner. Add to this the aids to
MANAGEMENT that are now being introduced in education increasingly,
it is clear that the computer's impact is already great and likely to grow
substantially.

(f) By encouraging IT capability across the curriculum

So far, I have been concentrating on ways in which the microcomputer or
other IT technology can contribute to the learning process more or less
independently of the subject or description. I do not apologise for that,
because it is this capability which makes a computer so important already
and will make it increasingly dominant in learning technology in the years
ahead. But there is also legitimately a need in schools and colleges to ensure
that those whom they are training and educating are prepared for adult life
and, in particular, the world of work. In the U.K., as I imagine many of you
may know, we have at last realised that we need a national curriculum. This,
I realise, is a fairly elementary concept which has been implanted for many
years in most other countries. But I suppose there are some advantages in
starting late, not least that we can learn from the experience of others. This
has led us to construct with some confidence a progression of attainment
targets, including some for the development of IT capability in our schools.
Through the national curriculum, we now encourage pupil development in
five cross-curricular areas where IT is making a special contribution:

1 communication and design;
2 enquiry and information handling;
3 modelling;
4 measurement and control;
5 applications and effects of IT.

In information handling, for example, we encourage children up to the age
of 11 years to gain experience of collecting and classifying data, of making
simple searches and drawing conclusions, of planning small-scale enquiries
and seeing them through to a conclusion. From 11 years, we increase
opportunities for pupils to speculate, to construct more complex investigation, to identify appropriate data collection techniques, to organise their
information, to adapt and manipulate the information, to examine conclusions and to consider their validity and ramifications.

Note that our progression is carefully framed in terms of the increasing complexity of tasks that students will face and in the combination of skills that are required – and *not* in terms simply of the complexity of the software that they will use. We continue to promote especially an approach which encourages students to identify and use the most appropriate tools, because this is a lasting skill which outdates the essentially ephemeral nature of specific software of the day.

WHERE ARE WE GOING WITH COMPUTERS, THE CURRICULUM AND THE LEARNING ENVIRONMENT?

One thing is already clear: computers are not just tools for curriculum designers; they are already changing the curriculum itself and the organisation of our schools and colleges. The educational and social impact can already be seen to be substantial and promises – or threatens – progressively greater change in the way we learn. Here are a few examples:

1 They are making more activities available *earlier*. We in the U.K. are already reconciled to having to adjust our IT capability attainment targets as new equipment and materials help us to embed higher level skills earlier. We are already putting tools in the hands of infant and primary children that enable them to control robotic devices, develop sophisticated spacial capabilities and plan and execute complex tasks. We are continually being surprised at how at every turn we find the potential for many pupils to do more and more earlier and earlier.

2 Computers are enabling us to bridge the home–school divide in compulsory education. Computers are introducing to the formalised and compulsory phases of education, the concepts of *not just flexible* learning, but *autonomous* learning – the self discipline that is needed for study in higher education and beyond and which is essential to so much of adult life. Our schools have not been too good at this in the past. We are expecting in the 1990s to have software which pupils can take home to work on, to adapt school work as necessary on their home machine and to return with it to progress further at school. Already parents are being influenced to buy machines in order to help their children's education. Yet they find little educational software they can readily understand or exploit, let alone readily use in direct support of school activities. All too often educational software for the home has trivialised the learning process. But important movement is taking place at the present time to improve the situation. Both through improved file compatibility and new software, we are expecting important breakthroughs in this area. At least, one major hardware supplier to schools is already beginning to exploit the potential of the home–school link in new ways which will not only develop the sales of its product, but also contribute to developing the partnership

between the teacher in the educational institution and parental support for learning at home.

3 Computers will also break down school walls (metaphorically!) in new ways. Improved communications through electronic mail, electronic conferencing and the potential for tutoring at a distance will make it possible to be much more flexible about access to classwork in schools and formalised learning in colleges. The technology is there and prices are already falling rapidly in, for example, optic fibre links of high bandwidth. The constraints of having to be in a particular place at a particular time are already becoming less severe in the field of adult learning and increasigly in schools where – in the U.K. certainly – flexible approaches to learning are gathering momentum. Improved authoring systems and computer administration systems will better enable us to prepare very adaptable, packaged materials which will allow a greater degree of personalisation of learning materials. I choose my words carefully: I am not suggesting that individuals learn generally best if they are on their own. On the contrary, experience dictates that that is not the case, but an important distinction can and should be made between tailoring learning materials to the needs of the individual and an individual learning in isolation. I should also mention the potential of mass storage systems which will help to promote an attitude of knowledge and learning which recognises the limitations of human memory and the limited power of humans to manipulate information. This in itself will encourage a focus beyond the confines of the classroom to much more varied and often distant resources.

All of this focuses our attention on the managers of our schools and colleges and the IT expertise which they will require in order to discharge their functions effectively. The greater the degree of autonomy which governing bodies are given, the greater is the danger that they will make ill-considered choices in fields like IT where a high level of expertise is needed. This is not in itself an argument against local autonomy, but a salutary warning that it needs to be backed by access to highly professional and specialised knowledge of the relationship between new technology and learning. Industry and commerce has learned the hard way that it is easy to make very costly mistakes and for schools particularly, with their restricted budgets, there is a high risk to the unwary and inadequately informed purchaser. I finish on this word of caution, because there needs to be available nationally, regionally or locally the quality of advice that is necessary to avoid costly mistakes being made repeatedly in a field of increasing complexity where simultaneous knowledge of learning processes and IT capability are not by any means always to be found. It is above all perhaps the most important role of my organisation – the National Council for Educational Technology – to recognise and provide for this need.

Chapter 27

New technology and its impact on classrooms

OECD

All the trends – technological, societal, environmental and educational – are interdependent. Changes in one area will have repercussions in others.

It is significant that the speed with which these trends will appear in practice will vary greatly from country to country. Some, especially in the technological section, are already at, or near to, implementation.

1 TECHNOLOGICAL TRENDS

In order to handle the very wide range of developments in this field, technological developments are subdivided into those related to computers and computing (including mass storage, and multi-media systems); satellites; and telecommunications. These divisions are recognised as being arbitrary, because, again, they are all interrelated and because computers, in some form or other, are an element in all of them.

Computers and computing

The computer market, with a current installed base of around 25 million personal computer systems, is estimated to be growing at a rate of 50 000 units per day worldwide. This growth rate is expected by trade sources to continue 'at least for the next decade'. The ratio of performance to cost has been increasing at a rate of some 20 per cent per annum over the past twenty years: it is expected to continue to do so. The implication of this growth in the market allied to decreasing cost in real terms, is that we can expect many school children (at least in the most developed countries) to have their own PCs, with something approaching the power and facilities of today's desktop business machines, by 2005.

Computer developments will continue at a pace similar to – or even greater than – that of recent years. They are likely to lead to:

– equipment which takes up less space, much of it designed to be truly portable (developments in battery technology are related to this);

- a substantial move towards flat-screen displays, which will eventually overtake VDUs based on cathode-ray tubes, with consequent savings in power consumption, heat generation, and space;
- the ability to present and manipulate three-dimensional images on screen (though this will probably remain an expensive and highly memory-consuming facility);
- improvement of speech recognition techniques so that speech input of commands and data becomes possible, thus reducing, or possibly eliminating, the need for keyboard skills (depending on success in developing both neural networks and artificial intelligence software);
- major improvements in the computer's ability to handle text: for example handling relational connections in full-text documents (through artificial intelligence techniques), or reproducing speech direct from text (using neural networks);
- the ability to receive data from short-distance radio transmissions will permit 'unwired' network connections;
- improvements in 'user-friendliness', for example the use of stylus and digitiser for control and low-volume data entry (like using a pen to point and write), speech input of commands and probably of text, and even greater use of icons in software;
- standardised software interfaces which will make it possible for different types of computers to exchange data over communications links.

Mass-storage developments will underpin all of the computer developments referred to above, because they will provide the large increase in memory required to provide the more complex facilities. Optical disc technology will continue to develop from the present 'publisher-manufactured' CD-ROM disc, through 'write once read many' (WORM) discs which can be produced by the user, but not altered once made, to mass-storage optical discs which can be recorded and erased (though these may not be reliable until near the end of the period covered by this report). It is reasonable to predict that storage capacity for data will not be a limiting factor on computer developments over the period under review.

An important spin-off from optical disc technology is the development of optical memory cards. These credit-card sized devices can already hold 2Mb of memory. Their potential value in educational and training uses seems likely to be considerable, especially if commercial use of these memory cards and other types of 'smart-cards' (which are already in use for financial transactions, for medical data, in portable and stand-alone terminals, in point-of-sale systems, and as removable memory in lap-top and pocket personal computers) expands as currently expected.

Interactive multi-media systems will continue their development from their optical-disc base. They will provide a new and powerful medium of communication through their ability to combine electronic text and high-level graphics with audio and full-motion video.

Whether the major market will go to the CD-I[nteractive] 'stand-alone player' development or to the DVI (Digital Video Interactive) which integrates existing PCs with CD-ROM storage, remains to be seen; as indeed does the possibility of developing an expert system to overcome their incompatibility. But in either case, a truly new and potentially very powerful medium of communication will exist.

Satellites and broadcasting

The use of satellites for the distribution of television and other material across much of the earth's surface will be commonplace. Although at present these facilities are most frequently used for commercial or entertainment purposes [it has been estimated that 9.5 million homes in Western Europe will be receiving satellite television (DBS) by the mid-1990s], education has already proved its ability to make good use of them, providing the costs are within its reach. Subject to that proviso, satellites will be used to:

- deliver television signals, including high-definition television, across national boundaries with sound commentaries in several languages (the problem caused by differing national television standards may remain);
- provide teaching and training programmes addressed to individual receiving sites, as well as for general reception;
- deliver a mixture of sound, text, data, graphics and full-motion video, probably with the capability of interaction from receiving sites using some or all of these media.

Satellites will enable, for example, the use of video-conferencing facilities over considerable distances (including internationally) as part of courses; the delivery of university-level courses to distant or isolated sites and to other nations; the co-operation of groups of schools from more than one country in the preparation and distribution of programmes and other materials in a variety of languages; and students to work on environmentally sensitive issues using live data about the earth and its atmosphere.

At a simpler level, they will permit the reception by educational institutions of general television broadcasts from a wide range of foreign countries. In this context, it can be expected that there will be widespread availability of personal television receivers (as with today's 'Walkman'-type radio and cassette players), many of which will be owned by students themselves.

Ordinary broadcast radio and television will continue to contribute educational programmes (although this will be increasingly dependent on national and commercial policy decisions about competing media and the tension between social and commercial pressures). Facilities such as the 'night hours' transmission of data, and the transmission of data and switching signals simultaneously with daytime broadcasts will also be available for use by education services.

Telecommunications

This is a technology which is developing rapidly. However, the speed of application of the new developments and the choice of which to use, are more dependent than any of the preceding technologies, on national policies, availability of funds for investment, and (in some cases) the terrain of the country. This makes prediction of the date by which particular technologies will become available very difficult, because it will vary from country to country. We can expect however that the telecommunications industry will be moving towards the following position by 2005–2010:

- Provision of integrated services digital networks (ISDN), which will end the division between voice (analogue) and data (digital) communications. ISDN will permit the simultaneous transmission of voice and data and give access via a variety of electronic devices to a wide range of services. In practice, this will mean, for example, that a user will be able to interrogate a database while talking to a client on the telephone and simultaneously editing the text which appears on the screen – all on a single ISDN line.
- The development of integrated broadband communications (IBC) which would permit the interworking of voice telephony, data packet transmission, ISDN, broadband video (interactive and distributive), satellite transmissions, and mobile (radio) telecommunications.
- Provision, either within another network (ISDN or IBC) or separately, of very high speed data links, with transmission speeds in the Gigabit/second range.
- Expansion and development of the mobile (cordless and cellular) telephone network, providing a small hand-held unit capable of transmitting data, fax, and low-rate video, as well as voice. This will operate within buildings (with interconnection through wireless PBXs) as well as out of doors, and will have a full interface with ISDN networks.
  These facilities will permit:
- a considerable growth in the use of facsimile (fax) for document transmission: personal computers will have integrated fax reception and transmission capability;
- integrated networks for electronic mail and for videotex systems (overcoming current incompatibilities).

The use of optical fibre to provide broadband transmission facilities will occur both within national telecommunications systems, and in separate cable systems designed primarily for the distribution of television to homes or to community facilities. Commercial broadband cable facilities will be able to provide the same data, voice and video transmission as the telecommunications system, but national regulations may not permit this.

2 SOCIETAL/POLITICAL TRENDS

The trends set out in this section are both derivative and selective: derivative in that they are based on a personal reading of other people's reports and predictions, and selective because they include only those trends which I think will have some impact on the main thrust of this report – the demand for and use of educational buildings.

Economic/industrial

The developed nations will move more and more towards a post-industrial 'information-based' economy which will lead to:

- Human capital becoming the key requirement of economic development: it has been suggested that by 2010 70 per cent of all jobs will be 'cerebral' with half of them requiring people with a university degree or professional qualification, and thus requiring a considerable expansion of higher education provision.
- Learning being the main work in three-quarters of all jobs – either people needing to absorb and act upon new information, or people helping machines to learn.
- The functional requirements of half of existing jobs changing completely in five years, creating a permanent training need.
- Increasing transience of workers in any particular organisation: it has been suggested that at any one time 36 per cent of workers in the United States will be changing or expecting to change their jobs – again resulting in an increased need for training.
- Women forming 45 per cent of the workforce, with the resultant provision of child-care facilities at the workplace.
- A considerable increase in the number of 'teleworkers': people who work from home, using telecommunications links to relatively remote offices. It has been suggested, for example, that 50 per cent of the London workforce will spend some part of the week working from home in this manner; it is city workers who will be most affected. The United States already has over 10 million self-employed teleworkers.
- The phenomenon of unemployment existing alongside job vacancies as the mismatch between workforce qualifications and level of training and the requirements of the new jobs continues to grow.

The move into a post-industrial, knowledge-based society will have an impact on a wide range of social activity.

- There will be increasing decentralisation of government and business activity. Telecommunications networks will mean that a person seeking information or service may well have that need met by someone hundreds of miles distant. All members of society, including children, will therefore become used to the idea of seeking information from a remote source over the telecommunications network.
- The use of powerful telecommunications facilities by governments and large businesses will put local, charitable, educational and public service activities at a disadvantage unless they can find the funds necessary to provide – or obtain access to – equally powerful networks.
- The widespread public availability of information from a variety of different sources, including sources outside the country, will cause increasing awareness of societal differences and will lead to increasing diversity in the social order itself. The problem of 'overchoice' available to people who have no experience in handling it, will be a concern.
- The availability of broadband networks will lead to increasing changes in shopping practices, strengthening moves to out-of-town shopping centres (dependent on computerised stock control and 'just-in-time' delivery of goods) and also to 'teleshopping' – purchasing from electronic catalogues. This could lead to towns losing their shopping 'heart', and to decisions to replace this with a cultural, leisure, and educational 'heart'.
- The potential isolation of individuals in their homes will be recognised by increased pressure to use leisure, shopping, cultural and educational activities as occasions for socialisation.

Environmental

National and international policies intended to protect or to improve the environment will have an impact on many aspects of daily life, not least because they are likely to be expensive and therefore to take a larger proportion of government funds. The most important effects from the point of view of this report are likely to be:

- restrictions of various kinds on the use of cars as private transport, both in order to reduce the emissions from exhausts and to reduce the clogging of towns and cities;
- pressure to reduce the level of commuting, by taking as much work as possible to people, rather than people to work;
- policies to reduce the consumption of power through the use of more effective thermal insulation of buildings; more efficient sources of lighting; materials for the construction of buildings, furniture and other goods derived from renewable or recycled sources;
- greater use of computerised control systems within buildings of all kinds to improve the efficiency of use of resources.

National identity

Satellite broadcasting and powerful telecommunications networks will not be constrained by national boundaries. It will be difficult – if not impossible – for a nation to isolate itself from the impact of other nations' cultures. Not only will the output of other (perhaps competitive) nations' broadcasting, educational and commercial concerns be receivable by anyone owning appropriate equipment, but it will also be open to individual citizens to obtain information direct from (for example) official statistical sources in other countries to compare with that provided locally.

There are likely to be two results from this. On one hand, there will be the possibility of attempts at cultural domination by nations prepared to invest heavily in their media industries and their technological facilities for communications. On the other hand, the very fact of what will be seen as 'cultural pollution' will lead to the use of the same channels of communication to strengthen the identities of smaller and smaller cultural groups. The technology will permit diversity and individual choice within the context of a growing international information flow.

3 TRENDS IN EDUCATION AND TRAINING

The difficulty in establishing trends in education and training systems is that they vary so much from country to country. The weight of history and cultural traditions lies heavily upon our educational provision – perhaps more than on any other aspect of national life. Any overview will inevitably describe trends which some readers will consider not to apply to their country or their system. Nonetheless, under the impact of the new technologies national and cultural boundaries are blurring. What is happening to some today, may well happen to others tomorrow.

Training is considered alongside education, not only because the boundary between those two elements is differently defined from country to country, but also because buildings currently described as 'educational' will increasingly be used for what is currently called 'training' – and vice versa. The distinction between the two terms is gradually losing significance.

Status and expectations

As the demands of an 'information-based' society become more apparent, governments are moving the education and training of their peoples higher up their list of priorities. They will call for a higher return from their investment in education and training facilities, both in terms of 'level of product' and in terms of value for money.

There will continue to be a tension between those who see education as primarily concerned with 'developing the whole person', and those who see it as primarily concerned with fitting people to work and live in their future society. Which of these two views predominates will depend on each country's view of the balance between the personal and spiritual benefit to its people as individuals and the economic benefit to its society as a whole.

Whatever the outcome of the tension between those views, there will be considerable changes in the demands made on the education and training system, because:

– The currently widening gap between the pervasive use of new information technologies in the world of work and leisure and their very limited use in educational institutions must be closed. It has been suggested that present educational methods are actually harmful in that they inculcate skills and methods of working opposed to those required by an 'information-based' economy (see also the section on teaching methods).

– The fundamental bases of education (all those things learned in the early years of schooling) will need to be grasped by children both more effectively and more quickly than at present, in order to underpin the more advanced and more individualised learning required as their education and training progresses.

– Pressure on national budgets will require education and training systems to be more cost-efficient. The use of sophisticated, computerised administrative networks will be commonplace, requiring inputs from teaching points as well as from the administrative office of the institution.

– The training/re-training cycle must be accelerated, with education and training becoming much more tailored to the specific needs of an individual, and increasingly provided on a 'just-in-time' basis. This can be done through the use of the new technologies; the constraint on doing so will come from educators' lack of understanding of how to make the most effective use of the technology, rather than from any deficiency in the technologies themselves.

– Individual people, perhaps from ages as young as 12 to 13 years, will become increasingly responsible for the progress of their own development and training, negotiating and working according to 'learning contracts' covering the content, duration and place of the various elements of their educational and training activity.

A word of warning may be necessary. Circumstantial evidence suggests that the new information technologies are not yet as much a part of the general culture of educators and politicians as they are in the culture of commercial and industrial leaders. Governments will increasingly be asking, over the next twenty years, for decisions and actions from the educational world which some of its leaders are ill-prepared to take. They themselves have a training need in this area.

Pressures of cost, staffing and demography

From what has gone before, it is obvious that as nations move towards an information-based economy, the cost of their education and training provision must rise. Equally it is obvious that strenuous efforts will be made by governments to keep this rise to a minimum.

In all education systems, the cost of teaching materials and equipment represents one of the smaller elements of overall budgets (around 10 per cent). If this element rises in order to cover the increased provision of computer and telecommunications-related equipment and their consequent day-to-day running costs, savings will be looked for from the major elements – premises (about 15–20 per cent) and teaching staff (about 50 per cent).

Individual governments will make different decisions about the balance of expenditure on various levels of education and training. In general, provision over the twenty-year timescale will probably favour further and higher education (those over 16 years of age) at the expense of those in the earlier years, and favour the training and retraining of adults at the expense of formal education.

The staffing structure of educational institutions will change in a variety of ways:

– Many countries will experience a shortage of qualified teachers, especially for children of the middle years (10–16). The reasons for this will vary between countries. In some, it will be caused by the drop in the societal status of the teaching profession and the consequent low teacher recruitmen in the 1980s; in others it will be caused by more attractive salaries and working conditions in the training departments of commercial, industrial and leisure concerns, or indeed within other aspects of those industries; and some countries will find that there is just not enough money to pay for all the teachers required.
– As educational systems make greater use of new technologies, they will need greater numbers of support staff. They will employ highly qualified information staff (currently librarians) who will have direct contact with learners, but whose skills will be quite different from those of subject teachers.

   There will also be managerial and administrative professionals with their own support staff. There will, especially, be technicians, to maintain the systems in optimum condition. These staff will be recruited and paid for at the expense of what are currently 'teaching' posts, as the division between those who manage and those who facilitate learning becomes more marked as a result of the move towards more pupil-directed learning methods.

Many countries will experience a drop in the number of children in school in the next ten years. Crude birth-rate statistics suggest that numbers will recover somewhat in the early years of the 21st century, but will not return to the levels of the 1970s. Demand for school places for those under the age of 16 therefore seems likely to be fairly stable at a little above current levels, but demand for places for those over 16 – the whole of the adult age-range – will increase considerably under the pressure for a more highly educated and trained workforce.

Teaching and learning methods and sites

It is worth remembering that even in a time of revolutionary change, many things remain much as they always were. There are still plenty of people who maintain that the introduction of new technologies will not suddenly reverse centuries-old educational practices. Others stress the process of alienation which takes place when students are confronted with technical artefacts instead of live human beings. Our estimation is that the first of these views will be overturned by the demands of governments and peoples facing life in the 21st century, and that the second may well apply to the present generation, but will not apply to the one currently entering school.

Because this section seeks simply to establish trends, the educational reasoning behind the changes in teaching and learning methods identified is not explained. All are extrapolated from current practice and writing: the arguments about their educational validity and effectiveness are published. One can expect to observe the following:

- A steady move away from class-based teaching towards individual responsibility for learning.

    The move will be progressive as the students get older (and therefore more able to take responsibility for their own learning), that is, with more class-based teaching at first school level to very little at young adult level.

    This move will be driven by the need for those living and working in the 21st century to learn – in controlled circumstances – how to construct knowledge from information in the course of ordinary life, and will be facilitated by the availability of powerful, computerised learning-management packages. (We can expect 'smart cards' to be carried by all older students not only as means of identification when using computer-based learning systems, but also as a means of recording progress within past and current courses.)

    The move will lead to much learning by older students taking place outside of school buildings, using open learning or supported self-study techniques; sometimes at home, sometimes in local 'drop-in' learning centres to assist peer-group interaction; but always with electronic access to tutors and resources in their base 'school'.

- Much more learning which involves contact between students and teachers from other schools and colleges, often in other countries.

  The walls of educational institutions will become transparent (educationally speaking) as: students obtain information from remote sources; learning materials are received from other countries; project work is shared between schools, involving the exchange of and interaction with, materials including text, graphics, video and sound; and tutoring of individual students is sometimes carried out by subject experts from other institutions. The concept of 'school' as a geographical entity will be eroded and may well disappear.

- The content of the school curriculum undergoing marked change because the fundamental thinking of current curricula will no longer match the skills needed for life in the 21st century.

  Today, learning and thinking is individual, sharing is considered to be cheating. But learning and thinking in the world of work is shared, and will be so increasingly as computerised management-information systems spread. Hand-written or printed text is fixed both in time and place, but electronic text is easily and immediately transferable and infinitely alterable, to ensure it is up to date.

  Memorisation still underlies much current teaching, but will it still be useful when information can be received on a personal computer-screen, which may be no bigger than a wrist-watch?

  Teachers, who are at present the major source of, or controllers of, the information needed for learning will find that they have become advisers on, and gatekeepers to a multitude of sources of information, many of which are outside their control. In much of their work they will be tutors, guides, counsellors, sources of judgement and experience, rather than providers. They will still be of vital importance, because they will be the people with whom ideas are discussed and tested, from whom encouragement and discipline are obtained, and above all who assess and aid progress. They will be the ones who teach the students to learn.

- The use of new technologies in the process of learning being pervasive.

  This has been prophesied before without it taking place. However, it may happen soon because of the widespread availability of cheap, powerful, portable microcomputers, often the property of students themselves. They will use them at home, not just for computer games and other leisure purposes, but also to obtain information, to book tickets for shows, and to buy goods. Their parents will do the same.

  This will match the world of work, where individual access to computer power 'at the desk' is already commonplace and a far cry from the strictly programmed session in the 'computer room' which is the current practice in schools. Indeed if schools do not make use of new technologies in this everyday way, young people will become alienated from their educational provision because they will find it more and more irrelevant to their daily life.

There will be great changes in the place where learning happens. This does not mean the end of school buildings – apart from any other consideration, there are already thousands of them across the OECD countries whose useful lives will extend into the middle years of the 21st century.

We may however see a proliferation of places where learning takes place, many of which will not be what we currently call schools. Homes, factory and office training centres, company child-care centres, public libraries, town-centre culture and leisure facilities all will find themselves providing for learners of various ages, including the very youngest.

We may expect to find new life breathed into small schools. Holland College, Prince Edward Island, Canada, may provide a pointer:

> The College is a multi-site institution with four major centres and supplementary centres spread over the Island . . . It thus has no campus as such, but uses a variety of houses, community buildings, redundant educational and industrial buildings for these centres. The buildings are seen as study centres where instructors conduct counselling services in suites which resemble 'live' work locations. Centres also act as a forum for student interaction and as resource centres.

Part V

Curriculum

Throughout the world the school curriculum has been at the centre of educational debate. If the early and middle years of the century can be associated with the expansion of schooling, and the structure within which this was achieved, the later years from the 1960s on have been preoccupied with the content or curriculum of that schooling. Malcolm Skilbeck opens this Part with a summary, taken from a longer review, of the international interest in defining core elements within the school curriculum. He suggests that *'core curriculum is a widespread phenomenon'* and one of the *'striking trends of the times across most industrialised countries'*.

HMI's *'Towards a statement of entitlement'* (Chapter 29 'The entitlement curriculum' in this volume) provided one of the key texts in the 1980s debate about establishing a national framework for the curriculum. It was widely read in schools and was seen by many as providing a blueprint for the legislation to come. The style and tone are markedly different from that adopted by polemicists of the right such as Oliver Letwin. His ideas, with their populist, traditionalist philosophy exemplify the pamphleteering of the 'new right', a small group of writers and tutors who came to have a significant impact on the way the national curriculum was set out in the 1988 Education Reform Act. Bob Moon describes the origins of this legislation and the way in which its formulation departed from that set out in the HMI document. He describes how *legislation was formulated in a context where political ideas and interest groups intervened to influence the final model adopted*.

Britain's educational performance in international comparison has been a recurrent feature of educational debate. Channel Four in the early 1990s commissioned a group to look at the education system. 'Academic drift – towards a new focus for the education system' is an extract from this report, which suggests that *Britain has failed to develop an effective educational system for the technological world of today and that a main reason for this is because education is still heavily focused on the needs of an academic minority*.

The need for a stronger vocational element within the curriculum of the compulsory years was argued, as well as a rethink of the curriculum in the post-16 phase. The development of new policies that link academic options in the 16–19 phase, perhaps conceptualised as a new post-14 phase of schooling, represents one of the liveliest of issues for contemporary curriculum debate.

Over much of this century assessment has been conceived of in terms apart from curriculum. One of the most interesting developments of recent years has been the attempts to develop an integrated view of these two inextricably linked dimensions of the teacher's role. Sally Brown, in the first of a group of articles on assessment, provides a summary of the changing practice of assessment. *Assessment*, she says, *is now seen as a much broader concept and fulfilling multiple purposes*. This, however, can lead to problems of a political, technical and curricular nature. The British Educational Research Association policy task group report on 'Assessment and the improvement of education', shows how these problems are manifest in the assessment arrangements for the national curriculum, and they point to ways in which existing models could develop from our experience of assessment reform. National programmes of assessment strive for accuracy and fairness. Patricia Murphy points to the way gender, however, came to influence the design of assessment. She points out how *changes in assessment practice have important implications for the perceived performance of boys and girls and she raises a number of important questions for the design of national systems.* John Marks, a writer who, like Letwin, has argued on behalf of the right on policy reform, introduces a cautionary note linking assessment practice to value for money. He sets out an advocacy for *public examinations and standardised group tests as the only realistic way of measuring attainment* and in polemical style, he argues that formal assessment need not be something which pupils dread, and he points to evidence that seven-year-olds have enjoyed testing under the new national assessment arrangements for England and Wales. Finally, and controversially, he argues that what they actually enjoyed finding out was 'what they knew and didn't know and how they stood compared with their classmates'.

Chapter 28

The core curriculum
An international perspective

Malcolm Skilbeck

One of the most striking trends we are observing in the curriculum field is the renewal of interest in a firm and clear national or system-wide framework: of goals and objectives: required subjects or subject areas for study; guidelines or procedures for assessment and a range of monitoring and accountability measures. Core curriculum is a widespread phenomenon. But what does the term 'core' connote in curriculum debate and school practice?

ANTECEDENTS

Changing assumptions about the nature and content of core curriculum parallel the vast expansion in the early to mid-twentieth century and onwards of our national systems of public education. This is most noticeable at the secondary school stage where the rapidly increasing number of students of much greater diversity than hitherto was, *inter alia*, a challenge to the classical model of the curriculum and pedagogy. This model presupposed a common body of knowledge, to be studied by all students, who would be taught by whole class methods and usually in a didactic fashion. Of course, there were exceptions, but the essential point is that the core curriculum meant the whole curriculum for all students.

The model collapsed [and] the question then arose as to whether there is any common body of knowledge, values or skills that, regardless of student aptitude and background, should or could form the nucleus of the variety of curricula that have emerged during recent decades. In fact, all school systems do have some prescribed core learnings although they are usually differentiated for purposes of teaching.

It is to the American literature that we must turn if we wish to trace the evolution of this process and the changing meanings of the term 'core'. Historical exegesis is not to our purpose here, but mention should be made of the principles that have informed core curriculum thinking. These include the beliefs that subject matter can be integrated through grouped or interdisciplinary studies; that there is a common set of social values and democratic principles that all citizens should imbibe; and that the core curriculum can be stated as a set of learning experiences and hence made personal to each and every student.

These aspirations for an integrated core of socio-cultural values and meanings and a new pedagogy were to be deflected, in the United States, by the post-Sputnik drives towards a subject-centred core curriculum.[1]

CURRENT MEANINGS AND APPROACHES

First, 'core' as widely understood across countries signifies system-wide (whether national or state/provincial) control and direction of defined, essential curriculum elements to meet national goals and objectives. Second, it signifies emphasis on predefined subjects or subject matter, structure and organisation in the curriculum. Third, it encompasses not only a defined content to meet specified goals or objectives but attainment standards and means of assessing them. Fourth, the approach being taken to core, with an insistence on compulsory subjects and standards, is a reaction to the fragmentation of the curriculum resulting from the 'cafeteria' approach whereby students assemble curricula by combining their choice of the subjects that please or suit them. Fifth, there is a belief in some countries that the core curriculum movement is a covert assault on innovations in curriculum and pedagogy such as integrated studies, controversial subject matter in the social, cultural and environmental areas, group work and inquiry-based learning.

There is little that is novel in the core curriculum movement. In the educational literature core curriculum has an ancestry dating back to antiquity. In all periods of history efforts have been made to analyse for purposes of schooling the fundamental elements of knowledge and understanding: the kinds of knowledge that seem to provide foundations for further learning; the intellectual and practical skills that serve as tools; and values and attitudes that seem to be of most worth to individuals and society. Inevitably, groups with power in society – whether church or state or professional bodies – will seek to control teaching and learning and the core curriculum is an obvious mechanism.

Since interest groups are involved, and value judgements enter into all these matters – and scientific knowledge of learning processes and of knowledge itself is limited – there always has been and there remains legitimate ground for debate about the core. Moreover, until recent times the debate did not have to take into account universal, compulsory schooling. This has added a dimension which is particularly evident in present endeavours to define required learnings for all, together with more advanced and specialised pathways for individuals and particular groups. The reform of examining, assessment practices and indicators of learning performance are also affected by extended participation in schooling. Consequently, the core is under great pressure.

In several countries where a nationally-prescribed core has been a feature, reviews have recently occurred of the overall scope, shape, content and organisation of the core to meet national priorities and needs and to respond to the changed context. Striking examples include Italy (elementary schooling), Turkey (secondary schooling) and Japan (elementary and secondary).

On the other hand, where there has been a tradition of local decision-making and where there has been variety or, until recent years, perhaps a slackening of commitment to nationally-declared curriculum priorities, as in the United States, England and Wales, Australia, New Zealand and Canada, there is now a very strong revivalist movement. The core curriculum in either a stronger or weaker form has as a consequence become a major educational priority.

In Canada, 'essential learnings' are being defined, computing courses in secondary schools increased in number, and stricter requirements introduced for the award of the high school diploma. At the level of subjects, core curriculum is now defined in all Canadian provinces at both elementary and secondary levels to include 'language arts, mathematics, sciences and social studies'. Compulsory studies are likely to be incorporated soon. It is emphasised, however, that subject labels are not enough in defining the basics. Increasing attention is being given to skills in handling information, problem-solving, critical thinking and so forth.

New Zealand has maintained a required core of subjects in both primary and secondary schools ever since the Second World War. However, this has been enlarged and varied – its critics would say diluted or fragmented – as a result of additions and variations which include health and peace education, computer studies, environmental education and others. The recent curriculum review has laid down principles and guidelines and indicated areas of study and approaches to teaching but has stopped short of specifying subjects and time allocations. The New Zealand authorities indicate that existing specifications on these items are being redrawn in light of their review. Moreover, the review draws the final years of secondary education firmly within the core curriculum net.

NEW NATIONAL ENDEAVOURS TO DEFINE (AND CONTROL) THE CORE

In countries that are moving to affirm or strengthen a clearly-defined, subject-oriented core curriculum, there is little if any disagreement over the desirability of facilitating students' access to knowledge and learning process skills (problem-solving, reasoning strategies, cognitive maps, co-operative and communication skills, etc.). The debate centres on whether knowledge access and process skills will be enhanced or submerged by the changes under way.

Great Britain has taken the unusual – for her – step of introducing legislation to specify the core areas and to empower the Secretary of State for Education and Science to monitor implementation, including the use of nationwide tests of student attainment at 7, 11, 14 and 16 (General Certificate of Secondary Education replacing the separate antecedent examinations). A set of specified subjects is required of all students during the years of compulsory schooling: mathematics, English, science, history, geography, technology, music, art, physical education and a modern foreign language (the latter only for students from 12 to 16). Effectively they constitute the core although that term is formally reserved for the three subjects of English, mathematics and science. There are radical delegations of financial and managerial decisions to schools: a neat reversal of the previous practice whereby the schools tended to control the curricula (allowing for the end of secondary school exams) while the outside authorities determined the budget details.

In the United States, while it is not within the power of the federal government to legislate a national core along these lines, the wave of national reports commencing in 1981 argued for a broad common core of studies for all youth and sketched their outlines.[2] By no means the first of such proposals, this series of documents nevertheless attracted interest and support of an unprecedented kind. *A Nation at Risk*, for example, advocated 'five new basics': English, mathematics, science, social studies and computer science. Of this five, only the last was a relative innovation, but the real novelty lay in the emphasis on systematic, continuous study of discrete subjects, all of them to be compulsory. Many United States school systems have moved in this direction.

The country reports for this study and other sources do not produce commensurate data sets on required subjects, time allocations and so forth, so systematic comparisons across countries cannot be incorporated here. The next phase of CERI work on trends in school curriculum includes a study of core trends and issues. More comprehensive and detailed data should be available then.

What is so different about the new advocacy of core? Most obvious in the United States has been the emphasis on standards of attainment in basic subjects to be achieved through:

- Greater concentration on key concepts
- Orderly knowledge structures
- Cognitive and practical skills
- Greater effort within schools by teachers and students alike
- More structured home study
- An explicit interest in cognitive learning strategies
- Evaluation and application of knowledge
- More rigorous, comprehensive and frequent testing of learning outcomes at all levels from individual schools to the whole nation.

In applying this agenda, the American public authorities and a number of private and professional organisations have embarked upon extensive critiques, reviews and developmental programmes in the humanities, sciences and mathematics. There has been a substantial development programme in assessment and evaluation and this has generated fierce controversy. As many commentators have pointed out, there can be a negative impact of this kind of activity upon the broader educational goals and values that have been widely promulgated across the nation. The American authorities are not blind to the dangers:

> Many educators are mindful that a great deal of instructional time has been diverted to testing. Practitioners, policy-makers, and researchers have all begun to question the appropriateness of the instruments used to gather the desired information, and the utility of the information once it is gathered.

The debate in Great Britain over the narrowness of the definition of the core and the move towards nationwide testing in the 'basic core' of English, mathematics and sciences continues as the government proceeds from plan to consultation to legislation to implementation.[3] This debate brings out a significant issue about curriculum and pedagogy. Priorities by their nature are translated into specific cognitive and affective changes and defined skills. These are separated out from the potentially much wider range of student learnings to which curriculum and teaching should minister.

It would be advisable for governments to examine more closely the implications of the inevitable narrowing of the curriculum that results from concentration on a handful of 'basic' subjects. Selections and choices must be made, and there are necessary economies of provision to achieve. But there is a risk of retrogressive reforms, with the solutions of the 1980s and 1990s referring to the problems of the 1960s and 1970s. It is not clear how the national drive towards compulsory subjects and testing will avoid a stultifying rigidity in teaching and learning or achieve the flexibility, independence and adaptability sought in the modern workforce or the cultivated interests needed for a leisure society. Studies in the history of pedagogy have indicated how difficult it is to achieve the experiential, student-centred learning of the kind that is needed.[4]

CORE AS AN ACCEPTED RESPONSIBILITY OF CENTRAL GOVERNMENTS

In many countries, indeed in all except some of the Anglo-Saxon countries, the concept of a nationally- or regionally-defined core curriculum is already quite familiar. There appears to be little interest in the question of whether or not there should be a government-determined core of subject learning required of all students. Rather, concern focuses on changes in its scope and context, the parties that participate in its determination, and procedural matters arising in the field of action. These include the definition of objectives, ways of ensuring compliance, procedures for assessing student performance and regional and local decision-making, support services, etc. Extensive developments in testing procedures, with national samples taken at every level of schooling, have been occurring in France for several years. This is but one example of such development.

In Finland, since the early 1970s there has been developmental work on core content to determine the essential and discard the peripheral. As mentioned above, the Finns are concerned about the undue weight given to mere information gathering and regurgitation. Accordingly, a major project, Formal Aims of Cognitive Education/Instruction was commenced in 1985 to find ways of developing students' thinking, problem-solving and intellectual curiosity and creativity within and across the core subjects. The Finnish cognitive project is not subject-specific, but addresses cross-subject learning process skills and cognitive strategies.

Development work on core subject areas, while still subject-related, illustrates a growing tendency across the OECD area. Systems are aiming to take a broader view and to clarify goals. In relation to them, efforts are being made to elaborate knowledge structures, cognitive strategies and style, learning processes and transferable skills such as problem identification, problem-solving and ways of applying and utilising knowledge. Examples are provided by the Netherlands, New Zealand, Germany and Norway. These emphases entail new roles and capabilities among teachers but it must be reiterated that there is no commensurate growth in provision and facilities, particularly for in-service education, which in the 1960s and 1970s were generally accepted as a necessary corollary of curriculum reform. The newer policy and planning approaches will not quickly take root in the schools unless this is remedied.

ADDRESSING NEW NEEDS

So far, the discussion of core has centred on the idea that fundamental and basic learnings required of all students are most readily expressed as a set of compulsory subject learnings in the framework of the school week and year. This does no more than acknowledge the way core curricula are frequently described in policy guidelines and regulations, and presented in school timetables. From the discussion of general curriculum concepts and approaches in the preceding chapter, it is evident that there are serious limitations to this approach. These are recognised to some extent where the specification of 'essential learnings' is not subject-bound but presented in terms of general understandings, critical thinking skills, values, intellectual flexibility and so on. Mention has been made of the Canadian provinces and the New Zealand approaches to the matter and there may be a trend emerging, but as yet it is submerged within the concept of 'core' defined as a set of discrete, timetabled subjects.

It is becoming increasingly obvious that more creative thinking, including more professional participation in policy studies, is required to clarify desirable directions in core curriculum planning and development. There are too many moves in [many] countries pointing towards a whole or cross-curriculum approach and to the need for fresh initiatives in pedagogy for this rather old-fashioned subject-centred and subject-timetabled curriculum to continue. It is the press of specialised and professionalised knowledge in higher education that has reinforced curriculum conservatism in the second-ary schools and the subject-centred regime of the upper secondary stage has similar effects lower down. Further changes will occur as a result of the drive towards vocational preparation in secondary schooling. Many of the pilot projects in this area are breaking the subject mould.

Are subjects to be abandoned, then? Certainly not. The point is, as John Dewey long ago pointed out, to draw upon subjects as a *resource* in the design of curricula and so to utilise and combine subject matters as to match the interests and experiences of learners and the socio-cultural world of which they are a part.

There are positive signs of a coming change. Thus, as has already been shown, the trends in contemporary educational policy development and the current concepts of curriculum include, but are not confined to, areas of subject knowledge. A comprehensive analysis of core in practice would incorporate both learning processes and learning environments, yet the specifications of core that are commonly made either deal scantily with these dimensions or, in the case of the second, frequently are completely silent. This is, as much as anything, an indication of the need for a more contem-porary and exact language.

As teachers know very well, what education authorities really regard as the fundamental and basic learnings is not necessarily those specified in up-front objectives and descriptions of what is to be taught. Their real concerns are to be found in the form and content of student assessments and in the kinds of monitoring that systems deploy in their quest for compliance. There ought to be, of course, a close correspondence between the two. This is more clearly the case in some systems (e.g. Finland) than others. The content and style of performance indicators, as they extend across education systems, will be most revealing. Teachers will teach to the requirements of the assessment system and students will learn accordingly. It is therefore of the utmost importance that the curricular and pedagogical reforms that are being sought should be fully reflected in the assessment, monitoring and accountability regimes.

We need to consider in a little more detail the trends in assessment – which seem to indicate that much of the current development work in education is occurring in that area (for example in the United States, the United

Kingdom, Canada, the Netherlands, Sweden and France). Evidence on school failure is growing as a result of monitoring work and forms the substance of major debate in some countries. In France, for example, an evaluation scheme for elementary education *(dispositif d'évaluation de l'enseignement à l'école élémentaire)* was launched in 1978 and a similar scheme for secondary school monitoring in 1980. Attention therefore needs to be paid to the devices being put in place to ensure compliance: accountability reports, the construction and application of performance indicators, monitoring and evaluating by the inspectorate and so on. Studies already carried out within the OECD on 'Quality', 'The Inspectorate and School Improvement', and 'Performance Indicators' are highly relevant and informative.

A crucial task in the core debate is the identification of the values, disciplines, areas of knowledge, skills and themes deemed to be essential for the modern world and for today's learners and tomorrow's citizens. These must not only be taught – they must be learned, and the effective translation of nationwide core requirements into individually successful and satisfying learning for *all* students remains one of the great unfinished tasks in education. The issue of the scope, content and organisation, teachability and learnability of the contemporary core of the curriculum requires more rigorous analysis than it generally receives. Supporters of the move towards the kind of broad compulsory core curriculum which is to be found in all school types in the German system question what they see as the looseness and mediocre overall standards of those systems which have encouraged great diversity, confining the most rigorous study requirements to a relatively small minority. Others, mindful of the wide range of student aptitudes, abilities, interests and socio-cultural backgrounds, are sceptical about the push towards a tough-minded academicism. Yet others see the shape of the core in terms more of social issues and life skills, as did the American advocates of 'life adjustment' education in the 1950s. There are, as a consequence, serious tensions in the general shift towards a core curriculum for all students, in all Member countries. They will not be resolved merely by the issuing of policy guidelines, frameworks or directives or even by legislation.

What is of most interest, educationally, in current debates about core curriculum are the attempts being made to introduce new forms and organisation of knowledge into the core itself: a reconceptualisation, in some measure, of basic and fundamental learnings. Noteworthy are the conceptual strategy approach adopted in the new Italian primary curriculum and the new Japanese concept of core as providing the basic building blocks of universal, lifelong learning. In Japan, there is a strong reaction to material affluence, hence a questioning of the effects of affluence on children, and a reassertion of humanistic values. *Seikatsuka* – the merging of elementary science and social-environmental studies, in the elementary school – is a bold new move. Overall, a brave effort is being made to find a central place in the core for creativity, logical thinking, imagination, inspiration, motivation to learn, enjoyment of learning, pleasure of accomplishment in face of the 'desolation' of contemporary Japanese education, and society.

NOTES

1 Goodlad, J. (1986), 'Core curriculum: what and for whom', in Gorter, R. J. (ed), *Views on Core Curriculum*, Enschede, National Institute for Curriculum Development.

2 For a review of the first wave of these reports, see Westbury, I. (1984), 'A nation at risk' *Journal of Curriculum Studies*, 16–4. pp. 431–445; and Goodlad, J. I. (1984), *A Place Called School*, New York, McGraw Hill; Berman, P. and McLaughlin, M. W. (1975), *Federal Programs Supporting Educational Change. Vol. 4, The Findings in Review*, Santa Monica, California, Rand Corporation; Kliebard, H. M. (1979), 'The drive for curriculum change in the United States, 1890–1958; From local reform to a national preoccupation', *Journal of Curriculum Studies*, 11, 12, pp. 273–281; and Kliebard, H. M. (1986), *The Struggle for the American Curriculum*. London, Routledge & Kegan Paul; McClure, R. M. (1971), 'The reforms of the fifties and sixties: a historical look at the near past', *Seventieth Yearbook of the National Society for the Study of Education: The Curriculum: Retrospect and Prospect*. Chicago, Ill., The Society, pp. 45–75; Giacquinta, J. B. and Kazlan, C. (1980), 'The growth and decline of public school innovations; a national study of the open classroom in the United States', *Journal of Curriculum Studies*, 12, 1, pp. 61–72; Gammage, P. (1987), 'Chinese whispers', *Oxford Review of Education*, 13, 1, pp. 95–109; An Roinn Oidachais (1971), *Curaclam Na Bunscoile (Primary School Curriculum)*, Dublin, the Stationery Office, Parts 1 and 2; Edelstein, W. (1986), 'The rise and fall of the social science curriculum project in Iceland, 1974–1984: reflections on reason and power in the educational process' *Journal of Curriculum Studies*, 19, 1, pp. 1–23; Edelstein, W. (1986), *art. cit.*, p. 3; see also Kliebard, H. M. (1986), *op. cit.*, Chapter 9, 'Life adjustment education and the end of an era'; U.S. National Commission on Excellence in Education (1983), *A Nation at Risk*, Washington, D. C., Government Printing Office. See also the U.S. Secretary of Education's 'progress report' on the reform movement that ensued: Bennett, W. J. (1988), *American Education: Making it Work*, Washington, Department of Education.

3 National Union of Teachers (1987), 'National curriculum', *N.U.T. Education Review*, 1, 2, Autumn; Lawton, D. and Chitty, C. (eds) (1988), *The National Curriculum*, Bedford Way Paper 33, London, University of London Institute of Education; Simon, B. (1988), *Bending the Rules*, London, Lawrence & Wishart.

4 Instructive on this point are two American studies: Cremin, L. A. (1961), *The Transformation of the School*, New York, Alfred A. Knopf; Cuban, L. (1986), 'How did teachers teach, 1890–1980', *Theory into Practice*, XXII, 3, pp. 159–165. Cuban notes that teacher-centred intruction prevailed throughout this period: 'far more teacher than student talk; the predominance of questions calling for factual recall and of whole class instruction; heavy reliance on textbooks with texts emphasizing factual recall of information: the margin of classroom change available to reformers is far narrower than expected in the elementary school and even slimmer in the high school. Historically, teaching practices have hewed to a teacher-centred pattern that persistently reasserts itself after reform impulses weaken and disappear.'

Chapter 29

The entitlement curriculum

Her Majesty's Inspectors

THE SOCIAL CONTEXT

Curriculum 11–16 (working papers by HM Inspectorate published in December 1977) began by stating the case for a coherent common curriculum in secondary education up to the age of 16. An important feature of the enquiry was to attempt to define what a pupil at the age of 16 might reasonably be expected to have acquired from a secondary school education. The following argument began to take shape:

> pupils have common needs to develop, with maximum enjoyment, skills and attitudes necessary for their individual autonomy now and in the future and for work and political and social participation in the democratic society to which they belong;
>
> they face the common experience of living in a world which is increasingly international, multi-ethnic and interdependent both economically and politically;
>
> their curricula should be based on a common framework which provides coherence, and, while taking account of individual needs and abilities, still ensures the provision of a broadly based common experience.

Accordingly it seemed essential that all pupils should be guaranteed a curriculum of a distinctive breadth and depth to which they should be entitled irrespective of the type of school they attended or their level of ability or their social circumstances and that failure to provide such a curriculum is unacceptable. This is the sense in which the term 'entitlement curriculum' was used in the partnership and continues to be used in this test.

AN OUTLINE SPECIFICATION

The work of the enquiry has led to the conclusion that any adequate specification of the curriculum to which all pupils are entitled up to 16 should include the following:

1 a statement of aims relating to the education of the individuals and to the preparation of young people for life after school;
2 a statement of objectives in terms of skills, attitudes, concepts and knowledge;
3 a balanced allocation of time for all the eight areas of experience (the aesthetic and creative; the ethical; the linguistic; the mathematical; the physical; the scientific; the social and political; and the spiritual) which reflects the importance of each and a judgement of how the various component courses contribute to these areas;
4 provision for the entitlement curriculum in all five years for all pupils of 70–80 per cent of the time available with the remaining time for various other components to be taken by pupils according to their individual talents and interests;
5 methods of teaching and learning which ensure the progressive acquisition by pupils of the desired skills, attitudes, concepts and knowledge;
6 a policy for staffing and resource allocation which is based on the curriculum;
7 acceptance of the need for assessment which monitors pupils' progress in learning, and for explicit procedures, accessible to the public, which reflect and reinforce 1 to 5 above.

AIMS

Clarifying and stating general aims is a necessary first stage and since much time can be taken in debate about what this term means, an *aim* was defined as a general statement of intent. For example, a school might aim to develop in children the ability to act and think independently. It needs to be noted, however, that clarifying aims involves discussion and the emergence of a degree of consensus about the values and principles of the society for which children are being educated. The example given above rests upon agreement about the worth of children learning to think independently, and the importance of this aim for schools and for a wider society. The way in which Wigan arrived at a consensus about the principles behind its aims is illustrated below in the statements which it made about two of its aims.

> '*Education must free the individual to enable the expression of human uniqueness.*'
> Education is responsible for fostering those conditions which afford all pupils the security to express emotions, feelings and thoughts which are peculiar to them. Education, therefore, must be based upon moral, spiritual and humanitarian values such as love, tolerance, altruism, freedom of speech, freedom from oppression. The fostering of these values, which are of supreme importance whether viewed from a religious or secular perspective, is vital to the nurturing of the human spirit.

'Education should equip people with the desire and skills to participate in a democratic society.'

Democracy, by definition, demands the involvement of people. Education has the responsibility of operating within a democratic system; of respecting and nurturing democratic principles; of being open to change by democratic process; and, perhaps most importantly, of encouraging within the young those qualities and skills which will enable them to participate in a democracy and ultimately to develop or change it.

During the enquiry, the aims most frequently identified by schools and LEAs were:

- to give children the experience of school as a caring, supportive community where life is enjoyable and where there is equal provision regardless of sex, race or culture;
- to enable all children to develop as fully as possible their abilities, interests and aptitudes and to make additional provision if necessary for those who are in any way disadvantaged;
- to allow children to develop lively enquiring minds, to be capable of independent thought and to experience enjoyment in learning so that they may be encouraged to take advantage of educational opportunities in later life;
- to develop appropriate skills in, for example, literacy and numeracy;
- to develop a curriculum which ensures contact with those major areas of knowledge and experience which will help children to know more about themselves and the society in which they live;
- to work in ways which will enhance the self-respect and confidence of young people and encourage them to take responsibility for themselves and their activities;
- to establish a partnership between the school and the community it serves and to develop understanding of the wider community and of the ways in which individuals and groups relate;
- to give children the skills necessary to respond effectively to social, economic and political changes and to changing patterns of work;
- to develop the social skills necessary to work successfully with other people;
- to equip children for their adult roles in society and to help them to understand the responsibilities of being parents, citizens and consumers;
- to encourage appreciation and concern for the environment;
- to develop interests and skills which will continue to give personal satisfaction in the use of leisure time.

The experience of the enquiry has been that aims are easy to write but hard to live up to. Nevertheless it remains true that if people want tolerance or consideration for others in society then these qualities have to be practised by teachers and pupils in schools. This is also part of the entitlement.

Objectives

Where an *aim* is a general statement of intent, an *objective* was defined as a more specific target which can be realised in practice and assessed with some precision and which is established to help to achieve an aim. For example, if a school were translating into objectives the aim to develop in children the ability to act and think independently, one objective might be to teach children to organise some of their work on their own. To achieve the aim more fully however, such an objective would not be sufficient on its own and others would need to be identified. Aims usually imply a series of objectives. For example, to achieve the aim 'to encourage appreciation and concern for the environment', one series of teaching objectives might be:

- to develop a range of skills for observing, describing, recording and classifying some environmental features in the immediate locality;
- to prompt pupils to ask questions about some environmental concepts, such as conservation and resource utilisation;
- to consider what attitudes to adopt towards such environmental issues as protection, pollution and restoration;
- to identify knowledge which can be used by the pupils in the ways indicated above, and which increases their understanding of the environment.

During the enquiry it has been found useful to identify objectives in terms of the skills, attitudes, concepts and knowledge which are to be taught. The working definitions which follow for each of these terms have been used throughout the enquiry.

Skills

A *skill* is a capacity or competence: the ability successfully to perform a task, whether intellectual or manual. The acquisition of a skill may be dependent on the possession of certain knowledge and/or concepts. Skills may be more or less specific; some are applicable in a variety of contexts. Often they hang together in clusters (for example, communication skills). There are degrees of skilfulness, and assessment of pupils' skills should take account of the appropriate level at which the skill needs to be practised. The following list includes skills identified by schools and LEAs during the enquiry. The list is not exhaustive, and schools and LEAs attempting a curriculum enquiry would need to consider where they wished to add further clusters of skills to the ones set out below.

Communication skills:
the ability to use reading, writing, oral, aural, non-verbal, and graphical skills to receive and convey communications without the risk of misunderstanding.

Numerical skills:
the ability to estimate and measure and to understand and use numerical relationships.

Observational and visual skills:
the ability to observe accurately; the ability to record distributions, patterns and relationships, using scale, perspective, shape and colour; and the ability to interpret observations.

Imaginative skills:
the ability to put oneself into other situations, whether of time, place or person; the ability to visualise other experiences; the ability to discipline imagination by evidence and experience; the ability to order and reshape experiences and images.

Organisational and study skills:
the ability to extract information; the ability to arrange in sequence; the ability to classify; the ability to weigh and interpret evidence and to draw conclusions; the ability to see relationships; the ability to make hypotheses; the ability to make the best use of time.

Physical and practical skills:
the ability to develop manual dexterity and a variety of coordinated body movements; the ability to select appropriate tools and items of equipment and to use them effectively.

Social skills:
the ability to cooperate; the ability to negotiate; the ability to express ideas in a variety of contexts; the ability to consider other points of view; the ability to recognise non-verbal communications.

Problem-solving and creative skills:
the ability to diagnose the features of problems; the ability to frame hypotheses, design experiments to test them and evaluate their results; the ability to draw on relevant ideas and use materials inventively.

A working group in one LEA identified skills and indicated how their acquisition might be coordinated by a school across the first year curriculum. They are shown in Table 29.1, and *Necessary Action 3*.

Attitudes

An *attitude* is a disposition to think or act in a particular way in relation to oneself and to other individuals or groups in society. Attitudes determine responses to problems, issues and situations. Examples are perseverance and tolerance.

The list on p. 239 indicates some of the attitudes identified during the enquiry, which schools thought pupils should be encouraged to form:

Table 29.1 Skill acquisition across the first year curriculum

English	Mathematics	Science	Humanities	CDT/HE Art	RE, Music, Drama	Modern languages	PE	Computer studies
oral work	graphs	**oral work**	extrapolation	problem solving	improvisation	**oral work**	inventing: games, rules	inventing: games, rules
small group activities	charts	**small group activities**	interpretation	transposing information	**cooperative activities**	presentation		modelling
reflective reading	diagrams	asking questions	**oral activities**	asking questions	presentation	**paired activities**	problem solving	editing
presentation	**small group assignments**	diagrams	reflective reading	blueprints	**oral work**	self-help	**paired activities**	rough draft
note making	problem solving	reflective reading	map-reading	modelling	display	display		programming
rough draft procedures	estimations	**note-making**	primary source work	presentation	comparison			**note-making**
display	predictions	predictions	field work	**oral work**	interpretation			**small group work**
			note-making	display	**note-making**			
			rough draft	**note-making**	reflective reading			
			small group work	**small group work**				

Notes: Stages in identifying cross-curricular skills
i.   Each department outlines the skills which will be promoted in the first year programme.
ii. The matrix reveals which skills are common to several departments.
iii. These major skills are selected for development.
iv. A Working Party, chaired by the Deputy Head, produces guidelines for teachers dealing with the identified skills.
See also necessary action (1)

Necessary action 1 – Skills
To ensure that all pupils have the opportunity to acquire and practise these and other skills, schools will need:

to agree descriptions of broad categories so that there is a basis for discussion in all departments;
to consider in each department the skills to which a planned structured and developmental contribution is made in each year, the necessary provision and the assessment of pupils' individual progress:
to cross-reference departmental contributions in order to identify mutual concerns and any apparent gaps or imbalance;
to appoint a senior member of staff to coordinate the acquisition of skills, and the assessment and recording procedures used.

Necessary action 2 – Attitudes
To ensure that all pupils have opportunities to develop such attitudes schools need:

to agree the definitions of the words used so that all staff have a basis for discussion;
to consider the classroom and extra curricular provision made for pupils to experience and develop the attitudes listed;
to ensure that year heads and form tutors consider what opportunities are offered for the development of attitudes;
to appoint a senior member of staff to consider the relationship of the responses made by departments and pastoral groupings.

Necessary action 3 – Concepts
To ensure that pupils are helped towards an understanding of concepts, schools will need:

to identify the general concepts that are important to their teaching;
to identify in each department the main subject specific concepts;
to establish a curriculum working group, not necessarily composed only of senior staff, so that cross curricular development of conceptual understanding may be identified and implemented.

adaptability	self-confidence	tolerance
commitment	self-discipline	empathy
cooperation	perseverance	consideration for others
reliability	curiosity	honesty
integrity		

The list is inevitably simplistic and there needs to be recognition that both the identification of attitudes and their acquisition is a complex process. For example, in considering 'commitment' it should be acknowledged that there are degrees of commitment and that the extent of commitment involves value judgements which must necessarily be related to other aims.

Concepts

A *concept* enables one to classify, organise and understand knowledge and experience; often it is the abstraction and generalisation from a number of discrete instances. Concepts may be used for predicting behaviour, for interpreting fresh phenomena and data in a particular field, and for perceiving connections between one area of study and another.

Some concepts are general such as energy or continuity, while others are more limited in scope, such as heat or shelter. Concepts are often subject specific or relate to the economic, social, political and cultural situation in which schools operate. Teachers will need to identify those which arise from particular subject studies and which they wish children to understand. For example, in English, appropriate concepts might be novel, poem, plot or sonnet. Others, such as continuity, change and causation might be identified by various subject teachers and require to be developed across the curriculum. However they are identified, it remains important that they are not trapped within subject boundaries but related to and explored in other subjects and wider perspectives.

Knowledge and its relationships to skills, attitudes and concepts

In this context *knowledge* is the information which is selected to develop skills, attitudes and concepts and to achieve aims identified in the curriculum. As well as knowledge selected for this purpose, other knowledge may arise from the spontaneous interests and enthusiasms of both teachers and pupils.

The main problem in making a curriculum up to 16 is that of deciding which knowledge all pupils need. Criteria are needed for the selection of the knowledge to be taught, and these are best located in the overall aims and objectives and in the eight areas of experience. It is essential to ask whether this selected knowledge leads to the acquisition of certain desired skills, attitudes or concepts, or is central to an area of experience to which children are being introduced, or is necessary for the understanding which society, parents or employers expect. These considerations are more important than whether the knowledge is, for example, traditionally part of classical studies or geography, history or mathematics, physics or woodwork.

This is not to suggest that subject organisation in schools is inappropriate. Subjects exist, teachers have been trained within them and learning is most often promoted by the enthusiasm and insight which the subject specialist teacher offers. It is to suggest, however, that the selection of knowledge and concepts from subjects for designated educational aims is of crucial importance for the making of the entitlement curriculum. For example, if the aim is to give children some understanding of the development of modern industrial society, it is not necessary to teach the whole of British social and economic history. It may be that selections from modern British and Japanese history, together with some principles of geographical location, elementary economics, and some understanding of technological developments will be more effective. Or if the aim is to make children numerate or even to give them a worthwhile mathematical experience, not everything that is currently prescribed in school mathematics courses may be necessary and a better selection of knowledge and concepts might be possible. Subjects provide the framework of knowledge but the selection of knowledge which is to become the content of the curriculum needs to be made by reference to the criteria provided by the aims, objectives and 'areas of experience'.

METHODOLOGY

The importance of methodology and classroom practices cannot be over-emphasised. If nothing happens in the classroom then curricular ideas remain paper exercises.

This is true of any curriculum but particularly so for the entitlement curriculum since its aims and objectives are of such a nature that they demand a whole range of teaching techniques and active learning opportunities. Where a curriculum has, as its predominant emphasis, the acquisition of knowledge or learning of information, a relatively narrow range of methods may be considered adequate. When, however, a curriculum emphasises the acquisition of skills, attitudes and concepts as well as knowledge, this is no longer the case. For example, physical skills cannot be acquired through theoretical exposition alone and conceptual understanding does not come with dictated notes. The aim to develop curiosity, creativity and independent thought will not be achieved by teaching which relies excessively on instruction and didactic methods. Teachers have shown that they need to adopt various teaching styles; they are at times listeners, at times partners, at times assessors; they need to question, cajole, encourage and guide and to know when, how, and when not to intervene. Teachers must have the means to enable the entitlement curriculum to be achieved.

Chapter 30

Grounding comes first

Oliver Letwin

I maintain that the strict duty of every school is to ensure that, by the end of their school days, every pupil has what I shall call a grounding. By this, I mean an understanding of those things which it is necessary to understand in order to take a properly independent part in the life of our society. To be such an independent actor, people must be able to read and comprehend information of divers sorts; otherwise, they are unable to make properly independent choices about their jobs, their houses, their everyday purchases, their travel and so forth. They must also be able to make sense of the newspapers, and the spoken words of public life, since how else can they hold independent, informed attitudes about their governors, and the political system? It is essential, too, that people should grasp enough mathematics to see the simple effects of their decisions upon their lives, since otherwise they are constantly at the mercy of others, who will use their ignorance as an opportunity for themselves. And, perhaps most important of all, people must be able to express themselves with sufficient clarity both on paper and in speech, to make themselves fairly understood, since they are otherwise virtually unable to cope with the choices which are the stuff of an independent life in our society, or to be recognised by others as possessors of an independent voice, worthy of being heard in its own right. A person who lacks such a grounding, and is therefore unable to take an independent part in the life of our society, clearly represents a failure on the part of the school or schools which he attended. If we care at all about living in a liberal democracy, in which people are permitted to make choices for themselves, then we are duty-bound to provide everybody with tools which enable them to make and express such choices, on the basis of understanding what is being chosen, rather than as mere arbitrary leaps in the dark. This involves enforcing schooling upon all potential citizens; but it also involves providing, in school, the grounding that validates such compulsion. A person who fails to receive a grounding represents a paradox, because he has been the subject of compulsory schooling which would be justifiable only if the life of our society is somehow dependent upon his having attended school; yet he has not received what would have justified such compulsion.

Grounding involves acquiring both a range of skills and a certain amount of knowledge – at a level where knowledge and skill are almost indistinguishable from one another. Reading and writing, understanding simple mathematics, and expressing oneself clearly, are of course skills: one has to know how to do them instead of merely knowing that something or other is the case about them. But, in the course of learning, one inevitably acquires certain specific items of knowledge. One learns that certain words refer to certain objects and activities, that $2+2=4$, probably also (on the way) that the moon is not made of cheddar cheese, and a number of other items of sheer information. Whether the skills are taught by teaching the information, or whether the information is acquired through teaching the skills, is a matter of teaching practice, rather than of teaching aim – or indeed, simply a matter of luck. But about the aim, the duty, there is no room for disagreement. Every child needs, by whatever method, to have acquired the combination of knowledge and skill which enables him to live in a liberal, democratic society.

The provision of such a grounding is, I believe, the only absolute duty of a school.

Many people concerned with education – and certainly almost all the present educational establishment – would deny this, to the point of finding it outrageous. They would argue that such a concept of schooling is hopelessly narrow, and that any school which provides its pupils with no more than a rudimentary grounding is failing miserably in its duty.

These arguments fail to recognise the extent of the opportunities which are opened up for someone who has a grounding. An individual is, in a most fundamental sense, someone who makes decisions for himself rather than having them made for him by others – someone who has sufficient access to the fruits of civilisation to enable him to understand something of what is on offer and to develop real preferences. That is just what a grounding enables a person to do. Like the working man at the Workers' Educational Association, and the audience at the improving lectures of the last century, a person with a grounding can go to the library and read, go to lectures and listen, ask questions and apprehend any answer that is given in clear English. A person with a grounding has what nobody without one can ever have – a basis upon which to build an understanding of the world.

Of course, a grounding is not the crowning achievement of a school in relation to the encouragement of individuality. A school which provides only a grounding has no right to claim that it has done all that could be done for its pupils' capacity to make independent judgements. That would be to suggest that individuality is an open and shut affair – which it most certainly is not. A person is not simply capable of individual judgement or simply incapable of it. Some people are more capable of it than others. As a person's understanding of his world, of the possibilities within that world, becomes larger, his range of choice widens: he becomes aware of possibilities which his imagination was previously unable to furnish. This is a product not of grounding, but of true education. The two aims of schooling, the essential duty to provide a grounding and the larger, hoped-for goal of enabling pupils to become educated both contribute – at different levels – to the encouragement of individuality.

Many educational theorists, and among them many who count themselves as conservatives of one sort or another, will no doubt argue that it is both wrong and dangerous to describe the aims of schooling in this very general and abstract way. They will complain that these aims make no mention of the teaching of English history, of scripture, of the encouragement of artistic creativity and musical ability, of training for jobs. Above all, they will complain that no mention is made here of the need for schools to teach sound morals to their pupils. But these omissions are intentional. Contrary to the prevailing fashion, it is neither safe nor right to lay down, from the pulpit or from Whitehall, a whole range of specific skills and items of information that should be taught by every school. Beyond a grounding, which is the indispensable prerequisite for playing an independent role in our society, there is no specific skill which needs to be acquired by every pupil: schools which fail to teach their pupils how to conduct physical experiments or how to speak French or how to play the piano may nevertheless be adequate or even very good schools. In some narrowly religious schools, for example, none of these things are taught. But still the pupils receive a grounding and (in some cases) emerge as educated people through their study of sacred texts, the languages of their own community and the traditions which are attached to these languages. On what basis has anyone the right to object if children are, by the choice of their parents, provided with a schooling so manifestly suited to their way of life and so clearly justified by its social results?

The idea that a school's aim is to train people for jobs is equally noxious. Acquiring a grounding is probably as important for most jobs that are now done, as it is for living as a citizen in a liberal democratic society; but there are still many jobs that can be filled adequately without any grounding; and there are many more that can be done well by people who are in no sense educated. This is an utter irrelevance from the point of view of schooling; if both grounding and education were unnecessary for every job in the world, that would not detract in the slightest degree from their importance. Jobs are done to provide those who do them and their customers with economic benefits which have some human value because they contribute to a civilised existence. Schooling, both in providing a grounding and in attempting to yield educated people, is making a direct contribution of its own to the sustenance of a civilised existence. It is therefore on a par with, not subservient to, economic work.

The teaching of sound morals is a much more delicate issue. The instilling of moral principles and practices is a prime aim of a school, in the sense that everything done in a school, not only in the classroom but also on the sports field and in the example set by the teachers should obviously encourage pupils to become better rather than worse people. In the days when it was taken for granted that every school had a duty to provide its children with a grounding, this moral aim could be stressed without danger. When Tom Brown was told that his moral education mattered more than any deep learning he might acquire, that was perfectly sensible, because it was assumed by his father that he would receive a decent grounding as a matter of course. But things are different now. It is not taken by any means for granted that every school will aim to provide a grounding for its pupils by the time that they leave school. Instead, a large number of teachers and 'educationalists' take the view that the provision of a grounding is unimportant so long as the children emerge as nice, compassionate, sensitive, socially progressive people. This is as dangerous as any educational doctrine that has been perpetrated during the last forty years. The pupils who attend schools dominated by this doctrine may emerge with delicate consciences; but they are likely to be so unsuited to play an independent role in society, that they will soon turn into embittered, miserable adults. Moral training is not therefore a substitute for providing a grounding. It is something that ought to go on through, rather than in addition to, the specific activity of teaching and learning.

Chapter 31

The national curriculum
Origins, context and implementation

Bob Moon

The Secretary of State's policies for the range and pattern of the 5 to 16 curriculum will not lead to national syllabuses. Diversity at local education authority and school level is healthy, accords well with the English and Welsh tradition of school education, and makes for liveliness and innovation.

(Better Schools: a summary, March 1985: 4)

The Government has announced its intention to legislate for a national foundation curriculum for pupils of compulsory school age in England and Wales. . . . Within the secular national curriculum, the Government intends to establish essential foundation subjects – maths, English, science, foreign language, history, geography, technology in its various aspects, music, art and physical education . . . the government wishes to establish programmes of study for the subjects, describing the essential content which needs to be covered to enable pupils to reach or surpass the attainment targets.

(The National Curriculum 5–16, a consultation document,
July 1987: 35)

The English, and the Welsh, now have a national curriculum. In July 1988 just a year after the publication of a consultation document the Education Reform Bill received Royal Assent and passed onto the statute books. The curriculum clauses survived the Commons committee stages and vigorous, early morning attacks in the House of Lords, to pass unaltered into legislation. The measures represent a remarkable political intervention to change the post-war consensus on curriculum control.

How did a centrally-prescribed national curriculum come to be established and, moreover, how can the *volte-face* in policy represented in the change from Better Schools to Baker Bill be explained? The answer lies partly in the evolution of some recurring, even predictable, curriculum policies, but arguably more significantly in the political opportunism of those who achieved positions of power and influence prior to and shortly after the 1987 Election. This chapter, therefore, will examine these events and speculate on how the system worked to produce what a few years ago would have been unthinkable policies. Curriculum management, to be fully effective, requires a broad understanding of the policy context within which national policies have evolved. This is essential if the *critical engagement* with implementation discussed in the introduction is to be promoted across the school or local community. It will be equally important in communicating and debating the issues with parents and others with a legitimate interest in the working out of the new programmes. Firstly, however, what form do the measures take?

Ten subjects make up the national curriculum; English,[1] mathematics and science, defined as *core foundation* subjects, alongside seven further *foundation* subjects: art, geography, history, modern languages (11–16 only), music, physical education and technology.[2] The Secretary of State is required by the 1988 Education Reform Act to establish programmes of study and define attainment targets for each of the subjects. The attainment targets provide the basis for national and school reported assessments at the ages of seven, eleven, fourteen and sixteen.

This simply-stated formulation summarises the English and Welsh national curriculum. The Act states that all schools must provide a balanced and broadly based curriculum which

> promotes the spiritual, moral, cultural, mental and physical development of pupils at school and in society
>
> prepares pupils for the opportunities, responsibilities and experiences of adult life.

Three new councils, a National Curriculum Council (NCC), a Curriculum Council for Wales (CCW) and a School Examinations and Assessment Council (SEAC) are established to provide advice to government on the implementation of the reforms and to oversee associated research and development activities.

The Education Reform Act contains little detail on curriculum, a point not missed in Parliamentary debate, with Lord Grimond railing against legislation only being comprehensible when read with a document that was not part of it (*Hansard*, House of Lords, May 1988: 711) and Lord Kilmarnock asking for some idea of the remit given to each of the subject area working parties (ibid.: 531) before making decisions about the Bill. These working parties represent a further innovative feature of the times. The Secretary of State has set up the national curriculum through subject working parties independent of the new councils and reporting direct to government. The reports are published alongside a preliminary ministerial response. The National Curriculum Council then consults on the document and in turn publishes a report. At that point the Secretary of State prepares draft statutory orders and after a brief further phase for comment these are laid before Parliament.

A NATIONAL CURRICULUM: THE LONGER VIEW

In many ways the subject basis of national curriculum is familiar, with origins stretching back at least to the nineteenth century. The historical line is traceable and well documented in general curriculum histories. The Newcastle Report of 1861, for example, led to the 1862 Revised Code of Robert Lowe and a stress on basic subjects, age-related programmes of study, and the notorious 'payments by results' system for teachers. Three years later the Clarendon Commission investigated nine leading public schools and advocated, in addition to the central study of classics, the introduction into the curriculum of mathematics, modern languages and natural sciences. The Commission even made an attempt to assess standards, and proposed examining fifth form boys. The replies from headteachers were terse and to the point:

> Your letter appears to be so seriously objectionable that I must beg to decline to entertain the proposal. The Dean of Westminster concurs with me.
>
> (Reverend Charles R. Scott, Westminster)

> Objectionable both in principle and detail.
>
> (Dr. Elwyn, Charterhouse)

More precise objections came from Moberley of Winchester:

> We should be deeply and unnecessarily wounded by having it put on record that we had passed a bad one.

and Balsham of Eton:

> This interference with the authority of the headmaster is calculated to cause evil.
>
> (Quoted in Sherwood, 1977)

In 1868 the Taunton Commission, after looking at 800 endowed grammar schools, recommended three types of school, serving three classes of society, with leaving ages of 18, 16 and 14. Each school would have a distinctive curriculum. The emphasis of the first grade school would be classics and preparation for university. In grade 2 the requirements of the army, business and the professions required a stronger emphasis on practical rather than abstract activities, whilst the sons of artisans in grade 3 schools had a less precisely prescribed curriculum, although the basics were essential.

The latter part of the nineteenth century, and the period of this century up to the Second World War, abounds with evidence of curriculum regulations.

Table 31.1 Subject regulations for 1904 and 1935

1904	1935
English language	English language
English literature	English literature
One language[1]	One language
Geography	Geography
History	History
Mathematics	Mathematics
Science	Science
Drawing	Drawing
Due provision for manual work and physical exercises	Physical exercises and organised games
(Housewifery in girls' schools)	Singing
	[Manual instruction for boys, dramatic subjects for girls]

Note: 1 When two languages other than English are taken, and Latin is not one of them, the 'Board' will be required to be satisfied that the omission of Latin is for the advantage of the school.

The Revised Code went through many versions, with Gladstone's fourth administration providing a significantly liberalising influence. The 1904 Regulations for Secondary Schools included detailed syllabuses specifying the amount of time to be allocated to each subject. A senior civil servant, Robert Morant, after a meteoric rise via the Court of Siam and a private secretarial position to Permanent Secretary of the Board of Education in just eight years, drafted the regulations. A workaholic ('the day is never long enough – I must soak all the time in varied educational juices') he is supposed to have recorded in his diary a liking for both centralised administration and for the widespread implementation in secondary schools of the classical curriculum model characteristic of the fee-paying public schools. Morant's political and bureaucratic manoeuvres succeeded on both counts, as well as markedly increasing the powers of Permanent Secretary in the revamped Board of Education. The table (31.1) of the subject regulations for 1904 and 1935 shows how successful he was and how lasting the early model was to be.

The 1935 regulations remained in force until the Butler 1944 Education Act. The elementary codes disappeared rather earlier, to be replaced by the Board of Education Blue Book, a *Handbook of Suggestions*, which went through a number of editions again until 1944.

The 1988 specification therefore looked remarkably similar to those of 1935, although planned to cover the whole rather than secondary years of compulsory schooling. What had happened in between? As far as secondary schools were concerned the pattern remained remarkably consistent. Survey after survey, culminating in the 1979 HMI Secondary School Survey, showed how lasting Morant's model was. The subjects of the national curriculum in 1988 were the subjects of the secondary curriculum in each of the four preceding decades. The grammar school model of the 1940s was copied by the secondary moderns of the 1950s and the newly established comprehensives of the 1960s and 1970s. Some brave attempts to provide otherwise, following the Newsom Report in 1963 on the average and below average attaining child, and the Raising of the School Leaving Age (ROSLA) programme in 1972 were soon reformulated in a subject structure. Even the more recent and prestigious Technical and Vocational Educational Initiative (TVEI), a national project promoting curriculum reform, was almost universally structured within a nine or ten subject pattern.

In primary schooling the picture was more varied. The abolition of the eleven plus examination helped generate a new approach to curriculum organisation. Strong advocates for a more child-centred approach to teaching, such as Alec Clegg in the West Riding of Yorkshire and Edith Moorhouse in Oxfordshire, received wide publicity for the primary school reforms in their local authorities. The Plowden Report, published in 1967, gave warm approval to these new directions, and for a few years English primary schools were inundated with international visitors. More recent evidence, however, suggests that the spread of these ideas was limited. An unpublished survey commissioned for HMI in 1988 showed that in the average primary classroom, over half the week was devoted to studying basic mathematics and English.

The school system therefore resolutely reflected subject traditions across more than a century of compulsory schooling. Government interest in the curriculum waned for only a few brief years following the 1944 Education Act, and up to the point in 1960 when David Eccles made his famous reference to the secret garden of the curriculum. There were then three attempts to provide national institutional structures for the curriculum. A Curriculum Study Group set up by Eccles in 1962 was soon replaced, in 1964, by the Schools Council. The rise, and fall, of this organisation as well as the way it tackled curriculum development has received considerable attention (see, for example, Plaskow, 1985). As an alternative focus of curriculum control, relationships with the DES were frequently strained. The influence of the local education authorities and the teacher unions, represented on the Council as of right, was a source of irritation to some DES officials and the politicians who came to power following the Conservative Party 1979 Election victory. Despite surviving a committee of enquiry chaired by the Principal of an Oxford college, the Council was closed down by Sir Keith Joseph and replaced by two separate organisations, one responsible for secondary examinations, the Secondary Examinations Council (SEC), and a Schools Curriculum Development Committee (SCDC) with the governing bodies of both appointed directly by the Secretary of State.

RED BOOK TO RED BOOK — A CURRICULUM CONSENSUS SHATTERED

The first indication of the form the national curriculum would take was published within a few months of the 1987 Conservative Election victory. The red consultation document, *The National Curriculum 5–16*, was greeted with forceful criticism. Although the time-scale for consultation was short, two months including the summer holiday period, thousands of responses were received. Comment ranged from the right-wing Institute of Economic Affairs (IEA) arguing that the market, not government, should determine curriculum, to the National Union of Teachers' fear of uniformity and conformity. The tone of the document was strident, and made for more interesting reading than many government publications. A model curriculum was proposed for the secondary school in subject terms. There was no discussion of how the subject curriculum would apply to primary schools. The need for a ten subject school curriculum was boldly asserted without qualification and without reference to the plethora of government and inspectorial publications that had appeared in the decade following James Callaghan's Ruskin College Speech of 1976. Ruskin is referred to in paragraph 4 of the consultation document:

> Since Sir James Callaghan's speech as Prime Minister at Ruskin College in 1976, successive Secretaries of State have aimed to achieve agreement with their partners in the education service on policies for the school curriculum.

This pointed political reference, implying a measure of cross party support and concern, is followed by a critical passage:

> progress has been variable, uncertain and often slow. Improvements have been made, some standards of attainment have risen. But some improvement is not enough . . . the government now wishes to move ahead at a faster pace.

It is interesting to look back to 1976 and trace the curriculum events that led to a national curriculum proposal. In the mid-1970s the signs of a breakdown in the post-war educational cohabitation between government, local authorities and to a lesser extent the teachers' unions were beginning to show. Political disillusion with the attempts at curriculum reform had surfaced in a confidential DES document prior to Callaghan's Ruskin speech. The widely leaked document (the Yellow Book) caused considerable consternation amongst educationalists. Callaghan commented in the speech on the interest aroused:

> There have been one or two ripples of interest in the educational world in anticipation of this visit. I hope the publicity will do Ruskin some good and I don't think it will do the world of education any harm. I must thank

all those who have inundated me with advice: some helpful and others telling me less politely to keep off the grass. . . . It is almost as though some people would wish that the subject matter and purpose of education should not have public attention focused on it nor that profane hands should be allowed to touch it.

and then proceeded, after a brief reference to the dedication of the teaching profession, to comment on:

the unease felt by parents and others about the new informal methods of teaching . . . the strong case for the so-called 'core curriculum' of basic knowledge . . . the use of resources in order to maintain a proper national standard of performance and the need to improve relations between industry and education.

The outcome from Ruskin was a series of regional meetings (the Great Debate), usually chaired by the new Secretary of State for Education Shirley Williams, and to which a wide range of groups, including industrialists, were invited to send representatives. For a short while the DES was clearly on the offensive in orchestrating national concerns; in policy terms, however, there was little outcome. The Labour government holding power for much of the time, with a small group of Liberals, found the local authority lobby powerful in opposing central government intervention. Attempts to distribute relatively small grants for the in-service education of teachers, for example, were rebuffed and in many LEAs the money was allocated to other, often non-educational, purposes. Any political momentum gained was in any case dissipated by the loss of power in the 1979 election. Ruskin did, however, represent a watershed in the post-war history of curriculum reform, and for two reasons. Firstly it brought into the open the ambitions of some DES permanent officials to increase central control over curriculum. In terms of Whitehall politics it heralded a decade of activity that many may see as one of the most significant forces in establishing a national and central curriculum. Secondly Ruskin precipitated a parallel debate amongst prominent interest groups about the way the school curriculum should be structured. Whilst the battles for control remained unresolved, a remarkable degree of unanimity began to emerge on this issue.

The consensus developed around the idea of curriculum entitlement expressed in terms of areas of curriculum experience. The influence of philosophers of education such as Paul Hirst at the London Institute and then Cambridge University, and John White also at the London Institute, was openly acknowledged. HMI were first in the field, publishing in 1977 what became know as the Red Book.

The discussion document focused on the Curriculum 11–16. After making clear that the papers included were not advocating a centrally controlled or directed curriculum, they go on to argue for a common curriculum constructed around eight areas of experience, listed they say in alphabetical order to make clear that none should be weighted more highly than the others:

- the aesthetic and creative
- the ethical
- the linguistic
- the mathematical
- the physical
- the scientific
- the social and political
- the spiritual

This model was soon taken up through the DES documents and, whilst it was still in existence, the publications of the Schools Council, and on the educational conference circuit. Rumours therefore of DES intervention in the late 1970s and early 1980s were associated in most people's minds with a framework based on areas of experience providing coherence and balance across the curriculum. Such a framework, it was assumed, would be interpreted according to school and local circumstances, and the publication of *Better Schools*, quoted in the introduction to this chapter, gave no reason to doubt otherwise.

At first sight therefore the presentation of a model curriculum, complete with possible percentage allocations of time, in the red 1987 consultation paper was in stark contrast to HMI's Red Book of a decade earlier. In 1977 HMI had asserted that curriculum construction through subjects was only acceptable when everyone was clear what was to be achieved through them (p. 6). The disappearance of 'areas of experience' from curriculum debate is one of the significant features of the 1987 consultation document and the debates that preceded and followed publication.

PRESSURE GROUP POLITICS 1986–7

Behind this change in curriculum policy was a radical shift in the balance of power between government and the interest groups that had been so influential in building educational policy in the post-war period. It is now becoming clear that in the months immediately before and after the 1987 general election, a small group of prime ministerial advisers, including or at least influenced by the pamphleteers and polemicists of numerous right-wing 'think tanks', exerted increasing pressure on the Prime Minister. The ideas formulated, first for the Conservative Party Election Manifesto and then the consultation document, bypassed Her Majesty's Inspectorate, the Association of County Councils, the Association of Metropolitan Authorities, the teachers' unions, the Society of Education Officers, and also the Schools Curriculum Development Committee (SCDC) and Secondary Examinations Council (SEC).

Government ministers and DES officials were well aware that none of these groups could subscribe to the form and style of the 1987 Red Book proposals. It was in line with government policy to marginalise the teachers' views and those of the local authorities, but few would have predicted the ruthless exclusion of HMI or SCDC and SEC from policy formulation. This, however, represented pressure group politics of a most active form, sustained over a significant period of time.

The way the national curriculum finally came to occupy an important niche in the Education Reform Act, and the form in which it was expressed, can be seen to date back to Sir Keith Joseph's final years in office. A more precise understanding of what happened will have to await the publication of personal diaries and testimonies of the sort that are now providing further information on the Ruskin speech. At this stage, however, it appears that there was impatience and disillusion within the Tory party about policy making in the Joseph era. Despite some radical ideas (set out, for example, in his 1982 speech to the North of England Conference) he had prevaricated over many decisions, and in his clumsy handling of the teachers' industrial dispute between 1984 and 1986 he had failed to show the clear and firm resolve expected of ministers in a Thatcher government. There may also have been something of a suspicion that despite the polemic and rhetoric of the times, he had earned a grudging respect from some parts of the educational establishment. The introduction of the common 16+ GCSE examination was one major source of concern in some quarters. Rumours of his departure circulated for a long period, and the Prime Minister herself was said to be showing an interest in education, particularly as her increasing impatience with local authority levels of expenditure, linked often to policies at variance with those of the government, was most starkly illustrated within the education service. It should also be noted that her own ministerial career, when she presided in 1970–74 over a record number of grammar school closures, was seen as hardly successful against the criteria of Thatcherism in the 1980s. This was a new opportunity to make amends.

The arguments put forward to and by her advisers were opportune and congruent with the way policy was being developed towards other parts of the Welfare State, most notably the Health Service. The polemicists of the New Right had waged a well-publicised campaign for a return to what they saw as traditional values. A number had been leading contributors to the late 1960s Black Papers, an earlier polemic against progressive and egalitarian ideas, and the prospect of a third Thatcher victory and active Prime Ministerial interest offered a unique opportunity to influence policy.

It is now widely accepted that regular informal contact was maintained between the Prime Minister's office and leading members from pressure groups such as the Centre for Policy Studies and the Hillgate Group. In formulating the election manifesto and determining the content and style of the consultation document, this influence was highly significant. A comparison between the Hillgate Group's 1986 pamphlet 'Whose Schools' and the content of the Education Reform Act shows just how significant. In their ideas Margaret Thatcher had detected a populist appeal, in public speeches she was quick to reassert the need for traditional approaches, whilst ridiculing certain attempts to combat some of the enduring curriculum problems. In her address to the 1987 Conservative Party Conference she talked of 'children who need to be able to count and multiply learning anti-racist mathematics – whatever that might be . . .', and promised her audience that the national curriculum would comprise '. . . reading, writing, spelling, grammar, arithmetic, basic science and technology'.

The consultation document therefore reasserts the primacy of subjects. Areas of experience smacked of the educational establishment, it allowed flexibility and local interpretation and it hardly made for a rousing address to the party conference. The consensus that had been building around the framework was ignored in the aftermath of a sweeping electoral victory. The symbolic importance of subjects overrode all other considerations.

THE NEW CURRICULUM – NATIONALISM, MANAGERIALISM OR THE MARKET PLACE?

The national curriculum in the form presented surprised and offended many in the educational world. It appeared to combine the continental traditions of subject prescription and the North American predilection for testing to create a particularly powerful, and for many threatening, proposal. The level of hostility was fuelled by the scarcity of information, fears about the way the statutory orders would be produced (would the working parties be given over to Hillgate?) and rumours about the form the testing would take. It was also apparent that the measures were to be vigorously pushed through, with compromise in the climate of the late 1980s interpreted as weakness. An ambitious Secretary of State had staked his political future on the passage of the Bill.

It is difficult, close to events, to clarify the way influence was exerted and motivation tapped in establishing such a major reform of curriculum policy. A number of themes, however, in the evolution of policy generally appear to be reflected in ERA and the national curriculum clauses. A brief review suggests that the events of 1987–8 were less surprising than reactions at the time suggested. Three processes in particular appear to have fused around the national curriculum: a long term staking-out of bureaucratic control; the drive for efficiency and accountability that had become the characteristic of government attempts to reduce public expenditure; and finally a formulation of policy that brought together competing interests among pressure groups on the right.

John Quicke (1988) has explored this final point in an interesting analysis of the politics and ideas of the 'New Right' towards education over the last decade. He points to the differences between neo-conservatives such as Roger Scruton, a member of the Hillgate Group, and neo-liberals such as Stuart Sexton, working within the Institute of Economic Affairs. Neo-conservatives, he suggests, advocate strong government and a hierarchical and disciplined view of society in which a concept of the national is central. Neo-liberals on the other hand emphasise individual freedom of choice through the free workings of the market. In terms of curriculum therefore, the neo-conservatives appeared to have been the most influential. A central, authoritarian prescription seems incompatible with a principle that permits the market (parents) to determine which form of curriculum prospers. The Institute of Economic Affairs in replying to the red consultation paper was clear:

> The most effective national curriculum is that set by the market, by the consumers of the education service. This will be far more responsive to children's needs and society's demands than any centrally imposed curriculum, no matter how well meant. Attempts by Government and by Parliament to impose a curriculum, no matter how 'generally agreed' they think it to be, are a poor second best in terms of quality, flexibility and responsiveness to needs than allowing the market to decide and setting the system free to respond to the overwhelming demand for higher standards. The Government must trust market forces rather than some committee of the great and good.

And the Institute sees the debate over a government-imposed national curriculum as detracting attention away from what really matters, namely the proposals to devolve management to schools. In establishing the curriculum proposals, these two groups appear to have been in tension. Margaret Thatcher is reported as wavering over the degree of prescription required for the national curriculum, reaching the view at one stage that English, mathematics and science should comprise the limits of regulation. Kenneth Baker, Secretary of State, is rumoured to have convinced her of the need for more widespread control. If Baker[3] did seek to convince in this way he may have exploited the argument of the neo-conservatives that, uncontrolled, the curriculum serves as a vehicle for the politically motivated, illiberal and indoctrinating tendencies of the left. This is a persistent theme running through both the pamphlets (such as the Hillgate Group's determined attacks on any curriculum activity described as studies – peace studies, multicultural studies) and speeches made by Margaret Thatcher and other ministers in the pre-election period.

For Quicke, therefore, the strategy of the neo-conservatives was to highlight those elements they had in common with all forms of liberal education, and to contrast the values they jointly espoused with those underpinning the radical left-of-centre ideologies said to be dominant in educational bureau-cracies, particularly at the local level. Despite the failure to convince market purists at the IEA, the approach was influential with the Prime Minister and with a minister keen to enlarge the role and responsibilities of the DES.

Hargreaves and Reynolds (1989) from a position on the left explicitly opposed to government reforms, provide a further perspective on the appar-ently contradictory policies of regulation and choice operating within the Act. They see nothing accidental in this juxtaposition, with centralisation and privatisation representing the co-ordinated arms of educational policy making. Centralisation of curriculum and assessment forces competitiveness around the values chosen by government. Ideological control is exerted, because to open up the next generation to socialisation by the free run of market forces runs social and political risks that no government could contemplate, particularly at a time of economic crisis and social uncertainty. For the neo-conservatives, therefore, the form and style of the national curriculum is paramount and helps explain their interest in the membership of the new national councils and their detailed scrutiny of ministerial and DES statements. It will be interesting to see how this surveillance can be sustained in the implementation of the national curriculum procedure.

A second influence on policy is the quest for measures that create accoun-tability and efficiency within the education service. From this perspective the national curriculum 'tidies up' the ground upon which cost and person-nel decisions can be made, and testing provides a basis for valid comparative judgements about efficiency of schools and classes. Donald Naismith, for-merly Director of Education for Croydon, is one of the few Education Officers to have gained the respect of groups such as Hillgate. He is unequivocal in seeing managerialism and efficiency as at the core of the proposals:

> The way the education service was organised after the war attached greater importance to the separation and distribution of powers and responsibilities between central and local government and schools than to bringing them together in ways which established a direct managerial link between investment in its widest sense and performance. The results were stationary or falling standards and higher costs. By reintroducing objec-tive standards and giving schools and colleges the means to attain them the Government believes it can combine higher standards with better management of resources, particularly as a school's results will be recorded and published in uniform ways, enabling comparisons to be made between schools and local authorities not only in terms of effective-ness but, more important, efficiency, the degree of success with which a school or local authority converts what goes into it and what comes out. We are going to hear a lot about performance indicators in the future.
>
> (1988)

It is through this perspective that the DES's preference for an objectives led curriculum, rather than HMI's 'areas of experience', becomes clear. HMI appear to have resisted many aspects of the pressure for comprehensive testing and assessment based on objectives. They would have been aware of the unresolved technical problems and the threat posed to time-honoured styles and inspection. There would also have been concern about a change in the working relationships with teachers and schools.

The curriculum clauses of ERA show, however, the DES in the ascendancy, a quite significant fight-back after years enduring Mrs Thatcher's reported suspicions of obstructionism and inaction, and the more recent activities of Lord Young who, at the Department of Industry and Employment, had launched through the Manpower Services Commission a significant challenge to DES authority over the education service. TVEI, one of the most prestigious of MSC projects, received only the briefest of mentions in the consultative process and represents another group excluded from the process of formulating policy in this period.[4] The ambitions of bureaucrats can develop a momentum of their own. Managerialism promotes bureaucratic activity and the DES prospered, not the least in new departmental structures and an expanded staffing.

The form in which the national curriculum was laid down represented a victory therefore for those on the right who had seized the political agenda for reform. It also represented a significant increase in the power and importance of the DES and it provided a yardstick against which new and more demanding forms of accountability could be introduced.

THE EARLY EXPERIENCE OF IMPLEMENTATION

The implementation phase has been characterised by an impressive weight and variety of curriculum development. Despite strident protests about the pace and extent of change, and the form of some of the subjects, surveys show that teachers have accepted the principle of a national curriculum. Professional and academic comment, however, has been critical of much of the development process. This comment has been borne out in practice by almost immediate changes in some key aspects of the structure and subject formulations. The style of development has implications for other countries contemplating core or national frameworks for curriculum. The main implementation problems therefore merit consideration.

First, the national curriculum was set up subject by subject through a series of working parties. Cross referencing between working parties, made up of government nominees, was discouraged and the setting up and reporting took place at different times and over varying periods of time. Mathematics and science came first with physical education and music last. Each subject, in addition to being defined through attainment targets was set out in four key stages, two for primary, two secondary, at the end of which there would be national assessments. Inevitably problems arose. Interpretation of the attainment targets varied from one group to another. The science working party defined attainment targets in terms of knowledge, the technology group by reference to processes. The number of attainment targets also varied, initially 17 for science, 14 for mathematics, 4 for English and 5 for technology. The capacity to organise the whole curriculum, particularly at the primary level became increasingly problematic. Schools were given responsibility about how the curriculum structure was organised but all the attainment targets in the statutory subjects had to be covered. Planning thematically or by topic in the early years became exceedingly complex. The science and mathematics programmes were, therefore, both rewritten almost immediately to reduce the number of attainment targets.

Second, the working parties and the subsequent consultation process became an area for political interest at the highest level. Prime Minister Thatcher intervened in the orders that were laid for both English and history – and this process has continued to the time of writing. The English curriculum in 1992 is being reviewed to take account of criticism from right of centre government advisers that it gives insufficient attention to basic skills. The new Secretary of State, John Patten, has indicated that Shakespeare should be a compulsory part of the curriculum for all pupils. The music curriculum, as with most other subjects, was the subject of controversial debate carried out primarily through the media. Despite the opposition of many leading music educators and musicians, led by conductor Simon Rattle, the curriculum was weighted towards musical theory and appreciation rather than practical activities.

Third, in some areas the national curriculum developed new approaches that involved a major restructuring of the organisation of the school curriculum. The thematic, topic work developed through the integrated day in most primary schools required major revision. The introduction of technology was also a new challenge for primary practitioners. Most significantly the technology statutory orders required the fusing of craft, design, technology, information technology, business studies and home economics at the secondary stage. The subsequent confusion has received widespread criticism. A report appeared with the memorable phrase, 'Technology and NC is in a mess' (Smithers and Robinson, 1992), and a major rewrite of the technology curriculum took place.

Fourth, the original subject blueprint limited the range of subjects. Dance and drama, for example, were not mentioned and had to be accommodated through English and physical education. At secondary level, given the normal English allocation of time of one tenth of the curriculum to each examined subject, it was clear that time was not available for subjects such as Latin, a second modern language or vocational options. Ministers have had to accept that the 10 subjects of the national curriculum go through to age 14 but many become optional thereafter. Policies on this issue have changed almost annually since 1989 making plans at the school level difficult to formulate. The different subjects were also expected to be implemented over differing time scales with the main pressure falling on the infant school to implement.

Fifth, the original formulation left out many curriculum issues that everyone acknowledged should be included: careers, personal and social education, for example. The National Curriculum Council has now produced a series of booklets to illustrate how these can be incorporated through the existing statutory orders, although this inevitably has led to some complex and retrospective attempts to achieve cross-curricular coherence.

Sixth, and of major significance, has been controversy surrounding assessment. The first government working party proposed assessment across 10 levels (each attainment target in each subject was subsequently divided into 10 levels of attainment) involving both formative and summative assessment through teacher assessment and national tests. The concept of teacher and formative assessment was accepted reluctantly by Mrs Thatcher but has subsequently been the subject of ongoing political and educational controversy. The idea of short and sharp 'pencil and paper' tests, favoured by some government politicians and all the right of centre 'think tanks', clearly clashed with the quest for more reliable and valid instruments that developments in assessment over the last decade suggested were required. In the assessment of seven-year-olds (key stage 1) the instruments used varied markedly in each of the first three years of implementation, and always towards the sort of instrument the Government favoured. The well-rehearsed difficulties (Murphy, 1990) of subsuming formative and summative proposals in the same instrument are being painstakingly relearnt through the national curriculum experience. At present, however, the form of assessment is still a matter of intense debate.

Finally, the separation of curriculum and assessment into two separate advisory councils led to a degree of infighting, much of which spilled out into the public domain, and led finally to a merged Schools Curriculum and Assessment Authority set up in 1993.

In the design and implementation of the national curriculum, curriculum developers can pinpoint major problems that have created enormous difficulties in schools. However, despite opposition and some derision the national curriculum is in place and is a major determinant of curriculum policy. It is a remarkable political achievement. One salutary conclusion is just how the agendas of government and most curriculum experts come to diverge so markedly. In this the judgement of history may suggest that burdens of responsibility are more equally spread than many contemporary commentators suggest.

NOTES

1 In Wales, Welsh can be an additional core or foundation subject.
2 Religious education is also compulsory, but defined by statutory requirements unique to that subject.
3 The rather obscure terminological distinction between core foundation and foundation subjects is said to date from this debate.
4 TVEI, or education relevant to working life, was strongly criticised by some traditional neo-conservative writers.

REFERENCES

Hargreaves, A. and Reynolds, D. (1989) *Education Policy: Controversies and Critiques*, Lewes, Falmer Press.

Murphy, P. (1990) 'National curriculum assessment: has anything been learnt from the experience of APU?', *The Curriculum Journal*, 1 (2), pp. 186–98.

Naismith, D. (1988) unpublished paper, A.S.C. conference, Gateshead, April.

Plaskow, M. (1985) *The Life and Death of the Schools Council*, Lewes, Falmer Press.

Quicke, J. (1988) 'The "New Right" and education', *British Journal of Educational Studies*, February.

Sherwood, P. (1977) 'Evaluating the English experience' in Houts, P. L. (ed.) *The Myth of Measurability*, New York, Hart Publishing Co.

Smithers, A. and Robinson, P. (1992) *Teaching in the National Curriculum: Getting it Right*, London, Engineering Council.

Chapter 32

Academic drift

Towards a new focus for the education system

*A. H. Halsey, N. Postlethwaite, S. J. Prais,
A. Smithers and H. Steadman*

We have seen that England has an education system firmly based on its academic origins, and geared to university entrance. Any attempts to make changes will have to reckon with the strength of that tradition. Many efforts at providing more practical/technical education have foundered because of a drift toward academic subjects. The prestige of academic study, for example, led to institutions created for technical or technological advancement becoming or aspiring to become universities, first the Colleges of Advanced Technology and then the Polytechnics. Further Education colleges are keen to demonstrate their worth by teaching A levels.

Most recently we have been seeing an academic drift or 'inappropriate intellectualisation' in relation to the teaching of 'technology' in our secondary schools. Technology as defined in the national curriculum is, as a matter of principle, deliberately general and 'context-free'. Even in relation to its most applied part (Attainment Target 3: Planning and Making, and the associated Programme of Study: Working with Materials) no specific materials are prescribed, nor is a degree of accuracy specified in the making of objects (comparable to the 0.5 mm typically prescribed in woodworking classes in Germany).

The reason often given for the changes in emphasis in Britain is that they make the subject more attractive to academically-inclined pupils. It can thus be taught, so it is suggested, 'across the whole ability-range' and made obligatory for all pupils. As it has emerged, it is less about actually *making* things, than about talking and writing about making them. British teachers of the established, more practical technology courses have expressed to us their serious concern that many pupils of middle and below-average academic attainment will suffer from these changes. Such pupils may excel in executing practical work but become dispirited in verbalising 'design briefs'.

The rise of technology as a school subject in the national curriculum has been at the expense of practical subjects, taught and examined in a practical way. At a few British secondary schools, courses that are more specific and more practically-oriented are still available (they were available at very many of them until overtaken by 'modern ideas'). They lead to GCSE examin-

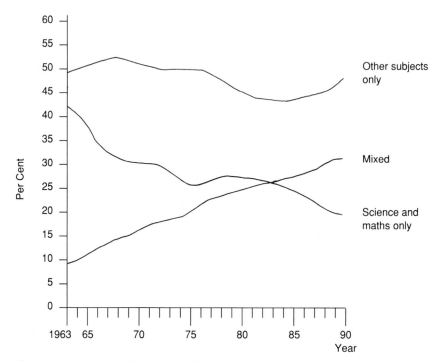

Figure 32.1 Trends in 'A' level studies

Source: Updated from Smithers and Robinson (1988) *The Growth of Mixed A Levels*, Manchester: Carmichael Press.

ations in subjects such as Technical Drawing, Engineering Workshop Theory and Practice, Motor Vehicle Studies, or Metalwork. (The examples are from the engineering side; corresponding examinations were set in other vocational areas, such as office or domestic work.) An estimated one quarter of all secondary school pupils passed examinations in such subjects in 1981 above CSE grade 4. These practical and specialised GCSE courses have gradually been replaced in the past decade by more general GCSE courses which go under the heading of 'Craft, Design and Technology', and are close to the new national curriculum requirements due to come into effect for 14–16 year-olds in 1993.

Although recent years have seen a marked increase in the numbers of young people continuing beyond school to higher education, this has not been true of all subjects. In particular, as Figure 32.1 shows, the swing against the sciences, identified 20 years ago in the Dainton Report, has continued. (Dainton Report, 1968, *Enquiry into the Flow of Candidates in Science and Technology into Higher Education. Cmnd. 3514.* London: HMSO.) The proportion of those taking A levels in 'science and maths only' has declined by more than half – from 44 per cent in 1963 to 21 per cent in

Table 32.1 Graduate output by country

Subject area	Per 1,000 of age cohort				
	UK (1985)	France (1981)	West Germany (1984)	Japan (1985)	USA (1985)
Engineering and Technology	18	20	28	45	25
Science, Maths and Computing	26	33	10	8	27
Medical and Health Related	7	5	13	12	15
Social Sciences, Law, Business Studies	37	58	45	91	87
Arts, Humanities, Education	36	77	37	55	43
Other[1]	14	9	6	18	33
Total	138	202	139	229	230

1. Mass communication and documentation, home economics, service trades, transport and communication, agriculture, forestry, fishing, other and not specified.

Source: Updated from Smithers and Robinson (1989) *Increasing Participation in Higher Education*, London, BP.

Table 32.2 Numbers qualifying[1] in engineering and technology in selected countries

	UK	France	West Germany	Japan	USA
Doctorates	0.7	0.3	1.0	0.3	0.5
Master's degrees	2	–	–	5	4
Bachelor's degrees	14	15	21	30	19
Technicians	29	35	44	27	17
Craftsmen	35	92	120	44	na

1. In thousands with raw numbers for Japan and USA reduced in proportion to UK population.

Source: Prais (1988) *National Institute Economic Review*, February, 76–83.

1990. This represents a decrease in actual numbers from 86,175 in 1985 to 68,358 in 1990. A major reason for the decline has been the pronounced shift towards combining the sciences with other subjects. The proportion studying some science in the sixth form has increased. This in itself is welcome. What is of concern, however, is that only about a fifth of those taking mixed combinations of A levels aim for the sciences and engineering in higher education, the rest tending towards business studies and the social sciences.

This is reflected in applications to universities which fell by nearly 20 per cent in engineering and eight per cent in the physical sciences in the period 1985–88 (the most convenient recent period over which like can be

Table 32.3 Vocational qualifications of workforce (percentages)

Vocational qualifications	France (1988)	Germany (1989)	Netherlands (1985)	UK (1988)
Degrees and higher diplomas[1]	14	18	18	17
Intermediate vocational qualifications[2]	33	56	44	20
None[3]	53	26	38	63

1. Degrees, Higher National Diplomas (HND), Higher National Certificates (HNC), teaching, nursing and equivalent
2. BTEC National, City and Guilds and equivalent
3. General education only (below Higher Education)
Source: Mason, Prais and Van Ark (1990) National Institute, Discussion Paper No. 191.

compared with like). While the number of entries is rising rapidly, those in physics, engineering and technology, have remained on a plateau, despite attempts to increase numbers.

The English system brings through relatively few young people to graduate level in engineering and technology compared to other countries. (Table 32.1). While in Japan there are five applicants for every place, in the UK there are barely enough people coming forward to fill the places available and it has not proved possible to increase supply by raising the number of places.

The National Institute for Economic and Social Research (NIESR) has argued, on the basis of international comparisons, that it is at the support levels of technicians and craftsmen that we fall even more seriously behind other countries (Table 32.2). Our schooling system does not set out to develop vocational–technical talents. This leads to fewer students in the UK than elsewhere (other than USA) studying for, and obtaining, intermediate vocational qualifications like the Business and Technician Education Council (BTEC) National Certificate or City and Guild Certificates. About two-thirds of the British workforce appear to lack vocational qualification compared to only about a quarter of the German (Table 32.3). This has obvious consequences for quality of workmanship, productivity, earning power and for full employment in a competitive and technologically progressive world.

The three tranches of reform – the 1944 Education Act, the Comprehensive Reforms of the 1970s, the Education Reform Act of 1988 – have failed to provide Britain with an effective education system suitable for the technological world of today. The paradox of change without change is brought about because education is still heavily focused on the needs of an academic minority. The education system worked well for this group in 1900 and it still does so today. The needs of the majority in relation to their subsequent working life have been given far too little attention.

Many with practical abilities vital to the economy become disillusioned with education and training long before they leave secondary school. They come to see education as not for them and truant or misbehave.

Curing the problem will be much harder than diagnosing it. There have been so many changes in recent years that more will not be welcome. But changes must come. Our national future depends upon it. These changes must be based on empirical evidence not on ideology. There is much we must learn from abroad.

Chapter 33

Assessment
A changing practice

Sally Brown

A SCENARIO FOR CHANGE

Change can be unsettling, sometimes overwhelming, but it can also be motivating and bring about real progress. In the field of assessment, a great deal of talk over the last decade has been about change and substantial attempts have been made to introduce new practices. Different practices usually reflect different ideological commitments, and one of the most salient features of the movement has been the recognition that assessment, as part of education, must be about promoting learning and opportunities, rather than about sorting people into social roles for society.

There are, of course, those who say that there has been no basic change in assessment practices, and indeed there is evidence of resistance from groups with vested interests in holding on to the past. This tendency to try to hang on to the traditional and tested methods at a time when a new philosophy and practice of assessment is being introduced has resulted, in some circumstances, in confusion and impossible demands on practitioners. However, it is important to emphasise that much valuable and ordered progress has been made in this field. Ideas about assessment are discussed and debated among policy-makers, practitioners and researchers more, and more openly, than in the past, and this has led to greater understanding of its role in, and effect on, the education of young people.

THE TRADITIONAL VIEW OF ASSESSMENT

It is not so long ago that the notion of 'assessment' in schools and colleges carried with it, in the United Kingdom at least, a vision of tests or examinations, certificates and grades or lists of marks. All of these were regarded as very important and as providing objective, reliable and precise measures of achievement. The use to which such measures were put was primarily one of the *selection* of young people for such things as further study, training courses, apprenticeships or careers. This system had the great advantage of administrative simplicity: it made comparisons among individuals (norm-referencing), and everyone knew that a grade B performance was better than a grade C and a mark of 49 was less than 51. It appeared to provide an effective means of sorting out those at the 'top', the 'middle' and the 'bottom', and of directing them towards an appropriate niche in society.

The assessment itself usually was carried out in a formal atmosphere and under strictly controlled conditions. Not all of it was undertaken under the auspices of national examination boards, but schools and colleges tended to try to replicate the boards' strict examination conditions: a large hall with an invigilator, no 'cheating', examination 'papers', a fixed allocation of time for responding in writing to the questions and the whole exercise undertaken at the end of something (a course, a term, a year or a school career). Teachers in 'non-academic' areas of the school curriculum without formal examinations tended to assert that they had no assessment. In some subjects, however, it was acknowledged that skills other than those which can be manifest in written answers may be important, and efforts were made to include practical examinations in, for example, home economics, music and science. Where examination boards took such initiatives, teachers were sometimes asked to administer the practical tests, but in strict accordance with instructions prepared by the board.

There were, of course, a wide range of activities going on in which teachers were trying to find out, often in classrooms and by informal means, what pupils had learned or could do. Employers too were making judgements about what apprentices had achieved. All of this we would now include within the concept of assessment, but that has been the case only in recent years.

Over the last two decades the ideas underlying the traditional concept of assessment increasingly have been questioned, and the last ten years have seen some dramatic changes in practice.

QUESTIONING PAST PRACTICE

The questioning of past assessment practice has been of several different kinds. Some of it has been concerned with technical matters and has asked: Are grades and marks reliable? Would another marker, or the same marker on another day, make the same judgement about the performance of a young person? Are the assessments valid? Do they assess all they claim to assess? Are they fair? Do they give recognition for achievement or are they more concerned with sorting people out? Perhaps the most searching questions, however, are about the purposes of assessment. Should the focus be on selection, or can it play a more constructive and educational role? If so, is the traditional form of marks and grades appropriate and adequate? And finally, there is debate about who has control of making and reporting the assessments, and of deciding which young people will have access to the benefits which any system of assessment might offer.

There has always been concern about whether tests and examinations are reliable, valid and fair. A substantial body of work of high technical quality has been undertaken, particularly in North America, which has ensured that much is now known about the conditions under which a group of items constitute a reliable test: that is, one which will give the same assessment of the performance of an individual no matter who marks it, and regardless of whether the individual takes the test this week or next. Objective tests with each item having one right answer are most likely to fill the bill; assessment instruments which have heterogeneous items, and subjective marking procedures (e.g. essays), are much less likely to do so. Indeed, measures of reliability on examination essay marking have sometimes produced results which are alarming, especially when it is remembered that the future career of a young person can depend on the outcome of an argument between two examiners about a grade. To avoid this problem, one approach has been to restrict examination questions to objectively marked items. But this may well distort the set of achievements which are assessed; some things which it is intended young people should learn or be able to do are not amenable to objective testing. The capability to create a literary idea, to understand a complex theory or to generate an imaginative artifact, may not be assessable by such means as answering a multiple choice question, or completing a single answer calculation.

A narrowing down of what is assessed to that which can be accurately measured may engineer some improvement in the reliability of a test, but it is likely to endanger its validity. One may ask what use is a grade or mark which is highly reliable but does not reflect the full range of achievements for which the course or set of experiences is aiming? Where such a grade or mark is used for selecting young people, what confidence can there be in its capability to predict that they will be successful in any subsequent course or career?

At a more general level, traditional tests are seen as having substantial limitations in the extent of their sampling of the variety of competences which it is intended young people should acquire. At one level, it is clear that a three-hour examination is an inadequate means of assessing, say, the learning from a two-year course. There are, furthermore, some kinds of performance which, in principle, cannot be assessed by traditional examinations, particularly where these are restricted to written tests. The validity of marks and grades as measures of performance in any given area, therefore, has been constrained by the form the assessments have taken. In particular, the assessment of practical skills, personal development, attitudes and performance in contexts other than conventional classrooms and laboratories has been neglected.

The matter of the fairness of assessments has been a continuing and agonising concern. Because the main aim of traditional assessments has been to spread out the performance of candidates (so that selection procedures could be carried out more efficiently), great emphasis was placed on choosing test items so as to maximise discrimination between the performance of the high achievers and those of the low achievers. This resulted in the omission of those items which everyone would get right, and so the lowest achievers were denied the opportunity to show what they were able to do. In some parts of the world this has been further exacerbated by the development of 'standardised tests'. Standardised tests are designed to spread out the performances and make no pretence to match the curriculum to which any given individual has been exposed. They are general tests within a broad area which discriminate well among the whole population of young people. High discrimination, however, is most effectively achieved by reducing the specific content of items; the greatest discrimination is to be found in those tests which closely resemble content-free IQ tests. As soon as a move is made in that direction, the validity of the test as a measure of *educational achievement* must be in doubt. A valid test of such achievement must clearly reflect all the qualities of which it claims to be a measure, and those qualities will be identified with the substance of the curriculum which has been followed.

Many of the characteristics of assessment in the past have resulted from the dominant purpose towards which it has been directed, i.e. selection. In recent years the question has been raised of whether there are not other, and more important, functions for it to fulfil. Since it is part of the educational process should it not have a more constructive role to play in teaching and learning? Should the very considerable efforts which are put into making assessments not be able to produce more, and more useful, information for teachers, students and others? If other functions are to be fulfilled by assessment, then it is unlikely that the traditional form of grades or marks will be adequate. An important limitation of that form is that while it enables comparisons to be made among the performances of individuals (norm-referenced assessment), it provides no information about *what* has been achieved. Any kind of function for assessment which aims to provide information which will help young people to learn, or teachers to teach, will require an evaluative description of what has been achieved (criterion-referenced assessment).

The question of who should carry out the assessment of young people has not been a matter for debate in the past. Most frequently it has been assumed that the teacher will be the assessor, although examination for certification (probably seen as the most important manifestation of assessment) has generally been the province of professional examiners. There are obvious constraints on the ability of a professional examiner, who under normal conditions would not see the candidate, to carry out a comprehensive assessment of that young person's capabilities in those areas where he or she has had the opportunity to learn. It has been suggested that the teacher will always be in a better position than the examiner to assess, but would that hold when the young people are out of school on, say, work experience or residential courses? The way in which educational aims have changed over the last few years, so that experiences of this kind are now commonplace in the school or college curriculum, clearly has implications for who should be the assessor. Furthermore, the fact that assessments may be carried out by a variety of people, with a range of perspectives, draws attention to the question of whether it is important to have a single measure of achievement for a young person in a given area, or whether it is more rational to accept that different people assess individuals differently, and that such differences should not be concealed within some compromise overall mark or grade.

The notion of young people themselves being involved in self- or peer-assessment has not been a facet of past practice. More recently the question of whether such involvement would be of value in helping to consolidate learning and to increase self-awareness is frequently mooted. For some aspects of personal and social development, which are currently receiving substantial emphasis in curriculum planning, it might seem that the young people are in the best position to make the judgements which assessment of such qualities calls for.

This debate on the possible inadequacy of the range of qualities assessed by traditional measures and the restrictions on who should carry out those assessments, has been accompanied by concern about the proportion of young people leaving formal education without any record of what they have achieved. The established (and academic) certificate courses were not designed for the whole population and, in any case, were unsuited to the educational aims for many young people. Educational 'qualifications', however, have become more and more important. If the curriculum is to develop in various ways to prepare everyone more effectively for their future in work and in society generally, then surely, it has been argued, *all* should have the opportunity to work for a certificate which recognises what has been achieved? And if everyone has the chance to earn a certificate, surely such recognition will have a motivating effect on learning and, perhaps, reduce the alienation from education characteristic of many of the low achievers?

The doubts and dissatisfactions with the traditional concept of assessment have resulted in more than academic debate. There have been substantial changes in practice, and the experience gained has led to greater understanding of the potential and the problems associated with assessment. Assessment now commands a much wider conceptualisation than in the past, and tends to be seen as an important and necessary ingredient of effective teaching and learning.

INNOVATIVE THEMES IN ASSESSMENT PRACTICE

The first theme concentrates on the way in which the concept of 'assessment' has progressed from the traditional notion of 'testing' for selection purposes.

Assessment is now seen as *a much broader concept and fulfilling multiple purposes*. It is considered to be closely integrated with the 'curriculum' (a concept which is itself conceived in very much broader terms than in the past) and its purposes include fostering learning, improving teaching, providing valid information about what has been done or achieved, and enabling pupils and others to make sensible and rational choices about courses, careers and other activities. Evaluation of pupils for various selection purposes will continue, but there have been major efforts to ensure that we progress from the simplistic notion that young people can be put in some kind of rank order by grades (frequently based on the results of a single examination). Assessment, therefore, now has several functions including the diagnosis of causes of young people's success or failure, the motivation of them to learn, the provision of valid and meaningful accounts of what has been achieved, and the evaluation of courses and of teaching. We are much more cautious these days about making claims for how effectively assessment in one context can predict the success of young people in other contexts at later dates. The emphasis has shifted away from assessment for summative purposes: that is a report at the end of a course or period of study which purports to predict future performance. Much more stress is laid on assessment for formative purposes: that is the use of the information gathered to improve the current educational process.

This multiple-purpose concept of assessment, which is closely linked to the totality of the curriculum, leads directly to the second theme. This theme is concerned with the considerable *increase in the range of qualities assessed and contexts in which that assessment takes place*. Stringent boundaries put on many assessment systems in the past are breaking down. No longer is it necessary for the qualities assessed to be 'academic' and strictly amenable to measurement. Assessment of personal, social and attitudinal characteristics is frequently under consideration, and what counts as 'achievement' within even traditional subject areas has expanded considerably. In addition, the contexts in which assessment takes place are much more diverse than in the past. No longer are examination halls the places which one immediately associates with assessment; long-overdue recognition is being given to the fact that most, and the most valuable, assessment is carried out on the site where the learning takes places. Changes in the curriculum have brought about acceptance that the place of learning is no longer always the school or college. The rise of work experience and community activities, for example, have opened up the issue of assessment for school pupils in the context of the workplace.

The third theme is directed to the rise of *descriptive assessment*. Much of this has manifested itself in the form of concern for criterion-referenced approaches which replace or complement traditional norm-referenced systems. The aim has been to provide descriptions of what has (or has not) been achieved rather than to rely on pupils' marks or grades, which have little meaning other than as a comparison with the marks and grades of others. Descriptions of this kind are seen as having the potential to help us understand what, and why, children are or are not learning, and to facilitate improved learning. Such descriptions may also be able to ameliorate the disadvantages of the competitive traditional system and to promote more cooperative attitudes to learning. Perhaps the most persuasive argument, however, has related to the anticipated value of the descriptive information to teachers and young people in making rational decisions about such things as courses to be followed, curricula to be reformed, work to be done, remediation to be carried out, and so on.

A fourth theme is concerned with the *devolution of responsibilities for assessment* to, for example, schools, teachers, work experience employers and young people themselves. Teachers have always carried out most of the assessment to which pupils and students are subjected, but traditionally the assessment which 'matters' (i.e. national certification) has been firmly in the hands of external examination boards. The recognition that at all levels internal assessment by educational institutions is of crucial importance is changing all that; but things are going further in some quarters. The concern with the assessment of a wider range of things some of which, like work experience, happen outside the classroom has led to the involvement of others, such as employers, in the assessment process. Furthermore, many of the arguments about the value of assessments to pupils themselves have suggested that the benefits will be greatest if the young people can be persuaded to undertake self-assessment.

A fifth and final theme focuses on assessment for certification. Much of the public debate and changes in government policy in the 1980s have supported the view that *certification should be available to a much greater proportion of the population of young people* than has been the case in the past. The nature of certification is also undergoing reform.

The innovations identified in these five themes are by no means restricted to assessment developments in the United Kingdom. Apart from the fifth theme, which reflects the substantially greater obsession with certification in this country compared with most others, there is a considerable and worldwide literature concerned with similar matters.

Chapter 34

Assessment and the improvement of education[1]

Wynne Harlen, Caroline Gipps, Patricia Broadfoot and Desmond Nuttall

PURPOSES AND PRINCIPLES

Those who support, through taxation, the provision of schools and various institutions for further and higher education and training have the right to expect that a high standard of education and training will be provided. Assessment plays important and different kinds of roles in fulfilling this expectation. Before enumerating these it is necessary to make explicit the meaning with which the term assessment is being used in this paper.

Definition

Assessment in education is the process of gathering, interpreting, recording and using information about pupils' responses to an educational task. At one end of a dimension of formality, the task may be normal classroom work and the process of gathering information would be the teacher reading a pupil's work or listening to what he or she has to say. At the other end of the dimension of formality, the task may be a written, timed examination which is read and marked according to certain rules and regulations. Thus assessment encompasses responses to regular work as well as to specially devised tasks.

All types of assessment, of any degree of formality, involve interpretation of a pupil's response against some standard of expectation. This standard may be set by the average performance of a particular section of the population or age group, as in norm-referenced tests. Alternatively, as in the national curriculum context, the assessment may be criterion-referenced. Here the interpretation is in terms of progression in skills, concept or aspects of personal development which are the objectives of learning, and the assessment gives direct information which can be related to progress in learning. However, the usefulness of criterion-referenced assessment depends on the way in which the criteria are defined. Too tightly defined criteria, while facilitating easy judgement of mastery, require an extensive list which fragments the curriculum. On the other hand, more general criteria, which better reflect the overall aims of education, are much less easily and reliably used in assessing achievement.

The roles of assessment in education

A number of roles of assessment in education are commonly identified:

- Assessment, as the means for providing feedback to teachers and pupils about on-going progress in learning, has a direct influence on the quality of pupils' learning experiences and thus on the level of attainment which can be achieved (formative role).
- It is the means for communicating the nature and level of pupils' achievements at various points in their schooling and when they leave (summative role).
- It is used as a means of summarising, for the purposes of selection and qualification, what has been achieved (certification role).
- It provides part of the information used in judging the effectiveness of educational institutions and of the system as a whole (evaluative or quality control role).

The discussion and recommendations in this paper are related to three of these purposes, maintaining a focus on assessment at the school level and on national curriculum assessment (NCA) in particular and omitting the certification role.

Issues

In previous papers (BERA, 1992), criticisms of the NCA have been laid out in some detail. The intention here is not to go over the ground of these criticisms but to use the earlier work as a basis for positive proposals about preferred alternatives to the present system. It is important, however, to bear the following key issues in mind:

- There is an unavoidable backwash on the curriculum from the content and procedures of assessment. The higher the stakes of the assessment, the greater this will be. Some countries are currently seeking to use the backwash effect to encourage the teaching of higher level skills such as problem-solving. For this purpose it is necessary to emphasise the use of assessment techniques capable of addressing the full range of knowledge, skills and attitudes which are embodied in the curriculum. But these more comprehensive measures are less easy to aggregate and thus do not readily provide means of reliably comparing educational outcomes in a statistical manner. By contrast multiple-choice and other paper-and-pencil tests provide results which are easily aggregated and compared but their use encourages teachers to ignore much of what pupils should learn as they 'teach to the test'.

- A major flaw in the NCA system which has been introduced is its use of the same assessment information for several purposes. Not all assessment purposes are compatible. Strong evidence from experience in the US, combined with that now accumulating in England and Wales, indicates that information collected for the purposes of supporting learning is unsuitable and unreliable if summarised and used for the purposes of quality control, that is, for making judgements about schools, and its use for this purpose severely impairs its formative role.
- There is likely to be a trade-off between, on the one hand, cost and quality and, on the other, effectiveness. The cheapest assessment techniques, such as multiple-choice, machine-markable tests, may be convenient instruments to use but provide poor quality information for the purposes of communication and little or no support for the learning process itself.

Key principles

These issues and the purposes of assessment are borne in mind in proposing the following set of principles to inform policy-making on assessment:

- Assessment must be used as a continuous part of the teaching–learning process, involving pupils, wherever possible, as well as teachers in identifying next steps.
- Assessment for any purpose should serve the purpose of improving learning by exerting a positive force on the curriculum at all levels. It must, therefore, reflect the full range of curriculum goals, including the more sophisticated skills and abilities now being taught.
- Assessment must provide an effective means of communication with parents and other partners in the learning enterprise in a way which helps them support pupils' learning.
- The choice of different assessment procedures must be decided on the basis of the purpose for which the assessment is being undertaken. This may well mean employing different techniques for different assessment purposes.
- Assessment must be used fairly as part of information for judging the effectiveness of schools. This means taking account of contextual factors which, as well as the quality of teaching, affect the achievement of pupils.
- Citizens have a right to detailed and reliable information about the standards being achieved across the nation through the educational system.

FORMATIVE ASSESSMENT

A major role identified for assessment is that of monitoring learning and informing teaching decisions on a day-to-day basis. In this role, assessment is an integral part of the interactions between teacher, pupil and learning materials. Because of this relationship, some teachers, who practise formative assessment well, may not recognise that what they are doing includes assessing. This may partly be due to holding an image of assessment as a more formal activity, distinct from teaching (Harlen and Qualter, 1991). A broader view is required, along the lines of the definition given above, which encompasses both the informal and the formal. Because of this difficulty of identifying assessment in its formative role in teaching, it seems helpful to provide a rationale and a brief illustration of its meaning in practice. These provide the basis for setting out the features of a scheme of genuinely formative assessment.

Rationale

It is difficult to conceive of teaching which does not use some information about the intended learners' starting point. In some views of learning and teaching the information is likely to concern what is and is not known and to be used to fill gaps and add to what is already there. However, much more is involved when the view of learning is one which regards it as important to 'take a child's initial ideas seriously so as to ensure that any change or development of these ideas and the supporting evidence for them makes sense and, in this way, become "owned" by the child' (DES/WO, 1988). For learning with understanding, according to this view, information about existing ideas and skills is essential.

In the notion of 'matching' learning experiences to pupils' abilities to benefit from them, the knowledge of pupils' present ideas and skills is a prerequisite. Here assessment is carried out to help, not to grade, pupils. Often pupils are unaware that assessment is taking place, but at other times they may take part in it explicitly through self-assessment.

Implied in these reasons for recognising assessment as essential to the educational process is that the information gathered is usable, and is indeed used, in making day-to-day classroom decisions. These decisions may be about 'the appropriate next steps' (DES/WO, 1988, para. 23) or about 'appropriate remedial help and guidance' (ibid.). Success and failure are not clear cut in the classroom, since performance is substantially influenced by context (BERA, 1992), so it seems to be preferable to use the single term 'formative' to encompass and replace what the TGAT Report (DES, 1988) described separately under 'formative' and 'diagnostic'.

An example

A teacher notices that a Year 7 pupil is making systematic errors in multiply-ing fractions. She questions him about his perception of what he understands $\frac{1}{2} \times \frac{3}{8}$ to mean in terms of real objects. His reply leads her to realise that he had not interpreted this as 'half of three-eighths' but was using an incor-rectly remembered algorithm. The intervention informed both teacher and pupil of the problem and the remedial action to be taken was clear to both of them.

The same story could be quite different: the teacher marks the pupils' sums wrong and, as this occurs often, comes to regard him as a poor performer in mathematics. This view soon becomes communicated to the pupil, adding to his discouragement from repeated failure. Neither pupil nor teacher find out why the pupil was having difficulty or what action to take to help him overcome it.

This brief example illustrates some of the requirements of a system of formative assessment. The teacher who uses it successfully is looking out for progress towards intermediate goals and is aware of underlying ideas and skills which are required for success. She brings together several obser-vations of the pupil's performance and finds patterns which help her to uncover shaky foundations by exploring understandings at earlier points. The teacher also uses techniques for uncovering these understandings which involve the pupil and avoid discouragement. She focuses on the specific aspect of response and does not label the pupil by generalising from this difficulty and making assumptions about other aspects of his mathematical ability.

Characteristics of a formative assessment scheme

Drawing together, and extending points from this example leads to the suggestion that what is required from a formative assessment scheme is information that is

- gathered in a number of relevant contexts;
- criterion-referenced and related to a description of progression;
- disaggregated, which in this context means that distinct aspects of per-formance are reported separately and there is no attempt to combine dissimilar aspects;
- shared by both teacher and pupil;
- a basis for deciding what further learning is required;
- the basis of an on-going running record of progress.

A report of recent practice in England suggests that it falls some way short of implementing assessment of these key characteristics. HMI report that, in 1990/1:

Many pupils were not being given a sufficiently clear idea of their progress or an indication of how they might improve the quality of their work.

(DES, 1992)

A scheme of formative assessment must be embedded in the structures of educational practice; it cannot be grafted on to it. Thus there are implications in the foregoing for the curriculum, for teachers, in terms of required supporting materials and pre-service or in-service training, and for record-keeping practice.

Recommendations

We conclude that effective formative assessment would be facilitated if the curriculum were to be expressed in terms of overall aims in the major and enduring areas of development and intermediate goals towards these aims, rather than, as at present, taking the form of separate statements of attainment with little articulation between statements at different levels. We therefore recommend that the curriculum should provide a description of progress, which enables teachers and pupils to map onto it the pupils' understanding at any time and to see the course of further development.

We further urge that steps be taken to provide teachers with the training and materials so that formative assessment can be carried out with the rigour and reliability necessary for it to be effective in improving pupils' learning (meeting the first two principles we identified on p. 275). These steps would enable teachers to be aware of and to use techniques for:

- *gaining access to pupils' present understandings and difficulties by observing them, analysing their written work and listening to their ideas;*
  advancing pupils' ideas and skills, based on the information about their present understandings;
- *discussing progress with pupils on a regular basis and involving pupils in keeping records of their learning;*
- *keeping regularly updated records of pupils' progress in the form of a detailed profile which is summarized for discussion with other teachers and with parents at the end of each year.*

SUMMATIVE ASSESSMENT

Summative assessment is similar to formative assessment in that it concerns the performance of individual pupils, as opposed to groups. In contrast with formative assessment, however, its prime purpose is not so much to influence teaching but to summarise information about the achievements of a pupil at a particular time. The information may be for the pupils themselves, for receiving teachers, for parents, for employers or for a combination of these.

There are two main ways of obtaining summative information about achievements: summing up and checking up (Harlen, 1991). The former is some form of summary of information obtained through recording formative assessments during a particular period of time and the latter the collection of new information about what the pupil can do at the end of a period of time, usually through giving some form of test. The nature and relative advantages and disadvantages of these are now briefly reviewed.

Summing up

This provides a picture of current achievements derived from information gathered over a period of time and probably used in that time for formative purposes. It is, therefore, detailed and broadly based, encompassing all the aspects of learning which have been addressed in teaching. To retain the richness of the information it is best communicated in the form of a profile (i.e. not aggregated), to which information is added on later occasions. Records of achievement (RoA) provide a structure for recording and reporting this information, combining some of the features of formative assessment with the purposes of summative assessment in that they involve pupils in reviewing their own work and recognising where their strengths and weaknesses lie.

Their defining aims are: (a) to address the full range of desired learning outcomes; (b) to make pupils partners in assessment so that they improve their willingness and their ability to learn; and (c) to provide a basis for decisions about future courses, career options and appropriate learning targets. Both the process of producing the record and its content are particularly valuable in meeting the pressing call from employers for assessment which can encourage a continuing process of personal education and development. As the DES/WO put it:

> The benefits to employers go wider than the availability of better information through records of achievement. The development of self-appraisal and self-management skills can help pupils not only to take increasing responsibility for their own learning whilst at school but also later on to be better equipped to present themselves for selection and interview for jobs; and later still, to manage their work in employment and evaluate their career performance.
>
> (DES/WO, 1989)

The establishment of records of achievement as a regular structure for summarising achievement at intervals during pupils' school careers would provide a natural base for the government's National Record of Achievement.

Checking up

No such additional benefits can be claimed for the 'checking up' approach to summative assessment. It is generally carried out through providing tests or tasks specially devised for the purpose of recording performance at a particular time. End of year tests or examinations are examples, as are the end of module tests for checking performance in modular programmes and external public examinations.

Checking up and summing up approaches have contrasting advantages and disadvantages. Tests used for checking up are limited in scope unless they are inordinately long and so are unlikely to cover practical skills and some of the higher level cognitive skills. On the other hand they do provide opportunities for all pupils to demonstrate what they have learned. Summative assessment which is based only on formative assessment depends on the opportunities provided in class for various skills and understandings to be displayed and, further, may be out of date in relation to parts of work covered at earlier points and perhaps not revisited.

This suggests that a combination of the two approaches may be the most appropriate solution. There are several advantages to having test materials available for teachers to use to supplement, at the end of a particular period, the information they have from on-going assessment during that time. The emphasis is on 'test materials' and not tests. These would ideally be in the form of a bank from which teachers select according to their needs. The items in the bank would cover the whole range of curriculum objectives and the whole range of procedures required for valid assessment. This provision would also serve the purposes of the non-statutory Standard Assessment Tasks (SATs).

The main advantages are that the availability of a bank of test material would provide teachers with the opportunity to check or supplement their own assessment in a particular area where they felt uncertain about what pupils can do. This would ensure that all aspects of pupils' work were adequately assessed without requiring extensive testing. Checking their own assessments against those arising from well-trialled and validated tasks would also build up teachers' expertise and lead to greater rigour in teachers' assessments.

Recommendations

The uniform testing of pupils across age groups, through SATs, is neither reliable nor valid and brings other well-rehearsed disadvantages for teachers and pupils. We consider them to be unnecessary since their purposes can be served through more educationally acceptable ways, meeting the second, third and fourth of our principles (p. 275).

We propose that a form of record of achievement should be used to report the profile of achievements of pupils at regular intervals throughout the primary and secondary school. These records would then lead to the government's National Record of Achievement. We also suggest that a bank of test material be available for teachers to use to check and supplement their own assessments, which will be the chief source of information in the record.

ASSESSMENT FOR EVALUATIVE AND QUALITY ASSURANCE PURPOSES

Assessment of performance at the national level

Information about pupils' achievement is necessary in order to keep under review the performance of the system as a whole – the quality assurance role of assessment. In the absence of such information it is possible for rumour and counter-rumour to run riot. For example, the argument about the levels of performance of seven years olds on reading (prior to the national assessment data) would never have been possible had there been a national survey of reading performance at the age of seven.

To serve this purpose, assessment has to be carried out in a way which leads to an overall picture of achievement on a national scale. It requires measures of achievement of a large number of pupils to be obtained and summarised. For this purpose testing in controlled conditions is necessary. However, if every pupil is tested, this leads to adverse effects both on teaching practice and on the curriculum and an over-emphasis on formal testing generally. Further, surveys which test every pupil cannot provide the depth of data required to provide a wide-ranging and in-depth picture of the system. Thus testing every pupil at a particular age is not appropriate for assessing performance at the national level.

To serve the evaluative role, assessment at the national level does not need to cover all pupils nor to assess in all attainment targets those who are included. The necessary rigour and comparability in assessment for this purpose can be provided by the use of a sample of pupils undertaking different assessment tasks. Following the pioneering work of the APU, it would be possible to obviate the 'excessively complicated and time consuming' approach of the SATs and still provide the comprehensive coverage of every subject area across a satisfactorily large sample of particular age groups of pupils.

The advantages of the APU were that:

– The surveys were able to assess performance in detail and in an 'elaborate' way, covering higher order skills and including practical and oral activities. The responses were marked by trained markers and the impact on teachers was minimal. By contrast, paper-and-pencil tests for all pupils, which must be carried out under examination conditions and marked quickly by teachers (as is necessary if all pupils are included), cannot assess in such a detailed way or cover such a range of skills and activities.

– Because only light samples of pupils and schools were included, the APU surveys did not have the negative side effects of high stakes testing programmes. They did, however, produce good quality performance data which provided pointers to curriculum development and some important in-depth analysis of differences (e.g. between girls and boys) on a scale not previously possible. This underlines the point that the use of light sampling and, if necessary, the anonymity of schools, reduces the undesirable effects of the testing (e.g. teaching to the test).

The arguments in favour of using APU-type surveys for evaluative purposes extend beyond the effects on schools to the quality of the information. Unless pupils' attainments are monitored over a broad range of performance, each of which is scrutinised in depth, a thorough and useful picture of national performance cannot be obtained. A system which has to test every pupil and yet is manageable can only provide us with a superficial picture of national levels of performance.

> The APU obtained their wide-ranging picture of performance by giving each of a small sample of individuals only a small selection of the total number of questions used in a survey. Since individuals' scores were not required the overall picture of performance could be aggregated over both questions and pupils. Had an individual been given the total range of questions used in an APU survey, about 30 to 40 hours of testing would have been required in each subject area. In fact, each individual took between one and three hours of a selection of the total amount of test material used in a survey.
>
> (SEAC, 1991)

In the experimental phase of SAT production, the attempt made to give every pupil a task for every aspect of performance led to the gargantuan testing of each pupil as depicted in this quotation. This was clearly not feasible, but it is equally clear that the much-reduced SATs will not give the detailed description of performance which is useful for national monitoring. The conclusion is that national curriculum assessment and testing for all pupils should be separate from and complementary to the collection of data for national monitoring.

The proposal to which this leads is that national surveys should be established at ages seven, eleven and sixteen, in English, mathematics, science and possibly technology, using a light sample (in the region of a 2 per cent sample), on a rolling programme so that every subject is assessed every three or four years. Much assessment material is already available, both that devised by the APU and from the pilot development of SATs. Use of this would provide good quality performance data on the core curriculum at significant educational stages. Feedback to teachers on performance in specific items would enable schools to interpret the achievements of their own pupils in terms of national standards. With light sampling and a large bank of items the notion of teaching to the test becomes entirely irrelevant. This bank could be open without invalidating its use and could constitute the resource suggested above for use by teachers, thus making the best use of carefully devised and validated items.

These proposals would meet two of the important principles outlined at the beginning of this paper: that assessment must be a force for good on the curriculum and that the nation has a right to good quality information about pupils' performance over a wide curriculum framework.

Recommendations

We propose that surveys of the APU type in the basic subjects should be resumed at intervals of three or four years in any one subject. Consideration should be given to making this bank of items open for teachers to use in supplementing and checking their own summative assessments of individual pupils (as recommended in the previous section).

Assessing school effectiveness

It is well established that the attainment of an individual is as much a function of his or her social circumstances and the educational experiences of his or her parents as it is of the effectiveness of the school or schools attended. To judge the effectiveness of a school by the attainment of its pupils is therefore misleading and unfair. What is wanted is a model that disentangles the effect on attainment of the school from that of the pupils' background. The value-added approach, that looks at the gain in achievement while the pupil is at a particular school (that is, the progress he or she makes there) offers a way forward and is, indeed, the basis of school effectiveness research such as that reported in *School Matters* (Mortimore *et al.*, 1988; see also McPherson, 1992).

The assessments of attainment used (both on entry to the school and on leaving) should be as broad as possible to ensure that school effectiveness is not reduced to efficiency in teaching test-taking skills but reflects the full range of the aims of the school. This would have been difficult to achieve even in the original plan for national curriculum assessment, which has since been abandoned as being too time-consuming, and would be far too narrow if based on the measures currently in use.

To counter the narrowness of outcomes implied by test results, even when shown in value-added form, it is suggested that schools should publish detailed reports covering such areas as:

- the aims of the school;
- details of recent inspection reports (if any);
- particular areas of expertise offered;
- cultural and sporting achievements;
- community involvement;
- destinations of leavers.

In short, the school should show its test results as part of its record of achievement.

Recommendation

The information used in assessing the effectiveness of schools should take the form of a profile featuring the academic achievement of pupils which is attributable to the effect of the school rather than other factors. Therefore pupil progress, as well as raw scores and a range of other achievements of the school and its pupils, should be published.

A MODEL BASED ON THE RECOMMENDATIONS RELATING ASSESSMENT PROCEDURES TO PURPOSES

In Figure 34.1 the proposals/recommendations put forward are related to the assessment purposes which they are intended to serve. The proposed open bank of formative/diagnostic assessment materials provides a resource to support teachers' on-going assessment as part of their teaching and the use of this assessment. These materials would include procedures through which assessment is planned into teaching and learning activities, examples of pupils' work, and descriptions of speech and actions, with interpretative commentaries, and suggestions of ways of including pupils in the discussion and assessment of their own work. Most importantly it would provide suggestions of 'next steps' for the teacher to consider. The use of this material in teaching supports the formative purpose of assessment.

Information collected during teaching informs teachers' summative purpose, through the summing-up route. When providing summative assessments of pupils' achievements at a particular time, the teacher needs to be sure that his/her judgements tally with those of other teachers. It is also necessary, in order for others to have confidence in teachers' summative assessments, that there is evidence of a common standard being applied. The 'bank' of test materials with national performance data serves two purposes: first, enabling a teacher to check his/her own judgements, by giving certain tasks to pupils as part of their activities and comparing the results with observations of the pupil in other activities, second, as evidence of performance at a particular level. The use intended here is not as a bank of tests, or of

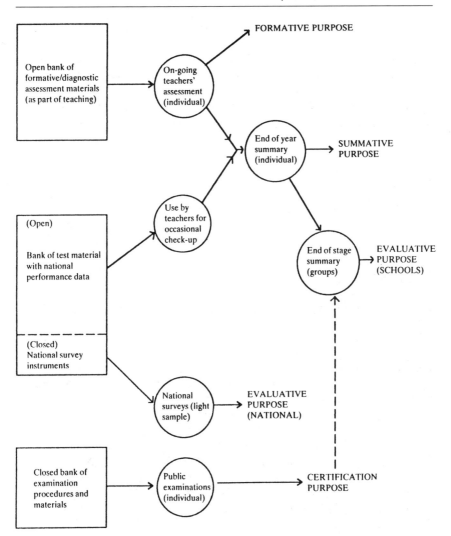

Figure 34.1 Assessment materials, procedures and purposes

materials to be put together as tests, but of tasks which teachers use to check their judgements.

The broken line separates the open section of the bank from items developed for use in the proposed national surveys. After use, these would be added to the open section, with their instructions for use, marking and performance data. It would be necessary to develop items or tasks for subject areas not included in the national surveys, for example for the social subjects, but since these need only sample the subjects in order to provide a check for teachers, there is no need to force onto them an inappropriate 'test' structure.

No changes are indicated by the closed bank of examination materials for the purpose of certification as the paper has not addressed this area of assessment. This bank is included to provide the full picture and to draw attention to the way in which results are presently used for school evaluation, via league tables. However, the proposals would not allow these 'raw' data to be used as measures of school effectiveness. The broken vertical line indicates that they should be subsumed in a profile of changes in a range of pupil performances which are attributable to the effect of the school.

NOTE

1 Based on the text of a paper prepared for the National Commission on Education by the BERA Policy Task Group on Assessment, February 1992.

REFERENCES

BERA (1992) Dialogue Series: *Policy Issues in National Assessment*. Avon: Multilingual Matters Ltd.

DES (1988) *The Task Group on Assessment and Testing: A Report*. London: HMSO.

DES (1992) *Education in England 1990/1: The Annual Report of the Senior Chief Inspector of Schools*. London: DES.

DES/WO (1988) *Science for Ages 5 to 16: Proposals of the Secretary of State for Education and Science and the Secretary of State for Wales*. London: DES/WO.

DES/WO (1989) *Records of Achievement: Report of the Records of Achievement National Steering Committee*. London: DES/WO.

Harlen, W. (1991) 'National curriculum assessment: increasing the benefit by reducing the burden'. In *Education and Change in the 1990s*, Journal of the Educational Research Network of Northern Ireland, No. 5, February: 3–19.

Harlen, W. and Qualter, A. (1991) 'Issues in SAT development and the practice of teacher assessment'. *Cambridge Journal of Education* 21(2): 141–52.

McPherson, A. (1992) *Measuring Added Value in Schools*. National Commission on Education Briefing No. 1. London: National Commission on Education.

Mortimore, P., Sammons, P., Stoll, L., Lewis, D. and Ecob, R. (1988) *School Matters*. Wells: Open Books.

SEAC (1991) *The APU Experience 1977–1990*. Ref. D/009/B/91. London: HMSO.

Chapter 35

Assessment and gender

Patricia Murphy

BIAS AND ASSESSMENT PRACTICE

Before we look at ways of interpreting gender differences in pupils' performance, let us first briefly consider bias – as a concept rather than a technical issue. There is consistency in the statements about bias in the national assessment documentation, i.e. that all efforts should be made to remove it. If assessors are to put this policy into practice, how are they to define bias? If we consider differences in group performance on an example of a reading test task (Hannon and McNally, 1986), the authors report that over half of the children who had English as a second language did not select what was judged to be the correct response.

> *An example from the reading test:*
> The man was very late and just managed to jump . . . the bus as it was pulling away from the stop.
>
> 1 at
>
> 2 up
>
> 3 *on*
>
> 4 by.
>
> (Hannon and McNally, 1986)

To consider whether the task was biased you have to ask why these children's response was as it was. Prior to asking the question, though, the performance has to have appeared aberrant in some way. For example, was the performance atypical? If the answer is yes, you may conclude, as the authors did, that the colloquial use of the word 'jump' when literally translated makes little sense. Jumping *by* or *at* a bus makes no more sense than jumping *on* one. For certain children, the task measures their lack of knowledge of colloquialisms rather than their ability to read.

The ability to explain a group difference on an assessment item enables us to make decisions about whether that item is biased. However, more often than not, we are unable to explain why certain assessment tasks demonstrate group differences. In international surveys of secondary pupils' science performance, boys have been found to perform consistently at a higher level than girls. Tasks where girls performed at a relatively higher level were few in number and exhibited no apparent common characteristics (Humrich, 1987). Consequently, they were assumed not to be biased. The overwhelming number of tasks which showed boys ahead of girls was taken as an indication of a significant difference in achievement. We tend to take a statistically significant trend in results as an indication that we are measuring something of educational significance and so we are reassured about the validity of our assessment.

Looking for atypical behaviour in assessment tasks is based on certain premises; commonly, that we expect a similar distribution of scores for groups of pupils. This interpretation is based on a norm-referenced view of the population, i.e. that some are able, others average, and half below average. The national assessment is criterion-referenced (DES, 1988a). In this paradigm, it is theoretically possible for the whole population to succeed or fail on any criterion with all shades of performance possible in between.

The APU science surveys were based on one of the few existing extensive criterion referenced assessment schemes and applied to a large proportion of the school population (DES, 1989a). A review of findings for populations of 11, 13 and 15-year-old pupils established that there was no criterion on which any group of pupils performed consistently. We have to consider, therefore, how on a criterion-referenced assessment, atypical behaviour can be identified. The premise that appears to be operating in national policy statements with regard to bias is that group scores for girls and boys, for example, are expected to be equal. Atypical behaviour is, therefore, signalled by differences between groups.

There are two further points embedded in this brief discussion which warrant consideration. We have mentioned that assessors tend to take homogeneity of group performance as indicative that the assessment is on target. Apart from the problems associated with criterion-referenced assessment, this position also needs to be challenged in terms of the values that determine what is assessed and how it assessed. The international survey results in science, referred to earlier, are a case in point. The cross-cultural uniformity of gender differences on multiple choice tests of science achievement have been subject to numerous interpretations. For some they represent a clear measure of boys' greater scientific ability; for others they indicate that, culturally, girls are not encouraged or expected to achieve as well as boys in science; yet others use them to argue that specific cultural factors which affect girls' and boys' science achievement must be in operation across cultures. For example, Kelly (1981) identified the 'masculine' image of science, common to most countries, as a contributory factor. She argued that as girls and boys have learnt to respond to gender appropriate situations, then a 'masculine' science will alienate girls and discourage their engagement with it. From this perspective, bias is inherent in the definition of the subject and the characterisation of achievement. The trend for boys to consistently outperform girls is evidence of this.

Another way in which we imbue assessments with particular values is in the choice of modes for assessment. Changes in assessment practice such as the introduction of multiple choice sections in public exams have affected not the numbers achieving success, but the people. In the case of multiple choice items, girls' success was negatively influenced (Murphy, 1982; Harding, 1979). The introduction of continuous course work assessment in GCSE has also led to a shift in the population achieving success which shows a marked gender difference. The pattern of performance is not uniform but there is a tendency for girls to outperform boys on course work even in subjects where boys tend to be ahead of girls on the written exam papers (Cresswell, 1990). Do we interpret these results as indications of bias or does their consistency suggest that something significant is being measured? What has to be asked, then, is whether what is being measured is what was intended and whether it is judged to be a significant element of subject achievement. At this point, our values determine our interpretations and a commonly-held view is that course work is a 'softer' option than the more 'objective' written forms of assessment. The devaluing of aspects of a particular group's performance can also lead to bias in assessment practice.

A final point concerns the notion of *group*. We have mentioned how our lack of awareness of significant factors in tasks limits our ability to explain both typical and atypical performance. If we are of the view that assessment procedures need to be individualistic to cater for individuals' meanings and ways of making sense, then bias is not a group issue, rather it is something we have to consider in interpreting each child's response. Our understanding of the concept of bias depends on how we view the way pupils create meaning and the extent to which we give priority to their meanings in assessments of achievements that we have identified as valuable. Any selection of technical treatments of bias will be informed by these perspectives.

INTERPRETING GENDER DIFFERENCES IN PERFORMANCE

The data discussed here is interpreted from a perspective that sees pupils as active participants in learning, striving to make sense of their own experiences by searching for patterns, regularity and predictability. Central to this perspective is the notion that children can understand other people's minds from a very early age because of the shared use of language. This follows because learning to use language involves understanding 'the implicit, semi-connected knowledge of the words, from which, through negotiation, people arrive at satisfactory ways of acting in given contexts' (Bruner, 1986, p. 65). To make sense of either learning or assessment tasks, pupils have to be able to construct meaning in them. To achieve this, assessors depend on a set of shared contexts and assumptions. Pupils' inability to understand a task can be interpreted either as a failing on the behalf of the assessor to provide appropriate cues to enable pupils to access their knowledge; or as an indication that pupils have not yet achieved the criterion being assessed. We look next at these two potential interpretations in the discussion of gender differences in performance.

DIFFERENCES IN EXPERIENCE

The APU science surveys at 11 and 13 showed boys and girls performing at the same level on assessments of the use of apparatus and measuring instruments. Evidence perhaps of an unbiased assessment. However, when performance on individual instruments was reviewed, girls as a group did significantly less well than boys on certain ones, e.g. microscopes, stop watches, etc. The number of instruments to show this effect increased as pupils went through school until, at 15, boys performed at a higher level overall. How do we interpret such results? Do we treat them as an indication that there are innate differences in the abilities of pupils which become more evident as the range and demands of the tasks increase? The viability of this interpretation will depend on the view we hold about the nature of individual ability and how it is distributed in the population. If, on the other hand, we assume that scores should be equal, what then? Do we statistically adjust scores to take account of this, reject certain tasks or attempt to generate others?

What was assumed in this case was that the tasks were assessing something significant. What that was had to be established before the results could be interpreted and used. Consequently, questionnaires were developed to find out what experience pupils had of the instruments outside of school that might be relevant. The results showed that boys' performance is better than girls' on precisely those instruments that they claimed to have more experience of. Thus, the assessment tasks themselves were not problematic, only the assumption that they were concerned solely with achievements acquired in school. A failure to collect such additional data would result in summative statements being misinterpreted. It would also make it difficult to meet the requirements of formative assessment which are to inform children's learning and teachers' planning. To understand and make use of assessment data, it is important that bias is considered as only one possible explanation of why responses are as they are.

If we are concerned to understand how pupils may or may not construct meaning in assessment tasks, it is important to consider the *nature* of their different experiences. Children using instruments outside of school will not only start to appreciate how to use them, but also when to use them and to what ends. An assessment task asking pupils to read off from an instrument is commonly judged to be measuring a relatively low level skill. Yet, such tasks assume that pupils understand: the variable being measured; the situations where the instrument is typically used; and the degree of accuracy that is appropriate. It is important to note that these assumptions cannot be overcome by minimal changes in assessment tasks such as rewording, or providing hints about instrument use.

This is a simple example of a difference in pupils' out-of-school experiences. Research studies have shown that these only account in part for the variation in scores between girls and boys (Rennie, 1987). Many people concerned with bias in 16+ examinations highlight the imbalance in the use of male and female names and the stereotypical portrayal of male and female roles. Such factors do contribute to bias in tasks, but are only the tip of the iceberg. A more significant issue is raised by the monitoring sub-committee of The Mathematical Association (1990). They commented on the use of names from ethnic minority groups in GCSE papers that 'those named appear to have totally accepted the values of the host culture'. If we are concerned with bias and consider that pupils have to construct meaning in assessment tasks then we need to ask how pupils' different values might influence this. Research into gender differences has looked at the relationship between different patterns of nurturing and how people subsequently learn to relate to the world (Chodorov, 1978; Harding, 1985). These learnt social rules determine: what we attend to, in relationships between people and between objects, and the content of our experience; and the values that we imbue and impart in social interactions. The implications of a gendered world are that children are not only channelled into gender appropriate experiences but also into gender specific ways of experiencing. As a consequence, children may not only have different experiences, but also different expectations and approaches to learning.

Earlier we mentioned that communication depended on shared contexts and assumptions. How does a gendered world view influence what is communicated in assessment tasks? An advantage of the APU item banks is in their scale extent. A comprehensive range of scientific criteria are assessed across a wide variety of content, using different contexts and varying modes of presentation, operation and response. The results showed that across the ages irrespective of what criterion is being assessed, questions which involve such content as health, reproduction, nutrition and domestic situations are generally answered by more girls than boys (Johnson and Murphy, 1986). The girls also tend to achieve higher scores on these questions. In tasks which have a more overtly 'masculine' content, e.g. building sites, race tracks, information from spare part catalogues, or anything with an electrical content, the reverse is true.

If we are assessing pupils' ability to interpret pie charts, for example, and set a question which looks at the varying proportions of different fibres in girls' school blouses, girls achieve higher scores than boys. If, on the other hand, the focus is on the proportions of different types of cars produced by a factory at different times of the year, the situation is reversed. Pupils' experiences outside of school lead them, unconsciously, to define areas of the curriculum where they expect to be successful or, conversely, unsuccessful. Areas where they expect to succeed they approach with confidence. Areas which promise failure are avoided either on the grounds of perceived incompetence, often the case with girls, or because the pupils reject them as being unimportant or irrelevant in terms of what they have learnt to value. This latter response is more typical of boys as White has reported on in the context of writing and assessment (White, 1986); and Murphy with regard to pupils' responses to practical science investigations (Murphy, 1988). The performance effects found by the APU science surveys arise from the combination of avoidance by some pupils and the heightened confidence of others.

So what are such questions assessing and how should we treat them? Deciding whether the use of certain contents disadvantages either girls or boys, and therefore constitutes a source of bias, depends on whether we judge the application of the criterion in that content area to be a significant aspect of subject achievement. In other words, how are we defining mastery of the criterion? This question has to be asked whether the assessment is for formative or summative purposes. An apparently fair assessment instrument which intentionally avoids particular content areas may be an invalid representation of achievement. Unfortunately, we do not know enough about primary and secondary pupils' criterion-referenced performance to be able to answer this. Furthermore, if we regard pupils' alienation from aspects of the curriculum as an unacceptable consequence of gender differences, we need to establish its effects in order to know how to address them. 'Biased' questions are, therefore, essential in a formative assessment instrument that seeks to inform the learner and the teacher about where to go next to progress. For national assessment purposes it may be judged appropriate that assessment should concern itself only with establishing that pupils demonstrate understanding of the criterion. It follows then that girls should be assessed on girl-friendly contents and boys on boy-friendly ones, i.e. build bias in. This may seem perfectly reasonable if we only concern ourselves with gender issues but even here the problems of reinforcing and fostering gender stereotypes are self evident. What we need to know is how the alienation of different groups and individuals is evidenced so that performance differences due to alienation are not interpreted as difference in ability. It is at the point of interpretation that bias has an effect.

GENDER DIFFERENCES IN PERCEPTIONS AND CHOICES

Most researchers into gender differences argue that with an appropriate learning environment, differences between girls and boys can be ameliorated. Is this the case for assessment and what are the implications for practice?

Perceptions of success

Girls' low self-esteem in maths and science is well documented and is seen as a contributory factor in their disengagement from these subjects in school. That girls underestimate their potential as writers is less well known (DES, 1985) and is more surprising as they consistently outperform boys on assessments of writing (DES, 1988b). Research has suggested that perceptions of success are influenced by the feedback that pupils typically receive in school. For girls, almost all the negative commentary they receive is directed at the intellectual quality of their work and so affects their academic self image. Boys, on the other hand, tend to receive comment on behaviour and presentation. A boy criticised for lack of effort is being encouraged to think that he can do better, irrespective of whether this is the case or not. Consequently, boys tend to overestimate their chances of success (Licht and Dweck, 1983; DES, 1989b). Confidence affects both pupils' ability to engage with an assessment task and the way in which they engage. For these reasons it is possible to consider some forms of *task presentation* as biased.

To enable girls to demonstrate their achievements it may be necessary to provide prior opportunities for them to succeed on aspects of tasks not being assessed. The actual assessment task could then be presented as a continuation of an activity in which they have already experienced success. Such a strategy would probably benefit most pupils in assessment situations. For boys, on the other hand, the need might be quite different. For example, when a class of 13-year-olds were faced with a science task involving a content already covered in class, boys were confident that they knew the answer whereas girls were anxious because they should know it (Murphy, 1990). This approach favours the boys on certain types of tasks. For example, on multiple choice items an ability to focus on the 'right' answer is an advantage. Girls tend to reflect on the ambiguities inherent in most multiple-choice distractors and so fail to find an answer or select several.

Recent innovations in assessment practice have looked at ways of assessing a broader range of achievements which probe the nature of pupils' understanding and how they apply it. Tasks to achieve this may, for example, ask pupils to provide a critique which draws on alternative viewpoints or focus on the range of observations pupils consider noteworthy in an open-ended situation. Gender differences in favour of girls on such tasks have been widely reported (DES, 1988b, 1989a, 1989b). In such tasks, boys may well need additional help in understanding what constitutes an expected response. This can be addressed to an extent in the presentation of tasks. However, changes in what assessors value as achievement have to be 'learnt' by pupils. It is unlikely that such understanding can be simply transmitted.

These suggestions about assessment procedures are based on a view of assessment as a process which can only represent snatches of pupils' potential achievements. In this view, assessment procedures should aim to 'elicit the individual's best achievement' (Nuttall, 1987). In the presentation of the SATs at key stage 1, the help that teachers can give children is controlled as it is considered to be a potential source of both invalidity and unreliability. Here you can see how one person's procedure to ensure reliability becomes another's source of invalidity due to the perceived potential for bias in the procedure.

Perceptions of tasks

In the last decade, assessment initiatives in the UK have attempted, with varying success, to develop procedures that reflect the principles of educational assessment, i.e. assessment that serves the learner constructively. The national assessment for England and Wales is an example of such an initiative. The national assessment tasks are intended to enable children to access their knowledge so that they can reveal what they know and can do. What would such tasks look like and how should assessors treat children's responses to be consistent with these intentions?

A consequence of pupils' differential experiences and ways of responding to the world is that girls typically tend to value the circumstances that activities are presented in and consider they give meaning to the task. They do not abstract issues from their context. Boys as a group, conversely, do consider the issues in isolation and judge the content and context to be irrelevant. How might these differences in approach affect pupils' perception of tasks?

A simple strategy for finding this out involved setting pupils open-ended design questions (Murphy, 1991). Examples of tasks used involved designing: a boat to go around the world; a new vehicle; a game for children; and an 'ideal' house. The tasks were given to primary and secondary pupils. The pupils' designs covered a wide range but there were striking differences between those of girls and boys. The differences reflected the different concerns that girls and boys are encouraged to attend to. The boys' boats were power boats or battleships, their vehicles army-type vehicles, 'secret agent' transport or sports cars. The detail focused on included elaborate weaponry and next to no living facilities. Other features included detailed mechanisms for movement and navigation, for example. The girls' boats were generally cruisers, their vehicles agricultural machines, family cars or children's play vehicles. The girls' designs included a great deal of detail about living quarters and facilities and essential food and cleaning supplies. Very few girls included mechanistic details.

Another strategy used a similar type of task but introduced it as part of the children's classwork. For example, children exploring patterns in buildings designed their ideal house and wrote an estate agent's description to accompany it. Again, girls' houses included many embellishments, e.g. curtains, vases, gardens and flowers. Their descriptions referred to pine fittings; cupboards for saucepans, vacuum cleaners and coats; matching curtains and wallpaper, etc. The boys' houses were generally stark but all had television aerials, notably absent in the girls' pictures. Their descriptions referred to the size of the garage, the availability of television in various rooms, including the bathroom, the distance away of the children's rooms and highlighted such amenities as the nearby motor racing track.

These images represent the type of detail that pupils, given an open situation, consider relevant. They help us interpret the content effects in tasks described earlier. More importantly, they show the very different world views pupils bring to assessment situations which alter what emphasis they place on assessors' cues and determine whether or not the cues provided enable them to access their knowledge. Can assessment practice deal with these differences and what are the consequences if it does not?

One important issue is that girls' attention to human concerns affects their ability to focus down on an aspect of a task. For example, moving from their boat design to investigate the load that a model boat would support made little sense to the girls as there remained other variables to consider. Even when girls focused on the narrow task, they remained committed to the original purpose for the boat, i.e. to take people around the world. Hence, they considered the stability of the boat in a range of conditions, seeking out ways to create effects, i.e. hairdryers to simulate hurricanes, watering cans for instant monsoons, spoons and buckets for creating whirlpools. In science assessments, it is common to consider girls' typical responses as inappropriate and off-task. Assessors generally look for correspondence with their world view and do not search for alternative perceptions in pupils' responses. Indeed a failure to correspond is taken as a measure of lack of achievement. Consequently even though girls' investigative strategies represent considerable scientific achievement, it typically goes unnoticed and unremarked. Generally, girls' attention to human needs and aesthetics at best is judged to represent other subject achievement rather than science. Other interpretations are possible and potentially more damaging. In these interpretations, girls' concerns with decor, diet, hygiene, etc., are viewed as trivial. It is interpretations like this which influence teachers' judgments and their treatment of girls. The following quote about girls' performance in maths is not untypical:

> Girls' tendencies to be distracted by powerful cues or true but irrelevant facts seem to reflect the 'hesitant, dependent, anxious, unmotivated, help-searcher' learner.
>
> (Levin *et al.*, 1987, p. 111)

If national assessment tasks, either SATs or teachers', are open-ended, then it will be essential to look for potential alternative tasks if pupils' performance is to be interpreted in terms of their achievements. If the degree of openness is restricted to enhance the reliability of the assessments, assessors need to consider how contextual issues and out-of-school experiences and interests might prevent pupils from seeing the task in the same way as the assessor. Again, this information is essential if pupils' performance is to be interpreted appropriately.

It is a potential source of bias when certain forms of achievement are accorded more status than others. The problem for girls and boys is not that one set of concerns is more valuable than another but that not having access to both limits what they learn and the uses they can make of their knowledge. For example, the girls who designed a pram with particular safety features are not using their knowledge inappropriately. Whereas the boys who computerised their pram to travel without an adult could be judged to be missing the point. In the same way, Sorenson's research study of children using circuits to light a house found that girls paid attention to the details of the model house and effectively installed the circuitry. Boys, on the other hand, were content to use Lego houses. Their circuitry was also perfectly adequate, but switches for the bathroom, for example, were located on the outside of the house (Sorenson, 1990). One can also see from these examples how in subjects such as design and technology, a typical 'boy's' view of relevance may lead to lower achievement and ultimately alienation and underachievement.

Other examples of how differences in what pupils are encouraged to attend to can lead to assessment bias relates to pupils' choice of expression. The APU language surveys (DES, 1988b) showed that girls choose to communicate in extended reflective composition. Boys, on the other hand, provide episodic, factual and commentative detail. Pupils' choice of expression was found to mirror their reading preferences. Depending on which subject is being assessed and the modes of expression favoured in that subject, girls' and boys' performance will create an impression of a 'good' or a 'poor' response. Presenting teachers of science and English with characteristic 'girls'' and 'boys'' descriptions of two butterflies showed a clear difference in what was valued. A girls' response tended to receive more credit from English teachers and a boys' from science teachers. Such interpretations help to foster images of gender-appropriate areas of the curriculum which influence teachers' expectations of pupils. The study of Goddard-Spear (1983) showed that the *same piece* of science writing when attributed to girls received lower marks from teachers than when it was attributed to boys. The attempt to move away from reporting achievement by scores to the use of more descriptive profiles will not have the beneficial effects hoped for if assessors do not disentangle features of style from the criteria they are attempting to assess.

SUMMARY

The implications for assessment practice that might be drawn from a discussion about gender differences will depend entirely on how learners and their learning are viewed. These views will also determine whether we judge an assessment task or procedure to be biased or not. From the position argued in this article, the commonly held view that bias in assessment is signified by 'unfairness' in tasks is not a particularly helpful one. The concern is not to find 'neutral' tasks which suit most pupils as this is not judged to be possible. To be consistent with a constructivist view of learning, assessment practice should rather aim to establish what the individual pupils' tasks are and to interpret their responses and their achievements in the light of these. Indeed, many children will have meanings, contexts and experiences in common but treating them as a homogeneous group is not appropriate in a constructivist paradigm. In other paradigms, where it is considered appropriate to treat children as a homogeneous group, it is odd that bias is an issue at all. On the other hand, if factors such as use of male and female names and role models are judged to affect pupils' performance then other influences that determine how they relate to the world must also matter.

If national assessment is to allow pupils to demonstrate what they know and can do then it has to consider how pupils make sense of tasks; and what purposes they might import if no purpose is presented to them or makes sense to them. How these then influence their subsequent engagement in a series of tasks also needs to be thought about. To achieve this assessment tasks need to be structured with children in mind so that they enable them to make the transition from their everyday understandings to respond to tasks in domain-specific ways. If we fail to do this, our assessments measure only our lack of understanding rather than children's lack of achievements.

REFERENCES

Bruner, J. S. (1986) *Actual Minds, Possible Worlds*. Cambridge, MA, Harvard University Press.

Chodorov, N. (1978) *The Reproduction of Mothering*. Berkeley, CA, University of California Press.

Cresswell, M. J. (1990) Gender effects in GCSE – some initial analyses. Paper prepared for a *Nuffield Seminar*. University of London.

Department of Education and Science (1985) *Language Performance in Schools – 1982 primary survey report*. London, HMSO.

Department of Education and Science (1988a) *National Curriculum Task Group on Assessment and Testing: a report* London, HMSO.

Department of Education and Science (1988b) *Language Performance in Schools: review of APU language monitoring 1979–1983*. London, HMSO.

Department of Education and Science (1989a) *National Assessment: the APU science approach*. London, HMSO.

Department of Education and Science (1989b) *Science at Age 13: a review of APU survey findings*. London, HMSO.

Goddard-Spear, M. (1983) Sex bias in science teachers' ratings of work. Contributions to the Second GASAT Conference, Oslo, Norway.

Hannon, P. and McNally, J. (1986) Children's understanding and cultural factors in reading test performance, *Educational Review*, 38(3), pp. 237–246.

Harding, J. (1979) Sex differences in performance in examinations at 16+, *Physics Education*, 14, pp. 280–284.

Harding, J. (1985) Values, cognitive style and the curriculum. Contributions to the Third GASAT Conference, London, England.

Humrich, E. (1987) Girls in science: US and Japan. Contributions to the Fourth GASAT Conference 1, Michigan, USA.

Johnson, S. and Murphy, P. (1986) *Girls and Physics: reflections on APU survey findings*. London, DES.

Kelly, A. (1981) Sex differences in science achievement, in: A. Kelly (ed.) *The Missing Half*. Manchester, Manchester University Press.

Levin, T., Sabar, N. and Libman, Z. (1987) Girls' understanding of science: a problem of cognitive or affective readiness. Contributions to the Fourth GASAT Conference 1, Michigan, USA.

Licht, B.G. and Dweck, C.S. (1983) Sex differences in achievement orientations: consequences for academic choices and attainments, in: M. Marland (ed.) *Sex Differentiation and Schooling*. London, Heinemann.

Mathematical Association (1990) *Bias in GCSE Mathematics*. A report on the 1989 papers prepared by the monitoring sub-committee.

Murphy, P. (1982) Sex differences in objective test performance, *British Journal of Educational Psychology*, 52, pp. 213–219.

Murphy, P. (1988) Insight into pupil's responses to practical investigations from the APU, *Physics Education*, 23, pp. 330–336.

Murphy, P. (1990) Gender differences in pupil's reactions to practical work, in: B. Woolnough (ed.) *Practical Science*. Milton Keynes, Open University Press.

Murphy P. (1991) Gender and assessment practice in science, in: L. Parker, L. Rennie & B. Fraser (eds) *Gender, Science and Mathematics: a way forward*. Oxford, Pergamon.

Nuttall, D. L. (1987) The validity of assessments, *European Journal of Psychology of Education*, 11 (2), pp. 109–118.

Rennie, L. J. (1987) Out of school science: are gender differences related to subsequent attitudes and achievements in science? Contributions to the Fourth GASAT Conference 2, Michigan, USA.

Sorenson, H. (1990) When girls do physics. Contributions to European and Third World GASAT Conference, Jönköping, Sweden.

Times Educational Supplement (1991) A new flexibility and freedom, January 11, p. 11.

White, J. (1986) Writing and gender. Paper presented at the *Co-ordinators Seminar, National Writing Project* (SCDC), Woolley Hall.

Chapter 36

Methods of assessment
Value for money

John Marks

The costs, especially the opportunity costs in terms of teacher time and teaching opportunities foregone, of different methods of assessment are very rarely considered in any systematic way. This chapter will discuss two recent examples where such costs have been very substantial – the original plans for national curriculum assessment and the extensive use of coursework in the GCSE.

The original plans for assessment under the national curriculum were based on the report of the Task Group on Assessment and Testing (TGAT) which recommended:

- the, by now familiar, ten level scale for all subjects with each level made up of a number of attainment targets which, in turn, contain a number of criterion referenced statements of attainment, all or nearly all of which must be achieved;
- tests which should be as far as possible indistinguishable from normal classroom practice;
- as many modes of assessment as possible should be used – verbal, oral, a wide variety of written modes, practical, open-ended, computer assisted.

The result of the thoroughgoing application of these principles, in conjunction with the complex series of attainment targets and statements of attainment defined by separate working parties for each national curriculum subject, was that the first pilot tests in the three core subjects for 7-year-olds in 1990 were a disastrous failure primarily because they were so time consuming. This was entirely predictable, given the TGAT ground rules, but apparently nobody had taken the trouble to do the simple order-of-magnitude calculations of the costs involved which are primarily those of teacher time. Simple estimates show that these costs are around £180 million for key stage 1 compared with a figure of only £3 million for simple pencil and paper tests taken by a whole class simultaneously (Marks, 1991). These costings are inevitably approximate but they clearly indicate that the differences in costs between different approaches to testing are very large indeed.

The benefits to be obtained from the more complex tests are also difficult to quantify. Indeed it could be argued that it is very difficult to see any important benefits at all, particularly when the substantial extra teaching time released by using the simpler tests is taken into account.

This conclusion is reinforced when the total costs in teacher time are estimated for all four key stages taken together. For the three core subjects alone these estimated costs amount to £860 million compared with about £18 million for simple pencil and paper tests. The additional costs for all the other foundation subjects are difficult to estimate but if similar approaches were adopted, as was the original intention, could well amount to a comparable figure. The total cost of national curriculum testing could then reach around £1.7 billion, which would be a substantial fraction of the annual teachers' salary bill of around £6 billion.

These conclusions are reinforced by HMI's findings on French primary schools in which written standardised group tests in French and mathematics are used as a matter of routine:

> These tests are reported as being very straightforward to administer, requiring no additional staffing or resources. They do not produce anxiety in teachers who cover the content of the programmes and feel secure in the knowledge that the tests will address the work covered. Pupils are not disquieted by testing because it is a regular feature of classroom practice.

Similar considerations apply to the substantial rise in the amount of coursework assessment in public examinations at 16 following the introduction of the GCSE in 1986. The costs of this change include the direct costs for the examination boards in arranging external moderation of coursework standards, which is potentially easy to quantify, together with the costs to schools and teachers of arranging systems for internal moderation *and* for supervising and marking coursework and ensuring that it is done. Once again, the major costs are for teacher time and for the opportunities for teaching and preparation which are foregone. Estimates are difficult to make and there is no data available from examining boards. However the indications are that these costs are considerable. For example, a strong supporter of 100% coursework assessment for GCSE English recently stressed that pupils' work:

> will be first assessed by the teacher, then moderated by other teachers, then sampled and remoderated. The sophistication (and the hard work) involved is far, far greater than that involved in final examinations.

> (Greenwell, 1992)

For a single subject taken by most of the cohort of about 600,000 pupils and wholly assessed by coursework, the costs, in addition to about £10 million for fees to the examination boards, may amount to about another £10 million for internal moderation in schools and as much as £150 million in teacher time for the very time consuming activities of marking and supervision. Such estimates are certainly compatible with reports of the pressure staff of secondary schools are under during the GCSE coursework moderation 'season'.

The greater costs of coursework – together with the fact that the more safeguards that are demanded by the need for fairness and reliability, the costlier coursework becomes – surely place the advantage with schemes of assessment which rely mainly on externally set and marked written examinations.

Here it is worth noting that almost every substantial piece of educational research, involving a significant number of schools, no matter from what ideological stable it has apparently emerged, has primarily measured attainment by using either public examination results or standardised group tests. The reasons surely are two-fold. First, researchers must believe that such tests do actually tell us something meaningful about attainment. But a close second is the factor of cost. It is so much cheaper to use these methods of testing and to make them reliable that, in nearly all cases, there is no realistic alternative.

Finally it is surely not true that formal assessment is inevitably something which pupils dread. Much comment has been made about the fact, which many seem to find surprising, that most British 7-year-olds enjoyed being tested in 1991. And the answer they mainly gave to the obvious follow-up question – What did you enjoy about the tests? – was that they actually enjoyed finding out what they knew and didn't know and how they stood compared with their classmates!

REFERENCES

Greenwell, B. (1992) 'Gradgrind's return', *New Statesman and Society*, 26 January.
Marks, J. (1991) *Standards in Schools: Assessment, Accountability and the Purposes of Education*, Social Market Foundation.

Part VI

Schools

In recent years there has been a sustained attempt to make school policies and practices more explicit and more open. The chapters in this Part in different ways reflect some of the impetus behind this move. More and more attention has focused on understanding schools as organisations. What, for example, are the structures and processes that characterise schooling, how do these interrelate, and how can they be changed to secure school improvement? Charles Handy and Bob Aitken provide an introduction to these questions in contrasting the type of organisational structures to be found in primary and secondary schools. They explore the internal and external world of school organisation *and focus attention on the way that individual teachers contribute significantly to the overall ethos and organisational health of the school.*

John Gray's contribution on school effectiveness exemplifies a new theme of educational research that emerged in the 1980s. In a chapter that first appeared as the text of an inaugural professorial lecture he reviews a range of work on the theme and argues that *'good' schools are characterised by a high proportion of pupils who achieve above average levels of academic progress, are satisfied with their schooling and have found a good relationship with one or more of their teachers.*

What evidence is needed to make judgements about how good a school is has been the focus of political and educational debate. The use of examination and test league tables to compare schools has been particularly controversial. Andrew McPherson draws on developments in research on school effectiveness to question some of the pitfalls in drawing conclusions from certain types of information. He explains the concept of measuring added value in schools, an idea that has attracted interest across the political spectrum. This he defines as the boost that a school's added value can give to a child's previous level of attainment, and he suggests that *any attempt to improve schooling by means of informed choice presupposes that parents are capable of understanding at least the complexity of an adjusted outcome score. To reject that possibility he sees as a rejection of the possibility of informing parents.*

Three researchers from the National Foundation for Educational Research (Foxman, Gorman and Brooks) address the same theme in exploring the politically vexed question of standards in literacy and numeracy. They point to the complexity of judgements about standards and argue, in a way that echoes the views of Cecile Wright, who also focuses on attainment and the continuing unease at the scholastic performance of Afro-Caribbean children. She reports a research study which *highlights how school practices, procedures and organisations can act as restraints upon black children of Afro-Caribbean origin*. The chapter quotes verbatim extracts from interviews with pupils to illustrate the way expectations, down to the minutiae of classroom life, can become prescribed in ways that work against equitable and effective forms of school organisation.

Brian Gorwood looks at the issue of continuity between primary and secondary schooling and addresses *the question of whether continuity between phases of schooling can ever be meaningful whilst fundamentally different philosophies of primary and secondary schooling exist*. Parents, like their children, have to make sense of different types of schooling and different phases of schooling. Alastair Macbeth produces a full analysis of the benefits that accrue from involving parents in schools. He includes within his review evidence to support a five-fold justification for seeing parents as relevant to what happens *inside* (his italics) school. For Macbeth *working with parents is not an optional extra, a favour bestowed on parents, it is at the very heart of the teacher's professionality*.

Chapter 37

The organisation of the secondary school

Charles Handy and Robert Aitken

The functioning of a secondary school depends upon the nature and quality of:

- organisation;
- relationships;
- support of the wider community;
- size;
- the advancing maturity of the students (including the fact that they have already had seven or so years of schooling);
- the increasing force of peer-group pressures;
- the demands of the examination system;
- employment expectations;
- the approach to adulthood.

Let us look further at some of these aspects.

Size

There are 4,553 secondary schools in England. They range in size from 45 to 2,001 students. Given a national average pupil-to-teacher staffing ratio of 16.5, this means that the average size of a secondary-school teaching staff is 54. For the larger schools (over 1,200 students) the teaching staff will number more than 80 (including part-timers). There may well be more than 50 other staff.

Secondary schools are therefore large organisations by any standards. In addition to the teaching staff there will be more non-teaching staff, more parents and families and additional outside interests. The spectrum of main interests and influences in the school as an organisation could be expressed as in Figure 37.1. The school has to be organised and managed so as to be able to 'box this compass'. And it has to be remembered that the students who are at the centre of these interests have to box the same compass. The management of the school has therefore to help each student to cope with the influences and values pulling him/her in different directions.

Figure 37.1

ORGANISATION

The tasks facing a secondary head in creating an organisation for her or his school are similar to those of a primary head:

- how to organise the students into learning groups;
- of what size, age mix and for what activities and stages;
- how to deploy the teaching and technical staff to these groups and activities;
- how to relate these to the space and facilities available.

The options are many and the answers are many (i.e. as expressed in the variety of forms of organisation being practised). The design (or change) of an organisation is a question of values. As for any designer, a decision to emphasise this or that feature determines the place and space left for other features. An order of importance – of what is valued in the organisation – is created. And the organisation goes on expressing those values. If, for example, specialist subject teaching is the prime basis of a school organisation, then, as we shall see, other aspects – such as the provision for pastoral care – may be debilitated. The choices and their consequences are many.

Commonly the five years' schooling between the ages of 11 and 16 is seen as two stages: providing in the first two or three years a general course for all students; with more differentiation (options) in the third and fourth years,

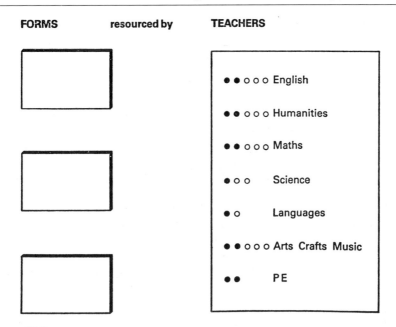

FORMS   resourced by   **TEACHERS**

● ● ○ ○ ○ English

● ● ○ ○ ○ Humanities

● ● ○ ○ ○ Maths

● ○ ○   Science

● ○   Languages

● ● ○ ○ ○ Arts Crafts Music

● ●   PE

Figure 37.2

usually dictated by choice of examinations to be taken. To maintain equality of opportunity and to counter over-early selection or specialisation (and therefore narrowing of the curriculum), many schools adopt all-ability groupings in the first year or so.

The basic model of the organisation of a school with three forms in the first year might be expressed as in Figure 37.2. This example relates to a small secondary school with about 90 students (three forms of entry) in the first year divided into classes of about equal size (30). The total number of staff (including part-timers) would be between 25 and 30, and some (indicated by ●) would be allocated according to their specialisms to teach first-year class/es. Some may teach more than one subject. For larger schools (e.g. eight forms of entry, 240 students per year) the number of classes would of course be greater, as would be the number of staff. The same model would to a greater or lesser extent express the organisation also of the second and third years.

There are obvious strengths and weaknesses in this form of organisation:

– the classes offer stability and security to the student groupings;
– the roles and responsibilities of staff are clear;
  but:
– the differences of style between seven or so staff teaching the same group can lead to differences of response *between subjects*;

- the differences of style between twelve or so staff teaching the same year group can lead to different responses *between classes in the same year group*.

That is not to say that roles are automatically clear or that different styles or responses can or should be avoided. These are potential consequences of the organisation adopted and are likely to need other organisational arrangements (e.g. meetings between all first-year staff under a head of year).

The same features and considerations will apply in the second and third years under this form of organisation. In larger schools the scale of the task of co-ordination is bigger, with possibly as many as thirty staff teaching first-year classes.

At the fourth- and fifth-year stage the tasks facing the organisation become yet more complex. It is necessary to arrange the teaching groups so as to match the examination courses or projects chosen by the students. Teaching groups therefore tend to be formed in relation to subjects (or groups of subjects), examination levels and syllabuses. There are several consequences of this:

- more student groupings;
- less stability and security in the teaching group;
- tendency towards polarisation of values (between subjects and levels of course);
- polarisation of expectations;
- greater differences in motivation (among students and staff).

The organisation has become more fractured, dispersed and unfocused; place and role in the organisation are less clear.

Taking the example again of a 450-student school the organisational 'chart' of the fourth year might look like Figure 37.3. The main groups (1–4) are clearly represented. The overlaps indicate regroupings for particular subjects, while the dotted line suggests the split between boys and girls for certain activities (e.g. physical education and some crafts). Potentially in this form of organisation there are between 12 and 18 different groupings of students. The complexities for a larger school are similar, except in scale.

The organisational problems of the secondary school intensify in the fourth and fifth year, driven by the demands of academic qualification and subject specialisation and the attitudes of students and parents. The school has to work harder to counter the contrary pressures that intensify too. There is a greater need to provide structures within the organisation to secure:

- co-ordination,
- continuity;
- commonality of styles and values;
- motivation.

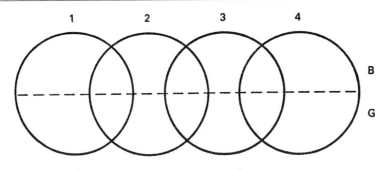

Figure 37.3

In the language of organisation theory, there must be enough *integrating devices* to match the necessary *differentiation*. These are difficulties that face any organisation. The larger and more complex the organisation the more difficult these nuts are to crack. And, as we have seen, secondary schools as organisations are both large and complex. They need careful and diligent managing if they are not to disintegrate.

The *differentiation* of secondary schools is forced upon them by the subject syllabus and the examination system. The dangers are that the imperative of academic qualification drives out other values cherished by the school, such as according equal respect and opportunity to all students: The reality is less than the ideology. So for example, attitudes develop among the people within the organisation (staff and students) that some subjects are more important than others, that some courses or classes are more valued than others, some teachers, some activities, some students more than others.

As always, what is important is how the organisation is perceived by the individual within it. What is his or her place, role, value? It can happen at this stage that some students feel teachers are competing for their time and minds against other subject teachers. It is unfortunately true that many students, particularly those with low or no academic expectations, feel unvalued at this stage. They are not motivated by the organisation (except to fulfil its low expectations of them) and are likely to retreat into the security or their peer group, whose anti-school culture becomes stronger than that of the school. When *motivation* and *identity* are lost within an organisation, other motivations and identities replace them.

Such dissonances can occur in any organisation. Fortunately it often happens that self-adjusting mechanisms begin to operate within the organisation. This is more difficult when the style of operation has become habitually engrained or when the organisation is subject to strong conditioning by external influences. Change is then a more difficult process and is slow in coming.

This is the snare that secondary schools are caught in to a considerable extent. Academic values and didactic method are deeply engrained, and these

---

Box 1 Splitting and binding

Organisations need to specialise their tasks but then need to bond them together. That seems to be an iron law of organising. But it goes further. The more you specialise the more bonding you need: for every split a binding mechanism.

Lawrence and Lorsch, in the United States, demonstrated that businesses in changing markets or changing technologies had to 'differentiate' their departments if they were not to lose out. The research people had to concentrate on the longer term, for instance, and not get distracted by the short-term fluctuations, whereas the sales force *had* to think short-term and concentrate on today's products and today's technologies. But they also found that those firms who matched the increased 'differentiation' with increased 'integration' devices – such as meetings, liaison groups, full-time co-ordinators, planning teams – were the most effective.

The message, however, is more general than that. Specialists inevitably tend to zero in on their specialism. Someone has to make sure that they are all pointing in the same direction, even if this means compromise for some. It is unwise, and unfair, to leave the end customer, or the student, as the one who has to pull it all together, the final integrator. Unfortunately the co-ordinating and integrating devices cost time and money; they are very visible. Logic says they shouldn't be necessary in a well planned state. Organisational reality says they always are.

---

are enshrined in an examination system that is based on subject knowledge. Since the examinations are marked against the average of those being examined, only a minority can ever come out top. And since the examinations are designed for only 60 per cent of the age group, there is a large bottom. These largely external factors contribute powerfully to the problems of internal organisation that we have described – particularly to the loss of identity and sense of anomie of many students in an organisation where such academic values are over-emphasised and other experiences and achievements are under-expressed.

The possibility that individual students could get lost in a large all-ability setting was recognised by the pioneers of the comprehensive school in the early 1950s. They built into the organisation a pastoral or house system whereby, for example, a school of 1,200 students had within it an organisation of ten houses each of 120 students. Tutors in the houses had responsibility for the welfare, discipline and pastoral care of their groups, including contact with families, the careers service, the courts etc. But it was not always clear whether the pastoral system was 'line' or 'staff', whether it was in charge or advisory.

This system of pastoral care has provided a strong integrating mechanism to counterbalance the disintegrating tendencies in a strongly emphasised academic structure. In addition to attention to matters of general welfare for the group it has enabled face-to-face counselling for individuals. But the pastoral care organisation has been under strain in recent years, especially since the school-leaving age was raised to sixteen in 1973 and in the face of developments in society including unemployment. In many schools the provision for pastoral care is as yet only 'bolted on' to the academic framework and accorded only one or two tutor-group periods per week. The adequacy and effectiveness of this are under question.

More recent developments in the pastoral care movement seek a more fundamental synthesis in their approach. They seek to acknowledge and use the resources of the peer group as a positive force in their own education. The main features of this for students are that they:

– work in tutor groups;
– learn by active and experiential methods;
– evaluate their own and the group's performance;
– have more determination of their own development.

Students, in other words, are being asked to learn by working in the kind of task groups that are part and parcel of work in the world outside. This requires a considerable shift of stance and method by teachers. They need to develop skills in group processes; to become enablers rather than instructors; to facilitate learning at first hand (through experience) rather than at second hand (by gathering others' knowledge). They need, in short, to become managers.

This is an example of a self-adjusting mechanism in operation: of positive organic growth within the secondary-school system to cope with a particularly difficult aspect of internal organisation. But such changes are not easily achieved. They threaten many established positions and practices. In those schools where this approach is more fully developed, *all* staff have a tutorial role, and learning in academic subjects is based on tutor-group processes. You cannot change the structure and the mechanisms of the school without affecting the roles, relationships, attitudes and skills of the people involved. Educational change inevitably involves an organisational shift, which has to be understood, planned for and managed.

RELATIONSHIPS

This example of 'tension' within a school organisation – in this case between the academic and pastoral aspects – throws up many issues of *internal relationships*. There is the need to maintain some commonality of will, style and understanding in all the expressions of the organisation, as well as continuity in the education and consistency of treatment of students and in the development of staff. The *issues* are intrinsically the same as for primary schools but more complex because of the nature and size of secondary schools. Because of this they are likely to require substructures within the organisation and some means of co-ordinating those structures.

Heads know how time-consuming and challenging this task of 'corporate management' – for that is what it is – can be. They leave their deputies and heads of faculty to share the responsibility, and the skills and experience of heads of department and pastoral heads. But, even more than in a primary school, factions and differences of values have to be faced. The definition of roles and responsibilities, the choosing of personalities, the vesting of authority and the creation of time and space for the exercise of responsibility are all essential ingredients of this pie.

But, again, that is not all; the senior management is not the whole organisation. The contribution and attitude of the 'ordinary' member of staff need to be recognised, especially in a professional organisation. The teacher in the classroom is the embodiment of the school. A wise head therefore values and creates space for 'hearing the voice' of ordinary members of staff, whether individually or collectively through trade union representation. Indeed, the trade-union angle is probably one that is under-valued, as a positive force, in school management.

Similarly the *external relationships* are more complex. There is still the need to recognise the 'bond' with the families of the students, including the aspirations of parents as their offspring approach occupational choices. But increasingly the students are reaching out beyond the family and the school and developing their own interests and aspirations. Adolescence can be described as a period of apprenticeship to adulthood. And this is likely to include experimenting with drink, drugs, sex, smoking, fashions and music, some of which may be stimulated by commercial pressures. The 'cultures' of home and school are themselves under pressure from the current youth culture.

There are two more formal external pressures. As the period of compulsory schooling approaches its end, students as individuals have to face the prospect (or lack of it) of employment. What kind of job or career to follow? What are the requirements of employers? What does 'going out to work' mean? What does it mean in terms of a particular occupation? This interfaces with the requirements of examining boards: not only GCSE, but also City and Guilds, Tec/Bec and RSA.

These are all issues that the secondary school has to address. They are points of contact or external relationships they have to maintain. They are the constituencies of the organisation, each one with different expectations of the school. And they need to find expression within the structure of the organisation. The boundary of the school never stops at the gate.

Chapter 38

The quality of schooling
Frameworks for judgement

John Gray

Those of you who like to review the health of the nation's schooling over breakfast will have noted that something is amiss. The *Daily Express* did not mince words. Commenting on the recent report from HM Senior Chief Inspector of Schools, Eric Bolton, it 'exposed' the 'Scandal of our rotten schools'. Even *The Guardian* was concerned: 'Schools must do better' was the line it took. It was left to *The Times Educational Supplement* to put a somewhat different gloss on the Inspectorate's conclusions: 'Less able most likely to be have-nots'.

With the passage of the 1988 Education Reform Act a concern with 'quality' in the education service has become something of an obsession.

As a direct result of the Act many LEA personnel see their main role in the future as monitoring and evaluating schools. I must confess myself worried as I see LEA after LEA establishing frameworks for judgement. In the rush to have something up and running by next September they run the risk of failing the very institutions such procedures are intended to protect.

'Quality' in educational circles is a potentially elusive concept. It undoubtedly has something of the 'best buy' features so assiduously researched and celebrated in *Which* magazine in relation to washing machines, TV sets and electric food mixers. Few people, however, would be happy with definitions that were restricted to these kinds of 'qualities'. They are undoubtedly looking for more. Articulating what that 'more' is will be a major challenge for the next five years but will come, I hope, to form the cornerstone of how schools find themselves judged over the next decade.

Different groups have different criteria for judging a school's quality. Rhodes Boyson is reported to have three 'instant tests'. The first is the amount of litter in the playground. The second is the amount and quality of graffiti in the loos. And the third is the angle at which children hold their heads, forty-five degrees being the optimum. Below that, they are clearly fast asleep. Beyond it, in open revolution!

SOME QUANTITATIVE INDICATORS OF QUALITY

In the attempt to understand quality many people turn to such traditional indicators of educational outcomes as exam results and staying on rates. Using the Youth Cohort Study of England and Wales, which we house in the Sheffield University department, I have picked out some relevant statistics [see Table 38.1]. Two of these are also available from official sources but the other two (the proportions of pupils truanting and pupils' attitudes) are not.

Table 38.1 Some traditional indicators of the quality of secondary schools (percentages)

Pupil outcome measure[1]	1987	1986	1985
Obtaining one or more 'higher grade' *exam passes* in 5th year	52	51	51
Staying on after 5th year	42	41	40
Truanting during 5th year 'seriously'	7	7	7
'seriously or selectively'	17	17	17
Saying: '*School was a waste of time*'	11	12	11

Note: 1 These various measures were obtained from the Youth Cohort Study of England and Wales.

Source: J. Gray *et al. Education and Training Opportunities in the Inner City* (Training Agency, Sheffield, Research and Development Series no. 51).

The picture over the three years 1985, 1986 and 1987 is a pretty stable one. Whichever of the four measures are employed things don't seem to have changed very much. (I need to make an aside here that when the full pictures from GCSE results in 1988 and 1989 come on stream we may find the 'improvement' so considerable that a new series of statistics to serve as benchmarks is required). Whatever the 'quality' in absolute terms of the education on offer in the secondary system, its quality (as judged by small and steady improvements over time) does not appear to have altered much in recent years.

THE VIEW FROM HM INSPECTORS

National responsibility for monitoring the quality of what goes on in schools is vested in members of HM Inspectorate. It was their report which provoked the recent outburst in both the press and parliament.

HMI follow events more closely than statisticians ever could. They visit institutions which are directly affected by events, both intended and unintended. Not surprisingly, their account is of a system which has had a bumpier ride. Policy initiatives actually affect what is happening.

So what did HMI actually say in their recent report regarding quality? They reported that:

> Across schools and colleges around 70%–80% of the work seen was judged to be satisfactory or better: roughly one-third of it at all levels was adjudged good or very good. That is *not* a profile of a service in great difficulty about its general standards of work. But . . . there are serious problems of low and under-achievement; of poor teaching; and of inadequate provision. It is particularly troubling that in schools some 30% . . . of what HMI saw was judged poor or very poor. Those figures, if replicated throughout the system, represent a large number of pupils . . . getting a raw deal.

(DES, 1990a)

These conclusions are undoubtedly disturbing and merit urgent attention. But what do the reports tell us about how quality has been changing over time? To establish this I looked back at the annual reports from previous years.

Anyone embarking on such a venture needs to be aware that comparing HMI judgements over time is not an easy matter. There are several reasons for this. The most obvious of these is that, attempting to capture the complete strengths and weaknesses of the educational system as a whole within a few pages of a report, much of the detailed basis for the judgements is inevitably omitted.

Table 38.2 HMI's judgements of school quality

Year	Proportion judged to be 'satisfactory or better'
1988/1989	'70% to 80% of work seen'
1987/1988	'Four lessons out of five'
1986/1987	'83% of work seen'
1985/1986	'81% of work seen'
1982 to 1986	'Nearly three-quarters of schools'

Note: 1 'Satisfactory' is the mid-point on a five-point scale running 'from excellent to poor'.

Sources: Sources were as follows. 1988/89: DES report published in 1990; 1987/88: DES, 1989; 1985/86 and 1986/87: DES, 1987; 1982–86; DES, 1988. All cited above.

But the difficulties are further compounded by the fact that HMI have, in fact, been using *three* summary judgements when they visit a school rather than just one. The report on the 1986 academic session provides the clearest discussion of this point:

– the *first* measure is an assessment of 'the overall quality of work in schools visited';

- the *second* is an assessment of 'the quality of provision for each class (or lesson) seen';
- the *third* is an assessment of 'pupils' response for each class (or lesson) seen'.

(DES, 1987)

Interestingly, HMI nowhere comment on secondary schools' exam results in their annual report. The focus is truly on the processes of teaching and learning!

The 1986 report suggests that for:

- 'overall quality' a figure of around 80% satisfactory or better is to be expected;
- for 'quality of provision' around 70%; and
- for 'pupils' response' around 80% – to their credit the pupils are apparently achieving in spite of the odds and the provision!

It is the evidence for the first of these three measures that I have attempted to assemble in Table 38.2. This was not always easy. The report on 1987/88, for example, refers to 'most of the work seen by HMI' rather than a specific percentage and the figure '4 lessons out of 5', the only quantified statement about secondary schools offered, relates in fact to their report on GCSE and is accompanied by the statement that this was 'a higher proportion than is usually reported in our inspection findings' (DES, 1989a).

By way of complete contrast the previous year's results (that is 1986/87) were quoted to a satisfyingly precise single decimal place. My confusions, I have found, are shared by one or two HMI as well. Probably the only useful conclusion to be drawn is that, over the years, HMI have consistently found that somewhere between 70% and 80% of the schools they have visited have been of 'satisfactory or better' quality.

In practice, as I shall argue later, broad judgements of this kind are the only useful ones to be made. What is important, when judging the quality of schools, is to note those occasions on which there are *marked* variations from the expected norms. Small fluctuations, one way or the other, are neither here nor there. At the national level at least, things do not appear to have changed very much in recent years whether one is looking at the quantitative indicators or the qualitative ones.

A 'POOR' SCHOOL BY ANY YARDSTICK

This is not to deny that there are marked variations in the quality of different schools, a point forcibly brought home by HMI's report on a Hackney secondary school. 'Only 20 per cent of the lessons seen reached satisfactory standards of teaching and learning. . . . As many as 50 per cent were of the poorest quality, lacking a clear sense of purpose, pace, progression or direction' (DES, 1990b). The gap between the national picture and the local one presented here is so stark that the apparent precision offered by the statistics is unnecessary. The school's 'overall standards' would surely be recognised as 'exceptionally low' by anyone. The environment in the upper school was 'squalid', the graffiti 'very offensive' and the toilets 'insanitary'. 'Many lessons failed to start on time' and 'pupils' attendance and punctuality gave serious cause for concern'. 'Teacher–pupil relationships . . . varied from the kindly, supportive, interested and positive to the distant, aggressive and, on occasions, the verbally abusive. Many teachers did not have the classroom management skills to maintain discipline'. 'Overall the school (was) not managed effectively and in some respects it was badly managed'.

Even by the standards of the measured language of evaluation employed by HMI it is clear that something had gone very wrong indeed. The 1983 HMI report on the Liverpool Institute for Boys was the last occasion on which I read about a similarly neglected institution. On this latter occasion, after almost 18 years of increasing neglect, the LEA eventually closed it down.

THE NATIONAL POSITION

How many secondary schools might be like these two nationally? The honest answer is that it is hard to say. The Hackney and Liverpool schools are doubtless at one extreme. There are nonetheless several pointers.

In their report on secondary schools in the early to mid eighties HMI reported that 'fewer than one in ten was judged poor or very poor overall' (DES, 1988). We ourselves noted, in our research for the Elton Enquiry into Discipline that 'teachers in fewer than one in ten (8%) schools thought that the discipline problems in their school were verging on the "serious" ' (Gray and Sime, 1988).

Again the national picture may well mask local differences. Back in 1986 the ILEA declared that the academic performance of almost one in four of its secondary schools gave 'cause for concern' (*The London Evening Standard*, 20 March 1986). The performance of the Hackney School, as it turns out, was at issue even then although it was not, it should be pointed out, one of the bottom ten which were 'carpeted' at that time. Of course, part of the answer to our question lies in how you choose to draw the line between the 'good' and the 'not so good'. To those who would maintain that the 'figures speak for themselves' I would merely observe that I have yet to find a single figure that could speak, let alone for itself.

Over the years I have noted a number of different strategies for drawing the line. HMI's preference, using a five point scale running from 'excellent' to 'poor', is to draw the line below the third category; hence 80% of lessons are 'satisfactory' (the mid point) or 'better' (good or excellent). By way of contrast most LEAs, in my experience, like to draw the line halfway down the list; this enables them to offer the insight that half the schools in the authority are above the LEA average and half below it.

My own preference is to draw two lines on the assumption that the majority of schools are performing at or around the average. I am looking, therefore, for ways in which schools may be said to differ from this average as well as for reasons; either they are a good deal above it or, alternatively, a good deal below. Most of the time there is nothing exceptional about their performance. They achieve what you would expect.

THE POLITICS OF SCHOOL EVALUATION

Setting the line is not just a matter of statistics or personal preference. As those who have tried to introduce improved strategies for schools' evaluation have found, more is at stake. In any system for evaluating schools there will be winners and losers. In selecting the overall approaches and the particular criteria this needs to be borne in mind. However, we could scarcely have a system more unfair than that which exists at present. By insisting that schools and LEAs publish their 'raw' exam or test results we run the distinct risk of rewarding schools for the 'quality' of the intakes they can attract rather than what they actually do with pupils.

Research on school effectiveness has something to contribute here. There are basically two ways in which the quality of a school's performance can be judged. The easiest way is to compare this year's performance with last year's and the year before that and so on. On the assumption that the intake has remained much the same over the years, how do the results compare?

The second approach is to compare like-with-like. How much progress have the pupils in this school made compared with pupils at similar starting points in other schools?

Ideally, one would use both approaches at the same time. In practice, most school effectiveness studies have concentrated on comparing like-with-like.

HOW MUCH DIFFERENCE DO SCHOOLS MAKE?

The debate about whether schools 'make a difference' has raged since the sixties. Like most such debates there has been ample scope for misunderstanding. The simple and unequivocal answer to the question whether they make a difference is a positive one – of course they do. The crucial questions are how much? and why?

Back in the early seventies Christopher Jencks argued that at least half the differences in pupils' performances in their late teens were due to differences in their social backgrounds and prior attainments; the remaining unexplained half he attributed to 'other factors' (Jencks et al., 1972). Whilst these 'other factors' undoubtedly included the schools young people attended, he maintained that no-one could actually identify which were the more effec-

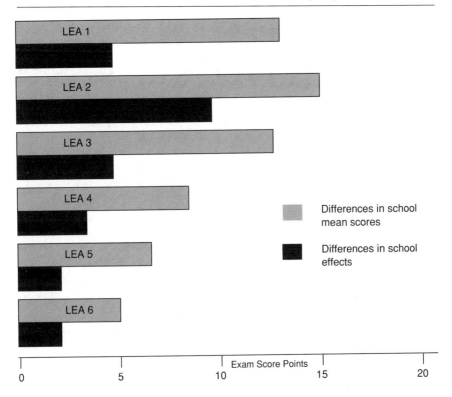

Figure 38.1 The size of school effects (inter-quartile ranges)

tive schools, prior to the event, or what precisely made them more effective. As far as predicting outcomes was concerned, schools, to all intents and purposes, made only rather small differences to life-chances.

Jencks' overall analysis of the *relative* importance of home and school continues to be the most comprehensive available and his conclusion that, relatively speaking, what pupils bring to school with them is considerably more important than what schools can do to or with them has scarcely been quarrelled with since then.

Our own most recent work confirms the sorts of estimates that have been made up till now (Gray *et al.*, 1990). Working with data from six different LEAs, and using the most sophisticated statistical techniques currently available (multi-level modelling), we found that when differences in schools' intakes are taken into account the differences between schools' results are roughly halved. We have seen this happen so frequently with the data-sets we have analysed that we have come to refer to this phenomenon as the 'rule of half'.

Figure 38.1 nonetheless shows that there were differences in the results of pupils attending schools of differing 'effectiveness'. The lightly shaded blocks show the difference in the actual exam performances of pupils attending different schools. These are the kinds of figures and differences the press reports.

The lengths of the heavily shaded blocks show the number of exam points difference between schools that just fell into the top quarter of 'effectiveness' in an authority and schools which just fell into the bottom quarter. In some LEAs, it can be seen, these differences were quite small (2 to 4 points); in one or two cases they were rather larger than this.

What causes the differences? Jencks was adamant that none of the things that policy-makers could directly influence 'made a difference'. 'We can see no evidence', he declared, 'that either school administrators or educational experts know how to raise test scores, even when they have vast resources at their disposal. Certainly we do not know how to do so' (Jencks et al., 1972).

When discussing the effects of policies and resources on pupils' outcomes he confined his attention to those 'school policies and resources that could be directly controlled by legislators, school boards and adminstrators'. In a brief but key paragraph he remarked: 'We did not look in any detail at things like morale, teacher expectations, school traditions and school "climate". While these things may well be associated with unusually rapid or slow cognitive development, policy-makers cannot usually measure them, and no one can be sure whether they cause achievement or only result from it' (ibid.).

FACTORS WHICH SEEM TO MAKE A DIFFERENCE

Almost two decades have passed since Jencks was formulating his conclusions and a decade since Rutter published *Fifteen Thousand Hours* (1979). Some of Jencks' conclusions have withstood the tests of time, others have been modified. Crucially, somewhat more is now understood about the nexus of relationships which Jencks was quick, perhaps too quick, to dismiss.

Whichever account one reads of research on school effectiveness a prominent place is given to the centrality of the institution's values. In a nutshell, the more effective or successful schools seem to know what they are about and where they are going. They have, as Lightfoot puts it in her account of six 'good' American High Schools, visible and explicit ideologies (1984). The particularly interesting (and with hindsight not unexpected) feature, however, is that staff and pupils alike can provide a reasonably good account of what the school is all about as well; the schools' aims and objectives are not merely the creation of, and confined to, their heads and senior teachers.

Teaching and learning are, of course, at the heart of any school's activities. What particularly distinguishes the more effective ones, Oakes argues in her wide-ranging review of the literature, is their 'press for achievement' (1987). Teachers expect their pupils to achieve and pupils, in turn, find themselves stretched and challenged in the classroom. Again there appears to be some mutuality of perceptions between pupils and teachers.

A third area in which the more effective schools make their contribution is in terms of relationships (Goodlad, 1984). Certainly, there is an absence of conflict between pupils and teachers; frequently there is some kind of mutual respect or 'rapport'. But crucially, at least in Lightfoot's study, there are plentiful opportunities for pupils to make good or, as she puts it, 'vital' relationships with one or more adults.

These sorts of things do not, of course, just happen; they are managed. Each of the various studies underlines, to a greater or lesser extent, the role of the school's leadership. Indeed I am still looking for a *research* study which demonstrates convincingly that the headteacher was not at the centre of things and yet the school, for which they were responsible, still functioned effectively.

More recently studies have gone beyond the headteacher to emphasise the role of senior management, the strategies that they implement and the ways in which they seek to support their more junior colleagues. A constant search for ways of evaluating and improving their institution's current performance also seems to be characteristic of the leaders of successful schools.

All four of these areas are ones to which Jencks paid scant attention. He would doubtless argue that the later research had given insufficient attention to the question of causal directions and there could be some truth in this charge. Taken collectively, however (and bearing in mind the qualitative accounts of how teachers and pupils actually behaved in the more successful schools), the balance of probabilities is that these things happened directly *because* of the efforts made by heads and their staffs. The most convincing demonstration would probably be to see how these factors were developed in a school over a period of time; but to date few researchers have been in a position to follow a school's development over this longer sort of period.

There is one area in which Jencks' conclusions have had to be modified a little, namely in relation to resourcing schools. This is the one area in which those responsible for a school, but nonetheless outside it, can influence matters directly. For much of the seventies it was fashionable amongst researchers and policy-makers to assert that resources couldn't buy success. Class sizes, for example, didn't make a difference; indeed researchers frequently reported that children did better in larger ones!

With hindsight nearly all the studies cited in support of these conclusions have been shown to be seriously flawed from the point of view of research design. One or two more recent studies (and notably the ILEA's Junior School Project in this country) have shown that smaller classes do make some difference, although the effects have not been startling (see Mortimore *et al.*, 1988). Within any one LEA pupil–teacher ratios are not usually allowed to vary by that much.

Adequate levels of resourcing, then, seem to be a necessary but not sufficient condition for a school to be effective; quite wide mixes of resources seem to be associated (and I emphasise the word associated) with success. Several caveats are, however, necessary.

The first is that in twenty years of reading research on the characteristics of effective schools I have only once come across a case of an 'excellent' school where the physical environment left something to be desired; interestingly, in that particular case, working on the environment of the school had been one of the new principal's first priorities, as indeed it appears to be with most new headteachers.

Second, in seven years of reading HMI's published reports on secondary schools I can only remember two or three occasions where their overall rating was highly favourable and the roof (or something similar) was in need of repair; and someone was always in the process of doing something about it.

Third, I have never read an account of a 'good' school which had serious staffing difficulties.

One further point needs to be made about the current research on school effectiveness. In general terms, it provides a relatively good introductory guide to the factors that make a difference. As a rule, schools which do the kinds of things the research suggests make a difference, tend to get better results (however these are measured or assessed). The problem is that these are tendencies, not certainties. In betting terms the research would be right around seven out of ten times, especially if it could be supported by professional assessments.

Around three out of ten times, however, schools seem to achieve 'good' results without scoring particularly highly on all the 'key factors' identified by researchers' blueprints. The collective wisdom of researchers and experienced practitioners is quite simply not good enough to hold individual institutions to account. To do so would be to run the risk of hampering, perhaps even damaging them.

The focus has tended to turn, as a result, from assertions about what schools must do to what schools must achieve. In particular, rather a lot of time has been spent debating the frameworks within which schools' performance will be judged.

SOME EARLY INITIATIVES IN RELATION TO PERFORMANCE INDICATORS

The initial push for the introduction of performance indicators in Great Britain came from the Audit Commission during the early eighties. Auditors are usually accountants by training and inclination. Naturally, therefore, they asked to see the accounts. The education service provided them with some fairly promptly. It was only several months later that it became clear that the education service's 'accounts' lacked the structure that a modern, performance-driven accountant might be seeking.

The accountant's dream that every educational activity and outcome could be allocated to a cost heading and given a precise cost was some way off becoming reality. To an accountant such imprecision is disconcerting. Before much progress could be made the education service needed to determine where it was headed and to establish some performance indicators by which it could be judged.

Much of the work that has gone on to date in relation to performance indicators is best described as 'ground-clearing'. The Coopers and Lybrand report, the CIPFA 'Blue Book' (1988) and, more recently, the DES's own pilot project (1989b) involving eight LEAs, have all produced lengthy lists of criteria which *might* be used to judge a school's performance.

Even if the DES had ever contemplated a 'grand design' for judging schools, it is clear that the experience of trying to orchestrate consensus during the pilot project contributed to the view that, in the context of the national curriculum and other major developments, a single set of recommendations was not appropriate. Schools were to be free to construct their own yardsticks. Whilst presenting the case for performance indicators, the Minister confined herself to the observation that each school should decide on 'a relatively small range of indicators for judging whether it is achieving its goals'.

Unfortunately, to date, schools have been given little advice about how they might make such decisions and, in the absence of such advice, they are not likely to find information about their own performance, in isolation from other schools, very helpful. Judgements about performance require a context within which they can be located. Equally importantly, given the firmly embedded nature of some existing approaches to school evaluation, they require some overall co-ordination, if publicly-credible judgements that have the power to challenge existing assumptions and prejudices are to be produced. Orchestrating such 'agreements' is not merely a technical activity but involves influencing the social organisation of 'educational knowledge' as well.

DEVELOPING SOME PRINCIPLES

Over the past year I and my colleagues had worked on these issues with members of about one in five of the English LEAs. A number of problems have emerged in our discussions about how their LEAs are responding to the new demands of the 1988 Education Reform Act. Things are a bit muddled at present.

First, few LEAs have sophisticated procedures in place already for judging the performance of their schools; indeed, as a recent HMI report confirmed, a majority of LEAs have not yet got round to establishing suitable procedures for interpreting schools' examination results (DES, 1989c). Lacking such approaches, they and their schools have recently found themselves falling victim to individuals or pressure groups who have been prepared to employ whatever crude yardsticks were to hand.

Second, they have only recently begun to develop procedures for systematically sharing information about schools' performances, let alone judging them. Few LEAs to date can rely on a consensus amongst their officers and advisers about what it is important to concentrate on. Should they, for example, look at outcomes as well as processes? And, in either case, which particular ones?

Third, even where the beginnings of some consensus have begun to emerge, there is considerable uncertainty about what precise evidence to collect. There is mounting pressure in many LEAs to use whatever happens to be on the shelf because time is short. But there is also widespread unease that what may currently be readily available or easily measurable is not necessarily central to the educational enterprise. Data collected for one purpose may not lend themselves to others.

Fourth, and most importantly of all, we have found it important to establish some general principles for the construction of performance indicators. Table 38.3 represents the latest attempt of my colleague David Jesson and myself to introduce some coherence to the debate by developing some general principles.

Table 38.3 Some general principles for the construction of performance indicators

---

Performance indicators should:
1 be about schools' performance
2 be central to the processes of teaching and learning
3 cover significant parts of schools' activities (but not all)
4 reflect competing educational priorities
5 be capable of being assessed
6 allow meaningful comparisons: over time and between schools
7 allow schools to be seen to have changed their levels of performance by dint of their own efforts
8 be few in number

The most important consideration relating to the construction of performance indicators is that they should *directly measure or assess schools' performance*. Many of the proposals we have encountered to date seem only indirectly related to actual performance.

They should be *central to the processes of teaching and learning* which we take to be schools' prime objectives.

They should *cover significant parts of schools' activities* but not necessarily (and certainly not to begin with) all or even most of them.

They should be chosen to *reflect the existence of competing educational priorities*; a school which did well in terms of one of them would not *necessarily* be expected (or found) to do well in terms of the others.

They should be *capable of being assessed*; we distinguish assessment here from measurement, which implies a greater degree of precision than we intend.

They should *allow meaningful comparisons* to be made over time and between schools.

They should be couched in terms that would *allow schools, by dint of their own efforts* and the ways in which they chose to organise themselves, *to be seen to have changed their levels of performance*; that is to have improved or, alternatively, to have deteriorated relative to previous performance and other schools.

Finally, they should be *few in number*; three or four might be enough to begin with. After some experimentation over a period of years one might end up with a few more. The processes that establish the wider credibility of the first ones will lend themselves to development if required.

THE THREE SHEFFIELD UNIVERSITY PERFORMANCE INDICATORS

In recent months we have come to recognise that there is an inverse relationship between the number of questions one chooses to ask and the quality of the evidence that can be collected in relation to each. The Sheffield Law of Performance Indicators states that 'too many questions drive out good answers'. Since 'good answers' are fundamental to the task of setting agendas for schools' further development it follows that we felt we ought to confine ourselves accordingly.

Table 38.4 The three Sheffield University performance indicators

Academic progress
   What proportion of pupils have made above average levels of progress over the relevant time-period?

Pupil satisfaction
   What proportion of pupils in the school are satisfied with the education they are receiving?

Pupil–teacher relationships
   What proportion of pupils in the school have a good or 'vital' relationship with one or more teachers?

Answer categories for all three questions

All or most		Well under half
	About half	
Well over half		Few

In the interests of economy, efficiency and effectiveness we have therefore restricted ourselves to the three questions listed in Table 38.4. The choice of 'academic progress' as one focus strikes us as largely unproblematic although, in the context of a national curriculum and related attainment testing in as many as ten subjects, it may be necessary to impose some restrictions.

Our second and third choices (relating to pupil satisfaction and pupil–teacher relationships) have been heavily influenced by our reading of the literature of school effectiveness.

In sum, we are arguing that a 'good' school is one where high proportions of pupils:

- make above average levels of academic progress;
- are satisfied with the education they are receiving; and furthermore,
- have formed a good or 'vital' relationship with one or more of their teachers.

We would agree with those who argue that these are not *sufficient* conditions for 'excellence'. As pragmatists we would argue, however, that it would be hard to imagine a 'good' school where these things did not happen in reasonable measure and furthermore that, where they happened frequently, the odds would be on the institution being a 'good' one. The concern that all aspects of schools' activities must somehow be brought in to complete the picture (and for justice to be done) needs to be resisted.

REFERENCES

Coopers and Lybrand (1988) *Local Management of Schools*, London, HMSO.

DES (1987) *Report by Her Majesty's Inspectors on LEA Provision for Education and the Quality of Response in Schools and Colleges in England 1986*, London, DES.

DES (1988) *Secondary Schools: an Appraisal by HMI: a Report based on Inspections in England 1982–86*, London, HMSO.

DES (1989a) *Standards in Education 1987–88: the Annual Report of HM Senior Chief Inspector of Schools Based on the Work of HMI in England*, London, DES.

DES (1989b) *School Indicators for Internal Management: an Aide-memoire*, London, DES.

DES (1989c) *The Use made by Local Education Authorities of Public Examination Results*, London, DES.

DES (1990a) *Standards in Education 1988–89: the Annual Report of HM Senior Chief Inspector of Schools*, London, DES.

DES (1990b) *Report by HM Inspectors on Hackney Free and Parochial Church of England Secondary School*, London, DES.

Goodlad, J. I. (1984) *A Place Called School: Prospects for the Future*, New York, McGraw Hill.

Gray, J. and Jesson, D. (unpublished) 'The negotiation and construction of performance indicators'.

Gray, J. and Sime, N. (1988) 'Findings from the national survey of teachers in England and Wales' in *Discipline in Schools: Report of the Committee of Enquiry*, London, HMSO.

Gray, J., Jesson, D. and Sime, N. (1990) 'Estimating differences in the examination performances of secondary schools in six LEAs: a multi-level approach to school effectiveness', *Oxford Review of Education*, June.

Jencks, C. *et al.* (1972) *Inequality: a Reassessment of the Effects of Family and Schooling in America*, New York, Basic Books.

Lightfoot, S. L. (1984) *The Good High School: Portraits of Character and Culture*, New York, Basic Books.

Mortimore, P. *et al.* (1988) *School Matters*, Somerset, Open Books.

Oakes, J. (1987) 'Conceptual and measurement issues in the construction of school quality', California, Rand Corporation.

Rutter, M. *et al.* (1979) *Fifteen Thousand Hours*, London, Open Books.

Chapter 39

Measuring added value in schools

Andrew McPherson

The publication of examination and test results, resulting in 'league tables' and calls for calculations of the contribution schools make to pupils' progress – the 'added value' they offer – raise a number of difficult questions. This first NCE Briefing describes the complex factors, values, and interests that should be taken into account when attempting to measure schools' performance.

This chapter draws on developments in research on school effectiveness to address questions about the value of information on schools' examination and test results. It identifies pitfalls and advocates certain methods. It argues that there is no single solution that can be recommended on technical grounds alone: even the best techniques have limitations. Value judgements will always be involved as well as issues of accountability and cost.

British schools have been required to publish their public examination results for over a decade. The current Education (Schools) Bill says that the government's purpose is to 'assist parents in choosing schools for their children' and to 'increase public awareness of the quality of the education provided by the schools concerned and the educational standards achieved in those schools'. Schools in Northern Ireland are likely to have to publish their results soon, and in addition English and Welsh schools must soon begin to publish the results of national curriculum attainment tests.

Many people are affected by these requirements: parents, pupils and teachers; school governors, school boards and education authorities; indirectly the employers, colleges and universities who select school leavers, and central government itself in Belfast, Cardiff, Edinburgh and London.

But does such information enable us to say with reasonable assurance that one school is better than another, or better or worse than it used to be? How can the information be used, and not abused? And how can we ensure that it will meet the needs of the wide range of interested parties? This briefing focuses on test and examination results at the secondary stage, but the main arguments can be generalised to other stages of education, and other measurable outcomes.

1 *By themselves, examination results do not show a school's added value.* Test and examination results differ from one school to the next. This is undisputed, and is one of the main reasons given by government for its concern with standards.

But schools also differ from each other in their pupil intakes. This, too, is undisputed. The type of school influences the gender and denominational composition of the pupil intake. The location of the school influences the ethnic and social mix. Type and location both affect pupils' levels of attainment on entry, as do many other factors.

A school's 'added value' is the boost that it gives to a child's previous level of attainment. 'Raw' outcome scores do not measure this boost. Test and examination results provide misleading indicators of added value if they are not adjusted for differences between schools in the attainment of their pupils on entry.

2 *Nevertheless, unadjusted results are informative.* Raw outcome measures are informative because they reflect actual attainment and activity. They tell one, for example, that a particular syllabus is being studied to a certain standard. But they convey information only when properly presented. They should be based on entire year groups of pupils and should identify any special cases or exclusions from the year-group base, such as pupils with special educational needs and transferred pupils.

Information about attainment on a subject-by-subject basis is often useful. But when one is looking at an individual pupil's attainment, whether overall or in specified areas of the curriculum, it must be aggregated, and this will entail value judgements. For example, it must be decided whether each grade level, or subject or type of examination, should be equally weighted or not.

Single outcome measures may not serve all users equally well and may thereby give one set of users priority over another. For example, summary measures of attainment may be too general to meet class teachers' or parents' diagnostic requirements for individual pupils. Similarly, judgements of value and priority are also implicit in the choice of a statistic to summarise outcomes: in the use of a mean or median, for example, rather than a distribution.

3 *Unadjusted outcome information should be accompanied by information on the school's contribution to pupil progress.* Parents need information on the value added by a school. School managers need information on the quality of the teaching input in a school. To meet such needs, one must take account both of the level of a pupil's 'prior attainment' before entry to the school or stage in question, and of other factors that might influence progress.

This cannot be done infallibly because there is no information available at present about methods through which schools boost attainment that can safely be assumed to apply to all schools in the future.

For example, studies typically find that about half of the variation among pupils in attainment in public examinations can be predicted from, or statistically 'explained' by, pupils' attainment on entry to secondary school. But such correlations do not necessarily tell us what caused the variations, or whether and how the pupils' prior attainment contributed to their later attainment.

If the cause lay solely with the pupil, then the school's boost, or added value, is the difference between the earlier and the later attainment. This is because the school was not responsible for the earlier level of attainment and its influence on later attainment.

On the other hand, the cause of the correlation between earlier and later attainment might lie partly with teachers. For example, teachers might wrongly expect from their pupils only levels of later attainment commensurate with their earlier attainment; and these teacher expectations might themselves then influence later attainment. If so, not all of a pupil's prior attainment should be subtracted when estimating a school's success in adding value.

The point is that the adjustment of outcome scores must always have a proper theoretical justification. Even the most 'commonsense' of adjustments is based on theory. Theories are not infallible, and therefore the particulars of any adjustment *may* be open to improvement and *must* be open to inspection and argument.

What is not open to argument, however, is that it should always be possible to adjust outcome scores for prior attainment. This is logically entailed in the idea of a pupil's 'progress'. Progress *is*, so to speak, an adjusted outcome score, the *difference* between an earlier and a later attainment. Schools are there to help pupils to make progress, so there can be no argument against the principle of adjustment if one wishes to know the added value of a school.

Nor can one dismiss the practice of adjusting outcome scores solely on the grounds that parents could never understand such adjustments. This would imply that parents could not understand the concept of pupil progress. Were this true, all attempts to inform parents would fail. A similar argument applies to adjustments for factors other than prior attainment, for example family background.

4 *Pupil progress is correlated with various non-teacher factors.*
Pupil progress may be correlated with *factors within the school for which teachers are not responsible.* An example is given in section 8. The history and religious denomination, if any, of the school may be associated with pupil progress as well.

Also correlated with progress are the characteristics of a pupil's *household*. These include: household size and adult composition; the educational level of the parent or parents; and the parents' occupations. Other factors associated with progress include the level of material and social (dis)advantage in the immediate *neighbourhood* of the home, and aspects of the wider *opportunity structure*, including the level and character of local employment opportunities, and the opportunities for further progress in education and training.

5 *The assessment of the effects on pupil progress of schools and other agents should be based on an explicit theory of good standing.*
There is substantial agreement amongst researchers, based on solid evidence, about a number of desirable features of any such theory. The first is that schooling is *longitudinal*. It takes place over time as pupils make progress and as schools maintain their effectiveness, improve or deteriorate. Any pupil can have a bad day, any school a bad year. Sensible judgements will therefore be based, not on snapshots, but on repeated measures of pupils and schools.

A second feature is that schooling is *multilevel*: pupils are grouped within classes, classes within schools, and schools within larger administrative and other types of grouping.

Both features are self-evident and should inform the way in which outcome scores are adjusted and used. Where they do not, adjusted scores will fail to inform the full range of users of the information; they may misinform them (see 7 and 8 below); and the statistical robustness of effects will be wrongly estimated.

A third requirement of a good theory is that it must be *multivariate* and *comprehensive* taking account of all factors involved. It is not sufficient to adjust outcome scores only for pupils' prior attainment. Outcome scores must be open to adjustment for other non-school factors that boost or retard progress.

The case for adjusting for non-school factors is not self-evident. But it cannot be dismissed by anyone who believes that a pupil's progress will benefit from the informed involvement of parents, or by anyone who believes that successful education is the product of a partnership between teachers and others. Adjustments are required if we are to avoid misinforming all parties to the partnership about the effectiveness of their several contributions.

6 *A single statistic may not be an adequate summary of a school's effect on pupil progress.*
There are two reasons for this. The first is that theories are always capable of improvement. Different theories entail different adjustments to outcome scores. This is already argued in section 3 in relation to adjustments for prior attainment. A similar argument applies to other adjustments, for example for family background. Whether or not an adjustment for family background, or any other factor, is invidious, depends on the theory underlying the adjustment.

The second reason is that, even when the theory or account of schooling is agreed, different users of the information may reasonably require different

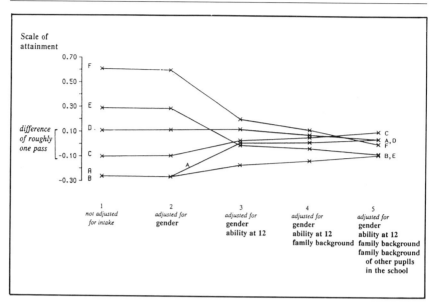

Figure 39.1 Average pupil attainment in six schools unadjusted for pupil intake, and with four adjustments

adjustments to be made. Two illustrations are given, one in each of the following two sections.

7 A school may boost the progress of different types of pupils at different rates.

One school may give a special boost to pupils who are already doing well or, alternatively, to pupils who previously have struggled. Another may succeed in spreading learning gains more evenly over all its pupils. A third may succeed in boosting the science attainments of girls in particular, whilst a fourth may give a particular boost to the language-related attainments of pupils from homes where the first language is not English.

All four schools could, nevertheless, achieve the same average attainment level and the same average amount of added value. In these cases, the averages would obscure as much about the school as they revealed. They would be of little help to a parent who wanted to make an informed choice for a particular son or daughter having a particular level of attainment and with a particular language capability.

In other words, a school may add different aspects and levels of value for different types of pupils. A method which can produce only one summary statistic for a school always runs the risk of misrepresenting that school's successes and failures and of misleading parents.

One advantage of a multilevel approach is that, subject to data availability, it allows one to test whether a single-statistic summary is adequate, or whether separate summaries are required for separate types of pupils.

Figure 39.1 shows the effects of four statistical adjustments for pupil intake on estimates of the quality of six secondary schools (schools A to F). The six schools are chosen from an education authority in which all schools are all-through comprehensives (showing more schools would clutter the illustration). Individual attainment is measured here by the number of passes in public examinations taken at sixteen, seventeen or eighteen years by pupils who were in their final compulsory year in 1983–84. The scaling of attainment is such that a difference of 0.2 corresponds roughly to one pass. Further information can be found in Lindsay Paterson's article (details below) from which this illustration is derived.

- With no adjustments for intake, schools A and B (coincident points) have the lowest average attainment scores, and school F the highest (column 1).
- Although females score higher than males on average, adjusting for the gender composition of the school does not change the estimates (column 2). This is because all of the authority's schools are co-educational and are more or less equally effective for males and females.
- Adjusting for gender and measured ability at the end of primary school does change the estimates, in two ways (column 3). First, it shrinks the range of differences between schools by about half. One reason for this is that ability on entry is correlated with later attainment. The other reason is that the six schools differ more from each other in respect of their pupils' measured ability on entry, than they differ in respect of the progress then made by their pupils. Second, the rank order of the schools is changed. School E, for example, now lies very close to A and C, though its unadjusted attainment score was substantially higher (column 1). (The close proximity of schools A, C and E in column 3 shows how misleading rank orders can be.)
- Adjusting additionally for the family background of individual pupils (various measures of parental and household characteristics) further shrinks the differences between schools (column 4).
- Finally, in column 5, an adjustment is made for the family-background characteristics of the school-leaver body as a whole in each school. This adjustment shrinks the differences between schools yet further and results in further changes in rank order. This is because, in this particular example, the attainment of a pupil having a particular set of characteristics (of gender, verbal-reasoning ability and family background), is also influenced statistically by the family-background characteristics of other pupils in the school (see section 8).

One way of interpreting column 5 is to say that the teachers in the school with the highest added value (school C) boosted the attainment level of their pupils by roughly one examination pass more than in the schools with the lowest added value (schools B and E). Such a conclusion, and the conclusions that can be drawn similarly from columns 3 and 4, are very different from any conclusions about a school's quality or added value *that could* be inferred from column 1.

Acknowledgement to, and further details in, Lindsay Paterson, *Socio-economic status and educational attainment: a multi-dimensional and multi-level study*, **Evaluation and Research in Education**, 5:3, 1991 pp.97–121.

Multiple summaries may seem complex. But any complexity is simply a reflection of the respect that good statistics must have for the individuality of the pupils and schools involved.

8 *The interests of parents and the interests of teachers may dictate mutually conflicting but equally valid adjustments to outcome scores.* A pupil's attendance at a particular school may confer advantages which have little or nothing to do with the action of teachers. Some studies have found that the characteristics of the pupil body as a whole are correlated with individual pupils' progress. In such studies, a pupil of, let us say, average prior attainment has tended to make more progress in a school where the prior attainment of all pupils was above average, than in a school where the prior attainment of all pupils was below average. Similar effects are sometimes observed for measures of family background.

Let us suppose that such correlations are wholly owing to peer-group effects outside the classroom: that is, to pupils learning from each other or preventing each other from learning in ways that a teacher could not reasonably be expected to influence. In summarising the effectiveness or added value attributable to teachers in a school, we would want to discount that part of a pupil's progress that was owing to such peer-group effects. This gives us a first added-value statistic for the school.

Parents, by contrast, will be interested in all of the advantages that will accrue to their child by virtue of their attendance at the school, whether these advantages arise from classroom teaching, from peer-group effects, or from anything else. It is not in parents' interest to discount peer-group effects when assessing the value of a school for their child. This gives us a second added-value statistic for the school.

Thus, a single-statistic summary cannot be presumed in advance to serve teachers and parents alike or, by extension, to serve education authorities and other interested parties. What is required is a multilevel capability – in this example a representation of pupils having certain individual character-istics, themselves grouped within schools so as to have certain collective or 'school-level' characteristics, namely the overall composition of the pupil body.

Again, there is a seeming complexity. We have two estimates of added value for the one school. But the complexity is simply an honest reflection of the different interests of two of the parties to the partnership of schooling. It is not a gratuitous imposition of the method.

9 *Features of a good indicator system.* A good indicator system must allow for the differences that characterise individual pupils and schools, for differ-ent explanations of these differences, and for the different interests of the range of parties to whom schools are accountable.

It is the job of statistics to produce the simplest and most economical summary of a school's value that is consistent with this variety and with the purpose or purposes of the indicator. The resultant summary might be simple or it might be complex. But complexity is not in itself an argument against aiming for the best possible indicator system.

Any attempt to improve schooling by means of informing choice presupposes that parents are capable of understanding at least the complexity of an adjusted outcome score. To reject that possibility is to reject the possibility of informing parents.

Nor is the cost of a good indicator system a decisive objection. We do not know the cost of the mistaken judgements, needless anxieties and fruitless 'further investigations' that are triggered by false signals from poor indicator systems. Misplaced complacency is costly too. In industry poor systems of quality control result in poor products and contribute to the very economic difficulties that better schools are expected to address.

A good indicator system will therefore aim to improve its own validity. It will not be content merely to 'indicate'. It will endeavour to describe outcomes and processes directly, to be valid in itself.

Whilst it is unrealistic to expect to build research enquiry into each and every application of an indicator system, the capability for testing its assumptions and improving its procedures should exist somewhere and should be available to everyone with an interest in better schooling. It will take quality to recognise quality.

CONCLUSIONS

1 Schools' test and examination results are informative, *but 'raw' results are misleading indicators of the added value of a school if they are not also adjusted for intake differences.*

2 'Raw' results should therefore be accompanied by *an assessment of the contribution a school makes to its pupils' progress.* The assessment should take account of each pupil's prior level of attainment and of other factors inside and outside of the school that may have influenced progress.

3 The basis of the assessment must be made clear, including any assumptions about the responsibility of teachers or others for the factors affecting progress; and *the assessment must have solid theoretical backing.*

4 *A single statistic may not adequately summarise progress.* Different types of pupils may progress at different rates. Parents and teachers may legitimately wish to know about different things. *What is needed is a good indicator system.*

5 A bad indicator system will hinder progress towards better schools and carry hidden costs.

6 *A good indicator system will:*
   - *take account of different needs and uses*
   - *be as simple as possible, while recognising the individuality of pupils, families and schools*

- *prefer measures of stability and change in performance to single 'snapshots'*
- *have built into it the means of monitoring and improving its own validity.*

ACKNOWLEDGEMENT

The CES is a Research Centre of the Economic and Social Research Council. The ESRC has supported many of the UK developments in school-effectiveness research on which this briefing draws.

FURTHER READING

Aitkin, M. and Longford, N. (1986) *Statistical modelling issues in school effectiveness.* Journal of the Royal Statistical Society, A, 149, 1–42.

Drew, D. and Gray, J. (1991) *The black–white gap in examination results: A statistical critique of a decade's research*, New Community, 17, 159–172.

Garner, C.L. and Raudenbush, S.W. (1991) *Neighbourhood effects on educational attainment: A multilevel analysis*, Sociology of Education, 64, 251–262.

Goldstein, H. (1987) *Multilevel models in educational and social research*, London: Griffin.

Gray, J., Jesson, D. and Sime, N. (1990) *Estimating differences in the examination performances of secondary schools in six LEAs: A multilevel approach to school effectiveness*, Oxford Review of Education, 16, 137–158.

Livingstone, J. (1990) *Performance indicators for Northern Ireland schools*, Summary Series No. 9, Belfast: The Northern Ireland Council for Educational Research.

Mortimore, P., Sammons, P., Stoll, L., Lewis, D and Ecob, R. (1988) *School matters: The junior years*, London: Open Books.

Nuttall, D.L., Goldstein, H., Prosser, R. and Rasbash, J. (1990) *Differential school effectiveness*, International Journal of Educational Research, 13, 769–776.

Raudenbush, S. W. and Willms, J. D. (1991) *Schools, classrooms and pupils*: International Studies of Schooling from a Multilevel Perspective, New York: Academic Press. Especially chapter 1 (Raudenbush and Willms), chapter 2 (Paterson), chapter 5 (Plewis), chapter 6 (Fitz-Gibbon) and chapter 7 (Paterson).

Smith, D. J. and Tomlinson, S. (1989) *The school effect: A study of multi-racial comprehensives*, London: Policy Studies Institute.

Willms, J. D. (1992) *Monitoring school performance: A non-technical guide for educational administrators*, Lewes: Falmer Press.

Willms, J. D. and Raudenbush, S. W. (1989) *A longitudinal hierarchical linear model for estimating school effects and their stability*, Journal of Educational Measurement, 26, 1–24.

Woodhouse, G. and Goldstein, H. (1988) *Educational performance indicators and LEA league tables*, Oxford Review of Education, 14.

Chapter 40

Standards in literacy and numeracy

Derek Foxman, Tom Gorman and Greg Brooks

SUMMARY

1 Reading standards among 11 and 15 year olds have changed little since 1945, apart from slight rises around 1950 and in the 1980s. Among 7–8 year olds, however, standards fell slightly in the late 1980s. In writing performance, there was no overall change during the 1980s.
2 Less than one per cent of school-leavers and adults can be described as illiterate. Basic literacy skills are however insufficient to meet the demands of many occupations.
3 British school students are above average in geometry and statistics, but below average in number skills, compared with other industrialised countries. Britain also has a wider spread of mathematics attainment, mainly due to the weaker performance of lower attaining pupils.
4 Nationally, there was a fall in attainment among 11 and 15 year olds in number skills between 1982 and 1987, and a rise in geometry, statistics and measures.
5 Attainment both in literacy and numeracy may need to rise considerably to meet the requirements of the next century.
6 We do not have an effective system of monitoring educational standards throughout the UK. Arguments about standards will continue until such a system is in place. National curriculum assessment is not best suited to monitor national performance: for this purpose, specially-designed, regular surveys are needed, using representative samples of pupils.
7 In addition to national monitoring, we need to compare ourselves with competitor nations, some of which are setting ambitious targets for the 21st century. The debate about standards of attainment must continue, but against a background of sound evidence.

1 INTRODUCTION

Public concern about educational standards is not new: criticism of standards has appeared regularly since the last century and is probably due to tensions between society's changing values and requirements, and the response made by the education service. Skills in literacy and numeracy are prerequisites for full participation in our society; it is not therefore surprising that public controversy about standards often focuses on them. This chapter asks what we mean by educational standards, and considers how they are measured and monitored. What is happening to standards in literacy and numeracy, and what will be the best way to monitor performance in future?

2 WHAT ARE EDUCATIONAL STANDARDS?

A 'standard' is a fixed measure against which performance is judged. A physical standard, such as a metre length, is objectively defined and is fixed over time, but educational standards in this sense, such as the letters denoting the grades attained in GCSE or the statements of attainment in the national curriculum, are less easily pinned down. Furthermore, the term 'standards' in educational discussion often refers not to particular criteria of performance but to the actual attainment of pupils: i.e. a mean score in a test or the proportion getting a question correct.

3 METHODS OF MONITORING STANDARDS

Monitoring implies attempting to determine changes over time in attainment. Five types of assessment have provided fuel for the debate on standards:

Public examinations, such as GCSE and A level, and Scottish Standard Grade and Highers, consist of different questions each year. Nevertheless, the letter grades awarded are intended to be comparable in standard from year to year and between examination boards. But the yardsticks that the grades represent are implicit; they are carried around in examiners' heads, and there are therefore no simple methods of determining whether the grade standards remain constant. Public examinations have other limitations as devices for monitoring standards: they are taken by candidates from more than one age group, and not all of the predominant age group are entered for the examination in any one subject.

National curriculum assessment (which applies to England and Wales) was carried out officially for the first time with 7 year olds in 1991 and will extend to 11, 14 and 16 year olds.

At all four ages, the assessments will consist of teacher assessments and externally set tests. The teacher assessments will vary inherently in content from school to school, and it is likely that the external tests will use different questions each year, although each question has to exemplify one of the statements of attainment which relate to a particular level in a particular subject. Since the statements of attainment are explicit, there would seem to be a lesser problem of comparability from year to year than in the present GCSE. However, as the system develops, points to watch in this regard will be the comparability of different questions supposedly exemplifying the same statements of attainment, methods of deciding when a statement of attainment has been achieved, and ways of aggregating statements achieved to attainment target level.

It is likely to be some years before the suitability of national curriculum assessment for monitoring can be fully evaluated, but it is already clear that only limited aspects of the national curriculum can be assessed in the external tests on each occasion.

There are also national assessment programmes in Scotland and in Northern Ireland, but these are more limited in scope than those in England and Wales.

Standardised tests consist of a fixed set of items relating to a particular area such as reading or mathematics. A test is initially given to a representative sample of the population whose attainment is to be measured. The results provide scores or 'norms' for particular ages of children against which the attainment of individuals can be measured. Attainment can then be monitored by repeating the test on representative samples at intervals. However, views on the nature of the content being tested may change and so the overall format of the test becomes outdated. In English, some items become outdated as language itself changes. Scores could fall as a result of these factors and be falsely interpreted as a fall in standards.

The surveys by the Assessment of Performance Unit (APU) represent the most extensive attempt to measure and to monitor performance nationally before the emergence of national curriculum assessment. The APU,[1] a unit at the DES, commissioned surveys in five subjects from independent agencies between 1977 and 1990, but only those in mathematics and (English) language will be mentioned in this chapter. These were conducted by the NFER on representative samples of pupils in England, Wales and Northern Ireland.

The APU surveys were very large-scale, each subject including written, practical and oral modes of assessment and assessing a wide range of knowledge, skills and processes. They gave a much more detailed picture of performance than had previously been obtained either by standardised tests or public examinations. A number of different methods were used to monitor change in performance over the period of the surveys: the principal one was comparing the results of the same questions used in different years. The APU programme was terminated by the government in 1990 when the national curriculum was introduced. The parallel programme in Scotland, the Assessment of Achievement Programme (AAP), began in 1983 and still continues.

International surveys. The rising importance of the global economy has produced increasing interest in comparative standards in different countries. International studies conducted over the past thirty years have compared attainment levels in some subjects in relation to the curricula in various countries and other factors in their schools and the home backgrounds of their pupils. There are obvious problems in attempting these comparisons: the test questions are likely to suit some countries more than others, translation can affect the levels of difficulty posed by specific questions, and comparable samples of pupils are difficult if not impossible to achieve because of the different features of education in the participating countries. The studies are also intermittent and the same countries do not always take part, so that monitoring changes in comparative differences is not easy. Despite these drawbacks there have been some very interesting results, especially in mathematics, as described below in section 5.

Trends in performance. In the following analysis of trends in literacy and numeracy, national curriculum assessment and public examination statistics will not be used as evidence for trends: the former because no data over time were available at the time of writing, even for 7 year olds, and the latter because although public examination statistics suggest a long-term rise in success rates, there are difficulties in interpretation.

4 TRENDS IN LITERACY

International studies of performance in literacy which included Britain have taken place (reading comprehension in 1967, written composition in 1983), but few conclusions can be drawn from these surveys about our performance relative to other countries. Consequently, this section focuses on data from national surveys and standardised tests.

Table 40.1 Performance by Year 6 and Year 11 pupils in APV reading and writing tests

Task	Year	Performance	
		Year 6	Year 11
Reading	1979–83	Slight rise	Slight rise
	1983–88	Slight rise	No overall change
Writing	1979–83	Slight rise	No overall change
	1983–88	Slight fall	No overall change

Literacy at age 7/8

For pupils in Year 3, national data are available only for England. They are available only for reading, and only for the years 1987 and 1991. In 1987, the NFER standardised a new series of reading tests, one of which was intended for pupils in Year 3. In 1991, the standardisation exercise of this test was repeated. The main finding was that average reading scores of pupils in Year 3 fell by $2\frac{1}{2}$ standardised points between 1987 and 1991.[2] This result corroborated on a national scale more localised findings, which showed a fall in particular LEAs of about one standardised score point in the average reading attainment of 7 year olds (Year 2) between 1985 and 1988, and again between 1988 and 1990.

Literacy at ages 11 and 15

For 11 and 15 year olds, national data on *reading* performance are available from several surveys using standardised pre-APU tests between 1948 and 1979, mostly conducted by NFER. APU surveys of the *reading and writing* performance of 11 and 15 year olds were conducted annually from 1979 to 1983 and again in 1988.

There was an apparent abrupt decline in average reading scores in the 1970/71 surveys, following apparently steady rises since 1948. This caused great concern about 'illiteracy' among pupils. But the decline was perceived only by overlooking the fact that most of the differences between the mean scores reported were statistically non-significant. When normal statistical criteria are applied, the proper conclusion appears to be that the aspects of reading of pupils in Year 6 and Year 11 measured by the tests then in use rose slightly between 1948 and 1952, then remained essentially unchanged until 1979.

The APU tests from 1979 were repeated in 1983, as were tests from 1983 in 1988.[3] The findings are summarised in Table 40.1.

Some findings for spelling were obtained in 1991/92 from samples of APU writing tasks undertaken by Year 6 pupils in 1979 and 1988, and by Year 11 pupils in 1980 and 1983. For the tasks examined (not a comprehensive set) an improvement in the performance of Year 6 pupils occurred and the performance of those in Year 11 remained the same. For all aspects of literacy the absolute size of the changes was small: the size of the APU samples ensured that even fairly small changes were statistically significant.

In Scotland the AAP[4] has conducted three surveys in 1984, 1989 and 1992. The results for 1992 are not yet available, but there was no change in the reading scores of Year 4 and Year 7 pupils from 1984 to 1989 and a small rise for Year 9 pupils. The same pattern was obtained for writing scores.

Literacy of adults

There have been two national performance surveys of the literacy attainments of young adults in Britain, in 1972 and 1992. The results of the 1992 survey, organised by City University, London, on behalf of the Basic Skills Unit (ALBSU), were not yet published at the time of writing. Since the tests used on this occasion were different from those used in 1972, they will provide no basis for an estimate of change over the intervening 20 years.

The 1972 survey used a version of the Watts-Vernon reading test. It was carried out as part of the continuing National Survey of Health and Development, the 1946 British birth cohort study which covered England, Wales and Scotland: the people involved were thus aged 26 at the time of the 1972 survey. This cohort had also taken the same reading test in 1961 when they were aged 15. The results[5] showed a general increase in reading scores, and an illiteracy rate 'as low as one per cent'.

Illiteracy

The best available information from the APU surveys indicates that less than one per cent of those leaving school (excluding pupils from special schools) are unable to read in the sense of being unable to answer correctly simple comprehension questions about a passage. This accords well with the adult illiteracy rate just mentioned. The APU surveys also indicate that up to three per cent of school leavers would be unable or unwilling to communicate in writing in the sense of being unable to compose a short paragraph that is intelligible on first reading.

Given these figures, it may be wondered where media reports of large numbers, usually millions, of illiterate adults in the population come from. Most such estimates between the 1950s and 1980s were based on extrapolation from the number of 15 year olds found to have a reading level at or below that of the average 7 year old or 11 year old. More recently, estimates of adult illiteracy have been based on self-report data from young adults on problems with reading and writing since leaving school. Neither form of extrapolation estimates basic literacy in the sense given in the previous paragraph.

Basic literacy is not, however, adequate for responsible involvement in the social, economic and political life of the present day, nor to meet the specialised demands of many occupations. Research in the United States has consistently found that the relationship between 'job literacy' and school-based attainment is poor. There are two main reasons for this. The first is that people with literacy difficulties usually find methods of coping with their difficulties, with assistance. Secondly, specific jobs require job-specific literacy or numeracy skills, some of which can be developed on task. Teachers cannot be expected to prepare students for specialised literacy and numeracy requirements of particular occupations. However, there is a need for literacy teaching in schools to include a higher proportion of non-literary texts, for example those addressing science topics and social studies issues.

5 TRENDS IN NUMERACY

'Numeracy' is the term invented to parallel 'literacy' and, like it, has been interpreted in various ways. One narrow way is to assume that it relates only to the ability to perform basic arithmetical operations. Here we shall take the broader approach, meaning not only an 'at homeness' with numbers, but also the ability to make use of mathematical skills which enable individuals to cope with the practical demands of everyday life. These skills must include some knowledge of spatial representation and data handling, as well as computational ability. In school, such skills may be used to a greater or lesser extent in a number of subjects in the curriculum. Given this broad definition of numeracy it is reasonable to consider the evidence on standards in Britain from APU national surveys of mathematics, supported by data from international studies.

National surveys of mathematics

APU surveys of the mathematics performance of 11 and 15 year olds took place annually from 1978 to 1982, and again in 1987. Between 1978 and 1982, performance on items common to the two occasions resulted in a small overall increase of 1.5 percentage points at both age levels. In the interval between the surveys of 1982 and 1987 there was a very general pattern of performance changes at both 11 and 15 years, with improvements in the APU categories of geometry, probability and statistics, and measures, and a decline in number and in algebra (there were some variations in the detail of this general pattern).[6] These changes were thought to have been influenced by changes in curriculum emphases since the publication of the Cockcroft Report[7] on mathematics education in 1982. Cockcroft, however, did not sanction a decline in number skills, but placed more emphasis on mental computation, estimation, and appropriate use of different methods of calculation than had been apparent in the curriculum.

In Scotland the AAP conducted surveys of the mathematics performance of years 4, 7 and 9 (secondary 2) in 1983, 1988 and 1991. There was a significant decline in all three year groups between 1983 and 1988,[4] but it differed in extent and in different areas of mathematics between age groups. There was no further change in 1991.

International surveys of mathematics

The International Association for the Evaluation of Educational Achievement (IEA) undertook surveys of 13 and 18 year olds in 1964 and 1981. Another organisation, the International Assessment of Educational Progress, carried out two later studies in 1988 and 1991 (IAEP 1 and IAEP 2). England (or England and Wales) has participated in all four of these international surveys. Scotland has usually been represented as a separate system, but was part of the 'UK' sample in IAEP 1.

The results have demonstrated two main features of England's (or England and Wales's) comparative performance (Scotland's pattern of performance is fairly similar to England's):

- A profile of performance across topics among 13 year olds which shows England to be below average in number and above average in geometry and statistics. This profile is consistent with the changes found by APU for 11 and 15 year olds during the 1980s.
- Our top-ability students at 17+ are among the highest scorers in mathematics, while our below-average younger students do less well than those in many other developed countries.

The results for 13 year olds are discussed first, since this age group is regarded as the basic one in international studies and so has been most frequently surveyed.

Mathematics at age 13

In the two IEA-surveys, separated by an interval of 17 years, over 30 questions were common to both occasions in the tests for this age group. Comparison of the results reveals a general decline among the 10 educational systems participating on both occasions in all but one of the categories tested: number, measurement, geometry, statistics and algebra. The exception was algebra, in which all countries except England and Wales improved their success rates. The relative position of England and Wales slipped in all categories between 1964 and 1981.[8]

Many changes occurred between 1964 and 1981 in the organisation of education in Britain and in the content and breadth of the curriculum, which could account for a general decline in respect of the questions common to the two occasions. Nevertheless, few of these seemed inappropriate for pupils in the later study.

In the international studies carried out since 1981, the same or similar cross-topic mathematics profile has been evident. For example, comparing the surveys carried out in 1981 and 1991 (IAEP 2)[9] England's position relative to the five other countries participating in both years remains the same: first in statistics/data handling and sixth in arithmetic/number and operations. Apart from the data handling area, Hungary and France were the highest scoring countries of the six in both years.

Mathematics at age 9

The 1991 IAEP 2 survey included 9 year olds – the first international study of that age group – and the results indicate that the same cross-topic profile is evident at this age as at 13 years. The participation rate of schools was low in IAEP 2, indicating the possibility of some bias in the results. If they are valid, we should question when the lower emphasis on number begins, especially as the survey teachers' perceptions of their emphasis on calculation conflicted with the results obtained.

Mathematics at age 17+

One of the older populations surveyed in the two IEA studies consisted of students in the Upper Sixth who were studying mathematics as a substantial part of their academic programme. Our students (who were about to take A levels) came third or fourth out of 15 countries in 1981, in each of the three topics in the test. Japan and Hong Kong were the leading nations. Eight countries participated at this level in both 1964 and 1981, and the rank of England and Wales was just slightly worse in 1981 than in 1964.

Innumeracy

Culturally it has always been more acceptable to be innumerate than illiterate. There are no definitions of 'innumeracy' as such, but APU and other mathematics surveys have shown that there is a very wide range of performance by age 11, and that the bottom 20 per cent of 15 year olds still have a very limited grasp of even the most basic mathematical ideas. Mathematics in some form has been reaching more areas of daily life and more individuals at home and at work in recent decades and is now regarded as a subject for all to learn in school, although what aspects and in what depth remain matters for argument.

6 HOW CAN FUTURE CHANGES BE MONITORED EFFECTIVELY?

There are two main reasons why there has been so much controversy recently about whether or not standards are changing: irregular monitoring and the use of unsuitable monitoring instruments. At present, no effective monitoring of educational standards is occurring in England, Wales and Northern Ireland.

To be effective, monitoring needs to:

- provide an accurate picture of performance;
- give early notice of rises or falls in curriculum areas;
- detect whether changes are 'blips' or becoming trends;
- be sufficiently wide-ranging in each curriculum area to detect whether performance in different aspects of a subject is changing in different directions, at different rates;
- be able to detect, for each age group monitored, whether changes are taking place in a particular attainment band, or operating throughout the range of attainment.

In order to achieve these aims, monitoring must be reliable, and should include nationally representative samples of pupils, tackling appropriate tasks repeated at regular intervals. Unlike national curriculum assessment, monitoring does not require data from every child in the age groups concerned, only from a small sample, and each pupil involved would take only a fraction of the total assessments in a survey. The total picture would be obtained by aggregating across the sample. For this purpose, it is essential that externally set tests and not teacher assessments be used, since standardisation of conditions for all pupils taking the tests is a basic requirement for the reliability of the results. In this fashion, monitoring surveys on the one hand, and national curriculum assessment on the other, could complement each other: the latter by providing detailed information on individual pupils, and the former an in-depth picture of the knowledge and skills of the nation's children. A future effective monitoring system could be designed not only to detect trends over time in overall attainment in various curriculum areas, but also to help check that the levels of national curriculum assessment (including the new-style GCSE) are being held consistent across years – this could be done by targeting some monitoring tests at particular parts of the national curriculum.

There needs to be a continuing debate on the standards of attainment we should aim for as we move towards the 21st century. Some countries are setting ambitious targets. For instance, in the USA the National Governors' Association has adopted the following goal: 'By the year 2000, every adult American will be literate and will possess the skills necessary to compete in a global economy and exercise the rights and responsibilities of citizenship.'

In these circumstances it may not be sufficient to say that standards are not falling, or are rising slowly; it may be necessary in certain areas to progress more quickly as requirements become clearer. However, this debate must take place against a background of assured knowledge not only about how our competitors are developing their pupils' educational achievements, but also, and more importantly, about how our school pupils are performing nationally. Such knowledge can only come from a system of regular and effective monitoring.

NOTES

1 Foxman, D., Hutchison, D. and Bloomfield, B. (1990). *The APU Experience*. SEAC. (Lists all works published under the aegis of APU.)
2 Gorman, T.P. and Fernandes, C. (1992). *Reading in Recession*. NFER.
3 Gorman, T.P., White, J., Brooks, G. and English, F. (1991). *Language for Learning: a summary report on the 1988 APU surveys of language performance*. SEAC.
4 Scottish Education Department. *Assessment of Achievement Programme. Reports on Mathematics* (1989) *and English Language* (1990). HMSO.
5 Rodgers, B. (1986) Change in the reading attainment of adults: a longitudinal study. *British Journal of Developmental Psychology*, 4, 1–17.
6 Foxman, D., Ruddock, G. and McCallum, I. (1990). *APU Mathematics Monitoring 1984/88 (Phase 2)*. SEAC (see pages 6 and 7).
7 Department of Education and Science (1982). *Mathematics Counts (Cockcroft Report)*. HMSO.
8 Robitaille, D.F. and Garden, R.A. (1989). *The IEA Study of Mathematics II: contexts and outcomes of school mathematics*. Pergamon.
9 Foxman, D. (1992). *Learning Mathematics and Science: The Second International Assessment of Educational Progress in England*. NFER.

Chapter 41

Black children's experience of the education system

Cecile Wright

Introduction

A readily discernible theme recurring through the increasing literature on black children's experience of schooling relates to their educational attainment. The past couple of decades have witnessed continuing unease at the scholastic performance particularly of Afro-Caribbean children. Numerous studies since the 1960s have suggested that they tend to achieve less well than children from other ethnic groups at both primary and secondary level. Various documented evidence (which includes the Rampton and Swann Reports), and the views of both black parents and their children strongly suggest that effective learning/schooling is not happening for most black children under the current education system. Rather black children's experience of the current education system is one of mis-education or ineffective schooling.

This chapter considers evidence from my research study[1] which highlights how school practices, procedures and organisation can act as restraints upon the attainment of black children, particularly of Afro-Caribbean background. The evidence is taken from an intensive ethnographic and statistical survey of two multiracial comprehensive schools over a two year period. A cohort of Afro-Caribbean girls and boys from both schools were studied in their fourth and fifth years at school. In addition to extensive classroom observations, assessment data accumulated on each pupil were analysed, along with an examination of the schools' allocation procedures. The observed classroom relationships between the white teachers and the Afro-Caribbean pupils are described below. The pupils' views on their schooling are also documented. Finally the pupils' experience of the school's practices and procedures is examined.

> TEACHER: Whenever I look up you're always talking.
> BARBARA: That's 'cause you only see us, everybody else is talking. Look at them [pointing to the boys playing with the computer game] they're

not even working. [Turning to the other Afro-Caribbean girls and talking in a loud whisper] Damn facety.

The Afro-Caribbeans burst into laughter at Barbara's comment to them.

TEACHER [shrilled]: Barbara and Jean will you leave the room.

The girls leave the room, closing the door loudly behind them.

TEACHER [to the class]: Will the rest of you settle down now, and get on with your work. I'll be gone for just a few minutes. [Leaves the room]

In an interview with the teacher after the lesson, she had this to say about the two Afro-Caribbean girls and the incident which had led her to send them out of the lesson:

TEACHER: Well I'd say perhaps I have more problems with them than most in the class, perhaps they are the ones whom I'm usually driven to send to Mrs Crane [deputy headteacher] for discipline. I'll put up with so much but they're inclined to become very rude sometimes, which others wouldn't do. They know their limits but those two frequently go over them. It's difficult because I've tried having them sitting separately which doesn't seem to improve things because then they just become very resentful and will try then to kind of communicate across the room, which is almost worse than this business here. As I've said before, they're quite good workers, when they get down to it they enjoy the actual work and they usually get good marks. Their work is generally handed in on time and nicely presented. As I've said, I've sent them out quite frequently and I know lots of other teachers have the same problems. I'm not sure what the solution is. I believe things are being done with them.

RESEARCHER: What happened when you sent Barbara and Jean out of the lesson and you followed them out?

TEACHER: I sent them down to Mrs Crane. I told them to take a note and just wait outside her room. They got into so much trouble last term, she [the deputy headteacher] threatened to bring their parents up. I don't know if it actually got to that. I never know quite what to expect, what sort of mood they will be in, they are either in a bad mood or a good mood. Yet I can't tell really, and I find it difficult because I resent having to jolly them along which I do slightly. Because if I just home in on them straight away at the beginning of the lesson and normally they do start their chattering and things right away. Well I try to put up with so much. They react, they just resent it, if I do tell them off. But then I mean they do accept it. In the past when I've sent them off to Mrs Crane, and after perhaps a blazing row, or having brought her up here [to the classroom], and we have had a big confrontation and I expect them to be quite cool for weeks afterwards, or really rude. And they haven't been at all. Really I have no reason to believe that they would not come in as charming as anything next lesson, or they'll be troublesome, it just depends on them more than me.

The teacher's conversation, when analysed, provides insight not only into possible factors underlying the incident between her and the Afro-Caribbean girls, but also indicates the criteria used for judging the girls as 'unteachable'.

First, the teacher considers the Afro-Caribbean girls' behaviour in class to be generally unpredictable, as her own comments suggest. She therefore invariably *expected* the girls to be 'troublesome' in class, and as a consequence, also expected to be engaged in frequent confrontation with them. Furthermore, this teacher appeared to use the experiences of other teachers with the girls, both to support and explain her expectations and judgement of them. As a result of her expectations, she was inclined to treat with a degree of suspicion any conciliatory act on the part of the girls towards her following a confrontation as being out of character, and subsequently dismissed.

Second, the teacher considers the girls to be academically able and cooperative in their attitude to work, and this was borne out by observations. Yet from her behaviour towards the pupils it appeared that these features received only secondary consideration from the teacher, compared to the pupils' alleged 'troublesome' classroom behaviour.

AFRO-CARIBBEAN PUPILS' VIEWS ON SCHOOL AND CLASSROOM LIFE

Conversations with the Afro-Caribbean girls and boys in both schools, in an attempt to ascertain their perspectives on school and classroom life and their adaptation to their perceived experiences, suggest that these pupils often wonder whether there is anything more to classroom activity for them than insults, criticisms, and directives.

A discussion with a group of Afro-Caribbean girls in which they talked vividly of their experience of some teachers supports this claim:

BARBARA: The teachers here, them annoy you, too much.
RESEARCHER: In what ways do they annoy you?
BARBARA: They irate you in the lesson, so you can't get to work.
GROUP: Yeah.
BARBARA: One day Mr Beresford gave the class a piece of work to do, I type fairly fast and so I finished first. I took the piece of work to Mr Beresford and told him I'd finished the work, he said that I wasn't the only person in the class and he had to see other children before me. I asked a question on the work and he gave me a funny answer saying 'I should know by using a typist's intuition'. I told him I wouldn't be able to know, if we were told to do straightforward copying, with that he threw the piece of paper at me. I was angry, so I threw it back at him. . . .
In the third year, I did sewing with Mrs Lewis, we got on well until one

day, she kept telling me off for talking loud, then she accused me of saying 'How now brown cow' and sent me down to Mrs Crane [deputy headteacher] for discipline. She insisted that I did call it Mrs Lewis, even though I kept telling her I didn't know what it meant and that I didn't even know a verse like that existed. I got sent out of the lesson for the rest of that year, which was about four or five months. . . . I was thrown out of sewing by Mrs Lewis, out of French for some reason I can't remember why, out of art, for a misunderstanding with the teacher about wiping glue off some scissors, out of office practice about three times for about a period of two to three weeks each time. . . . I've been in trouble all my school life, I think the girl who I used to hang around with gave the teachers the impression I wasn't worth the bother. I feel some teachers are prejudiced.

VERA: Yeah, I agree with her, take the cookery teacher.

SUSAN: For example in cookery, there were some knives and forks gone missing, right, and Mrs Bryan goes 'Where's the knives and forks?' looking at us lot [the Afro-Caribbean pupils in the class].

VERA: Yeah, all the blacks.

SONIA: Seriously right, in the past most coloured children that had left school they've all said she's prejudiced.

JEAN: She's told some kids to go back to their own country.

SONIA: Seriously right, if you go to another white teacher or somebody, an' tell them that they're being prejudiced against you, they make out it's not, that it's another reason.

JEAN: When Mrs Bryan told Julie to go back to her own country, she went and told Mrs Crane. Mrs Crane said that Mrs Bryan was depressed because her husband was dying.

SONIA: So why take it out on the black people. Then she's told black people to do many things, she even called them monkey.

RESEARCHER: Would you say that the Afro-Caribbean boys have the same experience with the teachers as yourselves?

VERA: The boys I know don't get the same treatment because most of the lads are quicker to box the teachers – than the girls, you see.

GROUP: Yeah.

Similarly a group of eight Afro-Caribbean boys were asked about their school and classroom experience. They responded as follows:

MULLINGS: The teachers here are too facety, they don't give you a chance.

MICHAEL: For example Hill [Afro-Caribbean boy] who was expelled.

PAUL: That just prejudice, he never did nothing wrong.

MICHAEL: He never done nothin' much you know. He's half-caste, but he was more to the coloured people dem.

RESEARCHER: Why was he expelled?

MICHAEL: What it is I think he got suspended three times and he was on report, kept getting bad grades, they just out him in front of the governors. Yet a big skinhead [white boy] right, he go in front of the governors three times already, right, they expelled him. He came back, and dem let him back in a de school yesterday.

PAUL: Teachers look down on you, Mr Parks, Mr Gordon, Mr Henry, Mr Gray, and some others. I can remember the time I was in metalwork, Mr Gray keep saying to me why you've a tan? Why have you got a tan? I say well I've been like this all me life. He say, well you should go back to the chocolate factory, and be remade or something like that [with anger] that's not nice at all.

MICHAEL: One day I was in there [in the classroom] so I don't know what happened between him and Errol, he came up to me and say, 'Why Paul, Errol, and Delroy is always giving us hassle' and all that. So I said, 'Oh well, you know how Paul and Delroy are, they won't take anything off you lot in'it. If anything, them like to stick up for them rights.' So he said to me, 'You know I like running a joke, Michael.'

KEITH: Mr Gray, right, he says it's a complete joke what he says to black kids, he said one day he was at lower school and he came in [the classroom] and said to this girl, this coloured girl was a bit upset, so he said to her 'What's wrong with you?' and he said, 'I'll have to send you back to Cadbury's to let them wipe the smile off your face' and the girl went home and told her father. And her father took her to the Race Relations Board, and he [Mr Gray] says he's to go to court.

KEITH: They don't give the half-caste kids no hassle, no hassle whatsoever. However, if the half-caste kids act black, they pick on them, hassle man.

ERROL: And the Asians.

GROUP: Yeah.

RESEARCHER: Are you all also saying that the Asian students are not treated in the same way by some teachers, as you suggest, the Afro-Caribbean pupils are treated?

KEITH: Because with the Asians, right, Asians just keep themselves to themselves like we now, we just want equality with the white people. Asians don't speak their minds, they keep it all in because they are afraid.

MICHAEL: They get fling around, they won't say nothing about it.

KEITH: Because of that Asians are better off than black pupils that's all I can say.

PAUL: Yeah, Asians aren't the ones what go around causing trouble with the teachers.

RESEARCHER: Are you all saying then, that the Afro-Caribbean or black children, as you put it, go around causing trouble?

GROUP: [defensively]: No, No.

KEITH: No, the thing that we want right, we want equality just like the white people, we want equal rights.

PAUL: I'm not saying that we cause trouble, but I'm just saying the teachers think black boys are always going around causing trouble. That's what they think.

KEITH: Teachers look down on you.

The Afro-Caribbean boys were asked to explain further how the nature of the relationship which they considered existed between some teachers and themselves affected their behaviour towards these teachers. Using their analysis the pupils felt that they were forced into a stimulus–response situation; as the dialogues that follow demonstrate:

PAUL: The school don't respect black students. We are treated badly, we are forever hassled. I can remember the time I was in (subject), Mr X keep saying to me 'Why you've got a tan?' I say, 'Well I was born like this.' He say, 'Well you should go back to the chocolate factory and be remade,' or something like that. To me that wasn't a nice thing to say.

KEVIN: We are treated unfairly, because we are black. They look after their flesh not ours.

MICHAEL: They look after them white people-dem, you know what I mean, but we get dash at the back all the time.

RESEARCHER: You have all said that you feel that you are treated unfairly in the school. How do you feel this makes you behave?

DELROY: Bad.

RESEARCHER: When you say 'bad' what exactly do you mean by this?

PAUL: It means that we turn around and make trouble for them.

DELROY: Yeah, we try to get our own back on them. We behave ignorantly towards them, and when the teachers talk to us and tell us to do something we don't do it, because we just think about how they treated us.

PAUL: Like when you walk down the corridor, and a teacher stops you, you just ignore him. When they stop you for no reason you just irate.

RESEARCHER: How about you, Errol?

ERROL: I try to keep out of trouble the best I can. If they cause trouble with me I cause trouble with them it's as simple as that. If you are a troublemaker, right, and you're pretty intelligent, they still keep you down. Look what they've done to Delroy, he's pretty intelligent, yet they keep him down, no wonder he causes trouble. I want to get on so I try to keep out of trouble.'

The Afro-Caribbean girls and boys in their conversations seem to be expressing similar complaints and dissatisfaction regarding their teachers' attitudes and behaviour towards them. Certainly similarities were observed in the way in which they responded to their teachers' treatment of them. For instance, in the classroom they were both prepared to openly confront and challenge the teacher, using Jamaican patois in their exchanges with the teacher. In this situation some teachers felt quite threatened by the pupils' use of a dialect they could not understand. The teachers' anxiety served only to accentuate their negative attitudes and behaviour towards those pupils who used patois. For the Afro-Caribbean pupils the use of a mode of communication outside the cultural repertoire of the teacher is intended to undermine the teacher's authority. In many instances this strategy was observed to be quite effective.

Another way in which the Afro-Caribbean pupils, particularly the boys, responded to the poor relationship which existed between them and their teachers was to organise into a large all Afro-Caribbean group which moved around the school at break time baiting the teachers and subjecting them to a barrage of patois. In the words of one pupil the purpose of their behaviour was to 'get our own back for what they [teachers] do to us'. Moreover, in behaving in this way, these pupils also entered into a self-fulfilling prophecy, which further appeared to justify the teachers' expectations of them.

THE OUTCOME OF THE AFRO-CARIBBEAN STUDENT–TEACHER RELATIONS

As argued so far the relationship between teachers and Afro-Caribbean pupils within both schools was often antagonistic. There is evidence to suggest that the quality of this pupil–teacher relationship may precipitate certain sanctions taken by the school against these pupils, the ultimate sanction being the removal of students from the school. Data examined on the suspension and expulsion for the year group studied for both schools reveal a higher proportion of suspension and expulsion amongst Afro-Caribbean pupils, even though they constituted the smallest ethnic group. In one school, for instance, over half the students from this year group suspended or expelled were Afro-Caribbean. In addition to this it was found that none of these pupils expelled from the school in the fourth year were offered alternative education provision, signifying that these pupils were thus entirely without formal education. Indeed, in the Afro-Caribbean students' conversations above, the issue of suspension and expulsion is emphatically discussed indicating how very real this issue is to their experience of schooling.

Another way in which the Afro-Caribbean students were also found to be denied educational opportunities as a consequence of the adverse relationship between them and their teachers, stemmed from what was found to be their teachers' faulty assessment of their abilities and achievements. Evidence suggests that in their assessment of the Afro-Caribbean pupils the teachers allowed themselves to be influenced more by behaviour criteria than cognitive ones. That is, the assessment given would be most likely to reflect the teachers' subjective involvement with the complex behavioural aspects of classroom relations. This in turn led to a situation where Afro-Caribbean students, more so than any other pupil groups, were likely to be placed in ability bands and examination sets well below their actual academic ability. This indicates that in their assessment of the Afro-Caribbean pupils' ability the teachers were less able to exercise professional judgement.

The apparent misplacement of the Afro-Caribbean pupils on the basis of their ability, would strongly suggest that within this school overt discriminatory practices were operating against the Afro-Caribbean students. This suggestion is supported by the view of one of the teachers, when attention was drawn to the placement of an Afro-Caribbean pupil in a CSE French examination set who otherwise, on the basis of her ability, should have been placed in an O-level set. 'This pupil has been on the fringe of trouble all year, her attitude to the teachers is not at all good, she can be a nuisance in class.'

It seems obvious from this teacher's statement that ability is a positive quality in some teacher's eyes, only if it is shown by a white, and possibly an Asian pupil.

Certainly, the Afro-Caribbean pupils in their conversations expressed anger that the teachers had low expectations of their abilities and in some cases prevented them entering for certain public examinations. However, they were optimistic that they would be able to undertake the courses at the college of further education, denied them by the school, as the following student's comment would appear to suggest:

I've been entered for all CSEs: typing, maths, English, social studies, and art. I haven't been entered for office practice and French. For office practice it was my teacher's decision. She said that I didn't have enough pieces of course work [project] to be recommended, even though a friend [white girl] of mine has less pieces of work and has been entered. I do feel a bit bitter about it but I've decided I will retake it when I go to college.

An analysis of the overall attainment in the public examinations (that is CSEs and O-levels) for all the pupils in the year group studied for both schools was undertaken. Figures show that the proportion of Afro-Caribbean pupils entered for, and thus gaining O-levels, was dramatically lower than for the Asian and white pupils. The educational attainment for the Afro-Caribbean pupils is particularly alarming when it is realised that in one of the schools the Afro-Caribbean pupils (for the year group studied) entered the school at eleven plus with an average reading age slightly above the whole intake for the year.

It is evident from the findings in this chapter that within the classroom, in allocation to sets, streams, or bands, and in examination entries, complex processes may be involved which serve to disadvantage black pupils, particularly those of Afro-Caribbean origins. Moreover, it is clear that assignment of pupils to groups undertaking a lower standard of work than they are capable of, and in turn entering them for lower level examinations or no examinations at all can affect the type of school-leaving qualifications attained.

The weight of evidence in this chapter highlights an experience of schooling which clearly places black children at a disadvantage in the education system. This situation is reflected in the minutiae of classroom interactions (particularly teacher–pupil interaction), the structures, policies and practices of the school. If black children are to benefit fully from the education system, therefore, it needs to be acknowledged that a reform of education, or alternatively a transformation of education is necessary. A transformation at the personnel and structural end is particularly desirable. This begs the question, whether the provision of the 1988 Education Act is the answer for the desired changes required to improve the educational opportunity of not only black children, but all children.

NOTE

1 This chapter is adapted from a report to the Department of Education and Science on 'The Educational and Vocational Experience of 15–18 Year Old Young People of Ethnic Minority Groups'.

REFERENCES

Wright, C. Y. (1985a) 'Learning environment or battleground?', in *Multicultural Teaching*, Trentham Books Ltd, Stoke on Trent.
Wright, C. Y. (1985b) 'Who succeeds at school – and who decides?', in *Multicultural Teaching*, Trentham Books Ltd, Stoke on Trent.
Wright, C. Y. (1987) 'Black students – white teacher', in *Racial Inequality in Education*, B. Troyna (ed.), Routledge & Kegan Paul, London.

Chapter 42

Primary–secondary transfer after the national curriculum

Brian Gorwood

At the time of transfer from primary to secondary schooling, many pupils experience difficulties because of extreme differences in curriculum between the two sectors. Theorists and HMI have been writing about this problem for many years; researchers have investigated it. Strategies for improving continuity have been suggested but the permissive nature of English education has resulted in piecemeal adoption. By its very nature, continuity demands that there should be general agreement to ensure that pupils move from one experience to another in a sequence of meaningful learning. General agreement about any aspect of education has always been difficult to attain, however, within a system so intent on affording freedom of choice to individual schools. With the advent of the national curriculum it was hoped that situation would change.

When the consultation document was published in 1987, the national curriculum was presented mainly in terms of raising standards but one of its objectives was concerned with continuity:

> A national curriculum will secure that the curriculum offered in all maintained schools has sufficient in common to enable children to move from one area of the country to another with minimum disruption to their education. It will also help children's progression within and between primary and secondary education and will help to secure the continuity and coherence which is too often lacking in what they are taught.
>
> (DES, 1987)

Such a positive statement, with the affirmative 'will', gave hope of a more effective approach to achieving continuity. But there have been many similar statements in the past and yet the problem remains.

REMAINING PROBLEM OF REPETITION

It is difficult to see how the requirements of the Education Reform Act can 'secure' continuity. As in former times, central government hopes to achieve continuity by guidance rather than by legislation. The assertive tone of that guidance is deceptive. 'Continuity is no longer an optional issue in planning the curriculum' declares the National Curriculum Council (1989). Yet associated schools continue to organise their curricula without reference to each other. The national curriculum has not been in place long enough for major research to have been undertaken but several studies by teachers in correspondence with the author suggest that it is likely to present a new variant of the 'stages' problem. In the late 1970s, I found pupils after transfer having to repeat SMP maths books they had already completed in the feeder school (1981). I now hear of secondary schools planning to start all pupils at national curriculum level three in mathematics. Their primary colleagues point out that some pupils may have reached level five, but secondary schools seem unable to adjust their teaching style to accommodate individualised approaches.

Provisions in national curriculum documents will do little to eradicate the major causes of discontinuity. There will still be unnecessary repetition and pupils will become bored; there will still be bewilderment from pupils who have missed out on previous essential learning; schools will still find it difficult to find a common starting point for pupils with different kinds of educational background. There is no legislation requiring schools to adopt particular kinds of curriculum organisation or teaching style. Yet it is these aspects of their education that cause pupils significant difficulties at the time of transition. Continuity is best achieved when receiving teachers take cognisance of what and how their pupils learned before coming to them. It is still very much an optional issue whether primary and secondary teachers communicate about the pupils in whom they have a common interest.

PLANNING BY SUBJECTS

Though the Education Reform Act may not 'secure' continuity, it will go some way to achieving it, particularly if schools move closer to each other in ethos. It is implicit in the national curriculum that subjects will form the starting point for curriculum planning (NCC, 1989). That has always been the dominant approach in the secondary school but not so in the primary sector. Certainly since the time of Plowden – and probably long before that – primary schools have centred the curriculum on the child and his or her needs. Schools Council projects for primary, middle and early secondary years rejected planning from subjects because there was too much to include if the curriculum was to be balanced. The emphasis was on skills, attitudes and values which would eventually feed into the subject-specific curriculum. If specialist subject teachers were to be too influential in planning curriculum for younger pupils, it was thought they would lean heavily on the learning of facts and skills to the neglect of the wider range of objectives that had been revealed by the curriculum development movement (Ross *et al.*,

1975). If we venture further back to the immediate post-war period, the Council for Curriculum Reform explored the relevance of subjects in the school curriculum and outlined problems of specialisation:

> Children must find the present time-table a very disjointed and piecemeal affair, mainly because of the traditional compartmentation of the subject matter. The means whereby this evil may be remedied demand careful research.
>
> (1945)

The notion of a subject, they concluded, was not a particularly helpful one. It was not until the learner moved into higher education that subjects as such started to have any real meaning. Out of such criticism there developed integrated approaches to curriculum, which seem now under threat.

There is, of course, little within the literature on the national curriculum to suggest that primary schools should modify practice. Indeed, the NCC assures, 'Planning under subject headings does not preclude flexibility of delivery across subject boundaries' (1989). It states, however, that subjects will form the starting point for curriculum *planning*. This is a significant change in method of planning for most primary schools which may, admittedly, approach mathematics and English as separate subjects, usually through the adoption of set schemes, but choose a topic method to treat other areas of the curriculum. It is difficult to see how national curriculum programmes of study in geography and history can be derived from topics such as 'toys', 'food' or 'ourselves' – themes tackled by the author's primary PGCE students during a recent teaching practice. There has been understandable criticism, particularly by HMI, of topic work which 'more often than not lacks continuity and progression, or any serious attempt to ensure that adequate time and attention are given to the elements said to comprise the topic' (1989). Even if topic methods survive, rigorous reappraisal of current forms of curriculum organisation will be needed. It is interesting to note that many of the local authority working parties set up to develop history and geography related in-service training are advocating either subject teaching or 'focused topic' approaches. Primary schools, therefore, are going to change and the change is likely to bring them closer to the subject-centred approach to curriculum characteristic of the secondary sector.

EFFECT ON MOTIVATION

Secondary schools are used to planning according to external criteria. The GCE and more recently GCSE have exercised a powerful influence on the curriculum not only of fifth forms but of young secondary pupils who are introduced to the techniques, if not the content, fundamental to passing external examinations. In the primary curriculum there has always been room to pick up some fortuitous happening. Children have been encouraged to talk about their interests, to bring artefacts into the classroom and to write about matters of pertinence to them. By so doing, teachers have succeeded in spurring pupils to maintain an interest in things educational; motivation has long been accepted as a powerful determinant of what happens in primary classrooms. The demise of the 11-plus released primary schools from external influences but with the advent of the national curriculum that is changing. Primary teachers and their pupils are being made aware that time is not always available to pursue particular interests; there is the national curriculum to be discharged. It will be some time before research can suggest the likely impact of recent curricular changes on primary pupil motivation. My informal discussions in primary schools, however, suggest that pupils welcome the more structured approach which is already taking effect. 'We do the same subjects now as they do in the secondary school', replied one proud pupil in answer to my queries about national curriculum changes. 'I like learning new things rather than doing topics', was one revealing comment. Pupils are aware that primary schools are being drawn closer to styles of working customary in the secondary sector and they seem contented with this situation.

TEACHER COMMUNICATION

Although the Education Reform Act heralded significant changes in schools, potentially more extreme in the primary than in the secondary sector, it could do little to influence what has been seen in all recent research as the main cause of lack of continuity: ineffective teacher communication. Teachers in associated schools seldom come into contact with relevant colleagues and there is mutual mistrust (Stillman and Maychell, 1984). There is an undoubted need for secondary teachers to have access to information concerning their pupils' achievements in the primary school but the transfer of records does not in itself ensure that such information reaches the appropriate staff or is used effectively. As Blyth points out, a teacher in a secondary school has many other things to do than to ponder over the records of new pupils (1990). Good continuity practice suggests, however, that schools which focus on transfer but fail to appreciate the need for wide discussion of curricular matters are least successful in satisfying the needs of transferred pupils. Rather than making continuity the concern of a Year 7 co-ordinator, secondary schools would do better, as the ILEA Secondary Transfer project recommended, to organise on a departmental basis (1988). A designated key-person within a secondary department would brief colleagues and keep them informed about developments and discussions between associated schools. Similarly, in the primary sector it should not always be the Year 6 teacher who takes part in continuity discussions, for curriculum continuity has to be considered within a school's total policy.

Some of the early extravagant claims for the national curriculum have been moderated in more recent statements. In 1987, it was projected that the national curriculum would 'secure' continuity. More realistically, it is now said to 'provide a framework for achieving continuity'. It is doubtful that significant improvements in continuity could ever have been achieved by a British form of national curriculum *per se*; by their very training, teachers in our schools have been encouraged to maintain fundamentally different philosophies of primary and secondary schooling.

REFERENCES

Blyth, A. (1990) *Making the Grade for Primary Humanities*, p. 145. Milton Keynes, Open University Press.

The Council for Curriculum Reform (1945) *The Content of Education*, p. 18. London, University of London Press.

Department of Education and Science (1987) *The National Curriculum 5–16*, a consultation document, London, p. 4.

Gorwood, B. (1981) Continuity – with particular reference to the effectivenes of middle school experience upon upper school achievement in Kingston upon Hull, unpublished Ph.D. thesis, University of Hull.

Her Majesty's Inspectorate (1989) *Annual Report of HM Senior Inspector of Schools for 1987/1988*. London, HMSO.

ILEA Research and Statistics Branch (1988) *Improving Secondary Transfer*, p. 26. London, ILEA.

National Curriculum Council (1989) *A Framework for the Primary Curriculum – Curriculum Guidance One*, York, p. 9.

Ross, A., Razell, A. & Badcock, E. (1975) *The Curriculum in the Middle Years* (Schools Council Working Paper 55). London, Evans/Methuen.

Stillman, A. B. & Maychell, K. (1984) *School to School: LEA and teacher involvement in educational continuity*. Windsor, NFER-Nelson.

Chapter 43

Involving parents

Alastair Macbeth

Parents are integral to schooling. Inevitably, by both example and instruction, usually for good but sometimes for ill, parents teach their children and through that teaching they influence the extent to which we, as teachers, can be effective. Further, parents, not teachers, are primarily responsible in law for the education of their individual child. They are therefore first-line clients of the school. They should not be lumped together with remoter interested parties, such as children's possible future employers or 'the community', which are largely outside the schooling process. The parental dimension of schooling is central to our professional performance as teachers. Yet it is often under-rated. In my view we neglect it at our peril, for our impact as teachers and our status as professionals may substantially depend upon the extent to which we take seriously the phrase 'partnership with parents'.

The Education Reform Act of 1988 for England and Wales[1] continued a trend to give more prominence in law to the roles of parents, a trend which had started with the 1980 and 1986 Acts. Yet much of this legislative action concentrated upon parental representation on governing bodies and upon parental rights, such as to choice of school and to information. These, of course, are important but they are less concerned with partnership between teachers and parents and ways by which parents can be involved both formally and informally in the child's education.

One cannot approach the practice of home–school relations without assessing *why* there should be partnership between parents and teachers. In the past many teachers have pursued whole careers with only minimal contact with parents, and some even now continue to do so. Reasons must be compelling if practice, involving energy, time and resources, is to be worth changing.

THE PARENTAL DIMENSION OF SCHOOLING

Parents are relevant to what happens *inside* school for five quite distinct reasons.

1   Parents are responsible in law for their child's education, and in that sense they may be regarded as the school's legal clients.
2   If most of a child's education happens outside school, especially in the home, and if parents are co-educators of the child with teachers, then it seems logical to make the two elements of school-learning and home-learning compatible, and for teachers to use that home-learning as a resource.
3   Research indicates that family-based learning influences the effectiveness of school on a child. It may be a significant factor among the complexity of forces associated with inequality of educational opportunity.
4   Besides providing a professional service for parents, the teacher is also an agent of the education authority and the state to some degree. There are implied functions of checking upon parents' fulfilment of duties (e.g. with regard to school attendance) and, arguably, of being an educational safety-net for pupils with incompetent or uncaring parents.
5   It seems democratically reasonable, in a decentralised system in which important decisions are made at school and class levels, that those with a stake in a school should influence (though not necessarily determine) the nature of those decisions. Parents are stakeholders on behalf of their child and should be able to influence school policy through representatives.

Each of these issues warrants separate actions. For instance, to have parents on a governing body may go some way to meeting the fifth point but is largely irrelevant to the other four; or to treat parents as clients may not necessarily do anything to make home-learning supportive of school objectives. Different reasons for partnership with parents require different sorts of responses at different levels of the system.

1. Parents' legal responsibility for their child's education

Freeman (1983, p. 4), discussing the rights of children, expresses the generally-accepted principle that 'interference with a child's liberty is an inescapable consequence of the biological and physiological dependence of children'. Given that children are necessarily dependent on adults, the question becomes one of who should have responsibility for their upbringing, including education. Of course traditionally (most would say naturally) that is the family, especially parents. Yet in theory the state could take over these functions. National and international pronouncements have resisted such a radical shift. The United Nations Declaration of the Rights of the Child (1959) states:

> The best interests of the child shall be the guiding principle of those responsible for his education and guidance. That responsibility lies in the first place with his parents.

Churches tend to enunciate the same view. For instance, the Second Vatican Council in its Declaration of Christian Education asserted:

> Since it is the parents who have given life to their children, it is they who have the serious obligation of educating their offspring. Hence parents must be recognised as the first and foremost educators of their children.

Most national laws similarly place responsibility for the child's education upon his/her parents, granting rights commensurate with the duty. For example, the Basic Law of the Federal Republic of West Germany (1949, Article 6.2) states:

> The care and education of children are the natural right of parents and the duty is primarily theirs. The national community shall check upon their endeavours in this respect.

In Britain we do not have such a Basic Law or a Bill of Rights to enunciate fundamental principles. Our laws tend to be administrative rather than philosophical, but the same concept is clearly there. Section 36 of the 1944 Act answers the question: who, in law, is responsible for the education of the individual child?

> It shall be the duty of the parent of every child of compulsory school age to cause him to receive full-time education suitable to his age, ability, and aptitude, either by regular attendance at school or otherwise.[2]

It should be noted that this applies to the *individual* child, not to children in general or to the provision of facilities in general, which are central government and education authority responsibilities. That is an important distinction. It may also be noted that although education is compulsory, schooling is not. Schooling may be (and normally is) used by parents to fulfil their legal duty minimally. That does not mean that schooling is the same thing as education, nor does it mean that schooling is obligatory.

Education authorities are required by Section 7 of the 1944 Act[3] to make educational facilities available. We may pose the question: for what purpose? If parents are responsible for their child's education, then the facilities must exist to assist parents in carrying out their legal duty. *In brief, parents may be seen as the school's prime legal clients, until the child is 16 years of age.*

That position is given emphasis by a section of the Act which is often quoted by parents, but which, in my view, is conceptually less important than the one which lays down their duty. This is Section 76[4] which requires (with qualifications about efficient instruction and the avoidance of unreasonable public expenditure) that education authorities (and therefore their school systems) are to 'have regard to the general principle that . . . pupils are to be educated in accordance with the wishes of their parents.' It is interesting that here, untypically, a general principle creeps into our law. It is not clear whether it is an inviolable and overarching principle or whether the words 'have regard to' mean, in effect, 'if it happens to be convenient', but what matters here is the relationship of parental wishes to parental duty. Educational provisions according to parental wishes is a logical consequence of the fact that parents bear prime responsibility for their child's education. It reinforces parents' client-status.

Laws are man-made and they can be changed. For instance, the state (through teachers as its agents) could be made responsible for the *schooling* of the individual child, leaving out-of-school education as the responsibility of the parents. Indeed many teachers behave as if that were the case now. But what would be the implications of such a change? I consider that they would be far-reaching, for they would set a precedent affecting not just parents' rights for the upbringing of their child, but would question current assumptions about the structure of our society and individual liberties within it. At present the family is regarded as the fundamental unit of our society. Parents, as the central figures in families, are given the prime right and duty to shelter, feed, clothe, educate and secure the health of their children. The state only intervenes and takes away that prime right in cases of negligence by parents. However, it provides *services* of housing, health, education and welfare which parents can use to carry out their duties. If those services were to be *imposed*, irrespective of whether there is negligence, that would seem to be a substantial incursion into both individual liberty and the concept of the family as the fundamental unit of society. I am not saying that such a change would necessarily be wrong. I am saying that it would be a major conceptual shift, not a minor adaptation.

Professionals, presumably, must operate within the law. I shall argue later that service to a client is one criterion of professionalism. If teachers are professionals, then they owe service to parents as clients (until the child is 16 years of age), and are required by law to have regard to their wishes.

2. Parents as co-educators of children in parallel with teachers

Besides being the legal clients of teachers, parents are the co-educators of children. As already mentioned, most education happens outside school. Much of it, especially in the early years, is experienced in the family, where emotional bonds make home-learning especially effective. Parents also influence the sort of community-learning which their child will acquire.

Since parents inescapably educate their children, surely a professional teacher cannot neglect the non-professional educators. Just as the dentist relies on parents to cooperate with regard to children's dental care, so must teachers seek to guide and to draw into partnership parents' impact on educational care. Parents are co-educators of children whether that suits our professional preferences or not.

3. The effect of home background on children's school attainment

Not only do parents largely create the nature of a child's out-of-school education, they also seem to influence (some would say determine) the extent to which their child benefits from *in*-school education. If teachers' effectiveness is linked to what families think, say and do, then an extra professional argument for collaboration with parents emerges. Unfortunately the evidence, substantial though it is, lacks the finality and precision which would enable us to define exactly which home-based initiatives would most heighten pupils' educational advance. It is therefore difficult to build closely-specified programmes of liaison based on it. Yet lack of fine detail need not deter us from action since much is already known.

Perhaps the strongest motivation for such action comes from the evidence that aspects of home background are the causes of unfulfilled potential and unequal chances in education. Equality of educational opportunity has been at the centre of educational thinking and planning for several decades, yet it has proved an elusive goal. It is difficult to define and even more difficult to attain. Despite the abolition of 11-plus selection, the creation of comprehensive schools, the increasing deferment of separating pupils with different abilities, and other structural initiatives, certain kinds of children continue to be more successful than others. Structural steps taken within the educational system have removed some *obstacles* to attainment, but they have not sufficiently stimulated the forces which *enhance* attainment.

What are these forces? What follows is necessarily an over-simplified sketch of complex environmental processes which are still not fully understood. It should not be misinterpreted as a statement that schools make no difference. Schools *do* make a difference. Studies such as those of Rutter *et al.* (1979) and Tizard *et al.* (1988) have shown that school performance can be more or less professional and that its effects on children's attainment can very accordingly. Although *Fifteen Thousand Hours* by Rutter *et al.* emphasised school influence, it did not deny the impact of home, indeed, having alluded to studies of home-related factors, it stated (p. 87), with tantalising brevity, 'We found the same.' It may be argued that *all* schools attain a basic level of beneficial influence and that what home learning is doing is affecting the *differences* of attainment between pupils. Yet, if equality of educational opportunity is the goal, then it is precisely those differences that matter whether they originate in homes or in schools.

The evidence of home influence on schooling began with studies which showed a general correlation between home background and in-school attainment. Home background differences often coincide with social class differences,[5] but researchers recognise that terms such as 'home background' and 'social class' are vague and difficult to measure. Further, there is some evidence that social class itself is not the causal factor (see Miller, 1971) and this is the foundation for optimism for it suggests that working-class children *can* do well, given the right circumstances. Questions then emerge about which elements of home background correlate with school success, whether they are causal and whether we can influence them.

What has emerged is a complex and by no means complete picture. Part of the difficulty stems from problems of measurement. Children cannot be manipulated experimentally like rats in a laboratory. Therefore controlling variables in a physical sense has to be replaced by statistical techniques to make allowances for the multiplicity of forces which might be causing an observed outcome. Even when a correlation exists between two phenomena that does not, in itself, tell us which is causing which, and indeed it does not necessarily mean that either causes the other, since a third factor may be causing both.

Further, some of the forces which researchers would like to measure are not susceptible to direct measurement and 'proxy measures' are used instead. For instance, the attitudes of parents have been advanced as a key element in pupil attainment, and it seems likely that they are; but can attitudes be measured? Since they are invisible, the best that we can do is to measure behaviour and to make assumptions about the attitudes which may trigger that behaviour. Alternatively, we can seek expressed opinions which may or may not reflect real attitudes, and these in turn have to be assessed in regard to the circumstances in which they were expressed, their strength and their persistence, all of them elusive elements. Next how do we assess educational attainment? Standardised test results and public examination grades are often used, but these tell us little about creativity, adaptability, determination and other facets of achievement. To take another example, father's occupation is often used as a measure of social class, whereas clearly it is not the same thing. Further, the involvement of researchers may itself affect the outcomes, while interpretation of results always involves value judgements.

The next problem is that the socio-psychological networks involved are intricate and variable, but as Osborne and Milbank (1987, p. 189) observe, enough is known to provide some guidance.

> It is important to recognise the interrelatedness of all these factors and the complex ways in which they can combine to either support or impede a child's educational progress. Each child is unique in the particular developmental path she follows yet some general principles can be discerned in the tangle of data which help to explain how some children succeed and others fail.

Thus, despite complexities, research is valuable. It provides essential indicators. Three rule-of-thumb tests may be applied which can help to decide how seriously to take a given set of findings:

1 Do several studies draw the same conclusions?
2 Is there a relative dearth of contrary evidence?

3 Do the findings accord with common sense and the experience of
  teachers?

The evidence that parents and family circumstances do influence children's
educational attainments appears to meet these tests.

Besides broad correlations between home background and in-school
attainment, research has suggested that particular features of background
could be especially important. Attitudes such as parental interest in children's education[6] and aspirations[7] have attracted special attention, while a
debate arose about the influence of language codes in coping with schooling.

One issue which has confused the picture has been the belief among some
teachers that because certain (often working-class) parents do not attend
school functions as avidly as do others, the former are 'apathetic'. As Mays
(1980) has pointed out, 'It is dangerously easy to use a phrase such as
"parental apathy" and leave it at that.' (p. 63). Rather, practical difficulties, deference to teachers, cynicism and a sense of alienation from the school
deter parents. Some studies (e.g. Cyster et al., 1979; Johnson and Ransom,
1983) show that some parents are hesitant and unsure of themselves when
confronted by the systems of schooling. But this does not necessarily mean
that they lack concern for their children's welfare and there is evidence of the
reverse (Lindsay, 1969). As Marland (1983, p. 4) has written '. . . not only
are the huge majority of parents *not* apathetic but very concerned, . . . the
nature of their concerns and the modes of their support have a great deal to
teach us teachers', a view more recently echoed by Tizard and Hughes
(1984) and Tizard et al. (1988). Yet Wolfendale (1983, p. 59) is surely to
some extent right when she asserts that 'between teachers' and parents'
expectations and presumptions lies unexplored territory'; for there is much
we still do not know about parental attitudes or actions in the home.

Several useful overviews of the evidence about the impact of homes on
schooling (Marjoribanks, 1979; Sharrock, 1970; Mortimore and Blackstone,
1982; Hewison, 1985) exist and it is not the purpose of the present book to
summarise the large and growing body of research into the impact of home-
learning on school-learning. However, a few generalisations do seem possible and these support (but do not determine) the practical actions discussed
in later chapters.

First, Marjoribanks (1979) drew attention to the great complexity of the
'network of interrelated family environment variables that are associated
with children's cognitive and affective outcomes.' However, having assessed
studies from three continents he concluded 'Environments for children's
learning will become more favourable when parents and teachers act as
partners in the learning process.' A model which might be sustained on the
basis of existing evidence could resemble that shown in Figure 43.1.

Secondly, there are signs from several studies[8] that the early years of
home-learning are especially important for subsequent attainment and

INFLUENCES ON CHILD   MEDIATING ELEMENTS

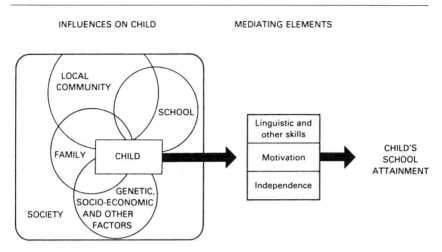

Figure 43.1

Tizard and Hughes concluded, 'Indeed, in our opinion, it is time to shift the emphasis away from what parents should learn from professionals, and towards what professionals can learn from studying parents and children at home.' (p. 267)

The third reasonable generalisation is that, if what happens in the home does have impact on overall educational attainment, and if average differences of attainment between children from different social class groups are linked to those home experiences, then presumably the goal of equality of educational opportunity cannot be approached merely by making changes within the system of institutional education which, as we have seen, represents only about 15 per cent of a child's waking and therefore learning life to age 16. The debate will doubtless continue whether it is material circumstances or learning circumstances which have *most* effect on that inequality; but irrespective of which is predominant, there can be no equality of educational opportunity without equality of parental input as one of the factors.

Finally, I would suggest that none of the practical steps considered in this book depends solely upon conclusions of research. Undoubtedly the studies to which I have referred have heightened educational interest in parents and have given new impetus to the quest for mechanisms of parent–teacher partnership, but parent–teacher partnership can be justified on other grounds also, irrespective of these socio-psychological findings.

4. Teachers as agents of the education authority

I have argued that much of a child's education is provided in or influenced by the family, and I have outlined the ways by which legal systems consistently make parents responsible for their child's education. However, parents vary in the conscientiousness and the effectiveness with which they meet their obligations, and a small minority of parents might be described as incompetent or uncaring. The state, having delegated responsibility to parents, must still monitor parents' performance: in the words of the German Basic Law quoted earlier, 'The national community shall check upon their endeavours in this respect.' The most obvious way that teachers do this on behalf of the state is by reporting instances of truancy; for parents, if they opt to use schools to fulfil their legal duty of educating their child, must ensure regular attendance. Further, persistent misbehaviour of a child will be reported back to parents on the grounds that they are responsible for their child's education; again it is teachers who act as agents of the education authority in reporting it.

In two other important ways teachers may represent the education authority (or the state). One is by providing educational expertise (knowledge, skills, understanding) which most parents will not have. Usually this will be with relation to the formal curricula. But the second is a pastoral care function in providing an adult alternative to the parent to whom the child can turn in times of need. Marland (1980, p. 157 and 1985 p. 82) has drawn attention to a combination of these two in what he calls the pastoral curriculum defined as 'the school curriculum looked at for the moment solely from the point of view of the personal needs of the pupil resolving his individual problems, making informed decisions, and taking his place in his personal world.' With regard to young people over the age of 16, and therefore responsible in law for their own education, there would be less or no need for teachers to involve parents in dealing with such issues. However, parents are responsible for the education (including schooling) of under-16 children and therefore whenever teachers are, as it were, filling the gaps left by parents they presumably have an obligation to contact parents on precisely those issues.

It is possible, however, to advance a quite contrary argument, namely that the school exists, in part, to *separate* the child from the family and to provide an induction to society. Taylor (1980, p. 12) has written:

> The primary school class emancipates the child from the basic emotional ties with his own family, encourages the internalization of social values and norms other than those current in the family home, and begins the process of selection and allocation relative to the adult role-system that will be continued and given great emphasis in the later stages of schooling.

This may be valid to some degree as a description of some current practice, but if rejection of family were to be an aim of the school, not only would it seem to be contrary to the spirit of current law, but it could well damage children's education. It is a major misconception, in my opinion, but a common one, to assume that being an agent of the education authority or state confers autonomy of action on the teacher. On the contrary, it implies an increased obligation to collaborate with parents.

5. Parents as stakeholders in their child's school

The fifth and final main reason why parents matter to schools is of an entirely different nature to the first four. It is democratic rather than educational. The principle is generally accepted in western democracies that those with a stake in an enterprise should have the opportunity to influence (though not necessarily to determine) decisions affecting that enterprise in proportion to their stake in it. We have a highly decentralised school system, and important decisions are taken at school, department and class levels. Politicians have a stake in the school as elected representatives of the community. Teachers have a stake in the school as employees, as co-educators and as taxpayers, among other criteria. Parents might claim to have a stake as clients, as co-educators and as tax-payers. The governing body is the main mechanism to enable those with a stake in a school to influence decisions about the school. However, it is worth noting that the families which jointly have children in one class might also have a similar stake in that class (or group) and the decisions made for it.

In one sense a school system is like an airline: it likes to create an image of individual service in what is, essentially, a group process. Perhaps parents should have more right to discuss and influence internal school processes than has hitherto been accorded to them for, whereas in an airline the passengers choose where to go and when, in a school parents have little choice.

LEVELS OF PARENT–TEACHER LIAISON

In the last section there was a conceptual leap from consideration of the individual child to consideration of school policy. I could have gone further to discuss parental influence on the education authority and in national and international policy-making. At this point different levels of liaison *within* a school will be considered.

There is a tendency to visualise parent–teacher liaison as a single entity, as one particular kind of activity. When a headteacher states 'We have excellent relations with parents here because we have a flourishing PTA', he may be exhibiting such one-track thinking. Alternatively, to someone else the term 'parent–teacher liaison' may conjure up a picture of little Johnnie's parents talking to his teacher(s) about his progress. There are different *levels* of partnership between parents and teachers, and at any given level several *modes* of contact may be possible. In any school there are four main levels of partnership: the *individual, class, school* and *representative* levels. Above the school there are the various 'political' levels.

NOTES

1 Scottish and Northern Irish reforms have been developing rather differently and comparisons will be made at appropriate points in this book.
2 Counterpart clauses in Scotland and Northern Ireland are Section 30 of The Education (Scotland) Act, 1980, and Section 35 of The Education and Libraries (Northern Ireland) Order, 1972. Wording is not identical but is similar.
3 and section 1 of the Education (Scotland) Act, 1980.
4 and section 28 of the Education (Scotland) Act, 1980.
5 e.g. Floud *et al.*, 1957; Fraser, 1959; Mays, 1962; Douglas, 1964 and 1968; Miller, 1971; Davie *et al.*, 1972.
6 Fraser, 1959; Wiseman, 1964; Douglas, 1964; Miller, 1971; Osborne and Milbank, 1987.
7 Rosen, 1961; McClelland, 1961; Miller 1971.
8 Wiseman, 1964; Davie *et al.* 1972; Schweinhart and Weikart, 1980; 1984; Tizard and Hughes, 1984; Osborne and Milbank, 1987.

REFERENCES

Cyster, R., Clift, P. S. and Battle, S. (1979) *Parental Involvement in Primary Schools*. NFER.
Freeman, M. D. A. (1983) *The Rights and Wrongs of Children*. Pinter.
Hewison, J. (1985) 'The Evidence of Case Studies of Parents' Involvement in Schools'. Ch. 3 in Cullingford (ed.) *Parents, Teachers and Schools*, Royce.
Johnson, D. and Ransom, E. (1983) *Family and School*. Croom Helm.
Lindsay, C. (1969) *School and Community*. Pergamon.
Marjoribanks, K. (1979) *Families and their Learning Environments: An Empirical Analysis*. Routledge & Kegan Paul.
Marland, M. (ed.) (1980) *Education for the Inner City*. Heinemann.
Marland, M. (1983) Parenting, Schooling and Mutual Learning: a Teacher's Viewpoint, advance paper for the EEC School and Family Conference, Luxembourg, 1983. Also published in Bastiani, J. (ed.), (1988) *Parents and Teachers 2: From Policy to Practice*, pp. 232–42. NFER-Nelson.
Marland, M. (1985) 'Our Needs in Schools', pp. 67–91 in Lang, P. and Marland, M., *New Directions in Pastoral Care*. Blackwell.
Mays, J. B. (1980) 'The Impact of Neighbourhood Values', ch. 4 in Craft, M., Raynor, J. and Cohen, L. (eds) *Linking Home and School*. Harper & Row.
Miller, G. W. (1971) *Educational Opportunity and the Home*. Longman.
Mortimore, J. and Blackstone, T. (1982) *Disadvantage and Education*, DHSS/Heinemann.
Osborne, A. F. and Milbank, J. E. (1987) *The Effects of Early Education: A Report from the Child Health and Education Study*. Clarendon Press.
Rutter, M., Maughan, B., Mortimore, P. and Ouston, J. (1979) *Fifteen Thousand Hours. Secondary Schools and their Effects on Children*. Open Books.
Sharrock, A. (1970) *Home/School Relations*. Macmillan.
Taylor, W. (1980) 'Family, School and Society', Ch. 1 in Craft *et al.* (eds) *Linking Home and School*, Harper & Row.

Tizard, B. and Hughes, M. (1984) *Young Children Learning, Talking and Thinking at Home and at School*. Fontana.

Tizard, B., Mortimore, J. and Burchell, B. (1988) 'Involving Parents from Minority Groups', pp. 72–83 in Bastiani, J. (ed.) *Parents and Teachers 2: From Policy to Practice*. NFER–Nelson.

Wolfendale, S. (1983) *Parental Participation in Children's Development and Education*. Gordon & Breach.

Acknowledgements

Chapter 2 'Why no pedagogy in England?', by Brian Simon, from *Education in the Eighties* (1981), edited by B. Simon and W. Taylor, reproduced by permission of B.T. Batsford Ltd.

Chapter 4 'The theory of multiple intelligences', by Howard Gardner, from *Handbook of Educational Ideas and Practices* (1990), edited by Noel Entwhistle, reproduced by permission of Routledge.

Chapter 6 'How children learn . . . implications for practice', by Neville Bennett and Elizabeth Dunne, from *Managing Classroom Groups* (1992), reproduced by permission of Simon & Schuster Education, Hemel Hempstead, UK.

Chapter 7 'Current views of the adolescent process', by John C. Coleman, from *The School Years 2nd Edition* (1992), edited by John C. Coleman, reproduced by permission of Routledge.

Chapter 8 *Sex Roles and the School 2nd Edition* (1990) pp. 44–9, by Sara Delamont, reproduced by permission of Routledge.

Chapter 9 'Acknowledging disadvantages', by Alec Clegg, from *About Our Schools* (1980), reproduced by permission of Basil Blackwell Ltd.

Chapter 10 'Cultural factors in child-rearing and attitudes to education', by Tessa Blackstone and Jo Mortimore, from *Disadvantage in Education* (1982), reproduced by permission of the authors.

Chapter 11 'Special needs education: the next 25 years', by Klaus Wedell, originally published as a National Commission on Education Briefing (No. 14, 1993) and reproduced by permission of the National Commission on Education, whose report, *Learning to Succeed*, is published by Heinemann in 1993.

Chapter 12 *What do Students Think About School?* (1993) pp. 61–8, by W. Keys and C. Fernandes, reproduced by permisison of the National Foundation for Educational Research.

Chapter 13 'What makes a good teacher?', by Roger Smith, first published in *Child Education* (December 1988), and reproduced by permission of Scholastic Publications.

Chapter 14 Adaptation of 'Implications of studies of expertise in pedagogy for teacher education and evaluation', by David Berliner, © 1993 by Educational Testing Service. All rights reserved. Adapted and reproduced under licence.

Chapter 15 'Teachers' first encounters with their classes', by E.C. Wragg and E.K. Wood from *Classroom Teaching Skills* (1984), reproduced by permission of Routledge.

Chapter 16 'Those who understand: knowledge growth in teaching', by L.S. Shulman, first published in *Educational Researcher* (February 1986), reproduced by permission of the American Educational Research Association.

Chapter 17 Exploring Teachers' Thinking (1987), pp. 1–3, by James Calderhead, reproduced by permission of Cassell.

Chapter 18 'Teacher expectations', by Peter Mortimore, from *School Matters* (1989), reproduced by permission of Open Books.

Chapter 19 'Teachers and cross-cultural counselling', by Jon Nixon from *A Teachers' Guide to Multicultural Education* (1989), reproduced by permission of Basil Blackwell Ltd.

Chapter 21 'Classroom variables', by William Taylor, from *Better Schools* (1986), reproduced by permission of the Controller of Her Majesty's Stationery Office.

Chapter 22 Managing Classroom Groups (1992), pp. 1–7 and pp. 109–15, by N. Bennett and E. Dunne, reproduced by permission of Simon & Schuster Education, Hemel Hempstead, UK.

Chapter 24 'Sex stereotyping in the classroom', by Sara Delamont from *Sex Roles and the School 2nd Edition* (1990), reproduced by permission of Routledge.

Chapter 25 'Managing classes', by Mick McManus, from *Troublesome Behaviour in the Classroom* (1989), reproduced by permission of Routledge.

Chapter 26 'Computers, curriculum and the learning environment', by Noel Thompson, from *Computers and Education* 16 (1), pp. 1–5, reproduced by permission of Pergamon Press Ltd, Headington Hill Hall, Oxford OX3 0BW, UK.

Chapter 27 New Technology and its Impact on Classrooms, OECD 1992, reproduced by permission of OECD, Paris.

Chapter 28 Curriculum Reform: An Overview of Trends (1990), by Malcolm Skilbeck, pp. 45–8, reproduced by permission of OECD, Paris.

Chapter 29 'The entitlement curriculum', HMI, from *Curriculum 11–16, Towards a Statement of Entitlement*, pp. 25–37, by permission of the Controller of Her Majesty's Stationery Office and the Department for Education.

Chapter 30 'Grounding comes first', by Oliver Letwin, from *Policies for the Curriculum* (1989), edited by R. Moon, P. Murphy and J. Raynor, reproduced by permission of Hodder & Stoughton Ltd.

Chapter 31 'The National Curriculum: origins, context and implementation', by Bob Moon, from *Managing the National Curriculum: Some Critical Perspectives* (1990), edited by T. Brighouse and R. Moon, reproduced by permission of the Longman Group.

Chapter 32 'Academic drift – towards a new focus for the education system', by A.H. Halsey, N. Postlethwaite, S.J. Prais, A. Smithers and H. Steadman, from *Every Child in Britain* (1991), reproduced by permission of Channel Four Television.

Chapter 33 'Assessment: a changing practice', by Sally Brown, from *Assessment Debates* (1990), edited by T. Horton, reproduced by permission of Hodder & Stoughton Ltd.

Chapter 34 'Assessment and the improvement of education', by Wynne Harlen, Caroline Gipps, Patricia Broadfoot and Desmond Nuttall, from *The Curriculum Journal* (1989) 3 (3), reproduced by permission of Routledge.

Chapter 35 'Assessment and gender', by Patricia Murphy, from *The Cambridge Journal of Education* (1991) 21 (2), by permission of *The Cambridge Journal of Education* and the author.

Chapter 36 *Value for Money in Education 15*, by J. Marks, reproduced by permission of the Campaign for Real Education.

Chapter 37 'The organization of the secondary school', by Charles Handy and Robert Aitken, from *Understanding Schools as Organizations* (London, 1986), pp. 11–33, © Charles Handy and Robert Aitken, reproduced by permission of Penguin Books Ltd.

Chapter 38 'The quality of schooling: frameworks for judgement', by John Gray, from *British Journal of Educational Studies* (1990) XXXVIII (3), pp. 1–16, reproduced by permission of Basil Blackwell Ltd.

Chapter 39 'Measuring added value in schools', by Andrew McPherson, originally published as a National Commission on Education Briefing (No. 1, 1992) and reproduced by permission of the National Commission on Education, whose report, *Learning to Succeed*, is published by Heinemann in 1993.

Chapter 40 'Standards in literacy and numeracy', by Derek Foxman, Tom Gorman and Greg Brooks, originally published as a National Commission on Education Briefing (No. 10, 1992) and reproduced by permission of the National Commission on Education, whose report, *Learning to Succeed*, is published by Heinemann in 1993.

Chapter 41 'Black children's experience of the education system', by Cecile Wright, from *Effective Learning: Into a New Era* (1990), edited by T. Everton, P. Mayne and S. White, reproduced by permission of Jessica Kingsley.

Chapter 42 'Primary–secondary transfer after the National Curriculum', by Brian Gorwood, from *School Organisation* (1990) 11 (3), pp. 283–90, reproduced by permission of Carfax Publishing Company.

Chapter 43 *Involving Parents* (1989), pp. 1–13, by A. Macbeth, reproduced by permission of Heinemann Publishers Ltd.

Notes on sources

Chapter 1 Commissioned for this volume.
Chapter 2 Based on B. Simon (1981), pp. 124–45 in B. Simon and W. Taylor (eds) *Education in the Eighties*, London, Batsford.
Chapter 3 Commissioned for this volume.
Chapter 4 H. Gardner (1990) 'The theory of multiple intelligences', in N. Entwistle (ed.) *Handbook of Educational Ideas and Practices*, London, Routledge.
Chapter 5 Based on ILEA Committee on the Curriculum and Organisation of Secondary Schools (1984), pp. 2–3 in *Improving Secondary Schools*, London, ILEA.
Chapter 6 Based on N. Bennett and E. Dunne (1992) 'How children learn . . . implications for practice', pp. 1–7 in N. Bennett and E. Dunne (eds) *Managing Classroom Groups*, Hemel Hempstead, Simon and Schuster.
Chapter 7 Based on C. Coleman (1992) 'Current views of the adolescent process', chapter 1 in J. C. Coleman (ed.) *The School Years* (2nd ed), London, Routledge.
Chapter 8 Based on Delamont (1990) pp. 44–9 in S. Delmont *Sex Roles and the School*, (2nd edn), London, Routledge.
Chapter 9 Based on A. Clegg (1980), pp. 84–7 in *About our Schools*, Oxford, Blackwell.
Chapter 10 Based on J. Mortimore and T. Blackstone (1982), pp. 42–52 in J. Mortimore and T. Blackstone *Disadvantage in Education*, London, Heinemann.
Chapter 11 K. Wedell (1993) 'Special needs education: the next 25 years', *NCE Briefing No. 14*, London, NCE.
Chapter 12 Based on W. Keys and C. Fernandes (1993), pp. 61–8 in *What Do Students Think About School?* London, NFER.
Chapter 13 Based on R. Smith (1988), pp. 10–11 in *Child Education*, December.
Chapter 14 Based on D. Berliner 'Implications of studies of expertise in pedagogy for teacher education and evaluation', © 1993 by Educational Testing Service.
Chapter 15 Based on E. C. Wragg and E. K. Wood (1984), pp. 47–62 in E. C. Wragg and E. K. Wood (eds) *Classroom Teaching Skills*, London, Routledge.
Chapter 16 Based on L. S. Shulman (1986), pp. 4–14 in *Educational Researcher*, February.
Chapter 17 Based on J. Calderhead (1987) 'Introduction', pp. 1–3 in J. Calderhead *Exploring Teachers' Thinking*, London, Cassell.
Chapter 18 Based on P. Mortimore *et al.* (1989), pp. 163–74 in P. Mortimore *et al. School Matters*, Wells, Open Books.
Chapter 19 Based on I. Nixon (1985), pp. 61–74 in *A Teacher's Guide to Multicultural Education*, Oxford, Blackwell.
Chapter 20 Based on P. Jackson (1979), pp. 21–5 in N. Bennett and D. McNamara

(eds) *Focus on Teaching*, Harlow, Longmans.

Chapter 21   Based on W. Taylor (1986), pp. 19–24 in *Better Schools*, London, DES.

Chapter 22   Based on N. Bennett and E. Dunne (1992), pp. 109–15 in N. Bennett and E. Dunne (eds) *Managing Classroom Groups*, Hemel Hempstead, Simon and Schuster.

Chapter 23   Commissioned for this volume.

Chapter 24   Based on S. Delamont (1990), pp. 55–63 in S. Delamont *Sex Roles and the School* (2nd ed.), London, Routledge.

Chapter 25   Based on M. McManus (1989), pp. 47–61 in M. McManus *Troublesome Behaviour in the Classroom: A Teacher's Survival Guide*, London, Routledge.

Chapter 26   N. Thompson, pp. 1–5 in *Computers and Education* 16(1).

Chapter 27   Based on OECD (1987) 'Long-term perspectives', *Individual Learning 4*, Paris, OECD.

Chapter 28   Based on M. Skilbeck (1990), pp. 45–8 in *Curriculum Reform: An Overview of Trends*, Paris, OECD/CERI.

Chapter 29   Her Majesty's Inspectors (1983) 'Towards a statement of Curriculum', pp. 25–37 in *Curriculum 11–16: Towards a Statement of Entitlement*, London, HMSO.

Chapter 30   Based on O. Letwin (1989), pp. 70–3 in R. Moon, P. Murphy and J. Raynor (eds) *Policies for the Curriculum*, London, Hodder and Stoughton.

Chapter 31   Based on B. Moon (1990), pp. 11–24 in T. Brighouse and R. Moon (eds) *Managing the National Curriculum: Some Critical Perspectives*. Harlow, Longmans.

Chapter 32   Based on A.H. Halsey, N. Postlethwaite, S. J. Paris, A. Smithers and H. Steadman (1991), 'Academic drift', *Every Child in Britain*, Channel 4 Television.

Chapter 33   Based on S. Brown (1990), pp. 5–11 in T. Horton (ed.) *Assessment Debates*, Milton Keynes, The Open University Press.

Chapter 34   Based on W. Harlen, C. Gipps, P. Broadfoot and D. Nuttall *The Curriculum Journal* 3 (3): 215–30.

Chapter 35   Based on P. Murphy (1991), *Cambridge Journal of Education* 21 (2).

Chapter 36   Based on J. Marks (1992), *Value for Money in Education* 15, London, Campaign for Real Education.

Chapter 37   Based on C. Handy and R. Aitken (1986), pp. 11–33 in C. Hardy and R. Aitken (eds) *Understanding Schools as Organizations*, Harmondsworth, Penguin.

Chapter 38   Based on J. Gray (1990), pp. 1–16 *British Journal of Educational Studies* 38(8).

Chapter 39   A. McPherson (1992) 'Measuring added value in schools', in *NCE Briefing No. 1* London, NCE.

Chapter 40   Based on D. Foxman, T. Gorman and G. Brooks (1992) *NCE Briefing No. 10*, London, NCE.

Chapter 41   Based on C. Wright (1990), pp. 65–75 in T. Everton, P. Mayne and S. White (eds) *Effective Learning: Into a New Era*, London, Jessica Kingsley.

Chapter 42   Based on B. Gorwood (1991), pp. 283–90 in *School Organisation* 11(3).

Chapter 43   Based on A. Macbeth (1989), pp. 1–13 in A. Macbeth *Involving Parents*, London, Heinemann.

Index